The Restless City

The Restless City

A Short History of New York
from Colonial Times to the Present

Joanne Reitano

 Routledge
Taylor & Francis Group
New York   London

Routledge is an imprint of the
Taylor & Francis Group, an informa business

Published in 2006 by
Routledge
Taylor & Francis Group
270 Madison Avenue
New York, NY 10016

Published in Great Britain by
Routledge
Taylor & Francis Group
2 Park Square
Milton Park, Abingdon
Oxon OX14 4RN

Taylor & Francis Group
is the Academic Division of Informa plc.

Visit the Taylor & Francis Web site at
http://www.taylorandfrancis.com

and the Routledge Web site at
http://www.routledge-ny.com

For Adam and Paul

Contents

Acknowledgments

Like New York City, this book has undergone many changes and benefited from the input of many people. Over three decades, the students at LaGuardia Community College of the City University of New York (CUNY) have been a constant source of inspiration and humility. They kept me grounded while motivating me to be as clear and concise as possible in the classroom as well as in print. Hence, a short history.

My colleagues at LaGuardia and in CUNY's University Faculty Senate Community College Caucus have encouraged my efforts over time. They understood too well the difficulties of doing research and writing while carrying an inordinately heavy course load replete with all the challenges of teaching underserved students. In addition, LaGuardia Community College and CUNY enabled me to complete this work through fellowship leaves and CUNY's Scholar Incentive Award.

The Web notwithstanding, historians remain deeply indebted to librarians. During the many years spent on this project, I relied on the expert staffs at LaGuardia Community College and its LaGuardia–Wagner Archives, New York University and its Tamiment Library/Robert F. Wagner Labor Archive, the New York Public Library, the New York Historical Society, and the archive at the City College of New York. In addition, my mother kept my personal library stocked with the latest books on New York City.

The final product has been strengthened by various individuals, none of whom should be blamed for my inadequacies. At Routledge, I have been privileged to work with Kimberly Guinta, Associate Editor for History, who was a solid advocate and skillful guide. She was ably assisted by Daniel Webb. Laura Lawrie did a dexterous job of copyediting, and Scott Hayes creatively resolved the art issues. As project editor, Sarah E. Blackmon was not only proficient and efficient but also responsive and gracious.

Bruce Hoffacker, Michael Nimetz, Christina Roukis-Stern, and Lawrence Rushing labored over the entire manuscript. Several other people read selected chapters in their various incarnations. Alexander Hoyt made useful recommendations at an earlier stage of writing. I thank them all for their diverse perspectives, acute perceptions, and constructive suggestions.

The anonymous scholarly reviewers raised excellent questions that tightened my presentation. Howard B. Rock offered gentle criticism and wise advice. Lewis L. Gould, David Nasaw, and Irwin Unger have been consistently supportive and helpful. Lord Asa Briggs greatly influenced my thinking and graciously corresponded with me although, of course, he bears no responsibility for my conclusions.

My sons, Adam and Paul, are wonderfully tolerant of their mother's academic obsessions. Now that they are adults, they also offer professional advice, humorous insights, editing suggestions, and technical assistance. I hope that, true to the spirit of their city, they will always be creative, humane, ambitious, and resilient.

1
Introduction

"Overturn, overturn, overturn! is the maxim of New York." As accurate in 1845 as today, this statement captures New York City's most basic characteristic. It speaks to everyone, especially to those who, like its author, former mayor Phillip Hone, regretted the relentlessness of rapid change. At the same time, it resonates with those who revel in change, the faster the better. Indeed, change itself is often cited as central to the city's complex history. New York, said Hone, exemplified "the spirit of pulling down and building up." It was chronically restless.[1]

Hone should have known. His own life reflected the city's rapid expansion as he rose above modest origins and acquired enough wealth in the auction business to retire in 1821 at age forty. After serving one term as mayor in 1826, he chaired numerous civic commissions, supported countless philanthropies, and became New York's most prominent citizen. Nonetheless, he was ruined by the Panic of 1837, forced to return to work, only to be ruined again by the fire of 1845. Depressions, crimes, epidemics, strikes, fires, and riots taught Hone that change was a mixed blessing. Despite his elite status and his contempt for poor immigrants, he worried about a society increasingly based on "two extremes of costly luxury and. . .hopeless destitution." Hone understood that although change brought progress, it also could cause conflict.[2]

According to the urbanist Lewis Mumford, conflict was embedded in the "creative audacity" that made cities so restless in the first place. By contrast

with the slow-paced, family-based village defined by continuity and conformity, the city was an unstable community that welcomed strangers, embraced
individuality, and was energized by change. It was bold and bustling, exciting
and inventive, arrogant and aggressive.[3]

Yet, Mumford observed that cities were schizophrenic. On the one hand,
they "enlarged all the dimensions of life. . .[and] became a symbol of the possible." On the other hand, they "packed [people] together under pressure."
While cities encouraged freedom and innovation, they enforced order and
regimentation. Although they depended on cooperation, they fostered competition. As a result of these internal contradictions, cities were in a constant
"state of dynamic tension and interaction."[4]

For better or worse, conflict characterized the restless city and complicated its sense of community. Mumford saw the significance of the "thousand
little wars [that] were fought in the marketplace, in the law courts, in the ball
game or the arena." Indeed, competition was so central to urban development
that "the city found a score of ways of expressing struggle, aggression, domination, conquest—and servitude." Ambition promoted a shared aggressive
culture, but community based on competition was inherently tentative and
volatile. Urban energy could be simultaneously positive and negative, constructive and destructive.[5]

So it was in Gotham. Over the centuries, New York City revised economic,
political, and social standards, nurtured controversial people, challenged cultural assumptions, weathered boycotts, strikes, and riots. Its conflicts were
violent and nonviolent, innovative and reactive. They spanned the scope of
urban diversity—poor versus rich, black versus white, male versus female,
immigrant versus native-born, worker versus employer, liberal versus conservative, rebel versus reactionary.

The constant jockeying of individuals and interest groups was natural in
a city with fluid political, economic, and social structures. In that sense, conflict reflected the special vitality of New York's multifaceted, ever-changing
community. It also exemplified what Frenchman Alexis de Tocqueville called
the American tendency to be "restless in the midst of abundance."[6]

Gotham's turmoil was perpetually stimulating, but it was particularly
unsettling for an optimistic nation steeped in myths of peaceful progress. As
the archetypical city of opportunity and equality, New York's tensions documented dissatisfaction and exposed the nation's fault lines. Consequently, the
historian Milton Klein concluded that Americans were always "scared of New
York City" because it represented "the present or future problems they themselves must face." Conflict was an essential, albeit disconcerting, corrective to
complacency.[7]

If conflict functioned as a warning, suggested the sociologist Lewis Coser,
it also could be an agent of change. In fact, most conflict presumed a desire

to improve and participate in, rather than overthrow, the existing system. Reformers and protesters wanted more democracy, equality, and wealth, not revolution. Of course, power holders resented criticism of the status quo and feared disorder. The ensuing struggle over the right to dissent spurred a long and still lively controversy over the role of police in a democracy.[8]

Much of the city's conflict was violent. In the colonial period, New York perpetrated the nation's most repressive response to a slave conspiracy. Then there were the Stamp Act riots of 1765, the antiabolition riots of 1834, the Astor Place riots of 1849, the draft riots of 1863, the race riot of 1900, the Harlem riots of 1935, 1943, and 1964, the Columbia College, CUNY, and Stonewall riots of the late 1960s, and the Hard-hat and Blackout riots of the 1970s. In addition, there were many minor riots. Violence was not just a function of the frontier.[9]

Riots were particularly controversial because they were extralegal, angry, and often deadly. They represented chaos and the breakdown of community. However, far from being irresponsible social aberrations, historian David Grimsted concluded that riots were actually "social exclamation points." For a brief moment, they gave voice to the voiceless and power to the powerless. Through what the historian Mary P. Ryan called "the social citizenship of the streets," they promoted popular participation in the polity and vented deeply felt, widely shared grievances.[10]

New York also experienced a substantial amount of nonviolent conflict promulgated by provocative individuals such as Alexander McDougall, Fanny Wright, Fernando Wood, Henry George, "Red Emma" Goldman, Adam Clayton Powell Jr., Edward I. Koch, Al Sharpton, and Rudolph Giuliani. They are discussed in this book because the controversies they caused over the changes they demanded reflected core urban and national dilemmas.

So did specific events such as the 1765 Stamp Act Congress, the 1911 Triangle Fire, and the 1975 fiscal crisis. More recently, the struggles over Ocean-Hill Brownsville, Howard Beach, Bensonhurst, Crown Heights, and Amadou Diallo were galvanizing. All were dramatic; all unmasked fundamental problems; all riveted national attention on New York City; and all had influence beyond the confines of one place. Together the extensive history of violent and nonviolent conflict showed that Gotham was, in the phrase of the sociologist St. Clair Drake, "the nerve center of American life."[11]

This book covers conventional time periods from 1609 to 2001 while emphasizing unconventional material. It selectively focuses on political, economic, social, and cultural developments that best capture the tensions of each era. The most striking events and personalities are examined most extensively, but are combined with less dramatic factors that help us understand change and continuity over time. Literary devices unify each chapter. Without trying to be comprehensive, the book demonstrates how various violent and nonviolent conflicts shaped a metropolis of unique vigor, creativity, resilience, and national influence.

Every chapter begins with an introductory unit that provides an overview of each era and offers a historical context for analyzing its conflicts. Omitting criminal exploits or natural disasters, the subsequent units of each chapter focus on people, events, or movements that illuminate the perennial debate over change and its effect on the relationship between materialism and humanitarianism, the private and the public interest. The core disputes involved the role of government and the police, the impact of economic growth, the nature of equality, the scope of reform, and the meaning of community. Because those issues remain unresolved, the disharmonies of the past ring true today.

Over time, broad patterns emerged. During the colonial and revolutionary periods, New York developed a uniquely open, pluralist society that was, nonetheless, torn by slavery and repression. This contradiction caused conflict and set the stage for the future. From the start, New York City was both the paradigm and the pariah for the development of capitalism and democracy in America. New York's complexity made it not only a symbol of optimism and opportunity, but also what British historian Lord Asa Briggs called a "capital of discontent."[12]

In the early and mid-nineteenth century, Gotham offered America a radical model of egalitarianism that applied beyond white men to include women, blacks, and immigrants while exposing deep fissures of class, racial, gender, and ethnic conflict. The result was so much violence that many people, including Hone, began to wonder if democracy could survive. Significantly, New York's Five Points, America's first slum, became the symbol of unrest in Jacksonian America.

By the late nineteenth century, New Yorkers were considered the prototypes of the Gilded Age—the greedy robber baron and the corrupt political boss. Nonetheless, in an era dedicated to social Darwinism, New York prodded the nation's social conscience through its "discovery of poverty" and aggressive labor movement. As Briggs observed, the problems of the industrial city "often overwhelmed people," but those problems also inspired efforts to better balance "economic individualism and common civic purpose."[13]

During the first half of the twentieth century, the Bohemian rebellion, the Harlem Renaissance, and Garveyism proclaimed New York's role as a center of cultural and social ferment by challenging artistic, social, and racial assumptions. At the same time, food riots, race riots, labor crises, and the Depression set the stage for a more expansive, more activist definition of community that came to fruition during the mayoralty of Fiorello H. LaGuardia. In all of these ways, New Yorkers were what the literary analyst Ann Douglas calls "the shock troops of modernity."[14]

The second half of the twentieth century brought the complications of change into greater focus as Robert Moses recast urban planning, not only by his bulldozing policies but also by reactions against them. Similarly, the city's upheavals over gender, race, education, and labor embodied both the sixties' revolution and the backlash against it. In the seventies, debt, crime, fires, and rats made New York the symbol of the nation's urban crisis. More than ever, Gotham seemed to be a community divided against itself.

The result was a new model of urbanism that emphasized order over the city's traditional flexibility. As Rudolph Giuliani shook New York to its foundations and acquired national fame, he provoked more conflict than any previous mayor. In the process, Giuliani underlined Gotham's seminal role in the American epic. The city's volatile mixture of people, profits, and politics inspired innovation even as it questioned the meaning of progress. Like the London described by Briggs, New York "posed the most exciting and alarming riddles about present and future."[15]

Gotham's conflicts had broad ramifications because it was the country's most watched, most controversial, most important metropolis. As James Fenimore Cooper noted in 1851, "New York is essentially national in interest, position, pursuits. No one thinks of the place as belonging to a particular state, but to the United States." In addition to its pivotal economic role, the city was a center for art, immigration, and communication. Consequently, New York's discord reverberated across the nation illuminating and influencing (if not necessarily resolving) its central challenges. New York was never irrelevant because it was always so vibrant.[16]

Conflict is hardly the only story and, as the historian Michael Wallace once remarked, not the story we prefer to recount.[17] By providing evidence of struggle rather than success, conflicts uncover inconsistencies that are often hidden or denied. That is why they are historically so important. In each era, urban disorder mirrors people's deepest anxieties about the urban order. The perpetual struggle over power, wealth, and status in America's premier urban center reminds us of the country's enduring aspirations and remaining agendas. Because conflicts are contests over the soul of the city and, by extension, the soul of the nation, they reveal how Gotham's ferment has invigorated the American Dream. In the end, New York City's restlessness was its greatest asset.

2

City of the Whirlpool, 1609–1799

In testimony to its vitality, New York has had more names than any other city. Each name reminds us that the history of the city is multifaceted and ever changing. Over time, people have tried to understand New York by labeling it. However, they have never quite succeeded because the city is too complex to be encompassed by any single notion. That complexity was often translated into conflict. Friction between different groups with different interests competing for power, wealth, and status was inevitable in a dynamic city. Although conflict could create chaos and strain community, it also could illuminate important grievances and stimulate constructive change. These positive and negative tendencies emerged in the colonial and revolutionary eras when the roots of conflict were planted.

The debate over New York's identity and significance starts with the very name of Manhattan. Legend attributes the word to the Manates, a Native American tribe considered particularly dangerous. As foreigners, the Europeans were never sure what the indigenous term really meant. It has been translated as "island," "small island," or "hilly island." Alternately, it may have signified a "place where timber is procured for bows and arrows" or a "place of general inebriation." The first three versions are similar and purely descriptive, but the latter two are quite different. Even at its inception, the infant city was perceived as a place of exchange, opportunity, profit, excitement, social rebellion, and, perhaps, depravity or exploitation.[1]

A sixth interpretation is even more provocative. Some sources suggest that the local tribe was known as the "people of the whirlpool." Apparently, the word "manahata" referred to "the place of the whirlpool," which was the narrow, treacherous channel between today's Astoria, Queens, and Wards Island where crosscurrents of the East River, the Harlem River, and Long Island Sound converged. In a ship named *Restless*, Dutchman Adriaen Block navigated through the channel in 1614. It was so dangerous that he called it Hell Gate, a negative antecedent of the more positive modern term, the Gateway City. Both concepts capture the essence of New York as a place of new beginnings offering as much peril as possibility. A whirlpool, therefore, is an excellent metaphor for a port city forever flooded by changing tides of humanity and engulfed by the rapid swirl of events.[2]

The colonial and revolutionary eras were particularly turbulent for New York. They established the patterns that gave New York City its distinctive characteristic not only as a fast-paced, flexible society dedicated to commercial success but also as a center of ferment. Controversies over political, economic, and social freedom lay the foundations for democracy. Yet, the colony encouraged slavery and violently repressed a purported slave conspiracy. Decades later, New York played such an important role in the pre-Revolutionary conflict that it became both British headquarters during the war and the United States' first capitol after the war. Throughout its various incarnations, New York embodied the dilemmas of the new nation.[3]

Unlike the other seaboard colonies, New York was constantly buffeted by European imperial ambitions as shown by its various names. Called New Amsterdam by the Dutch who arrived in 1624, it was taken over by the British in 1664 and renamed after the Duke of York to whom the English king had granted the land. In 1673, it was reacquired by the Dutch and labeled New Orange in honor of the ruling House of Orange. When the colony was returned to England a year later, it resumed the title of New York despite a pro-Dutch coup from 1689 to 1691. From the start, New York was complex and hotly contested. According to the historian Milton Klein, its fluid society and international context made colonial New York a microcosm of what the nation would become.[4]

New Amsterdam was formed, not as a religious refuge, but as a trading post of the Dutch West India Company. A magnificent harbor centrally located along the coast with river access to inland resources held limitless economic potential. Trading fur with the Native Americans provided a hint of the colony's future development as a commercial center. However, the process of economic growth was initially so slow that, in 1629, the Company offered large land grants to wealthy men, called patroons, if they would sponsor fifty new settlers. In 1640, the offer was extended to men who could sponsor only five settlers, but still the colony floundered.[5]

The need to attract settlers made New Amsterdam a uniquely poly-glot society where over eighteen languages were spoken. This "confusion of tongues," as described by a Jesuit missionary, was paralleled by an empha-sis on flexibility and competitive individualism that contrasted sharply with Boston's cohesive religious community and Charleston's structured social hierarchy. Consequently, wrote the historians Henry Kessler and Eugene Rachlis, New Amsterdam became "a home for the restless." It attracted "the dissidents, the nonconformists, the rebels, the adventurers, the freebooters, the disenchanted." Its social contract came to be based on a live-and-let-live principle, or what the founding father James Madison called a "multiplicity of interests" that checked and balanced each other. New Amsterdam's special sense of community was born in diversity and prone to conflict.[6]

Struggle was endemic to settlement. Hostilities between Native Americans and Europeans began in 1609 when Henry Hudson first sailed into the Lower Bay and one sailor was killed. Conflict was also embedded in Peter Minuit's famous 1626 "purchase" of Manhattan, which had only 270 European resi-dents at the time. From then on, New Amsterdam maintained an uneasy bal-ance between trading with and warring against the Native Americans. Liquor, a staple of Dutch culture and trade, quickly became both an antidote to and an aggravator of intergroup conflict. To make matters worse, from 1641 to 1645, Dutch Governor William Keift instigated such frequent and brutal combat with the Native Americans that 1643 was called "the year of the blood" and the colony was almost abandoned.[7]

Even after the Dutch West India Company replaced Kieft with Peter Stuyvesant in 1647, skirmishes occurred regularly. The colony so feared aggression from Native Americans and the British that in 1653 Stuyvesant ordered the colony's slaves to construct a wooden wall, later known as Wall Street. Then, in 1655, a Dutchman shot and killed a Native American woman who was taking some peaches from his fenced-in orchard. In retaliation, two thousand Native Americans invaded the city beginning three days of violence that extended to Hoboken, Jersey City, and Staten Island. At the end of the Peach Tree War, one hundred colonists were dead and one hundred and fifty others had been captured, including six at Hell Gate. Twenty-eight farms lay in ruins and five hundred cattle were lost. Native American fatalities remain unknown but are estimated at sixty.[8]

The Peach Tree War pitted the self-determination of one group against the self-preservation of another. It epitomized the complications of coloniza-tion. Symbolically and practically, the biggest problem was the fence because it divided shared resources from private property, Native American culture from European culture. On the one hand, the Peach Tree War ended Native American attacks in Manhattan. On the other hand, it inaugurated the long struggle over place, power, and profit that inundated life along the banks of the Hudson throughout its history. (See Figure 1 following page 150)

Turmoil created a vortex of contradictory traditions. Individualism, liberalism, and tolerance were offset by exploitation, riots, and repression. Wealth mocked poverty; slavery belied opportunity. Straddling North and South, the colony struggled with all the dilemmas confronting the New World. If New York typified the complexity of American history, it also was unique. In a nation largely defined by agrarianism and homogeneity, the polyglot city stood out, notes historian Thomas Bender, as "a center of difference." It was precisely this characteristic that made New York so prone to conflict. It was precisely this propensity to conflict that engaged the city in a maelstrom of rebellion and reinvention. It was precisely this perpetual tempest that made the city so dynamic, so fascinating and so important. The whirlpools of city life perpetually refreshed even as they roiled the nation.[9]

PRACTICAL TOLERATION

Peter Stuyvesant was considerably more rigid and narrow-minded than many of his Dutch compatriots. By the time he became Manhattan's Director General in 1647, he had lost one leg in battle, but he had gained valuable experience in the Dutch Caribbean as an administrator with a penchant for order. A severe, righteous man, Stuyvesant brought honesty and efficiency to New Amsterdam, albeit autocratically. As a result, he confronted resistance from a lively, competitive, multiethnic community that thrived on diversity, flexibility, and freedom from authority. The problem New Amsterdam faced was how to maintain the delicate balance between private interest and public need, freedom and order.[10]

Many of Stuyvesant's initiatives were widely supported improvements for the common good such as establishing a fire code, a school, a post office, a jail, and a poorhouse. In addition, he organized a rattle watch comprised of nine men patrolling at night with wooden noisemakers to signal danger. Social controls were much less popular, such as requirements for attending church and limits on work and leisure activities on Sundays plus harsh physical punishments for fighting, cohabiting, and committing sodomy. The nine p.m. curfew for bars and inns was openly defied as the spirit of discontent spread.[11]

Stuyvesant promoted economic development by solidifying the shoreline, building a pier, extending the streets, and expanding the markets. At the same time, he tried to regulate the economy too closely. There were rules for setting wages and prices, brewing beer, baking bread, and slaughtering cattle. There also was a prohibition on letting pigs and goats roam the streets, even though they were essential sources of household survival and doubled as the colony's sanitation department. In addition, cartmen were required to walk rather than drive their wagons through the streets (except on Broadway) in order to reduce accidents.[12]

Protests against these regulations were loud enough to reach Holland. In response, the Dutch West India Company counseled Stuyvesant to be less restrictive so that people "may not be discouraged" from doing business in New Amsterdam. They understood that "the expectation of gain" was a major motivation for migration. The ground was broken for a community based on commerce and profit where individual initiative, free enterprise, and economic opportunity would become articles of faith.[13]

Similar patterns emerged regarding ethnicity and religion. A strict Calvinistic adherent of the Dutch Reformed church, Stuyvesant opposed religious diversity and unsuccessfully resisted the settlement of Lutherans in 1653. When twenty-four Brazilian Jews landed in 1654, Stuyvesant tried to have them expelled from the colony as members of a "deceitful race." However, the Dutch West India Company rejected his request pointing out that Dutch Jews were investors in the Company itself and that the colony had a labor shortage. Economic pragmatism prevailed over religious prejudice.[14]

The Company instructed Stuyvesant to grant Jews the same privilege they had in Holland—the right to worship privately. Although compelled to pay higher taxes than other residents, Jews slowly won rights to own property, to become traders and retailers, to build a synagogue, and to have their own burial ground. The Dutch respect for "freedom of conscience" had been transported across the ocean and an important precedent had been set. It provided the basis for the liberalism that would come to define the new colony replete with its open-minded emphasis on individual freedom and tolerance of difference.[15]

Stuyvesant did not share those values. He banned Quakers from the colony and sent their boat off toward Hell Gate, but they left some settlers behind. As their numbers grew, Stuyvesant personally authorized their arrest, trial, fine, and torture. Even so, the Quakers persisted and met secretly in Flushing, Long Island (not far from Hell Gate), at John Bowne's home, which is still an historic site. When Bowne himself was arrested and sent back to Europe, he took his case directly to the Dutch West India Company. Again the trustees told Stuyvesant "not to force peoples' consciences" in order not to discourage immigration.[16]

During this controversy, thirty-one non-Quaker residents of Flushing made a remarkable contribution to the establishment of New World liberalism. In 1657 they protested against Stuyvesant's repressive tactics and issued the Flushing Remonstrance. Defending the Quakers' right to freedom of religion, they preferred "not to judge least wee be judged, neither to Condemn least wee bee Condemned, but rather let every man stand and fall to his own."

Out of conflict had emerged a commitment to the principles of freedom and a policy of what Milton Klein labeled "practical toleration."[17]

Stuyvesant's autocratic leadership style also led to a radical new departure in colonial self-government, an initial step toward democracy. According to the author Russell Shorto, an anti-Stuyvesant protest movement was orchestrated by Adriaen van der Donck, who took his complaints straight to officials in Holland. In 1653 they granted the colony its first city charter, which established an advisory council of seven men to represent community interests. Although Stuyvesant appointed the council members, he no longer acted alone and the principle of popular representation began to take root. However, van der Donck did not get to see it flower because two years later he lost his life in the Peach Tree War.[18]

In 1664, the English sailed into the harbor and assumed control of the colony, which by now numbered fifteen hundred persons. Resistance was minimal because there was so much dissatisfaction with Stuyvesant's rule and because the inhabitants did not want their city to be attacked. In order to ease the transition, the British cleverly merged existing guarantees of Dutch self-government with their own traditions of town government by allowing the city to elect some administrators and make most local laws. Nonetheless, the Crown retained ultimate control through a royal governor who appointed key local officials including the mayor. Requests by the city to elect the mayor were summarily dismissed. Although the 1731 charter called New York "a free city of itself," it would take another century to get the right to elect its own mayor.[19]

The shift of imperial control posed additional problems. In New York City, which served as the colony's capitol, the old Dutch majority resented the new British minority with their aristocratic ways, their lucrative mercantile connections, and their Anglican church. The Dutch were joined by other urban ethnic groups who resisted domination of any sort. The British felt equally beleaguered by the variety of peoples and religions with which they had to contend. As one British settler observed, "Our chiefest unhappiness here is too great a mixture of Nations, & the English the least part." Ethnic antagonisms grew within the city as well as between the city and surrounding areas where the Dutch remained powerful.[20]

Anger peaked when the British appointed a Catholic governor and set up the Dominion of New England, which lumped seven colonies into one governing unit. Resistance against this restructuring and loss of autonomy broke out in Boston, Long Island, Queens, Westchester, and New York. Seizing the moment, Captain Jacob Leisler, a wealthy, German-born, anti-Catholic, anti-British merchant, took over New York in 1689 and ruled it for thirteen months. His political coup reflected the rivalries of the time, or what British Governor Benjamin Fletcher called the "heats and animostyes" of New York politics.[21]

Leisler's Rebellion was the outgrowth of twenty-five years of mounting Dutch hostility toward the British compounded by the new taxes they levied and the new rules they imposed. In order to undermine their authority, Leisler abolished New York City's monopoly over packing flour, which had been granted in 1683 to the great benefit of English traders. In addition, he freed debtors from prison, sought a more democratic city charter from England, and appointed artisans to serve as his deputies. His short rule was a protest against the rise of a British aristocracy in the colony.[22]

The rich got the message, especially after some Leislerians took to the streets and plundered their homes. In return, the anti-Leislerians branded their foe as an unruly drunken mob, an ethnic slur against the many Dutch taverns that dotted the city. By 1691, the British resumed control, arrested Leisler, tried him by a British jury, and hung him without delay. It was reported that local carpenters refused to provide the ladder needed for his climb to the scaffold. They understood the larger significance of Leisler's interregnum and its bid for the democratization of New York politics.[23]

That effort was strengthened when the printer John Peter Zenger won his famous case for freedom of the press in 1735. Two years earlier, Zenger had started the *New York Weekly Journal* as an alternative to the *New York Gazette,* a paper formed in 1725 by William Bradford, who was the royal governor's official printer. In criticizing the governor, Zenger gave voice to anti-English sentiment and was arrested for seditious libel. After the judge disbarred Zenger's New York lawyers, the printer was represented by a renowned eighty-year-old Philadelphian named Andrew Hamilton. His eloquent appeal for freedom of the press established the vital democratic principle that public officials are not exempt from public criticism.

The issue, said Hamilton, was "not a small or private concern. . .not the cause of a poor printer, nor of New York alone." Rather, it was "the cause of liberty. . .the liberty both of exposing and opposing arbitrary power. . .by speaking and writing truth." The Zenger case stimulated the publication of newspapers and pamphlets, thereby foreshadowing New York's role as a communications center. Most important, it served notice that the people, as represented by the jury, would not automatically defer to the power holders, as represented by the judge and the prosecution. Although freedom of the press was not yet complete, its spirit had prevailed.[24]

Liberal principles also were promoted by the controversy over establishing King's College. From 1752 to 1756, New Yorkers waged a major debate over whether the colony's first college should be controlled by the Anglican Church. After all, Harvard and Yale were Congregational and the College of New Jersey (later Princeton) was Presbyterian. Only Benjamin Franklin's Philadelphia Academy (later the University of Pennsylvania) was secular. To the Anglicans, a college in New York would complement their existing southern base at the College of William and Mary in Virginia. Moreover, it would affirm their power over the notoriously diverse colony and, because of New York's central location, over the colonies as a whole.[25]

Underlying and complicating these larger issues was a local power struggle between two prominent colonial families. The DeLanceys were merchants, Anglicans and Tories, or, as they preferred to be called, loyalists to the British crown. The Livingstons were landowners, Presbyterians and Whigs, or those who were more critical of the Crown. It was significant that the British party labels, Tory and Whig, were transposed to the colonies even as they were being redefined in the context of new circumstances, new priorities, and the development of a new nation. The King's College controversy embodied this tension between continuity and change.[26]

The acting governor at the time was James DeLancey, who was the judge in the Zenger case and who granted the charter for the new college to the Anglicans. This decision spurred an aggressive counterattack by three prominent Presbyterian lawyers, two of whom were the lawyers disbarred in the Zenger case. The most important of "The Triumvirate" was William Livingston, Yale graduate and later a signer of the Constitution as well as a governor of New Jersey. Through pamphlets, essays, and a weekly newspaper significantly called the *Independent Reflector,* Livingston instigated a lively public debate over what was at the time a radical blueprint for higher education in the New World.[27]

Sharply breaking with existing practice, Livingston wanted New York's college to include all Protestants but be dominated by none. Although still requiring attendance at some Protestant weekly service and remaining closed to Catholics and Jews, the plan was intended to separate church from state in academia through a secular curriculum. Critical of "gloomy pedants," Livingston proposed that faculty be chosen for their knowledge, not their religious affiliation, and that they be allowed to evaluate ideas rather than just reiterate dry dogma. He envisioned a college located in the city so that students could learn from real life, prepare for a variety of careers and become civic leaders. Moreover, he insisted that the college be incorporated by and answerable, not to royal authority, but to the representatives of the people sitting in the colonial assembly.[28]

The Triumvirate's campaign was only partly successful because the Anglicans joined the conservative wing of the Dutch Reformed Church to get an Anglican-controlled college established after all. Indeed, the college's first home was at Trinity Church. Nonetheless, its administration was not exclusively Anglican and it enrolled students of all Protestant denominations. Refusing to serve on the Board of Trustees, Livingston made sure that the college was underfunded. After the Revolution, King's College was redefined as the sectarian Columbia College supervised by a new public body, the

Regents of the University of the State of New York. Created in 1784, it marked America's first endorsement of college education as a civic responsibility in a democratic nation.[29]

Once again, conflict in New York had broad ramifications for the development of liberalism in the New World. Bender observes that a publicly supported, secular college open to diverse people, shaped by civic interests and enriched by civic discourse, was a distinctly urban idea. It reflected a city in which, as Livingston explained, people "are split into so great a variety of opinions and professions" that controversy was inevitable. For Livingston, encouraging, not repressing, debate would promote "a perfect freedom" for all. In this context, conflict was constructive and progressive. Altogether the opposition to Stuyvesant's authoritarianism, Leisler's Rebellion, the Zenger case, and the King's College debate legitimized liberalism. These nonviolent conflicts shaped the special character of the new settlement, which now became a symbol of and model for pluralism, tolerance, secularism, and democratic self-government. It was, says Shorto, "a new kind of spirit. . .something utterly alien to New England and Virginia," something uniquely New York.[30]

SLAVERY IN THE CITY

Ironically, while New York was nurturing liberalism, it was also promoting slavery. In fact, noted Milton Klein, "race prejudice was to become worse in the very centers of ethnic diversity which bred tolerance for whites. Colonial New York mirrored the national disease." Slavery in the city created endless ethical and practical dilemmas. It resulted in two violent conflicts—a slave rebellion in 1712 and the brutal repression of a slave conspiracy in 1741. These episodes betrayed the weaknesses of a liberal colony pursuing illiberal policies, of a profit-oriented people plagued by the problems that invariably accompany economic oppression. Slavery revealed the limits of both democracy and capitalism in America.[31]

The first sixteen male slaves were seized from a Portuguese ship in the colony's first year, 1626. Like other residents, they became employees of the Dutch West India Company, which controlled all of Holland's commerce with Africa and the New World. The names of Simon Congo, Paul D'Angola, and Anthony Portugese reflected the international nature of the slave trade. Although their status was not rigidly defined by the Dutch, there is no question that they were held in bondage and that, as an active agent of the slave trade, the Dutch West India Company wanted to increase their numbers. Faced with a lack of agricultural workers and the expense of importing European colonists, the Company viewed Africans as a cheap, reliable labor force. Over the years, the Dutch settlers became increasingly dependent on slave labor. In this case, pragmatism bred intolerance.[32]

Evidence indicates that slavery in New Amsterdam was extensive enough and institutionalized enough to require an overseer and to designate separate slave living quarters. At the same time, slavery during the Dutch period was complex. In 1644, eleven of the original slaves petitioned for and were granted their freedom but with a catch. They were obliged to make an annual payment of farm products or be returned to slavery. Moreover, their children were expected to serve the Company until adulthood. Stuyvesant aggressively promoted the expansion of slavery in New Amsterdam and owned forty slaves himself. Nonetheless, he freed four of them and, just as Dutch rule was ending in 1664, he granted eight of the original male slaves full freedom and land near his own farm, which encompassed today's 5th to 20th Streets from Fourth Avenue to the East River.[33]

Contradictions abounded. Because few colonists were financially able to maintain slaves permanently, they were hired out as seasonal laborers in a form of "half-freedom." Unlike slaves in the South, slaves in New Amsterdam could testify in court, possess land, belong to the militia, and marry legally. However, the colonists feared that baptizing slaves would make them equal in the eyes of the church and, therefore, undermine slavery itself. Greed trumped faith as shipments of slaves increased during the last twenty years of Dutch rule. By 1660, claims historian Graham Russell Hodges, New Amsterdam was "the most important slave port with the largest population of slaves in North America."[34]

Spurred by affiliation with the Royal African Company, slave trading and slave owning grew under British rule. Slaves were a vital part of the burgeoning trade network that brought flour, meat, and lumber from New York to the West Indies in exchange for sugar, molasses, cotton, and spices, which were sold in the colonies or in England. As more slaves were imported from the West Indies, the colonists adopted more severe measures of controlling them. A market flourished at the foot of Wall Street where slaves were sold and hired out on a daily basis, thus competing with white laborers. Although restricted in numerous ways, slaves lived throughout the city, one or two in each master's home. They worked not only as cooks and servants, but also as farmers and skilled artisans. Unlike the isolated plantation, the city presented ample opportunities for slaves to associate with each other, to meet free blacks, and to run away. Consequently, controlling them became a major problem. As slaveholders everywhere understood, slaves were truly "a troublesome property."[35]

In 1706, reports of disorder among blacks in Brooklyn motivated the governor to order that all suspects be caught "and if any of them refuse to submit themselves, then to fire on them, kill or destroy them." In 1708, a Native American slave and his African wife committed the "Barbarous Murder" of a slave owner at Hell Gate. In addition to two alleged African accomplices, the couple was promptly executed—one by hanging, the other by burning.

According to the records of the time, they were intentionally "put to all the torment possible for a terror to others."[36]

Racial tensions were exacerbated by the importation of 185 new slaves between 1710 and 1712. In early April of 1712 a full-fledged rebellion occurred when forty to fifty people—African and Native American slaves plus at least one free black—ignited a building, killed eight whites who came to put out the fire, and injured another dozen. After the whites counterattacked, the slaves fled north of the wall. Some escaped, but at least seventy were captured. Of the latter, six committed suicide immediately, some were deported, and eighteen were executed. The trials united whites across ethnic boundaries and preoccupied the city until late May.[37]

Punishment was quick and cruel, including "one by slow fire in torment for eight to ten hours. . . , one to be broken upon the wheel. . . , and one to be hung in chains without sustenance until dead." For weeks, the victim's heads were on display as a grisly deterrent to anyone intent upon revenge. According to the historian Richard Hofstadter, this incident was a prime example of the "purposive brutality" used by governments to reinforce race relations. The shock was that it occurred in a Northern city already reputed for its liberal traditions. It so upset other colonies that both Massachusetts and Pennsylvania took steps to limit the importation of slaves.[38]

Motivated by "the Late Hellish" events, the colony passed laws as harsh as the Southern Black Codes for regulating slave behavior. It became illegal for slaves to gather more than three at a time, walk at night without a lantern, "strike any Freeman or Woman," use guns or trade without their master's consent. Towns were authorized to hire a "public whipper" and punishments for violating the law were severe. It became prohibitively expensive to set slaves free and more restrictions were placed on blacks already free. In 1730, these laws were strengthened in the belief that "many Mischiefs had been Occasioned by the too great Liberty allowed to Negro and other Slaves."[39]

The problem, of course, was exactly the opposite. Suffering from a lack of liberty, slaves rebelled in little ways every day by visiting each other, frequenting taverns, trading on the black market, committing minor crimes, forming gangs, and meeting surreptitiously. They found allies among poor whites who also were struggling to survive in a city where almost half of the wealth was controlled by 10 percent of the population. In 1736, the city built a poorhouse, but allocations for this purpose never seemed adequate and the extremely cold winter of 1740–1741 worsened the situation.[40]

News of a large slave rebellion in Stono, South Carolina during 1739, of slave plots to incinerate Charleston in 1740, and of several slave conspiracies in nearby New Jersey provoked an already anxious New York. When a Spanish ship was captured, its free African sailors were sold into slavery. These men threatened rebellion and the Spanish crew aroused the colonists' fears of a foreign, Catholic invasion. Restlessness pervaded the city and one slave was overheard saying, "God damn all the white people; if I had it in my power, I'd burn them all." New York was about to demonstrate that a society built on slavery could be consumed by the very terror it practiced.[41]

During the spring of 1741, a robbery was followed by several fires over the course of a month. With reports of similar incidents being blamed on slaves in Hackensack, New Jersey, white New Yorkers feared a "Great Negro Plot" to destroy the city. Hundreds fled to farms above Chambers Street while the authorities rounded up 150 slaves along with twenty-five whites. The drama then moved from the streets to the courthouse rivaling the Salem witch trials in its miscarriage of justice. Judge Daniel Horsemanden was determined to prove the existence of a conspiracy. Lacking hard evidence, he found a substitute in a teenage indentured servant named Mary Burton who agreed to testify when promised a reward plus her freedom.[42]

Mary became the star witness and, like other witnesses who testified under compulsion, made inconsistent statements implicating a variety of people in the supposed plot. At the center of the conspiracy, she placed the white owner of a disreputable tavern serving a mixed-race clientele plus his wife, two slaves, and an Irish prostitute who had born a child by one of the slaves. These five were quickly executed—the three whites by hanging and the two blacks by slow burning at the stake. The crowd was intense and their spirits were savage.[43]

Thus began a brutal summer marked by a death sentence issued almost every day and executions carried out every week. The dead were left hanging in chains until the stench forced the city to remove them. The journalist Roi Ottley called it "the biggest lynching in the history of America." All of New York's adult male slaves were suspect and almost half were arrested. The "Spanish Negroes" were considered particularly dangerous and fears of "a Spanish and popish plot" were magnified by reports from other colonies that Spanish privateers were seizing English ships and that Spanish spies were infiltrating English settlements. In return, the other colonies reported on events in New York with evident concern that the spirit of rebellion might spread.[44]

Mary warmed to the task and, after naming scores of free blacks and slaves, identified a Latin tutor named John Ury as a coconspirator. He was accused of covertly baptizing blacks, plotting a Catholic coup, and organizing the whole conspiracy. The New York Weekly Journal expressed particular anger "that white People were privy to and fomentors of so unparalel'd a Villany." Despite efforts to defend himself, the tutor was hung. However, his was the final execution as panic waned and Mary began incriminating prominent Protestant members of the community. Suddenly the trials ended and, given her reward, Mary disappeared.[45]

The peculiar partnership between a servant girl and a judge left a grue-some legacy of thirty-four executions and seventy-one deportations. The con-spiracy itself was never confirmed, but the city's reaction to it remained the most severe response to a slave rebellion in American history. At the very least, it showed that New York was at war with itself—white against black, rich against poor, Protestant against Catholic, English against Dutch, Spanish, and Irish. The diversity that was New York's unique strength also could become its weakness when marred by inequality and intolerance. The entire episode, observed the historian Thomas J. Davis, exposed "a seldom-seen, dark side of life in colonial America."[46]

REVOLUTION

The 1760s brought a different kind of turmoil to New York. Protests, riots, fire, and war kept the city in chaos and its population constantly on the move. Although not considered quite as central as Boston, New York City had a sig-nificant impact on its sister colonies during the revolutionary era. As the site of the first Sons of Liberty organization, the first intercolonial congress, the first boycott of British goods, the first fatal skirmish with British soldiers, and the first national capitol, New York City's key role in the rebel cause was unde-niable. According to the historian Michael Kammen, "New York served as a fulcrum of the American Revolution." Internally divided, yet geographically pivotal, New York could either cement or shatter colonial unity.[47]

Its port, mid-coast location, postal service, and wealth entangled New York in imperial politics, leading to the name of the Empire State. Although benefited by British military spending during the French and Indian War (1756–1763), the city faced depression after the war as British expenditures decreased and trade restrictions increased. Resentments against the King smoldered in a bustling port that chafed under economic limits. Ethnic diver-sity further undermined loyalty to England and factionalism energized politi-cal participation. As a result, New York experienced constant conflict during the revolutionary period.[48]

British policies inspired resistance. The 1764 Sugar Act hurt New York by enforcing the collection of import duties on sugar and molasses, items essen-tial to the West Indian trade. In response, the colony sent sharply worded petitions to the King and Parliament. Women started making their own homespun cloth rather than use imported textiles from England. The 1765 Quartering Act was particularly offensive because it required colonists to provide food and housing for British troops, many of whom were stationed in New York, which was British military headquarters. Tension between resi-dents and soldiers mounted daily in the form of petty vandalism and sporadic violence. The city's nerves were raw.[49]

In 1765, the Stamp Act created a crisis, especially for New York. The act hit both rich and poor by directly taxing items used in professional and personal life such as customs papers, legal documents, licenses for selling or marrying, as well as ordinary goods such as newspapers, dice, and cards. Stamps verifying that the taxes had been paid were tangible tokens of taxation and, therefore, became targets of protest. Moreover, the revenues collected from the stamps were intended to support the very British troops that the colonists found so objectionable.

The fact that the proposed taxes were light was less important than that they were to be enforced. Regulation of any sort was anathema in a city dedicated to individualism and competition. For all these reasons, the Stamp Act heightened a sense of common grievance against the Crown across classes and factions within the colony. It strained the limits of colonial patience and reinforced the perception that economic and political freedoms were, as John Peter Zenger put it, intrinsically "interwoven."[50]

Defiance mounted when New York merchants took the lead in organizing colonial opposition to the new imperial policies. They initiated communication with their counterparts in other cities and called for a meeting in response to the new taxes. The result was the Stamp Act Congress, which was the first time that delegates from different colonies joined to discuss their grievances. By assembling at City Hall on October 7, 1765, other colonies acknowledged New York's importance as port and as protester. Deliberating for almost three weeks, representatives of nine colonies passed resolutions affirming their rights as Englishmen, especially the right not to be taxed without their own consent.

The Stamp Act Congress did not advocate rebellion, but it did signal a new level of aggressive, coordinated opposition to Parliament. Merely by calling this extralegal meeting, the colonists declared their right to assemble without directions from the Crown. The implications were clear to British General Thomas Gage who "feared. . .that the Spirit of Democracy is strong amongst them." As a bold assertion of self-determination, the Stamp Act Congress was an important step in the march toward revolution.[51]

While the ink was drying on the petitions of the Stamp Act Congress, the stamps arrived in New York Harbor. Such a large crowd gathered at the Battery in protest that the stamps were secretly unloaded during the night and locked up in the fort under British guard. Posters throughout town warned that anyone who tried to enforce the Stamp Act put his person and property at risk. Two hundred New York merchants met to adopt the colonies' first non-importation agreement, which was followed by similar boycotts in Albany, Philadelphia, and Boston. Reminding the mother country that trade had to be reciprocal to be profitable, the colonies cleverly used economic means for political ends.[52]

Other New Yorkers took to the streets in the Stamp Act Riots, which were the most extensive expression of mass protest since Leisler's Rebellion. (See Figure 2 following page 150) They lasted for five days. Businesses were closed, the port was paralyzed, and the Stamp Act became a life and death issue. Flags flew at half-mast, people wore mourning, houses were draped in black, and a coffin labeled "Liberty" was carried aloft. Marching through the dark streets in funeral procession with six hundred candles casting eerie light, the mob burned the British governor in effigy and his elegant coach in actuality right in front of the fort where the British military was stationed. As a "sacrifice to liberty," they also ransacked the lavish home of the fort's commander, who had indiscreetly vowed to "cram the stamps down the throats of the people." Church bells tolled and the city was consumed by resolve.[53]

Mobs roamed the streets day and night. Sympathizers arrived from New Jersey, Connecticut, and the countryside, where tenant farmers were rebelling against their Hudson Valley landlords (including the Livingstons). Rumors spread that a full-scale war might break out. Finally, the stamps were delivered to City Hall with thousands watching and officials pledging not to use them. The Stamp Act Riots were over and New York had proven to be as turbulent as Boston. The colonists moved closer to rebellion as the very act of riot repudiated royal authority and legitimized local leadership. Their survival as a community seemed to be at stake.[54]

The riots were neither spontaneous nor haphazard. They elicited widespread support and were well planned with activities selectively directed at symbols of ostentation and imperial authority. Merchants and lawyers condoned the violence and tried to control it, but the mob itself was dominated by seamen who lived a precarious life prone to impressment and unemployment. Being forced to work on British ships made British tyranny quite personal. Having to compete for jobs with British soldiers moonlighting as dockworkers made matters worse. Economic interests intensified the protests and bridged class distinctions; political ideas cemented the bond.[55]

The protests in New York and other colonies proved successful when, pressured by British merchants suffering from the boycott, Parliament repealed the Stamp Act in 1766, even though it reserved the right to tax the colonies "in all cases whatsoever." As part of the celebration, a Liberty Pole fashioned from a ship's mast was erected in the Commons (today's City Hall Park) across from the British barracks. Modeled on a Liberty Tree used in Boston, the pole became a bone of contention between the troops and the colonists. It complemented the negative death metaphor with a positive, uplifting symbol for collective action. As New York's special revolutionary icon, it acquired such lasting significance that liberty poles were still being used in urban politics during the 1830s.

In 1766 and 1767, the pole was repeatedly cut down by British soldiers and resolutely restored by colonists in an ongoing guerrilla warfare exacerbated by a new Quartering Act, new taxes, and new trade restrictions. The issue of soldiers' moonlighting on the docks particularly rankled the colonists and fomented frequent conflicts. After the soldiers destroyed the first Liberty Pole, three thousand people attended a massive protest meeting on the Commons called by Isaac Sears, merchant and former privateer. A riot erupted during which soldiers used their bayonets freely, leaving many colonists badly injured and inciting them to sweep through town in pursuit of soldiers working in the port. Over the next year and a half, these antagonisms toppled two more Liberty Poles.[56]

New York's Liberty Pole was the brainchild of the Sons of Liberty, a loose group of mechanics, artisans, seamen, shopkeepers, and self-made men like Sears. They orchestrated the Stamp Act Riots and were a vital force in New York's mounting opposition to Parliament. Moreover, they spawned similar groups along the coast thereby fostering crucial cross-colonial communication. Although at times New York's Sons of Liberty cooperated with the well to do, they had their own grievances, leaders, and methods—many of which challenged the authority of the upper class. For example, they kept careful watch over and put pressure on merchants suspected of avoiding the boycott of British imports. Their nightly street demonstrations included the destruction of an elegant theater, which, like the private coach, was resented as an offensive display of wealth among people experiencing economic hardship.[57]

In 1770, the Sons of Liberty clashed with British troops over the fourth Liberty Pole in the Battle of Golden Hill, which took place on a rise located near the intersection of John and Williams Streets. After days of effort, the soldiers destroyed the pole and deposited its remnants in front of Montayne's Tavern on Broadway, which was frequented by the Sons of Liberty. The challenge provoked what was technically the first conflict of the American Revolution. Six weeks before the Boston Massacre, a New York sailor became the first fatality in the long struggle over trade. Three weeks later, the Sons of Liberty defiantly erected a new Liberty Pole on land purchased by Sears near the Commons. With great ceremony, they reinforced the pole with iron hoops and topped it with the word LIBERTY. This fifth pole was the focal point for rebel parades, protests, and meetings throughout the pre-Revolutionary period. It survived until the British took over the city in 1776.[58]

Three weeks after the Battle of Golden Hill, Alexander McDougall provided another cause for conflict in New York City and for unity across the colonies. A merchant of working-class origins, a leader of the Sons of Liberty, and an ally of the Livingston family, McDougall was arrested because he had written a pamphlet in 1769 criticizing the DeLancey–controlled colonial assembly for authorizing taxes to support the new Quartering Act. Not only were the requisitions "taking money out of our Pockets without our Consent," he said, but they were also fostering a corrupt alliance between the DeLancey family and the Crown. In essence, McDougall argued, the Assembly was legitimizing Parliament's right to impose taxes and undermining colonial protest.[59]

The pamphlet was a sensation. It galvanized popular support for the Sons of Liberty and won many admirers for McDougall. Among them was a precocious King's College scholarship student named Alexander Hamilton. Born illegitimate and orphaned at age thirteen, Hamilton emigrated from the Caribbean island of Nevis in 1774 at age nineteen and soon joined the rebel cause. The Livingstons also defended McDougall, partly for their own political advantage, partly because they connected their campaign for a more democratic college with McDougall's call for a more democratic government. However, McDougall was considerably more radical than both Hamilton and the Livingstons and, like Leisler, tapped a growing reservoir of resentment against all elites, including Livingstons.[60]

With the Zenger case as a precedent, McDougall was accused of seditious libel. After bail was set high by the same judge who presided over the 1741 conspiracy trials, McDougall dramatized his case by going to jail. He compared himself to the renowned British radical, John Wilkes, whose criticisms of the British government had recently earned him an arrest for seditious libel that fomented riots, strikes, and a Parliamentary crisis in England. According to his biographer, Roger Champagne, McDougall's arrest not only mesmerized the city but also made him an intercolonial hero.[61]

Although the case was ultimately dropped, it spurred revolutionary fervor, sparked street demonstrations, and dominated New York's press throughout 1770. The impact of the affair was so great that McDougall's pamphlet may have been important to New York as Tom Paine's *Common Sense* was to America. Moreover, it resonated beyond New York and became a cross-colonial rallying cry covered by newspapers from South Carolina to Pennsylvania to Massachusetts. McDougall's arrest was a timely reminder, said one colonist, that "our freedom & rights are invaded by Serpents and Harpies that We foster and Nourish in our Very Bowels."[62]

In 1773, the Tea Act provoked eight weeks of protest in New York City. There was a boycott of tea by women and, like Boston, a tea party in the harbor. McDougall kept the political pot boiling with broadsides condemning the East India Company's monopoly on tea as politically corrupt and commercially disastrous. In addition, he helped mechanics and craftsmen form their own extralegal political organization as a counterforce to the existing merchant-dominated power structure. By meeting often and supporting candidates for office, the city's middle and working classes affirmed their right to participate in politics. As the historian Carl Becker observed long ago, the developing revolution over "home rule" was accompanied by an equally significant revolution over "who was to rule at home."[63]

In 1775 an extralegal Committee of One Hundred, comprised of both moderates and radicals, took over the city government. With a mob in tow, Isaac Sears commandeered the port and domineered the streets. Many Tories left the city. Even Whig merchants who previously condoned mob action "now dread[ed] Sears' Train of Armed men." As one merchant complained, the Sons of Liberty had become the "Sons of Discord." The well-to-do of all persuasions understood that antiauthoritarianism was the subtext of riot. They feared that protests against Parliament would boomerang if, as conservative Gouverneur Morris put it, "the mob begin to think and reason." Then the upshot just might be "farewell aristocracy."[64]

Hamilton's rebel leanings notwithstanding, his contempt of the "turbulent and changing" masses led him to oppose mobs of any sort. Accordingly, in 1775 he distracted a rebel mob so that the Tory president of King's College, whom he had often criticized, could escape unharmed. In that same year, he protested against a mob attack led by Sears against the Tory printer James Rivington. Although Hamilton disliked Rivington, he disliked anarchy more and thought that fickle public sentiments should always be offset by the more stable sensibilities of the elite. This opinion inured him to mobs, aligned him with the aristocracy, and earned him an antidemocratic label even though he aggressively supported the revolution.[65]

New York endorsed the Declaration of Independence on July 9, 1776, the last colony to do so. Reflecting the ambivalence of a community that sought economic freedom and political autonomy, but that also served as imperial headquarters and depended heavily on trade with the mother country, New York was always betwixt and between. By the same token, the city's rebels eagerly joined the First New York Regiment led by McDougall while Hamilton dropped out of King's College in order to command a rebel artillery unit himself. Mobs tore down the royal coat of arms on City Hall and the King's statue in Bowling Green.[66]

However, their joy was short-lived because that fall New York City was occupied by the British despite defenses at the Battery, Fort George, and Hell Gate. Landing on the loyalist stronghold of Staten Island, the British drove General George Washington and his troops from Brooklyn up through Manhattan and over to New Jersey in retreat. In the wake of conquest, a suspicious fire decimated five hundred buildings covering a quarter of the city, symbolizing both the heat of battle and the fervor of anti-British sentiment. News of the fall of New York horrified the other colonies, which wondered whether the rebel cause could survive the blow.[67]

As a conquered city throughout the Revolution, New York served not only as headquarters for the royal army but also as a refuge for British loyalists fleeing other colonies. Many rebels left the city and the fifth Liberty Pole was taken down. Trade with England resumed, colonial court life revived, and elegance reigned. However, the profits were not widespread. Ordinary people struggled with housing shortages created by two major fires, food shortages because of wartime blockades, plus a series of horrible epidemics. British soldiers took over rebel houses while tent cities for the poor rose among the rubble and trees were cut down for fuel. The situation was grim. New York reeled from the repercussions of revolt.[68]

The city remained under martial law until peace came in 1783. Again the historic tide was reversed and loyalists left as the rebels reentered the city. The British flag flying from the Liberty Pole was quickly replaced by the American flag and several small riots against loyalists broke out. McDougall, now a general, joined the military escort to welcome Washington, who celebrated victory at a tavern on Broad Street run by Samuel Fraunces, a West Indian immigrant (reputedly a mulatto) who later became the president's steward.[69]

As an important center of rebellion and as imperial headquarters, revolutionary New York was caught in the crosscurrents of conflicting interests. Although the Stamp Act, the Liberty Pole, and the Tea Party drew the community together, the DeLancey-Livingston dispute, the Sons of Liberty and the McDougall affair tore it apart. Meanwhile, the Stamp Act Congress, the various riots, and the ad hoc self-governing committees embraced extralegal activism, which undermined empire and nurtured new definitions of democracy. No wonder Massachusetts' John Adams, founding father and future president, suggested in 1776 that New York was "a kind of key to the whole continent."[70]

POST-REVOLUTIONARY CONFLICTS

After the revolution, New York continued to struggle with the dilemmas of playing a national role while maturing as a local community. The sense of perpetual crisis diminished. Although it suffered more damage than any other American city during the war, New York reconstituted itself. Houses were fixed, streets were extended, trade was revived, and its population reached 24,000. The city was the capitol of the state and, for fifteen months, the capitol of the nation. City Hall became the first Federal Hall where George Washington took the oath of office as America's first president in 1789.[71]

The new nation's first Department of Foreign Affairs was headed by John Jay, a colonial leader who would become chief justice of the state and federal Supreme Courts, as well as two-term governor of New York. A graduate of King's College, he was William Livingston's son-in-law, a Livingston law partner, and Hamilton's close friend. Believing that justice should prevail over revenge, Jay and Hamilton were the only lawyers willing to defend the property rights of former loyalists in the post-Revolutionary period. Together, they later supported the nation's first trade treaty that Jay negotiated with England in 1795. It was, however, so controversial that it caused a riot in New York by those who thought it favored English trading rights and impressment policies. When Hamilton tried to calm the crowd, they threw stones at him. He then began a six-month campaign in the political press that helped get the treaty ratified by Congress, but did not dampen the spirit of protest in New York.[72]

Hamilton, who was Washington's right-hand man for most of the war, embarked on a spectacular career as a public servant after the war. His nationalism is usually attributed to his orphaned background, immigrant origins, and military service. Undoubtedly, it also resulted from his identification with New York City's ambitions, which, paralleling his own, were always expansive. Despite Hamilton's belief that the new Constitution should have been more aristocratic (maybe even monarchical), he was the only New Yorker to sign the document. Fearing for the nation's survival, he joined Jay to fight for ratification of the Constitution in New York State and to write the powerful essays of the *Federalist Papers* that marshaled opinion across the states.[73]

In New York, Governor George Clinton led the opposition to a central government. Historians agree that, without Hamilton's brilliant and relentless (albeit often arrogant) advocacy of strong government, the state might have split in two, with the southern section surrounding New York City seceding from the whole. Alternately, the state might not have joined at all and, therefore, could have destroyed the union. As it was, the vote of thirty to twenty-seven ratifying the Constitution by New York's convention delegates was closer than in any other state. Hamilton was honored when a huge mock ship named after him led the victory parade in 1788. For all his reservations about democracy and his fear of mob rule, he had effectively defended the Constitution as the last, best hope for the infant country.[74]

Appointed America's first Secretary of the Treasury in 1789, Hamilton secured the establishment of two financial institutions—the Bank of the United States and the Bank of New York, where he installed McDougall as president. Both banks were designed to stabilize the economy by binding the interests of the rich to those of the body politic. In addition, Hamilton advocated a protective tariff to encourage manufactures, internal taxes to raise revenue, and the federal assumption of state debts. The debate over Hamilton's aggressive economic program fueled the development of America's first political parties and created political crises for decades to come. In order to defend his policies, in 1801 Hamilton founded the *New York Evening Post*, which remains the city's oldest paper and is a testament to Hamilton's multifaceted, enduring legacy.[75]

Earning him much criticism as an elitist and ruthless materialist, Hamilton's economic policies reflected his ties to a city based on trade and finance, not to mention his personal affiliation with the rich. Indeed, Hamilton's climb from poverty to wealth had been sealed by marrying the daughter of a wealthy New York landowner, General Philip Schulyer, and acquiring a large country estate called Hamilton Grange located between 141st and 145th Streets from today's St. Nicholas Avenue to the East River. Nonetheless, Hamilton's reputation was damaged in 1792 when his friend William Duer was caught in a massive, fraudulent bank scheme that plunged New York's economy into chaos and cost hundreds of investors their savings. Hamilton recouped by using his influence to buy government securities in order to rescue the banking system rather than his friend who ended up in debtor's prison. His commitment to national economic stability was predominant; New York's pivotal economic role was evident.[76]

As New York moved forward, it still struggled with old problems, some of which had been intensified by the sense of a "right to riot" that emerged from the Revolution. A case in point was the 1788 Doctor's Riot, which was a protest against the practice of grave robbing at night by medical students seeking specimens for dissection. Hamilton and Jay were injured trying to control the mob during its two-day rampage against doctors and students at Columbia College. Finally, the militia was called up and, for the first time in New York City history, was authorized to fire on the crowd. With one in twenty New Yorkers participating in the riot and three rioters being killed, the Doctor's Riot ranks as one of the most serious conflicts of the era. At the same time, by successfully pressuring authorities to prohibit grave robbing, it demonstrated the continuing power of popular protest to get results.[77]

Class conflict (with an undercurrent of ethnic conflict) colored the 1796 Keteltas riot when two Irish ferrymen were arrested and jailed for refusing to carry a prominent Protestant alderman across the East River ahead of their scheduled departure time. In a trial with no jury and no defense attorney, the ferrymen were convicted of being rude to an alderman and sentenced to months of hard labor. One was also flogged twenty-five times. Two weeks later the ferrymen escaped, but their cause was taken up by a self-appointed advocate named William Keteltas, a latter-day McDougall.

Calling the case "the most flagrant abuse of rights . . . since the Revolution," Keteltas wrote articles for the press and petitioned the State Assembly for redress. When he appeared before the legislature, he was escorted by two thousand supporters. When he was jailed for slander, a mob protested in the name of "The Spirit of '76." The case exposed the underlying components of class conflict that complicated the shared commitment to revolutionary ideals. In refusing to defer to the elite, the city's workingmen reaffirmed the self-dignity of the masses that democracy promised.[78]

The issues of race and gender equality revealed yet more limits of communal consensus. After the war, New York State adopted a representative government modeled after the federal Constitution. Although state legislators granted liberal voting rights for white men, they did not abolish slavery or enfranchise free blacks and women. Actually, the status of women had declined since the early colonial period when, because of a labor shortage, women could become artisans, shopkeepers, and merchants. By contrast, laws now restricted women's options making Hamilton, who never forgot his own mother's struggles for self-sufficiency, an early advocate of women's rights. He seemed to understand that women were experiencing what the historian Elaine F. Crane described as "dependence in the era of independence."[79]

The plight of women was illuminated by the Bawdyhouse Riot of 1793, which originated when Lanah Sawyer reported being raped by a gentleman, Harry Bedlow, at Mother Carey's bawdyhouse. Sawyer was the daughter of a popular ship captain, a seamstress, not a prostitute. Bedlow was a known bon vivant and frequent customer at Mother Carey's. In court, his lawyers attacked Sawyer as a typically weak, loose, lower-class girl who should have recognized seduction when she saw it. After considering the evidence for fifteen minutes, the jury acquitted Bedlow.

The verdict sparked three days of rioting in the Red Light district, sardonically referred to as Holy Ground because it was located near Trinity Church. Hundreds of working-class men destroyed several brothels, particularly Mother Carey's, and attacked the homes of Bedlow's lawyers. No one was hurt, but the protesters effectively registered their hostility to the entrenched power of wealth. It was a striking example of the undercurrents of class and gender conflicts in a nascent democracy.[80]

Race remained controversial even if did not cause violence in this period. Opposition to slavery in New York had been mounting for decades. In 1737, Zenger urged the city to import more indentured servants instead of slaves. In 1767, Flushing's Quakers declared slavery unchristian and vowed to combat it. In 1774, a widely read pamphlet penned anonymously by Hamilton criticized slavery as "fatal to religion and morality," anathema to reason and "industry," the source of "misery and indigence." The spirit of the Revolution motivated some men to free their slaves, whereas others could no longer support slaves once they themselves had to flee.[81]

The biggest impetus for change came when the British offered freedom to slaves who would serve in the royal army and New York State felt compelled to make an equivalent counteroffer. (Hamilton supported a similar policy for the Continental army.) The result was that runaway slaves from the North and South gravitated to New York to form their own military units or to assume various civilian jobs. Although some blacks improved their situation, the majority remained oppressed. Shrewdly did the Long Island slave poet, Jupiter Hammon, encourage whites who "were so much engaged for liberty to think of the state of the poor black, and to pity us."[82]

Some did. Although he had married into a slaveholding family, Hamilton continued to oppose "the peculiar institution." With Jay (who owned five slaves) and McDougall, Hamilton helped establish a New York Manumission Society in 1785. It sponsored the first African Free School in 1787, petitioned for the end of the slave trade, and protected runaway slaves from capture. In 1788, New York State adopted a new, more liberal slave code and slowly granted slaves legal protection to marry, own property, and have a jury trial in capital cases. As a response to segregation and as a statement of self-determination, the African Methodist Episcopal Zion Church was formed in 1796 under the leadership of Peter Williams, a former slave.[83]

The election of John Jay as governor of New York State in 1795 set the stage for a contentious, extended debate over emancipation. The solution was a compromise gradual emancipation act by which all children born of slaves after July 4, 1799 would be considered free. Nonetheless, they would continue to serve their parents' masters until age twenty-four if female and until age twenty-eight if male. Existing slaves were not freed but children, the aged, and the sick could be released to the local overseers of the poor. As a result, some slaves were abandoned and many were sold in order to avoid financial loss later. Others managed to buy themselves or negotiate work agreements premised on freedom. Slavery began to die in New York City although equality remained elusive and racial violence was hardly over.[84]

Conflict in the colonial and revolutionary eras strained social consensus and raised questions about how to maintain social order. Provisions for policing New York City hardly met the needs of a rapidly growing, regularly disrupted community. Whether it was the rattle watch of the Dutch period or the citizen's watch during the English and Revolutionary eras, the number of men protecting the city was small. In some periods they were paid; in others service was an expected part of residency with the proviso that the rich could always pay for a substitute. During the Revolution, citizens created their own watch to compensate for the inadequacies of the city's watch. Nonetheless, because there was considerable resistance to recreating a repressive Old World military force, policing remained weak until well into the nineteenth century.[85]

From the start, the colony's diversity fostered adversity as exemplified by the city's reaction to the slave conspiracy of 1741. This episode foreshadowed the development of a tradition of repression and intolerance that would cast a dark shadow over New York and American history. At the same time, the city that was derided in 1776 as a "motley collection of all the nations under heaven" nurtured a tradition of practical toleration most evident in the Flushing Remonstrance, the Zenger case, and the King's College debate. These episodes projected the brightest lights of the American vision.[86]

The tension between the two trends kept New York vibrant and volatile while nurturing a third tradition—one of conflict. The more New York cherished liberty, the more it incited protests by people whose liberty was limited by local or foreign foes. Disputes over slavery, the Leisler Rebellion, the Stamp Act crisis, the McDougall Affair, and the post-Revolutionary riots put New York City at the center of that tradition. In trying to balance private interests with the public good, the city often heeded McDougall's call to "rouse" itself. Consequently, New York helped crystallize the resistance that became revolution and promote the patterns of popular rule that strengthened democracy.[87]

In many ways, Alexander Hamilton was the essential New Yorker—the typical immigrant, the ultimately ambitious, restless man. He has been described as "turbulent and explosive, . . .ruthless and aggressive," qualities that also defined his city. Hamilton embodied New York's pivotal contribution to the developing nation replete with all of its contradictions. He was liberal and conservative, aristocratic and democratic, materialistic and humanitarian, idealistic and pragmatic, local and national. As a result, contends biographer Ron Chernow, Hamilton became "the flash point for pent-up conflicts" of the age. Primarily a student of difference, Hamilton knew that self-interest could divide and unite, corrupt and motivate. Where better to learn these lessons than New York?[88]

By virtue of its complexity, New York City was repeatedly swept up in its own whirlpool of political, economic, and social conflict, which, in turn, kept it from ever becoming stagnant. Throughout the colonial and revolutionary eras, New York wrestled with the challenges of development. Its vitality and resiliency derived from the fact that, as Governor Thomas Dongan observed in 1687, it was "generally of a turbulent disposition." New York City's crises commanded widespread attention because they reflected the most fundamental dilemmas of the emerging society—its most inspiring ideals set in the context of its most disturbing inconsistencies. A model of pluralism, liberalism, and capitalism, New York was also a seedbed of enslavement, ethnic tension, and repression. This combination of opposites made New York, in the words of the historian Bruce Wilkenfeld, not "merely a precursor but. . .a paradigm" of the new nation.[89]

3

Gotham

The Paradoxical City, 1800–1840

We can thank the satirist Washington Irving for giving New York City its most enduring and endearing nickname, one replete with historical double meanings. In 1807, Irving equated New York City with Gotham, an old English town whose residents pretended to be simpleminded in order to keep the king from taking over their village. As the English put it, "more fools pass through Gotham than stay in it." This name lasted because it captured what the historian William R. Taylor called "the ironic persona of the city." It suggested a place that was at once "unique and representative," a part of the nation, yet different from it. In being "outlandish, crazy, yet somehow typical," New York provided perspective on America and much material for satire throughout the early national and Jacksonian periods.[1]

The English origin of the term was paradoxical because Irving, who was named after America's first president, wrote in the post-Revolutionary period and promoted the development of national identity through a national literature. In fact, he insisted on using "the original Indian name, Manna-hatta," as a mark of independence from Europe. Furthermore, his *History of New York* (1809) was notable, not just for its humor, but also because it drew on the pre-British past of the nascent nation. While mocking the rotund, contented Dutch, he was also criticizing the lean, aggressive British and their Yankee descendents. Irving cleverly used the colonial era to reflect on postcolonial dilemmas. In the process, he suggested that New York and America were more complicated than they seemed.[2]

So was he. Despite his nationalism, he was skeptical of the republicanism of his age. Despite being unsuited for politics, he sought and accepted political appointments. Despite focusing on local subjects and being the first writer to achieve financial success in America, he spent much of his life abroad—flitting between London, Madrid, and New York. Even in New York, his time was divided between the city and his country home in Sunnyside. As a result, Irving's significance lies in his own "ironic persona." Like Ichabod Crane, his fictional schoolmaster, Irving was peripatetic and paradoxical, haunted by the history he was creating. Like Gotham in the early nineteenth century, he was torn between past, present, and future, between myth, ideals, and reality.[3]

In New York City, the first four decades of the nineteenth century were tumultuous because change was too vast and too fast to either control or comprehend. Gotham was characterized, said one observer, by "the perpetual motion of the busy." In Irving's *History*, city streets were created by grazing cows before burghers had a chance to plan them. Similarly, the city fathers mapped out a street grid in 1811, but failed to put marble on the back of city hall because they did not envision the city expanding that far. In fact, New York was growing so quickly that efforts to shape it often seemed futile. Certainly, its policing system was a joke. The difference was that although Irving's Dutch colonists did not seem to care very much about the future, post-Revolutionary New Yorkers cared a great deal. They cared so much that they embroiled the city in constant conflict.[4]

Early-nineteenth-century Gotham was a colorful, if confusing, combative, and contradictory, place. It had the best theaters and the worst water, the fanciest mansions and the filthiest slums. As the city shifted from a simple to a complex economy, the rapid growth of population, trade, and industry created both opportunity and chaos. Flux bred controversy and the democratization of politics brought discontent into the public arena. Consequently, no other period witnessed so many incidents of violent struggle. Gotham was a far cry from the sleepy, self-satisfied town that Irving's history extolled. Perhaps that was his point.

Tension mounted from 1800 through the 1820s, reached a peak in 1834, which is called "the year of the riots," followed by another riot in 1835, leading to "the year of the strikes" in 1836. The period culminated with economic depression and a final riot in 1837. Protracted conflict was actually an appropriate expression of Jacksonian-era convictions that the common man should participate in public affairs. The radical feminist Fanny Wright insisted that this principle apply to women too. "The Jacksonian attitude," explained the historian Arthur M. Schlesinger Jr., "presumes a perpetual tension in society, a doubtful equilibrium, constantly breeding strife and struggle."[5]

Newspapers played an important role in the violence not just by reporting on events but also by taking sides and competing with each other to influence popular opinion. One editor even participated in the riots and several were accused of fomenting them. The press war was waged among mainstream newspapers geared toward the well-to-do as well as between the mainstream papers and the new penny papers geared toward the working classes. Long before radio and television, the metropolitan press was the key source of information and opinion in a city that had grown too big and too complicated to be deciphered by word of mouth. As new technology facilitated printing, newspapers multiplied, became more accessible to more people, and shaped Gotham's rise as the nation's media center.[6]

New York was not the only city that experienced conflict during this time period. In fact, an epidemic of riots swept the nation from 1834 to 1836. However, it is significant that the most rioting occurred in Gotham and that the Five Points, America's first slum, became the symbol of the nation's dilemmas. According to historian Carl Prince, these riots "alarmed a nation" because they revealed how much society was in stress and how many people were in distress. They exposed the complications of egalitarianism and the quest for dignity by workers, women, blacks and Irish Catholics. Consequently, the early nineteenth century was a precarious period for a young city in a young nation seeking political and social stability in the midst of exciting, if unsettling, economic change. New York was never more contested.[7]

The struggle over change was latent in another term that Irving bequeathed to Gotham. The surname of his narrator, the purported historian, Diedrich Knickerbocker, quickly became a synonym for New Amsterdam and ultimately for New York. By the time of the 1849 edition of his *History,* Irving proudly noted that Knickerbocker had already become a household word, and was being used as a New York label for everything from businesses and bread to the first baseball team formed in 1842.[8]

At the same time, Knickerbocker was a moniker for resistance to change, particularly by prominent old families of Dutch lineage who resented the Yankee families of Anglo-Saxon lineage who were capitalizing on Gotham's growth. Responding to social clubs formed by New York's New England transplants, Irving started his own club comprised of old-line families like Stuyvesants and Roosevelts. His conflict with Yankees struck at the heart of New York's metamorphosis as a mercantile center. However, Irving himself admitted that it was a weak defense against men who "out-bargain them in the market, out-speculate them on the exchange, out-top them in fortune, and run up mushroom palaces so high that the tallest Dutch family mansion has not wind enough left for its weather-cock."[9]

The economic changes were so striking that by 1815 New York surpassed Philadelphia to become the nation's premier metropolis. By the 1820s, Gotham had cornered the east coast steamship trading route, enriching Cornelius Vanderbilt in the process. Instituting regular packet service to Europe brought wealth to the Grinnell family. Developing an efficient auctioneering system did likewise for Philip Hone who was mayor when the Erie Canal opened in 1825. As New York became the link between the mid-west and Europe, New Englanders flocked to the city to build fortunes as merchants. They included Anson G. Phelps and William Earl Dodge in metals, Stephen Whitney in shipping, and Lewis and Arthur Tappan in silks. Ten years later, the harbor was bursting with over a thousand ships representing over 150 different ports and New York dominated both the nation's import and export trades.[10]

The development of external commerce had great internal implications. In the fifteen years between 1820 and 1835, the city's population more than doubled from 124,000 to 270,000. Hotels, theaters, newspapers, and stores multiplied accordingly. The city's mercantile sector spawned an industrial sector to build ships, refine sugar, print books, and sew clothing. There were savings banks for the middle classes and investment banks for the rich. When the Stock Exchange was established in 1817, it magnified New York City's core financial functions. Gotham's growth seemed limited only by the fact that the Bank of the United States (BUS) was located in Philadelphia where policies undermined New York's interests although New York's revenues provided much of the bank's resources.[11]

The city expanded as profits exploded. The wealthy were already abandoning downtown in favor of upper Broadway when the 1822 yellow fever epidemic propelled them to Greenwich Village, which was absorbed by the city in 1825. Land speculation was so profitable that, by 1830, John Jacob Astor ranked as the nation's wealthiest man comfortably situated on a thirteen-acre estate at Hell Gate. The area would soon be named Astoria after the man and his west-coast trading post, which was chronicled by none other than Astor's close friend, Washington Irving.[12]

However, the poor who were squatting on land that was previously considered public property faced disaster. Dislocated by the sale of lands and the erection of fences, people angrily tore down fences throughout the 1820s. Hundreds rioted to protest the fencing of Stuyvesant family land in 1828. These land riots were fitting sequels to the Peach Tree War, which, in Irving's opinion, had previewed a propensity for "discontent" in an "ambitious little province" bent on expansion "far into the regions of Terra Incognita."[13]

The clash of values over the meaning of progress in early-nineteenth-century New York also was evident in the dog and hog riots. Trying to address urban problems such as disease and dirt, unpaved and unlit streets, foul water and fires, the city government began expanding its supervisory role. It required licenses for numerous jobs, promoted cleanliness, and set standards for selling in and transporting goods to the marketplace. In 1811, the city mandated that all dog owners pay a tax as well as tag and leash their animals. In 1821, it banned hogs from the streets altogether.[14]

The city fathers saw loose dogs and hogs as dirty pests, even if they helped clean the streets of garbage long before a sanitation department existed. To poor New Yorkers, the dogs were pets while the hogs were sources of food and revenue. When dog catchers rounded up the animals in 1811, riots ensued; some dogs were freed but over two thousand were killed. Nonetheless, the city relented and the law was not strictly enforced until 1818 when more riots occurred. This time, however, the roundups were smaller and so were the mobs.[15]

The situation was different with the hogs, which were vital sources of income and nourishment for the poor. Municipal efforts to capture hogs sparked riots from the 1820s to the 1850s. These riots were more violent than the dog riots. Both the hog catchers and the marshals protecting them were beaten up and the hogs were freed. The rioters were those most affected by the law such as butchers and residents of the city's poorest sections, including artisans, women, African Americans, and Irish immigrants, all of whom the press dismissed as "the swinish multitude."[16] (See Figure 3 following page 150)

The issue was bigger than hogs. The land, dog, and hog riots revealed that urban growth was pitting segments of the city's populace against one another. Although the propertyless were trying to uphold the tradition of public use of public streets and public land, the propertied classes were rejecting old concepts of communal rights in favor of a new emphasis on private rights backed by public authority. At the same time, by moving uptown, they were abandoning the patterns of residential proximity that had previously kept rich and poor within range of each other. The historian Elizabeth Blackmar explains that economic polarization was being translated into a geographic polarization that minimized contact and magnified distrust between classes. As the interests of the rich increasingly outweighed the interests of the poor, New York City's social contract seemed to be unraveling.[17]

Immigration added a new dimension to the dynamics of change and further frayed the urban fabric. The 1820s and 1830s brought German and Irish Protestants fleeing political and economic problems in their own countries and looking for new opportunities. Irish Catholics responded to the call for workers to help build canals and railroads. As a result of the rapid population growth, the infamous Five Points district emerged as the nation's first slum marked by poverty, crowding, filth, disease, and crime. Located behind City Hall on the site of an old filled-in pond where five streets converged, it witnessed at least two dozen disturbances or riots during the 1820s.[18]

One group taking advantage of these changes was the Society of St. Tammany, a social club formed in the 1780s that later evolved into a powerful political club synonymous with the Democratic Party. Eager to win the immigrant vote, Tammany men met the immigrant ships, helped people find dwellings and jobs, and aided them in completing naturalization papers. In return, the immigrants supported Tammany at election time and considered themselves Americanized.[19]

By contrast, the Whig Party came to be identified with nativism, that is, opposition to immigrants, especially Irish Catholics. Historic prejudices brought over from England surfaced in employment directives that "no Irish need apply" and in several blatantly anti-Irish Catholic riots. When the rate of immigration soared in the 1830s, antagonism surged. Anti-Catholic associations were formed, anti-Catholic literature was widely distributed, and rumors were spread of a papal plot to take over the city.[20]

Religious reformers pursued a different strategy by sending missionaries into the slums. In 1829, the popular preacher, Charles Grandison Finney, made Gotham a center of Evangelical Protestantism counting the Tappan brothers among his followers. Finney's work spurred efforts to eliminate taverns and prostitution. Religious organizations distributed hundreds of thousands of pamphlets designed to rescue the poor from sin. Sabbatarians like Arthur Tappan waged a campaign to ban all entertainment and drinking on Sundays. These ills were associated with poverty and the slums, which were associated with Irish Catholics.[21]

The Irish Catholics did not take such insults lightly. They broke up meetings of anti-Catholic organizations and defended themselves in street brawls. In an 1828 New Year's Eve riot, a mob of four thousand marched down the Bowery making noise, breaking windows, destroying carts, and creating general chaos. They also tore down the iron railing around Battery Park in order to make it more accessible to "the sovereign people." The mob was in control and showed no fear of the police who twice retreated before them.[22]

Tension built until it erupted in the Five Points Riot of June 21, 1835, which began when sabbatarians tried to stop a Sunday saloon fight. The result was that thousands of Protestants and Catholics took to the streets and fought for three days. Irish Catholics were chased; their homes and stores were sacked; the mayor was assaulted and two men were killed. Religious and ethnic conflict branded the Five Points an urban battleground, thereby earning it the nickname, the "Bloody Sixth" Ward.[23]

The city was exploding under the pressures of change. Clearly, the old order was history and the traditional form of crowd control was pitifully inadequate. Night watchmen served at the pleasure of district commanders who served at the pleasure of the city councilmen. Not only was the watch small and subject to political whim, but it also was used as a dumping ground for people otherwise unemployable. Competence and professionalism were irrelevant. Of course, there had been no need for police in the Dutch era when people happily smoked their pipes, dozed, and grew fat. After all, Irving asked, "Who ever hears of fat men heading a riot, or herding together in turbulent mobs?" For him, the past was a golden age of simplicity, tranquility, and community that, he feared, "never more will dawn on the lovely island of Manna-hatta."[24]

FANNY WRIGHT AND EQUALITY

There was no greater contrast between past and present than the person of Frances (Fanny) Wright, a woman who so challenged convention that her name became both a rallying cry and a term of opprobrium. While workers proudly voted for the Fanny Wright labor ticket, most prominent citizens condemned Fanny Wrightism as a dangerous, deluded, and debauched ideology. Former mayor Philip Hone predicted that her "doctrines would unsettle the foundation of civil society, and subvert our fundamental principles of morality if people were fools enough to believe them." Much to his dismay, her influence spread in and beyond New York as she insisted that Jacksonian democracy be extended across race, class, and gender lines.[25]

Wright was a Scotch radical feminist who gave a series of controversial lectures in New York City and around the country from 1829 to 1830 and again in the mid-1830s. Orphaned as a child, she was raised by wealthy relatives in London, but followed her father's dedication to the revolutionary ideas of Thomas Paine. As a young adult, she visited and wrote about the United States and, amidst rumors of impropriety, traveled with General Marquis de Lafayette in France and America. Her most important American lecture tour began in 1828 when she was thirty-three. A year later, she came to Gotham believing that it was "the most central spot both with respect to Europe and this country."[26]

The first woman of note to speak before men in large public gatherings in the United States, Wright was the opposite of Irving's fat, frivolous house frau. She was utterly unorthodox in style as well as substance. Replacing the constraining garments of the day with a simple, loose-fitting Grecian toga, she impressed listeners with her intelligence, eloquence, sincerity, charisma, and melodious voice. Later in life, the poet Walt Whitman remembered her as "graceful, deerlike. . .beautiful in bodily shape and gifts of soul."[27]

In association with utopian reformer, Robert Dale Owen, Wright advocated cooperation and cooperative living as an alternative to the competition and exploitation that she believed characterized capitalism. Consequently, she supported workers' organizations and opposed oppression in every form. These commitments led her to become a gradual abolitionist and to establish two communal farms for freed slaves—one in Tennessee and one in Haiti. When both ventures failed and were clouded by interracial sexual innuendo, they proved costly to her inheritance and her reputation.[28]

More successful was the *Free Enquirer,* her widely read, appropriately named New York–based journal dedicated to Right Reason and coedited with Owen. It contributed to the rise of the penny press by widely disseminating information through an inexpensive mass-oriented newspaper in contrast to the existing expensive, elitist papers. From 1829 to 1831, the *Free Enquirer* attacked the rise of big banks and the decline of small businesses, the materialism of the clergy and the misery of the poor, the ruthlessness of employers and the powerlessness of workers. Sparing none, Wright criticized both the established and the evangelical churches. She deplored the development of a "professional aristocracy" of lawyers, priests, and politicians who pursued their own interests at the expense of the people. It was, she said, "a war of class. . .where. . .the ridden people of the earth. . .are struggling to throw from their backs the 'booted and spurred' riders."[29]

New York City's workers were organizing politically just when Wright was at her peak in 1829 and they comprised the bulk of her audiences. Intensified by declining economic status in an increasingly insecure job market, artisan activism drew on a tradition of ad hoc political participation by mechanics, seamen, and other workers during the revolutionary era. As the historian Howard Rock demonstrates, working-class politics in New York City matured during the post-Revolutionary era when artisans secured the right to vote and run for office. Intent on making the promise of democracy real, they refused to defer to the presumed superiority of the mercantile class. Their political motivation was strengthened by their economic concerns. Building on these themes, in 1829 the radical Workingman's movement became the nation's first radical Workingman's Party, often called the Fanny Wright Party. Opponents ridiculed it as the party of "Wright Reason" led by "Ichabod Ragamuffin" who was supported by "Rag, Tag and Bobtail."[30]

Nonetheless, the Workingman's Party did exceptionally well in the state elections of 1829 with over six thousand votes cast for several radical candidates. Wright herself received twenty write-in ballots. Although few actually won seats, the new radical political activists upset the traditional parties by proving that they could hold the balance of power in local elections. New York's 1829 election results showed the strongest correlation between wealth and voting patterns of any election during the Jacksonian era. Historians conclude that it signaled a new level of class-conscious politics in the state.[31]

The Workingman's Party faded from the scene by 1831, but its members remained politically active. In 1835 they led a bolt from Tammany whose men turned off the gaslights during a nominating convention in order to derail the labor insurgency. Lighting their Loco Foco matches, the laborites affirmed their independence by selecting their own slate and forming an Equal Rights party. Immediately, "Loco Focoism" was equated with "Fanny Wrightism." Although Fanny Wright did not ignite this fire alone, she definitely fanned its flames and, notes the sociologist Alice S. Rossi, was the only nineteenth-century woman to become part of the nation's political vocabulary.[32]

Wright's program of educational reform was particularly controversial. "Equality! Where is it, if not in education?" she asked. Her answer was that the American Dream would never become reality as long as "we see endowed colleges for the rich, and barely common schools for the poor." Accordingly, she proposed a national, tax-supported boarding school system where all children, boys and girls alike, would get the same food, clothing, and lessons regardless of economic background. Parents could visit, but their role would be limited. Ability, not inherited advantage, would shape children's futures and the resulting egalitarianism would strengthen democracy. Although Wright's specific program was widely criticized and never materialized, she helped make universal public education a central cause for both the labor movement and the antebellum reform movement.[33]

Wright's base in New York City was the Hall of Science, so named as a rebuke to religious institutions. True to her deist, free-thinking commitments, it was a temple of reason designed to empower the masses through the promotion of knowledge. Located in a former church that she purchased on Broome Street off the Bowery, it housed a bookstore, a library, a medical clinic, and an auditorium for twelve hundred. It also provided classes for adults, a nonsectarian school for children, and scores of well-attended lectures. Democratizing the literary society, secularizing the mission, and anticipating the settlement house, the Hall of Science was the nation's first holistic haven for working-class radicals.[34]

Many admirers called Wright the "female Tom Paine" and packed her lectures, not only in New York City, but also in Albany, Baltimore, Buffalo, Cincinnati, Louisville, Philadelphia, and St. Louis. Others considered her dangerous and tried to stop her. At one lecture, a barrel of oil was ignited filling the hall with smoke and causing a stampede; at another, the gas was turned off forcing the audience to light candles. Outside the hall, mobs harassed Wright's followers and there were several near riots. Cartoons derided her as a "downright gabbler, or a goose that deserved to be hissed." (See Figure 4 following page 150) The more she was pilloried by the press, the more people flocked to her lectures, including otherwise respectable women and prominent men like former mayor Hone. Even William Leete Stone, conservative editor of the *New York Commercial Advertiser*, went to five of her lectures and had to admit that, although her ideas were revolting, she was an "unrivalled...public speaker."[35]

Wright was an outspoken supporter of women's rights when there were none. Two decades before the 1848 Seneca Woman's Rights Convention and three-quarters of a century before Margaret Sanger's birth control campaign, Wright advocated full equality for women, including sexual equality. She criticized marriage as an institution, excoriated the economic exploitation of women, and deplored laws that denied married women the right to own property. She even condoned amalgamation and free love. In return, she was condemned as the "Red Harlot of Infidelity" and "a voluptuous preacher of licentiousness." William Cullen Bryant's *New York Evening Post* parodied her as "one bold lady-man" less interested in social reform than in "buxom boys with peachy cheeks."[36]

Wright may have had a particular impact on female workers. Indeed, it was reported that women comprised a large part of her audience, which was rare for public lectures in the early nineteenth century. Even though, as Wright acknowledged, the situation of women was better in America than in Europe, their roles were severely circumscribed. It was an era when women were expected to be pious and passive, domestic and demure. Ironically, being placed on a pedestal meant that opportunities for education, employment, and self-development were contracting for women, just as they were expanding for men. Indeed, women's sphere was limited to philanthropy, religion, reform movements, material consumption, and social life, especially for the upper and middle classes.[37]

The situation was much more difficult for working women. Although the culture emphasized their dependence on men, reality often left them on their own, especially in the city. As they migrated from the farm, either within the United States or from abroad, women lost their customary productive functions and had to seek new sources of survival. However, men monopolized work outside the home and were themselves struggling to earn a living wage. Women tried to adapt in a variety of ways. At home they took in boarders and laundry or sent small children to scavenge the streets. Venturing out of the home, women and girls could peddle goods they bought or cooked. The more fortunate could rent stalls in the local market; the less fortunate might have to enter the almshouse or turn to prostitution.[38]

The "oldest profession" had long flourished in New York City. As the city prospered, so did landlords renting to brothels, among them a member of the Livingston family. Prostitutes and madams proliferated, but their ostentation and independence threatened male notions of superiority. The result was violence against brothels during the 1820s when inebriated groups of men burst into brothels, destroyed furniture, and beat or threatened to rape the women. The aggressiveness of these riots reflected the new expansion of prostitution, its commercialization and the ways in which both developments undermined the prevailing presumption of women's subservience. The brothel riots proved Wright's point that competition and hostility between the sexes were the inevitable "fruits of inequality."[39]

In the clothing trade, one of the few industries that employed women at all, some women workers began to protest against their plight. The best jobs were dominated by men tailors who made only men's clothing, leaving women to make dresses, shirts, and clothing for children. Many women did piecework at home, which saved the employers overhead costs and enabled them to underpay or fire workers at will. The situation was somewhat better inside the shops where wages were higher, but the labor was hard, the days were long, and the pay was still too low for survival. Scorned by male tailors and employers alike, young women wondered, "If we do not come forth in our own defence, what will become of us?"[40]

Marking a turning point in the history of the city and the nation, the New York tailoresses mounted the first woman's strike in 1825. It did not last long, but in 1831 they managed to hold out for over a month. Fully aware of the significance of their actions, they recognized, said one striker, that "it needs no small share of courage" for women to act so boldly in public. Although these workers were not physically violent, they, like Fanny Wright, did violence to conventional notions of women's role in society.[41]

Fanny Wright was a flashpoint for the sensitivities of her era. Both the message and the messenger created what her biographer, Celia M. Eckhardt, calls "the hysteria she inspired in New York" and made her "the most controversial woman in America." Wright's analysis of society was audacious. She took on the powers that be in all their manifestations, attacking America's most venerable political, economic, and social institutions. In tune with prevailing republicanism, Wright believed in equality, democracy, and the perfectability of humankind, but she pushed their definitions well beyond those of the day. Yet, rather than being summarily dismissed, Fanny Wrightism commanded attention across boundaries of ideology, class, and gender. The term itself was widely used to advocate or denigrate social change.[42]

As a female, Wright added a dynamic new dimension to public debate and irritated delicate cultural nerves accordingly. In her very being—articulate, pretty, educated, eloquent, self-confident, impassioned, idealistic, defiant, and independent—she personified protest against present realities and offered a promise of future possibilities. She provided proof that a woman could become, in her own words, "a vigorous tree" rather than just "a fragile vine clinging ... [to men] for support." Consequently, Rossi concludes that Wright was America's "first woman radical leader."[43]

Ironically, although Irving was conservative and Wright was radical, they shared some common characteristics. Both spent most of their lives outside New York City, but both were identified with it. When Irving traveled in Europe, he was considered a literary ambassador for America via New York. When Wright traveled in America, she symbolized the intellectual ferment, working-class radicalism, unconventional social mores, aggressive women, and spirit of dissent that defined Gotham.

Hardly a match for Irving's wit, Wright nonetheless penned her own satire. Using a biblical format to promote her secular program, she assailed the greedy "merchants and money-makers" who, together with the "soothsayers" (the priests) and the "perverters of words" (the press), ruled New York and enshrined false idols for the people to worship. "Then did a woman raise her voice in the midst of the city" and help the downtrodden see how rich men "devoured the fruit of the people" who were the real "strength of the land."

These ideas so infuriated the powerful that they determined "to poison her in the eyes of the people." However, instead of being fooled, the people rose up and resolved "to choose their rulers from among themselves." Thus, did Wright claim to inspire "the first awakening of the people in the great city." Thus, did she offer hope that all could attain "equal knowledge, equal protection, equal maintenance, equal privileges, equal enjoyments." Thus, did she expose the hypocrisies of her age, radicalize Jacksonian democracy, and reinforce the American Dream.[44]

THE 1834 ELECTION RIOT AND POLITICAL CHANGE

1834 was called "The Year of the Riots" because it was marked by repeated incidents of civic unrest that unnerved both the city and the nation. The April election riot was the most volatile of New York's frequent election riots and a symbolic test of Jacksonian democracy. The July anti-abolitionist riot provided chilling evidence of the racial and socioeconomic tensions of the antebellum era. The October Stonecutters' riot reflected the agonies of America's shift to an impersonal, capitalist economy. New York's riots were part of a national phenomenon. Two dozen major confrontations, sweeping from Portsmouth, New Hampshire and Charlestown, Massachusetts to Newark, Philadelphia, Baltimore, and New Orleans, involved more people in mass protest than ever before in the nation's history. Violence threatened to overwhelm reason in the era of the common man.[45]

Much was at stake. It was an exciting time when the nation's definition of democracy was being expanded. President Andrew Jackson set the tone by advocating equal rights (for white males) as opposed to special privileges, opportunity rather than monopoly, and the interests of the many over those of the few. According to the historian Robert V. Remini, Jackson's popularity derived from his fervent moral conviction that the majority must rule. However, to French observer Alexis de Tocqueville, that fervor could also create a "tyranny of the majority."[46]

The riots of 1834 gave credence to both perspectives. On the one hand, they reflected the aggressiveness of ordinary people determined to express their opinions on the critical political, social, and economic issues of the day. On the other hand, the riots demonstrated that popular participation could descend into a very undemocratic repression of minority groups. The intensity of the conflicts revealed the significance of the changes that were, noted Irving, "eternally keeping society in a ferment."[47]

The April election riot mirrored the political, economic, and social changes of the period. Participation in public affairs was stimulated in 1821 when New York State extended the right to vote to all white males (although imposing a property qualification on black males). Rallies and parades enlivened the three days allotted for elections in April and November, which led to fights at the polls and often escalated into riots throughout the 1820s and 1830s. In 1833 New York State finally authorized New York City to elect its own mayor, who had previously been appointed by the governor. The promise of long-delayed local home rule heightened excitement about the mayoral election of 1834.[48]

At the same time, the local election was part of a national conflict over the Bank of the United States (BUS), whose recharter was vetoed by President Andrew Jackson in 1832. The debate over the bank polarized the commercial metropolis and defined the 1834 election. Some New York merchants and businessmen supported the Whig Party, the BUS, and the economic stability it represented. Others sided with the Jacksonians in opposing the BUS as a symbol of federal interference in the local economy and as competition to local banks. They also believed that killing the Philadelphia-based BUS would secure New York City's dominance of national finance.[49]

Many workers felt compelled to stand by their Whig employers who backed the BUS or risk losing their jobs. However, in the Loco Foco spirit, more workers aligned with the Jacksonian Democratic Party and its local Tammany arm in opposing the BUS as a symbol of aristocracy and monopoly. It was imperative, claimed a campaign song, that "Mechanics, cartmen, laborers/ Must form a close connection/ And show the rich Aristocrats/ Their power at this election." To Fanny Wright, the BUS was the ultimately elitist institution antithetical to the welfare of the poor. The issue was joined and the nation's leaders (including the president himself, Massachusetts' congressman and former president, John Quincy Adams) Kentucky's Senator Henry Clay and New Hampshire's Senator Daniel Webster, agreed that the country's economic future depended upon "the great struggle which is to take place in New York."[50]

The voting extended over three days in early April 1834. On the first day, the Whigs marched through the city with a model ship called the "Constitution," which was matched by a Jacksonian boat named "Veto." Street theater and symbolic rhetoric became violent when the Jacksonians invaded a Whig political office and beat up several party workers. James

Watson Webb, editor of the Jacksonian *New York Courier and Enquirer,* proclaimed a "REIGN OF TERROR" and falsely reported that one man had been killed. Events escalated that night when a brawl broke out between hundreds of people attacking and defending their respective ships. Arrests stopped the chaos temporarily.[51]

On the second day, merchants closed their shops out of fear of more violence. According to the Democratic *New York Evening Post,* however, their real motivation was to foment violence by sending their employees into the Five Points to prevent the Irish from voting against the BUS. Webb himself led two hundred men into the center of the fray. As nativists marched their ship through the streets, they made derogatory comments about "the low Irish" and "the damned Irish." Elite observers like former mayor Hone saw the Irish Catholic mob as barbaric savages and applauded all efforts to subdue them. With a great deal of effort, the mayor, the district attorney, the sheriff, and assorted marshals kept the polls open; thirty people were placed under arrest.[52]

The riot raged into a third day. During the morning, there were more street fights over the ships and Mayor Cornelius Lawrence was wounded. At midday, the competition became intense when the ships passed Masonic Hall, located on Broadway between Duane and Pearl Streets, where the Whigs were meeting. As hundreds of Whigs rushed out of the hall to chase away the Jacksonians, they instigated a full-scale riot that lasted for two hours. Rich as well as poor fought hand-to-hand, club-to-club. The police were powerless and several suffered severe beatings.

Whigs looted stores, seized guns, and proceeded to the nearby state arsenal where they confiscated more guns. The Jacksonians intercepted them and soon thousands of people were fighting in the streets. One watchman was killed and eight others were hospitalized. The mayor called for peace and requested that the governor send a thousand state militiamen to restore order. In the end, the vote was close. With the Jacksonians winning the mayoral election and the Whigs carrying the Common Council, both sides claimed victory.[53]

The whole affair gave credence to Washington Irving's contempt for the democratic political process. An election, he wrote in 1807, was not a rational enterprise, but a form of "violent internal warfare" defined by "the discordant revelry of his majesty, the Sovereign Mob." Sadly, all the noise emanating from "the puffers, the bawlers, the babblers, and the slangwhangers" only proved that an election was a "great political puppet-show." William Cullen Bryant disagreed. Although the riot itself was regrettable, the editor of the *Post* concluded that "the principle of universal suffrage has undergone a fiery ordeal, and it has nobly stood the test." Democracy might be messy, but it worked.[54]

Yet, even Bryant had to admit that the process had been unsettling, and he wondered about the implications of the riot for the city's long-range future. Bryant particularly deplored the tendency to pit rich against poor, native-born against Irish. Self-interest seemed to have eroded the social contract on which urban peace depended. This was particularly problematic, he said, because of the very nature of a crowded city where people are "easily excited" and "dissension runs like wild fire." The most explosive political riot of Gotham's history showed how fragile the booming, aggressive city really was.[55]

THE 1834 ANTI-ABOLITIONIST RIOT AND SOCIAL CHANGE

More conflict was in the offing. Three months after the election riot, New York City experienced the worst violence it had yet witnessed and would witness until the Civil War. For eight days, controversy over the status of African Americans in Gotham and the movement to end slavery in the nation exploded in and around the Five Points. White mobs broke windows, smashed church doors, ransacked houses, and demolished stores. They viciously attacked blacks and their white supporters. New York, said one observer, was drowning in "an ocean of madness."[56]

Strangely, the city fathers did not react to the mayhem until the mob seemed totally out of control and a danger to property holders everywhere. Most prominent citizens actually applauded the Mayor's recalcitrance and criticized the abolitionists, not their attackers. Of all of Gotham's newspapers, only the *Post* lamented that the riot would "inform the whole people of the United States of the additional and deplorable blot" which defiled New York City's image.[57]

The violence began on a hot July 4, 1834, when anti-abolitionists broke up a racially integrated abolitionists' meeting commemorating the seventh anniversary of slavery's official demise in New York State. The site was the Chatham Street Chapel, located a block south of Chatham Square right near the Five Points. A former theater renovated by the wealthy evangelical abolitionists Arthur and Lewis Tappan for revivalist preacher Charles Grandison Finney, the chapel was a regular meeting place for abolitionists.[58]

On July 5, there was a fight between a butcher and the English stage manager of the Bowery Theater who cursed all Yankees. This was offensive at any time, but was now complicated by British support for the American abolition movement. When a white choral group and a black choral group were scheduled to meet in separate rooms at the Chatham Street Chapel on July 7, a major fight erupted. On the next day, an abolitionist's store was set on fire and another integrated abolitionist meeting was disrupted.[59]

On July 9, the mob invaded a third abolitionist meeting at the Chatham Street Chapel and ransacked Lewis Tappan's home. They caused so much chaos at the Bowery Theater that the popular American actor, Edwin Forrest, had to be called in to calm the crowd. July 10 and 11 brought general mayhem. The mob attacked homes, businesses, and churches associated with white abolitionists, including Arthur Tappan's store, and demolished five Mulberry Street brothels serviced by black women. They also destroyed black churches, a black school, black-owned stores, and black homes in the Five Points district. Despite numerous appeals to the Mayor to act, the state militia was not summoned until July 12. No one was killed, but sixty houses, six churches, and several other buildings were destroyed.[60]

The riot was perplexing. To be sure, it occurred when the city was in a state of general unrest created by the April election riot, a recession, labor strikes, and ethnic tensions. However, unlike most riots, this one lacked a precipitating event. Furthermore, the victims were not only blacks but also whites who challenged the nature of race relations in antebellum America. One wonders why the riot was so intense and prolonged. Was it just an exceptionally hot July? Was the city government too weak to act? Were the abolitionists too threatening to too many economic, political, and social interests? Was racism so systemic as to justify violence? Was violence so endemic to Gotham that riots no longer fazed anyone? Or was it simply proof that, as Washington Irving had warned, a democracy was "nothing more or less than a mobocracy?"[61]

There is no doubt that this local, short-term conflict reflected larger, long-term national struggles. It occurred at a key moment in the nation's torturous path to Civil War, just when abolition was gaining strength and voice. Boston's William Lloyd Garrison, a frequent presence in New York, had been publishing his controversial abolitionist paper, the *Liberator,* since 1831. That year also brought Nat Turner's rebellion in Virginia, which spurred the South's frantic restrictions against educating slaves and distributing abolitionist literature. In 1833, America was shaken by the abolition of slavery in the British West Indies and by a polarizing sectional debate between the protectionist North and the free trade South. The nation was on edge.

New York City acquired a pivotal role in the national abolition movement when the Tappans helped form the New York Anti-Slavery Society in 1833 followed by the American Anti-Slavery Society in 1834. Although the abolition movement is often associated with well-to-do evangelical reformers such as the Tappans, evidence from antislavery petitions indicates that there also was significant support from middle-class artisans and shopkeepers. This broad base perpetuated the city's liberal traditions while disproving James Watson Webb's claim that New York's abolitionists were just a few fanatics. Consequently, the abolition movement constituted a rising independent force in city politics, one that the city fathers may not have been too interested in protecting.[62]

Abolitionists were offensive on other grounds as well. When they distributed literature supporting immediate abolition, they antagonized people who favored either colonization or gradual emancipation. When they held integrated meetings, they threatened all whites who took segregation for granted. In addition, many prominent New Yorkers had close mercantile ties with the South and preferred to avoid the issue of slavery altogether. New York's abolitionists were repeatedly charged with fomenting disunion. Increasingly they were demonized as dangerous agents of social disaster, political disorder, and financial deficits.[63]

For all of these reasons, the abolition movement was especially controversial in New York City and some "gentlemen of property and standing" were actively involved in July's events either as organizers or as actual rioters. Certainly, the Tappans were widely reviled and it was no accident that the mob attacked Arthur Tappan's Hanover Square store and Lewis Tappan's Rose Street house during the riots. Although the store escaped serious damage because it was defended by Arthur and his armed employees, Lewis's home was gutted and its contents ignited in the streets. The night watchmen failed to intervene. Afterward, Lewis insisted on leaving the wreck untouched throughout the summer as "a silent anti-slavery preacher" for all to behold.[64]

Black abolitionists were also active in the city, further irritating many whites. David Ruggles, for example, aided numerous runaway slaves (including Frederick Douglass in 1838). In addition he opened the first bookstore, library, and literary society for African Americans. In 1827, *Freedom's Journal,* the nation's first black newspaper, was started in New York City. Despite segregation in jobs, schools, and churches, in the poor house and the graveyard, on street coaches, and in stores and restaurants, there was a small black middle class and several stable black communities, including Weeksville in Brooklyn. Whites who felt threatened by these developments feared that abolishing slavery would enable Southern blacks to migrate north and flood the job market. Significantly, the 1834 rioters carefully targeted black churches, homes, schools, and small businesses, as if expressing their hostility to black self-sufficiency.[65]

The riot was laced with irony. Existing racial tensions made whites susceptible to suggestions that, as in 1741, blacks were plotting to "burn the city." They believed false reports that a "Negro Riot" was taking place when whites were actually the aggressors. Events were complicated by the fact that, segregation notwithstanding, blacks and whites lived in close proximity throughout the poorer wards. As a result, when the rioters wanted to attack black homes in the Five Points, they had to ask whites to identify their houses by placing candles in the window. Another curiosity was that, although frequently blamed for riots, unskilled Irish laborers living in the Five Points did not dominate the mobs in 1834. Rather, most rioters were native-born skilled laborers and tradesmen living in nearby neighborhoods who saw free blacks as a threat to their already fragile economic status.[66]

These twisted realities were highlighted by a shockingly strident, racially charged debate that made the 1834 July riot unique. Much of the blame for the controversy has been laid at the door of James Watson Webb. His *Courier and Enquirer* editorials repeatedly used incendiary language to equate abolition (the elimination of slavery) with amalgamation (interracial marriage). In his opinion, racial mixing meant "mongrelization," which he found so "disgustful" that he sanctioned violence against anyone who dared support integration and thus "outrage public feeling."[67]

When the Reverend Samuel H. Cox (who was white) openly supported integration by opposing "Nigger pews," that is, segregated church seating, and announced that Jesus was probably of dark skin, Webb was enraged. Nothing could be more appalling, he said, than to suggest that "the Saviour of mankind was a negro." No wonder Cox's church at Laight and Varick Streets was demolished during the July riots along with the Spring Street church of another abolitionist Presbyterian minister, Henry G. Ludlow, who had supposedly married mixed couples.[68]

Webb had good company in the person of William Leete Stone, editor of the *New York Commercial Advertiser* and secretary of the New York Colonization Society, which advocated resettling blacks in Africa. On July 7, 1834, in the midst of the riot, he published an offensive satire on amalgamation. In a mock misspelled letter to the editor, a black man, purporting to be "a good skoller," solicited a white wife in the interests of "equal rites." He requested that she be "young and handsum and of good health for de sake of de posterrity." Moreover, she should "be clean and free from smel, because I don't tolerate any smel bout me." Most important, she should "hab plenty money. . .be in de highest circles and a member ob de Bobolition Society." This ribald parody reinforced prevailing prejudices and helped make amalgamation the major topic of private and public discussion during the summer of 1834.[69]

After the riot, the complexity of the controversy became more apparent than ever. Reverend Ludlow officially denied performing interracial marriages or supporting amalgamation. So did Peter Williams Jr., the nation's first African American Episcopalian minister and pastor of St. Phillip's African Episcopal Church on Center Street, which was savaged by the mob. Moreover, Williams was compelled to resign from the American Anti-Slavery Society or relinquish his ministry. Public pressure was so strong that the American Anti-Slavery Society itself issued a formal statement, over Arthur and Lewis Tappan's signatures, that it did not "promote or encourage intermarriages between white and colored persons." The anti-abolitionists had triumphed over New York's psyche as well as on its streets.[70]

In essence, amalgamation became a code word for the destruction of an entire social, economic, and political structure steeped in racial distinctions that were threatened by abolition and the prospect of integration. The July riot demonstrated that amalgamation was as much a psychological trigger point in the North as in the South. Derived from a history of anxiety over interracial sex and slavery, it explains why the 1834 riot was the most extended and emotionally charged, although not the most lethal, racial conflict of the era. (It also may help explain why the Supreme Court did not end all prohibitions on interracial marriage until 1967.) At the very least, the 1834 riot seemed to validate de Tocqueville's comment that "slavery recedes, but the prejudice to which it has given birth is immovable."[71]

New York's anti-abolitionist riot was echoed by similar race riots in New Jersey, Connecticut, and New Hampshire. Violence was narrowly avoided in Brooklyn during July but raged in Philadelphia during August. Newspapers in Boston, Detroit, Utica, and Newark blamed New York's abolitionists for all the trouble. By contrast, de Tocqueville's collaborator, Gustave de Beaumont, confirmed his conviction that mob violence meant the "tyranny of the majority."[72]

To Southern newspapers, the riot suggested widespread Northern resistance to abolition. However, in Washington, D.C., it was viewed as the prelude to an inevitable struggle between slave and free labor, between North and South. New York's 1834 anti-abolitionist riot intensified the nation's racial agonies and, through the issue of amalgamation, showed how convoluted the race question really was. The riot brought to the surface passions and insecurities that had haunted the city since its inception and offset its traditions of tolerance.[73]

THE 1834 STONECUTTERS' RIOT AND ECONOMIC CHANGE

Although the Stonecutters' Riot was the least dramatic confrontation of 1834, it represented some of the most disturbing changes of the era. The problem was that Jacksonian dreams of equality and opportunity conflicted with the new mass production, industrial economy. As the small shop was replaced by impersonal work settings, the skilled craft worker was being displaced by unskilled labor at uncertain daily and seasonal wages. Ironically, labor was losing status in the very era that celebrated the common man. "The arrogance of wealth," observed Irving, seemed related to the "heartburnings of. . .poverty."[74]

Stonecutters were skilled craftsmen facing wage reductions in the open market. For several decades, skilled craftsmen such as bakers, carpenters, and printers had been defending themselves against a loss of status in the local economy. In 1801, bakers had struck against city pricing regulations and in 1803 a cross section of artisans had opposed a plan to establish public workshops designed to train the poor to make shoes and hats. In both cases, the artisans were trying to protect their autonomy in the open market. Similarly, the stonecutters were struggling for survival in the 1820s. In 1823 and 1824, they held peaceful strikes for wage increases, but, by 1829, they were more desperate and attacked men who refused to strike. Three days of combat ended in twenty arrests. The use of prison labor further undercut wages and, in 1830, led to a one-day demonstration by two hundred stonecutters followed by meetings and parades.[75]

Then in 1833, New York University recruited prisoners to construct its new building on Washington Square. The stonecutters asked the State legislature to ban prison labor saying that it "took the bread out of their mouths." Their appeal fell on deaf ears. By October 1834, they were so angry that 150 men marched to the office of the contractor who employed the prison labor and, appropriately enough, stoned the building. The National Guard was summoned to quell the riot and camped in Washington Square Park for the next four days in order to prevent further disturbances. According to the historian Daniel Walkowitz, "for New Yorkers, the Stonecutters' Riot was an unsettling introduction to the American industrial revolution."[76]

The Stonecutters' Riot bridged the labor activism of the 1820s with the labor crisis of 1836. It was one episode in a larger, longer struggle over the dignity of labor. A weavers' strike in 1828 was particularly significant. First, the strikers sent an anonymous note to "Boss Nox" warning the city's largest textile employer, Alexander Knox, to raise wages or close up shop. When he refused, fifty rioters paid an uninvited, threatening visit to his home. They caused considerable destruction in Knox's shop and in the homes of weavers still working for him. By being violent, acting anonymously, and using the term "Boss," the strikers expressed the alienation and hostility that had developed between themselves and their employers. More than a century before unions became legal, these workers embraced, as the historian Sean Wilentz put it, "collective bargaining by riot."[77]

At the same time, workers understood the need for broader reforms, especially when they faced a serious economic recession in 1829. Accordingly, they entered politics independent of Tammany and started the New York Workingman's Party. Fanny Wright's lecture series energized the movement and influenced its distinctly radical platform, which called for public education, popular election of the mayor, salaries for local political officials so that the poor could serve, the end of imprisonment for debt, and the elimination of licensing regulations that limited job opportunities. The "Workies" garnered more votes than anyone expected in 1829, but the party fell victim to internal squabbles and died two years later.[78]

In 1833, workers formed a General Trades Union, which brought large numbers of skilled and unskilled white men together across crafts in a moment of labor unity that would not be seen again until the 1950s. In 1834, radical workers joined Tammany forces in the April election riots. In 1835, they bolted from Tammany through the Loco Foco, antimonopoly, equal rights movement. Workers understood that their daily struggles were part of broader changes requiring bolder, more concerted activism. Consequently, there were nineteen job actions in New York City during the five years from 1829 to 1834 and eighteen job actions in the single year of 1836. By then, two-thirds of Gotham's workers belonged to unions and Wilentz concluded that "If 1834 was New York's year of the riots, 1836 was the year of the strikes."[79]

The first strike of 1836 was in February by tailors angered at their employers' refusal to uphold the previous year's wage agreement. Rumors that other employers were planning to follow suit motivated clothing cutters, house carpenters, and hatters to plan strikes also. Soon thereafter, dockworkers walked out and marched along the waterfront accumulating new recruits at each ship. On the next day, a melee erupted between the police and two hundred dockworkers, while a second group of five hundred laborers briefly walked off their construction jobs and marched menacingly around the downtown area. On the third day, the mayor called for the militia, marking the first time that the military was used for strikebreaking in New York City.[80]

The angry workers called a mass meeting on the fourth day to affirm their right to strike. The meeting was important because it included both skilled and unskilled workers and because it threatened the first general strike in New York City history. That big strike never materialized, but numerous smaller strikes erupted throughout the city. Several were violent, especially between striking tailors, strikebreaking tailors, and the police. In March, a grand jury indicted the tailors' union on charges of conspiracy to restrain trade. The tailors responded with a huge procession of several thousand workers along Broadway. Each group carried its own trade insignia and signs critical of banks, monopolies, politicians, and employers. All asserted the workers' right to control their own wages. The conservative press feared that the city was "on the eve of another revolution."[81]

Tensions rose during April as employers organized their own trade associations to fight against the workers' organizations. Disregarding the risks involved, tailoresses joined the tailors' three-month strike. In mid-May, the tailors' trial began with an openly antilabor judge presiding. By early June, the jury decided that the tailors were guilty of conspiracy and that labor unions were illegal. To the workers, this ruling meant not only that they "no longer have any rights in the community" but also that "the freemen of the North are now on a level with the slaves of the South." A "Coffin of Equality" symbolized their anger. In one of the largest mass meetings in Gotham's history, a crowd of thirty thousand (about 20 percent of the city's population) gathered at City Hall in mid-June for speeches and resolutions. As in the pre-Revolutionary riots, they hung the judge in effigy. Strikes continued throughout 1836 and more conflict seemed inevitable.[82]

However, 1837 dealt a deathblow to the New York City labor movement in the form of the nation's first major industrial depression. To Irving, the economic crisis demonstrated the dangers of America's "universal devotion" to "the almighty dollar." Three factors fed the crisis. First was the decimation of the mid-Western wheat crop by Hessian flies in 1836. As the nation's key middleman in the production and distribution of flour and flour-based goods since the opening of the Erie Canal in 1825, New York's economy was heavily dependent on flour. The crisis threw thousands out of work while raising consumer prices, thereby hitting the working classes doubly hard. Second, the city was still recovering from a massive fire that had devastated downtown in 1835 causing housing shortages that raised rents all over the city. Third, a national economic panic triggered a serious depression that spelled economic collapse for many local bankers and businessmen, including Arthur Tappan.[83]

The result was unemployment for about a third of the city's labor force and the 1837 Flour Riot. Shortages and inflation hit all items needed for daily survival; winter made the situation worse. In February, a call went out for a mass protest meeting of "all friends of humanity, determined to resist monopolists and extortionists" responsible for the high prices of "Bread, Meat, Rent, Fuel." On one of the coldest days of the year, a crowd of five thousand converged on City Hall for a rally organized by the Loco Focos. The speakers criticized landlords, merchants, and other "aristocrats" whose wealth accumulated while the poor starved. They advocated old notions of a "moral economy" where the good of the whole community prevails over the interests of the few. By this reasoning, prices and rents should have been reduced so that the poor could sustain themselves in hard times. It was a notion in direct conflict with the profit orientation of a market-driven economy.[84]

One speaker suggested that a local merchant, Eli Hart, was hoarding flour and that the crowd might visit his store in protest. As a result, hundreds of people rushed down Broadway to Washington Street where they stormed the premises. This new tactic of targeting private property horrified the wealthy. Mayor Lawrence and the police tried to control the situation, but the crowd fought fiercely and the mayor fled. Flour barrels were seized and thrown to the crowd who scooped up whatever they could into boxes, baskets, or aprons. The flour sifted onto the street a foot deep. Some of the rioters then attacked other flour stores and only the arrival of the militia stopped the pillage. The Flour Riot was a collective cry of despair over the practical implications of economic change.[85]

Instead of dissipating, the depression deepened and dragged on into the 1840s. Ward-based relief committees were so swamped with hungry applicants that their funds ran out. Church-based efforts were limited both by funds and by a belief that the poor caused their own difficulties. Sharing this conviction and afraid to attract the poor from neighboring states, the city leaders barely increased aid appropriations despite an almost threefold increase in the number of the destitute. Not only was the idea of a public works program rejected, but all existing state public construction was stopped.[86]

Nonetheless, former mayor Philip Hone, who chaired the city's Flour Riot investigation, understood that the situation was dire for everyone, especially when he faced financial ruin himself. Contemplating the economic devastation that paralyzed his beloved city, Hone mourned over "Poor New York!" Ironically, the commercialism that was responsible for New York's long-range rise also could spell its short-range demise. The year of the riots, the year of the strikes, and the depression of 1837 all proved that the city's sensitivity to change caused pain as well as profit.[87]

The first four decades of the nineteenth century had been tumultuous for Gotham. The rise of Five Points, the prevalence of riots and strikes, the controversy over Fanny Wright, and the furor over amalgamation were outgrowths of major challenges to concepts of economic, political, and social democracy. According to the historian Paul Weinbaum, these struggles made New York a seething caldron of "a quarter million disharmonious people."[88]

At the same time, conflict showed that grassroots activism could effectively register popular discontent and promote participation in public dialogue. Metropolitan mayhem over whether to extend equality to Catholics, women, blacks, and workers was simultaneously a positive and a negative expression of Jacksonian democracy. By pushing that idea to its limits, New York called attention to its deficiencies and helped set the democratic agenda for the future.

Washington Irving had anticipated the difficulties that accompanied urban growth. Comparing the history of New York to the life of a person, Irving noted that periods of childhood simplicity and contentment are short. "Cities, like men, grow out of them in time, and are doomed alike to grow into the bustle, the cares, and miseries of the world." Although he knew that all parents want their progeny to acquire "magnitude and importance," Irving cautioned against "the dangers of the one and. . .the calamities of the other." He was right. As New York matured, its problems multiplied and its conflicts intensified. Oddly enough, those challenges seemed starker and greater because New York remained, in Irving's phrase, America's foremost "city of dreams and speculations."[89]

4

The Proud and Passionate City, 1840–1865

Walt Whitman, America's first urban poet, celebrated New York as a "city whose gleeful tides continually rush or recede, whirling in and out with eddies and foam!" He understood that the restless harbor, the crowded streets, and the busy people made New York a "proud and passionate city—mettlesome, mad, extravagant city." For him, it was a unique place that would "submit to no models" and tolerate no limits. Like the river currents, its power came from being both "hurried and sparkling."[1]

The period between 1840 and 1865 proved Whitman correct. Rapid economic growth, significant population shifts, and intense political struggle created a series of conflicts over religion, education, labor, and home rule. Two of the most violent riots of New York's history were compounded by several small riots. The sum total of all of this chaos raised doubts about the civility of the city and the nature of progress. People wondered whether a democratic system could control disorder while preserving liberty and opportunity. Nonetheless, the chaos was constructive because it meant that the city was confronting rather than ignoring the complex human dynamics of change.

Although Whitman waxed eloquent about "the aboriginal name," Mannahatta, he understood how much the city valued the new over the old. For him, it was always a city "of things begun" and never "finished." By mid-century,

New York was rapidly surpassing its rivals here and abroad. From 1820 to 1860, its population increased sevenfold to over eight hundred thousand. Swelled by rural migrants and European immigrants, mostly from Ireland and Germany, over half of New York City's population was foreign born by 1860 as compared to only 11 percent in 1825. The influx was so great that, in 1855, the city established the nation's first immigration depot at Castle Garden. Demographic change gave Gotham a diversified urban culture and provided a large labor supply for the burgeoning economy. In Whitman's words, New York was becoming a "city of the world."[2]

Whitman was its most ardent student. Born in 1819 of Dutch and English Quaker ancestry, he grew up in Brooklyn. Starting at age thirteen, he held a variety of jobs as printer, teacher, penny press editor, journalist, novelist, and, from 1846 to 1848, editor of the *Brooklyn Daily Eagle*. Whitman appreciated the variety of humanity, the individual in the mass, and the nobility of the ordinary person. These he celebrated in the poetry that came to dominate his life after the publication of *Leaves of Grass* in 1855. Although sometimes critical of urban anonymity, Whitman extolled New York as the pinnacle of civilization, which to him meant the embodiment of democracy. It was with great pride that he proclaimed: "This is the city and I am one of the citizens."[3]

As it grew geometrically, the city also was proud of itself. Horse-pulled street cars were enabling New York to expand uptown from Houston Street to 42nd Street where, in 1842, the massive stone Croton Reservoir provided the city's first decent water supply and, in 1853, the Crystal Palace welcomed the nation's first World's Fair. Further uptown, Central Park was begun in 1857 to provide "the lungs of the city." Frederick Law Olmstead and Calvert Vaux envisioned a beautifully landscaped haven where rich and poor could mingle. It was to be cherished, said Mayor Fernando Wood, as "one place" in Manhattan "not given up to mammon."[4]

In all other ways, Gotham seemed thoroughly dedicated to mammon, that is, money. By 1850, New York City dominated the nation's economy as its biggest market and the center for investment, insurance, credit, and retailing. So, too, New York was America's premier east coast railroad hub and, by 1860, it also controlled three-quarters of the nation's ocean steam tonnage. Moreover, manufacturing sector employment doubled from 8.5 percent in 1840 to 16.4 percent in 1850. Stores and banks complemented the sewing machine, the railroad, and the steamship to create a robust, diversified economy. Consequently, millionaires mushroomed, including the financier August Belmont and the merchant A. T. Stewart. As the new rich moved from Broadway to Fifth Avenue, their houses became increasingly extravagant, thereby magnifying New York's wealthy image. The city's economic predominance was unquestioned.[5]

At the same time, progress brought problems. The concentration of wealth at one end of the economic spectrum spelled struggle at the other end. By 1845, the top 1 percent of New York City's population owned half of its wealth, and the top 4 percent accounted for fully four-fifths of its wealth. The contrast between rich and poor was stark. In 1842, the English writer Charles Dickens depicted the "poverty, wretchedness, and vice" of the Five Points, which was the nation's first slum centered around the juncture of five streets near Chatham Square. Others decried the gangs, brothels, dance houses, billiard saloons, and opium dens. Poverty and crime fashioned an ominous partnership.[6]

Above all, observers condemned the Old Brewery, a dilapidated structure built in 1797 to make beer but turned into a tenement by 1837. The last refuge for the poorest of the poor, it was branded "the wickedest house on the wickedest street that ever existed in New York. . .in all the country and possibly all the world." Newspapers reported so regularly about the drinking, gambling, brawling, mugging, and killing that respectable people dared not venture into the Five Points except at their own risk. Dickens himself had two police escorts. To make matters worse, riots in and beyond the Five Points reinforced Gotham's growing reputation as an unmanageable, unconventional, unsavory place. The "democratic turbulence" of New York City, admitted Whitman, had a truly "fierce" side.[7] (See Figure 5 following page 150)

THE ASTOR PLACE RIOTS

The 1849 Astor Place Riots captured the tensions of mid-nineteenth century Gotham. In their aftermath, twenty-two people lay dead, with another nine dying later. There were over 150 serious injuries and more than 100 arrests. Originating in a petty, personal quarrel between two actors, the whole affair was a mixture of farce and tragedy. Although the immediate cues seemed ridiculous, the riots actually dramatized a complicated social script about power, status, and ethnicity. According to the historian Michael Kaplan, the Astor Place Riots were "the most direct and explosive collision between the world" of New York City's upper and lower classes. It was oddly fitting that the theater became the medium for expressing social anxiety in America's most culturally rich city.[8]

The Performers

William Macready was a prominent English actor and competitor of Edwin Forrest, a popular American actor about whom Horatio Alger wrote a biography. Macready cultivated a subtle, elegant approach to drama associated with the upper classes, whereas Forrest preferred a more emphatic, down-to-earth style that appealed to the lower classes. Their feud was long-standing and accentuated existing social tensions. In 1817, 1825, 1831, 1832, and 1834, New Yorkers rioted against English actors who were targeted as vestiges of royalty, symbols of aristocracy, and competitors to American actors. In addition, the English actors were sometimes seen as representatives of abolitionism, especially after slavery was abolished in the British West Indies in 1833.[9]

The Place

In May 1849, the two actors accepted separate but simultaneous engagements for Hamlet and the stage was set for conflict. Macready was scheduled to perform at the new Astor Place Opera House located at 8th Street and Lafayette Place. Its uptown site replete with lavish decor and strict dress code made it a symbol of the wealthy. Named for the nation's first millionaire, real estate speculator John Jacob Astor, the Opera House was the pride of the rich—the first collective demonstration of their economic prowess. Conversely, it was ridiculed in song as "de spot of de eliteet." Forrest was scheduled to perform at the more ordinary Broadway Theater located downtown between Pearl and Worth Streets. The contrast was clear and highlighted the differences between culture, class, and nationality that colored the conflict.[10]

The People

When the doors opened at the Opera House on May 7, the crowd rushed in, but, aside from the rich seated in their boxes, it was not the customary Opera House clientele. Most of the audience seemed to be the new type of self-assertive, gang-affiliated workingman called the Bowery B'hoy. Instigated by Captain Isaiah Rynders, former riverboat pilot, gambler, and politically connected gang leader, the hall soon resonated with the sounds of catcalls and stomping feet. When the play began, the crowd threw rotten eggs and potatoes, but Macready glared at them and stood his ground until several chairs hurled in his direction convinced him to leave the stage. The curtains fell on the first act of the Astor Place Riots.[11]

The city's better classes were mortified. Men like former mayor Philip Hone were determined that a disreputable mob not be allowed to determine what actors respectable people could watch. Accordingly, several prominent citizens (including *New York Times* editor Henry J. Raymond plus writers Washington Irving and Herman Melville) signed an open letter urging Macready to try again and promising him protection. In response, Forrest's supporters posted signs on the streets asking "Shall Americans or English rule in this city?" and urging people to express their opinions at the "English Aristocratic Opera House." A huge crowd assembled before the imposing building on May 10, the night of Macready's next performance, and a number of Forrest supporters were admitted because they had tickets. However, the police were there, too, and, by infiltrating the crowd, managed to foil an attack on Macready. When the rabble-rousers were ejected from the theater, their treatment further infuriated the crowd outside.[12]

The Panic

At this point, 350 members of the state militia arrived only to be greeted with missiles of rocks and paving stones. The horses got frightened, forcing the cavalry to leave, and the infantry sustained severe injury. Just as the troops were contemplating withdrawal, the sheriff, pressured by a sense of crisis, gave orders to fire. The first warning volley went into the air prompting one man to shout "Fire, if you dare—take the life of a free-born American for a bloody British actor!" Fire they did, this time directly into the crowd with fatal results. By the fourth volley, the second act of the riots was over and twenty-two people, innocent bystanders among them, lay dead in the bloodstained streets. On hearing the shots from his nearby house, Mexican War General Winfield Scott supposedly exclaimed in dismay, "They are shooting down American citizens!"[13]

The Postscript

On May 11, rich and poor gravitated to the scene to contemplate the disaster. Thousands viewed the bodies on display in the area. That night a massive protest rally, the third act of the riot, was held in City Hall Park. After resolutions condemning the shootings were passed, Captain Rynders branded the violence "murder" perpetrated on behalf of "the aristocrats of this city against the working classes." Mike Walsh, radical political defender of the workingman, called firing into the crowd "an atrocity" unthinkable even by the Czar of Russia. When he finished speaking, an angry crowd surged up to Astor Place, but a solid flank of two thousand soldiers, nine hundred policemen, and one thousand newly deputized special constables kept them at bay.[14]

Perspectives

The Astor Place Riots immediately became a national issue. The fatalities were disconcerting enough, but the riot also raised disturbing questions about the state of American society and the future of democracy. At mid-century, New York City seemed to suffer simultaneously from what the urbanist Ralph Conant called "under-control and over-control." There was a strong sense that democracy needed to be saved from itself by repressing mob action, upholding the law, and protecting property rights. From this perspective, the problem was under-control by government forces. The Unitarian minister, Henry

Whitney Bellows, justified using "the whole power of the State" to contain "the most atrocious mob since the abolition riots." Others believed that, in a democracy, people should be able to protest without being killed, that civilian and military spheres should be kept distinct, and that personal rights should take priority over property rights. From this perspective, 1849 was a prime example of governmental over-control.[15]

The fourth act revolved around the trials of those arrested in the riot. Distinguishing between anarchy and liberty, despotism and democracy, the district attorney proclaimed that the mob had "struck a blow at the American character" by undermining law and order. This theme was echoed by conservatives in the city and around the country, from the pulpit and in the press. Newspapers in Rochester and Boston recommended shooting directly into the mob from the first signs of disorder. James Watson Webb, editor of the *New York Courier and Enquirer,* applauded such tactics in order to reassure Europeans that their investments were still safe in New York City. Overall, the business community was relieved that the crisis had been quelled. Nonetheless, Hone recognized that "the lesson has been dearly bought."[16]

The 1849 riots raised real questions about the nature of civil society and the social contract. Why, asked several Philadelphia papers, had the city not tried to avoid using the militia by closing the theater, arresting the mob leaders, or otherwise preventing mobs from gathering? Why, asked several Albany papers, was the military called in when no revolution was threatened? Above all, why were the troops allowed to fire on civilians?[17]

Although the police force had been reorganized in 1845 with its first police chief and eight hundred new policemen, they were still low-salaried, untrained patronage appointees unable to handle the 1849 riots. Yet, the use of soldiers evoked the tyrannies of old Europe and seemed to subvert American liberties. The ethnic aspect of the conflict underlined this issue by evoking the revolutionary struggle between patriots and royalists. Consequently, Kaplan concluded that "unleashing the military into a civilian population had turned a local riot into a matter of national importance."[18]

The 1849 riots also heightened awareness of the new social realities of American society. Numerous observers commented on the class context of the protests. They saw the feud between Macready and Forrest as a substitute for the antagonism between capitalists and workers, rich and poor. Across the nation, the riots rang an alarm bell. They left one with the "feeling," said the *Philadelphia Public Ledger,* "that there is now in our country, in New York City, what every good patriot has hitherto felt it his duty to deny—a high class and a low class."[19] (See Figure 6 following page 150)

Parallels

Reflecting on the Astor Place Riots a few years later, *New York Tribune* editor Horace Greeley concluded that the lesson of 1849 was the need for social reform. Although he would have preferred that the unemployed "Go West," he understood that the working classes needed to have a stake in the city. In fact, their efforts to achieve precisely that goal reached a climax in 1850.[20]

Labor had been organizing since the depression of 1837–1843 ended. In 1843, Irish construction workers formed a mutual aid society for unskilled workers, the first of its kind in the city. In 1844, men struck in four different trades and tailors led a torchlight parade of two thousand workers. In 1845, a short-lived but bold Ladies' Industrial Association brought seven hundred women together "to stand up for our rights." In 1846, Irish dockworkers struck in Brooklyn. In 1847, the New York Protective Union promoted cooperative shops run by workers themselves.[21]

All of this labor activity provided a backdrop for the Astor Place Riots, raised parallel class-based issues, and served as a prelude to the dramatic events of 1850. Spring witnessed the formation of cooperatives and protective unions in a variety of trades. Parades and mass meetings dramatized the struggle. So many workers organized (including carpenters, shoemakers, tailors, confectioners, quarrymen, painters, porters, and printers) that the conservative press feared the advent of socialism. They were taken aback by the widespread resentment of workers toward their employers who, as one man put it, "make use of us like machines."[22]

In June 1850, a New York Industrial Congress was created to coordinate under one umbrella all the city's labor organizations. Soon, ninety groups supported its platform, which included better wages, public baths, and public reading rooms. In early July, nine hundred German, Irish, and American tailors struck for better wages. When a fight broke out during a march on Nassau Street, the city's newly enlarged police force clubbed and arrested protesters. Angry rallies in City Hall Park denounced police brutality and called for a general strike. As the tailors continued their protests against hostile employers, police attacks increased. They peaked in early August when three hundred marchers were assailed on Ninth Avenue at 38th Street resulting in dozens injured, forty arrested, and two killed. For the first time in American history, labor protesters met death at the hands of the urban police.[23]

Angrier than ever, the strikers stood firm and soon the employers capitulated, although several later abrogated their agreements. Even so, the labor crisis of 1850 was significant. By bringing white, male workers together across lines of skill and ethnicity, it affirmed their potential organizing power and laid the groundwork for future activism. As an extension of the class-consciousness evident in the 1849 Astor Place Riots, the labor struggles of

1850 placed New York City at the center of the nation's class conflict. Not surprisingly, Walt Whitman concluded in 1852 that, "at this moment, New York is the most radical city in America."[24]

CULTURAL CONFLICT IN THE 1840s AND 1850s

Although Whitman applauded the fact that "all races are here, all the lands of the earth make contributions here," the truth was that cultural conflict racked New York City during the 1840s and 1850s. It was largely the result of changing demographics as 1.6 million Irish Catholics crossed the ocean, with 200,000 of them settling in Gotham. Although New York City was always diverse, it had long been dominated by Anglo-Saxon Protestants, the very people whom Irish Catholics considered their enemies. At mid-century, old and new inhabitants competed to define their own identity, their city's identity, and, ultimately, the nation's identity.[25]

Fleeing economic disaster caused by a potato blight, the Irish Catholics arrived impoverished. They quickly became a source of cheap labor displacing not only African Americans as domestics and dockworkers, but also white Americans in unskilled jobs. Consigned to the bottom of society, they comprised 50 percent of people arrested and 70 percent of people receiving charity in New York during the 1850s. One response was the expansion of private help organizations such as the Association for Improving the Condition of the Poor, formed in 1843, and the Children's Aid Society, formed in 1853. However, the former tended to blame the poor for their poverty and the latter sent poor Catholic children to Protestant homes away from the city. Neither group endeared itself to the Irish Catholics.[26]

Another response to the increased immigration was nativism, a national movement of some American-born, Protestant whites who blamed the Irish for all social problems by raising a three-headed specter of economic competition, papal domination, and social disintegration. Locally, nativism led to the development of street gangs such as the American Guards, who were quickly countered by the O'Connell Guards. Gangs multiplied and, fueled by a common culture of alcohol consumption, both sides contributed to the tough, unruly, riot-prone image of mid-nineteenth-century New York.[27]

As Irish Catholics grew in numbers, their conflicts with mainstream society acquired new importance, especially when they began challenging the prevailing public education system. New York City's schools were run by the Quaker-inspired, supposedly nonsectarian, Public School Society. However, instruction was heavily imbued with Protestantism—in the version of the Bible that was read and the anti-Catholic concepts that were taught. Requests that the Public School Society expunge anti-Catholic material from its texts and hire at least one Catholic teacher went unheeded. Consequently, the

Catholic Church established eight schools but, because the community was poor, the schools were underfunded.[28]

In 1840, after Governor William H. Seward expressed support for public aid to religious schools, Bishop John Hughes mounted a campaign for public funds. The immigrant son of a poor Irish farmer, Hughes had worked himself up from gardener to prelate fortified by a spirit of determined defiance that proved useful in urban politics. He engaged in public debate, pressured city power holders, and organized a campaign to petition the New York State legislature for Catholic school funding. Cleverly combining ethnic, religious, and democratic themes, Hughes accused the Public School Society of being an aristocratic, anti-Catholic monopoly.[29]

Several small riots between Protestants and Catholics erupted during the summer of 1841. Hughes had little support in the city except from Catholics and Jews. Typical opposition sentiment was expressed by Whitman whose poetry preached tolerance, but whose politics condemned the "coarse, unshaven, filthy Irish rabble." In the fall of 1841, Hughes announced that Catholics would only vote for those candidates who supported their cause. Politicians and the press were irate, but victory for ten Democrats backed by Hughes convinced Tammany that Catholics held the balance of power in city elections.[30]

The point was driven home again in the spring elections of 1842 when the mere threat of a Catholic bolt forced Albany to think seriously about reforming the New York City school system. On Election Day, there was a riot in the Five Points. Protestants and Catholics brawled on Centre Street and, although St. Patrick's Cathedral on Barclay Street was spared (because its wall was heavily guarded), Hughes's home was sacked. Whitman voiced approval, but the Catholics had made their mark. Still refusing to fund religious education, the State legislature nonetheless replaced the old Public School Society with an elective Board of Education.[31]

In the short run, nativists organized to dominate the school board, to form the nativist American Republican Party, and to elect publisher James Harper as mayor from 1844 to 1845. However, the ethnic conflict of the 1840s seemed so alien to the city's traditions of religious tolerance that it discredited nativism. In the long run, by establishing a nonsectarian school board, the Catholic school conflict created a more ecumenical educational system for all New Yorkers. In 1847, the city went even further by establishing a nonsectarian Free Academy (later the City University of New York) to educate "the children of the whole people."[32]

Cultural tensions festered during the 1850s. Determined to convert Irish Catholics, Protestants established numerous religious missions in poor neighborhoods. They handed out Bibles with bread, admonitions with alms. One of the most ambitious efforts to save the slums was the Methodist's Five

Points Mission, which replaced the notorious Old Brewery building in 1853. Originally, the Reverend Louis M. Pease ran the Mission, but broke with it when he saw the need to do more than preach. He started a school that enrolled a hundred children for whom he provided bathing facilities, food, and clothing. In addition, he opened a House of Industry on Worth Street near Baxter Street to offer job training, work, and lodging for destitute women. Good intentions notwithstanding, these reform efforts caused widespread resentment among Irish Catholics.[33]

The result was violence in the form of three riots during 1853. The first occurred on July 4 when two patriotic parades took place—one by native-born Americans and the other by Irish Catholics. When conflict erupted, the police arrested only Catholics who were easily identifiable because they were dressed in green. The city remained tense for months and that fall the Catholic Church established a school designed to absorb all the Catholic children in Reverend Pease's school. The second riot erupted on October 9 when mobs tried to keep Catholic children from attending Pease's school where teachers were assaulted and books destroyed.[34]

The 1853 riots fueled an ongoing controversy over Protestant Evangelical street preaching in Catholic neighborhoods. The openly anti-Catholic message of the preachers inspired conflict instead of conversion. Nativist gangs protecting Protestant street preachers fought Catholic gangs on Sundays throughout the fall of 1853. Consequently, more Protestant street preachers descended upon the Five Points and on December 11 there was a third full-scale riot involving five thousand people. At a massive nativist rally in City Hall Park a few days later, one Protestant preacher resolved "eternal war upon the Catholics and upon everything that is foreign."[35]

The anti-Catholic, anti-immigrant, nativist sentiment was complex. It harnessed real anxieties fed by a substantial population shift accompanied by ethnic and religious differences. These demographic and cultural factors were further complicated by competition for jobs in a changing economy made more volatile by recurrent recessions. In the process, nativism acquired a powerful psychological dimension that demonized Catholic immigrants while exalting native-born Americans. Once again, intolerance undermined the city's tolerant traditions.[36]

Irish Catholics responded by developing strategies to counter prejudice. Through street battles, school wars, and political mobilization, they resisted assimilation. By 1858, they were established enough to begin construction of a huge cathedral on Fifth Avenue at 50th Street. Indeed, during the 1850s, the St. Patrick's Day parade became a sizable, all-day affair that disrupted the city in a bold assertion of organized power and ethnic pride. By insisting on their own parade, separate from existing omnibus parades (such as on July 4), Irish Catholics were consciously extolling their own community while broadening the definition of what it meant to be a New Yorker and an American. At mid-century, Gotham proved to be much more "proud and passionate" than Whitman and his compatriots had expected.[37]

FERNANDO WOOD AND THE FREE CITY

One politician who capitalized on the complexity of mid-nineteenth-century New York City was Fernando Wood. Charming and eloquent, clever and corrupt, Wood allied alternately with wealthy merchants, petty politicians, reformers, nativists, immigrants, workers, and the underworld. Real estate speculations and other financial ventures brought Wood the prosperity he craved to offset his humble origins. However, numerous accusations of bribery, forgery, and dishonesty permanently tarnished his Horatio Alger success story. From his Woodland mansion, located on Broadway between 77th and 78th Streets, he pursued respectability, courted the powerful, and led a long, colorful career as political boss, mayor, and congressman.[38]

During his three terms as mayor in 1854, 1856, and 1859, Wood modernized his office in both positive and negative ways. On the positive side, he sought more control over municipal affairs from the state while reaching out to the urban masses. He tried to address the suffering of the poor and opened up municipal employment, especially the police force, to Irish Catholic immigrants. He also promoted the improvement of city services regarding building codes, piers, sanitation, health, transportation, and education. An ardent advocate of Central Park, Wood was a city booster who saw New York as "an empire within itself—the metropolitan city of the Western Hemisphere. . .the city of splendor. . .the great mart of the world's commerce."[39]

On the negative side, Wood was corrupt and power hungry. When he protected Central Park, he may have been thinking about how it enhanced his property values. When he naturalized immigrants and gave them jobs, he expected them to contribute to his campaigns and vote for him. In order to guarantee the outcome, he gave gangs free reign on election days. Regularly accused of bribery and double-dealing, Wood nonetheless bounced back from every defeat and became the city's first truly strong mayor. He pursued power both for its own sake and because he believed that only central leadership could coordinate the city's many conflicting forces. As his biographer Jerome Mushkat notes, Wood's "mixture of good and bad made him the most controversial politician of his generation."[40]

Wood's leadership was sorely tested during 1857 when riots roiled the city in June, July, and November. The police, liquor, and bread riots were the outgrowth of social, political, and economic tensions. They involved struggles over the city's internal priorities as well as its external relations with the state and the nation. At stake were crucial issues of home rule conflated with ethnic tensions complicated by political and economic self-interest. The riots spanned the spectrum of urban life. Moreover, they reflected the dilemmas of the city in a national system that made municipalities creatures of the state rather than autonomous political entities. The greater New York City grew, the more intense its conflicts with New York State became.

While Wood was competing with urban reformers and his Tammany party rival, William M. Tweed, for control of the city's affairs, his most spectacular struggle was with Republicans over home rule, temperance, and corruption. Long contemptuous of Democratic downstate urbanites, the upstate-dominated Republican State legislature passed several bills in 1857 that were designed to humble New York City and its brazen mayor. For Wood, these acts were as offensive as the Revolutionary era Stamp Act and justified creating a "free city" in order to escape the tyranny of the state. The mere idea revealed how serious the conflicts of 1857 really were.[41]

Albany's 1857 bills weakened the city. One established a system of state-appointed commissions to supervise the development of Central Park, the harbor, and a new City Hall. A revised city charter reduced the power of the city's Common Council and removed the mayor from the Board of Supervisors while taking away his control over city finances and city property. City residents were not allowed to vote on the merits of charter revision. In addition, an Excise Law made liquor license fees too expensive for small-business men, restricted the sale of alcohol by the drink, and forbade its consumption on Sundays and election days.[42]

A direct attack on the drinking traditions of German and Irish immigrants, the liquor law also was part of the larger nineteenth-century temperance movement that blamed all social problems on alcohol consumption, especially in cities. By mid-century, the movement had turned to legislation as the best way to reform society. Maine led the way in 1851 with a law totally prohibiting the sale of alcohol, followed by thirteen other states in New England and the Midwest. New York State passed a similar law in 1855 but, after it was declared unconstitutional in 1856, the legislature was forced to adopt new tactics.[43]

The 1857 Excise Law was targeted at Wood, who had ordered his policemen not to enforce the 1855 act. Opposing the law curried favor with immigrant voters who readily saw the connection between nativism and temperance. Perhaps more important for Wood was the fact that saloons and the many grocery stores that sold liquor were centers of political activity. They even served as polling places. Because the saloons also were havens for gangs and because gangs were politically connected, an intricate (and often violent) link existed between alcohol, gangs, and politicians. Wood was despised by reformers for openly exploiting this relationship to build support and control voting. Anti-Wood to the core, the 1857 Excise Law was designed to curb political corruption and alcohol consumption simultaneously.[44] (See Figure 7 following page 150)

Another (and even more controversial) directive coming from the New York State legislature in 1857 was the Metropolitan Police Act, which created an Albany-controlled police district that combined New York City with Westchester, Richmond, and Kings counties. By making the police department independent of the city, the act eliminated one of Wood's key sources of patronage and weakened the entire city government. This strategy was the brainchild not only of upstate lawmakers but also of the City Reform League, a group created in 1853 to combat political corruption, especially among city legislators who were known as the Forty Thieves. The League's roster of prominent men included *Times* editor Henry J. Raymond, merchants William E. Dodge and Stephen Whitney, plus industrialist Peter Cooper, who had just broken ground at Astor Place for Cooper Union, his free mechanics' institute.[45]

Wood filed a lawsuit claiming that the Metropolitan Police Act unconstitutionally deprived the city of its historic right to home rule. He refused to disband the existing city police force and made policemen choose whether to stay with his Municipal force or join the state's Metropolitan force. Dividing along ethnic lines, the immigrant policemen stood by the city, whereas the native-born switched to the state, resulting in eight hundred Municipals against three hundred Metropolitans. Throughout early June, the two forces vied for power on a daily basis. They fought over control of station houses and, when one force arrested a criminal, the other would release him. Chaos flourished.[46]

Further defying the state-imposed charter revision, the mayor would not relinquish his appointive powers. When he insisted on naming a new street commissioner, the Metropolitan police commander, George W. Walling, tried to arrest him for violating the law. The Municipals then threw the Metropolitans out of City Hall, but the latter returned with reinforcements and an outright battle took place between the two forces on the steps of City Hall. Numerous Wood supporters joined in the fray and the hand-to-hand combat was vicious.

Helped by a passing militia regiment, the Metropolitans ultimately won and arrested Wood, this time also charging him with inciting a riot. To some, he was a bold defender of municipal rights; to others he was a brash rabble-rouser. Although soon released on bail, Wood lost his battle in the courts when the Metropolitan Police Act was ruled constitutional on July 2. Reluctantly, the mayor disbanded the municipal police on July 3, minus their June paychecks.

A mere twenty-four hours later marked Independence Day, traditionally an occasion for celebrating, carousing, and drinking. It also happened to be the day on which the new liquor law was scheduled to take effect. Emotions were already high after months of altercation, but now the entire Municipal police force was unpaid and unemployed. Although hundreds of men were immediately enlisted as Metropolitans, with many extras hired just for the holiday, they did not include former Irish-born Municipals. Few of the Metropolitans had much experience on the job; all of the Municipals were angry.[47]

These factors coalesced when an Irish gang, supposedly called the Dead Rabbits, confronted the Metropolitan police who took refuge in the quarters of a nativist gang, the Bowery Boys. A three-hour battle ensued along Bayard Street with barricades erected by the Dead Rabbits at Mulberry Street and by the Bowery Boys at Elizabeth Street. Bystanders increased the number of combatants to over one thousand. Bricks and bullets flew with fatal effect. Even Captain Isaiah Rynders failed to stop the violence and, reversing his 1849 position, ultimately asked the police to call out the militia. The riot ended only after each side was tricked into believing that the other was ready to quit. However, at least twelve people lost their lives and at least one hundred were injured, thirty-seven of them seriously.

The next day, Sunday, July 5, witnessed another riot in the Five Points area where the state of unrest almost seemed like a "civil war." With three to four thousand people mingling in the streets, an hour-long battle broke out at Centre and Worth Streets resulting in fifty wounded, but no deaths. That evening, the militia marched through the city, bayonets ready, clearing the streets and closing stores, especially those that sold liquor. The peace was fragile.[48]

Several small incidents occurred during the following week with real rioting resuming the next weekend. This time it was not in the Five Points area, but in Kliendeutschland, the German immigrant community of what is now called the East Village. Like the Irish, the Germans valued the social role of the beer hall and considered the liquor law insulting. Therefore, when the Metropolitans swept through the neighborhood on the night of Sunday, July 12, a major confrontation erupted. Shots rang out, killing a German blacksmith who was just an innocent observer.

On Monday, furious Germans spilled out onto Avenue A between 2nd and 4th Streets to express their anger at the police. The crowds hurled bricks at the police captain and assaulted several Metropolitans. The authorities sent in hundreds of policemen with three units of the state militia standing by. On Tuesday, there were less violent demonstrations of indignation via testimony at the coroner's inquest in the morning, a funeral march that afternoon on Broadway by ten thousand mourners, and a protest rally in the evening. Three thousand people met to condemn the police, but resolved to be lawful and to stop rioting. Ironically, both the inquest and the rally were held in a popular local beer hall.[49]

If the 1857 riots were largely a protest by downstate against upstate, they also were part of an internal struggle to control the city. It was significant that mainly Irish Catholics were arrested in the riots and that the Irish Dead Rabbits gang, which may not have even existed, was blamed for the riots. Although widely condemned as the worst elements of society, the historian Carol Pernicone has shown that the rioters were really artisans and laborers. They lived in communities characterized by tight family structures, not disorder and degradation.[50]

Irish and German immigrants had registered their protest against ethnic stereotypes perpetuated by upstate and downstate Protestant elites as well as against ethnic economic hostility harbored by local native-born workers. Altogether, the riots reflected the ongoing polarization and politicization of New York City life. In the process, they revealed the frustrations created on every side when new circumstances and new groups challenged the existing order. The city thrashed in the throes of change.

The 1857 police and liquor riots challenged the city's complacency. Admitting that the events might have been protests by poor people against "the selfishness of churches and the avarice of the rich," Henry Raymond's *Times* wondered whether the poor deserved "something more at the hands of the State than a scarcity of whisky and volleys of musketry." The prominent lawyer and diarist George Templeton Strong did not know whom to blame for the disorder, but he sensed that the city was "in a very perturbed state." Indeed, the sheer volume of conflict motivated the *Times* to call it "a civic rebellion."[51]

That fall brought yet more problems in the form of a financial downturn that was so severe it engendered the Panic of 1857. When banks, which had given out too many loans, tried to call them in, they started an economic domino effect, which wrecked other banks, which, in turn, ruined bank-dependent businesses such as shipbuilding, construction, manufacturing, retailing, and publishing. Almost a thousand merchants declared bankruptcy. With 150 business collapsing each week and at least 100,000 unemployed in New York City and Brooklyn, disaster loomed.[52]

Mayor Wood responded to the Panic of 1857 by insisting that the crisis be addressed. Offering a new version of the social contract, he suggested that the city provide jobs for the unemployed in constructing Central Park, fixing streets and docks, or building police and fire stations. This was the most ambitious proposal for helping the unemployed that the city had ever witnessed, and it was defended in the most radical language that the city had ever heard from a mayor. Sounding Marxist, Wood observed "that in New York those who produce everything get nothing and those who produce nothing get everything. They labor without income whilst surrounded by thousands living in affluence and splendor who have income without labor." Under these circumstances, he asked, "Now, is it not our duty to provide some way to afford relief?"[53]

Most prominent New Yorkers said "No." Contending that charity should be private and that aid should be given sparingly in order to prevent dependency, they rejected the idea of a positive public role to combat suffering. Many were taken aback by Wood's rhetoric and accused him of pandering to the poor. To be sure, Wood was a wily political animal, nicknamed "the Fox" by his enemies, and was always alert to his political advantage. Nonetheless, here he was consistent, having made similar proposals and used similar language in 1855. In addition, the situation in 1857 was truly tragic. When desperation turned into demonstrations, Wood's progressive proposals were supported by businessmen and politicians who reluctantly recognized that "the people must be taken care of."[54]

In early November there were a series of rallies in Tompkins Square, at City Hall, and on Wall Street that led to the 1857 Bread Riot. Four thousand gathered one day, five thousand the next. On November 5, fifteen thousand people convened in Tompkins Square Park and marched down to City Hall in the largest of several demonstrations held in cities across the nation. They asked not for charity but for work as an inherent part of "the right to live." However, it was only after mobs of hungry people stormed bakers' wagons and food stores that the government agreed to hire some men to work in Central Park. The 1857 Bread Riot convinced the city fathers that, for the moment, a few jobs were the best antidote to violence. At the same time, jobs for white workers came at the expense of African Americans who were forced off Central Park land that they had owned since the 1820s.[55]

The controversies surrounding Wood were magnified by the three major riots of 1857 and cost the mayor reelection. However, Wood won again in 1859 after mounting an ambitious challenge to Tammany Hall. He defiantly created his own Democratic Party organization, called Mozart Hall because it met at a hotel named after the German composer located on Broadway and Bond Street. Effective grassroots organization, clever campaigning, and the liberal use of hard cash brought victory. Aided by resentment over the charter changes of 1857 and anxiety over the city's economy created by the Panic of 1857, Wood deftly blended ethnic pride, political indignation, and economic self-interest. He capitalized on the widespread feeling that both the state and federal governments were hostile to the city's welfare.[56]

The final, most powerful, ingredient in Wood's 1859 electoral formula was the debate over slavery. Abolitionists were active in the city, but New York as a whole was hardly an abolitionist stronghold. In fact, a significant segment of New Yorkers supported slavery. Many workers feared the job competition that might materialize if freedmen flocked to the city. Many merchants, shippers, industrialists, and bankers were closely tied to Southern cotton and tobacco, which were sent to England or turned into manufactured goods.

Moreover, although New York State abolished the institution of slavery in 1827, New York City was the center of the illegal slave trade during the 1850s. Isaiah Rynders, now U.S. marshall, was notoriously lax about enforcing trade regulations. Accordingly, New York City money financed Brazilian, Portuguese, and Cuban ships bringing slaves from Africa to the Caribbean Islands. Not only were profits immense, but, as part of this network, Southerners owed New Yorkers over $125 million in debt. No wonder William Cullen Bryant's *New York Post* deduced in 1860 that "the City of New York belongs almost as much to the South as to the North."[57]

After the Panic of 1857, New York City became increasingly dependent on its Southern connection. Determined to prevent their trade from being diverted to Charleston, South Carolina, Wood and his business allies vociferously proclaimed their sympathy for the South. In December 1859, twenty thousand merchants signed the call for a meeting at the Academy of Music, a lavish opera house built in 1854 at Irving Place and 14th Street to supersede the old Astor Place Opera House. Key figures included the financier August Belmont and prominent merchants A. T. Stewart, William E. Dodge, Arnold Constable, Stephen Whitney, William B. Astor, and John Jacob Astor Jr. As the historian Philip Foner pointed out, the meeting was strikingly pro-slavery in tone. It not only endorsed intersectional commerce but also condoned slavery as natural, necessary, "just, wise, and beneficent."[58]

Wood appreciated the political importance of these sentiments and, in 1861, with the city confronting another economic downturn and the nation poised for war, he affirmed New York's common cause with the South by resurrecting his "free city" program. It was high time, he said, for New York to dissolve "the bonds which bind her to a venal and corrupt master," the Republican Party. As an independent entity, the city would finally be able to govern itself and to pursue prosperity with all nations and all sections, including "the slave states." Economic, cultural, and political grievances reinforced by local and national circumstances made urban secession as compelling to New Yorkers as sectional secession was to Southerners.[59]

Although many New Yorkers dismissed Wood's "free city" proposal outright, enough people supported it to warrant considerable discussion in the press, at the Chamber of Commerce, in private circles, and even by preachers. It delighted the South and dismayed Washington, which feared that secession by New York City would seriously weaken the Union cause. Ultimately, the idea died when the Civil War actually began and the city's businessmen decided that their best long-range interests lay with a national economy. However, the internal divisions revealed by the "free city" debate remained. In opposition to Tammany's War Democrats, Wood (aided by Isaiah Rynders) became the leader of the city's pro-South, pro-slavery Peace Democrats.[60]

Wood remains an enigma. His corrupt practices, unabashed self-promotion, lust for power, and support of slavery made him seem an unsavory manipulator. At the same time, his defense of home rule, efforts to develop the city, support of Irish Catholics, and sympathy for the poor rendered him an aggressive, responsive, modern leader. Although dedicated to New York's economic development, he refused to leave the future entirely to the free market. Instead, Mushkat points out that Wood "tried to alleviate the human traumas that New York's commercialism. . .had created." Basically a transitional figure, Wood promoted the worst aspects of urban bossism while also previewing the potential of positive government. In the process, he demonstrated that contentious methods could be used for constructive ends.[61]

THE 1863 DRAFT RIOTS

The destructive aspects of metropolitan conflict were never more evident than during July 1863, when mobs ruled the streets in the worst riot in the history of the United States. Records document that over one hundred persons were killed, including at least four blacks who were lynched. Seventy soldiers and policemen plus a minimum of 128 civilians were seriously injured. Hundreds of people were burned out of their homes, thousands fled, and untold numbers were dumped into the rivers.[62]

Estimates at the time suggested that the fatalities surpassed one thousand. Even if an exaggeration, this figure accurately measures the way in which the 1863 Draft Riots exposed the trauma of a nation in the midst of Civil War and a city torn apart by class, racial, ethnic, political, and economic strife. New York's inability to control its passions was blatantly self-evident. "To contemporaries," comments the historian Mary P. Ryan, "the civic tumult of mid-century only underscored, with more force than ever before, that urban democracy was a belligerent affair."[63] (See Figure 8 following page 150)

Circumstances

The immediate cause of the riots was the inauguration of a national draft. Facing bitter military combat and declining enlistments, Congress authorized the nation's first draft. Antidraft rallies called by Fernando Wood were blamed for inciting the mob to attack the provost marshal's building on Third Avenue and 47th Street where the draft lottery was being conducted. Overwhelming the few police on hand, German and Irish rioters, led by firefighters who were angry about not being exempt from military service, destroyed the draft apparatus and, ironically, set the building on fire. As the flames spread, the draft was halted, but twelve thousand people swarmed through the Upper East Side and business was paralyzed.[64]

The draft was intertwined with other issues, one of which was class. To most workers, the draft was unfair because it allowed rich men to avoid service by buying a substitute for three hundred dollars, a sum that no worker could afford. Immediately, the Civil War was labeled "a rich man's war and a poor man's fight." It was significant that the draft riots began with a major coordinated labor stoppage in which hundreds of skilled and unskilled men refused to report for work. Instead, they marched up Eighth and Ninth Avenues compelling other workers to join them, tearing down telegraph lines and tearing up streetcar tracks.[65]

Rich people were chased off the streets and many fled the city by boat or train. The first day brought the pillage, destruction, and arson of several mansions on Fifth and Lexington Avenues plus elegant shops and jewelry stores on Broadway. On the second day, there was a battle over the expensive Brooks Brothers clothing store on Catherine Street, which was looted and sacked. In an extension of the 1850s culture wars, two Protestant charitable institutions, the Five Points Mission and the Magdalene Asylum on 88th Street and Fifth Avenue, also were destroyed.[66]

A second riot theme was political. The draft was the work of the national Republican Party that, like the state Republican Party, seemed to be invading urban life. Consequently, the mob targeted sites associated with Republicans, including Columbia College at 49th Street and Fifth Avenue and Mayor George Opdyke's house at 79 Fifth Avenue. An attack on the Union Steam Works, a rifle factory on 21st Street and Second Avenue, which was owned by the wealthy Opdyke family, resulted in hand-to-hand combat and a major fire costing thirteen lives.[67]

The Park Row offices of the most prominent Republican newspapers, the *New York Times* and the *New York Tribune,* were attacked on both the first and second days of the riot. Several attempts were made to seize the antislavery, pro-Union, pro-draft *Tribune* editor, Horace Greeley. Taking no chances, Henry Raymond personally manned one of three Gatling guns he installed to defend the *Times'* building. As local representatives of Republican authority, the Metropolitan policemen were particularly vulnerable. The mob beat Police Superintendent John Kennedy to a pulp and attacked any Metropolitans they saw. On the second day, they brutalized and killed Colonel Henry O'Brien, an Irishman considered a turncoat because he was a Metropolitan police officer, and gave the order to fire at a battle on East 32nd Street during which a mother and child had died.[68]

The third and most volatile of the rioters' grievances revolved around race. From the very first day, African Americans were the mob's special targets. On Monday, rioters yanked blacks from streetcars, assaulted them at work, and attacked them on streets. A Mohawk Indian, who was assumed to be black, died from wounds inflicted by the mob. Roaming through the city, white workers warned employers not to hire blacks. That evening, rioters mobbed the Colored Orphan Asylum at 43rd Street and Fifth Avenue. Although the children were safely evacuated, the building was demolished and set ablaze. All black men seen along the waterfront were immediately attacked. Several were chased into the river, with at least one (perhaps three) being lynched and roasted over a fire.[69]

Tuesday brought wider attacks on the African American community and cries of opposition to "nigger, Abolition, Black Republicanism." Tenements, boarding houses, brothels, dance halls, and stores owned by or serving blacks on the waterfront and in Greenwich Village were targeted, with their owners chased out of the neighborhood. Blacks in Minetta Lane mounted a valiant defense but to little avail. A black sailor was murdered on an Upper West Side pier by a crowd of people who alternately jumped on him, knifed him, and smashed him with rocks. The son of an interracial couple was stripped, beaten, and almost lynched until rescued by some Germans. Attempts were made to burn the home of a black abolitionist. The *Tribune* called it "a perfect reign of terror."[70]

On Wednesday, there were three lynchings of African American men on the Upper West Side, but a fourth was thwarted by an Irishman. In one case, a shoemaker was brutally beaten, stripped, tarred and feathered, and then hung. A second victim had his fingers and toes cut off. The third was a handicapped coach driver who was beaten, strung up from a lamppost, cut down by soldiers, hung up again, then cut down and dragged through the streets by the genitals. The writer Horatio Alger found the sight "so disgusting—so revolting" that it literally made him sick.[71]

African American churches and homes were set afire, forcing hundreds to flee for their lives to police stations or across the rivers to Brooklyn, Long Island and New Jersey. Echoing the riot of 1834, the mob harassed anyone associated with abolition or amalgamation, especially white women affiliated with black men. Soon the mobs began targeting Jews, Germans, and Chinese. Prejudice knew no bounds.[72]

Context

The context for these atrocities was both long and short range. Ethnic and economic animosities may have dominated the 1840s and 1850s, but, by the 1860s, race was the paramount issue. In fact, ethnic, economic, and racial tensions were intertwined. For many northerners, the 1863 Emancipation Proclamation had radically altered the nature of the Civil War by making it less a war for union and more a war for abolition. Racial prejudice in the North was exploited by antiwar forces who warned that freedmen would flee the South and undercut Northern white labor. A steady stream of such doomsday predictions spewed forth from the *New York Herald,* edited by James Gordon Bennett, and the *New York Daily News,* run by Fernando Wood's brother, Benjamin.[73]

This economic appeal built on insecurities resulting from the labor struggles of the 1850s during which employers had used African Americans as strikebreakers. In 1862, there had already been riots and attacks on blacks by white workers in New York City, Brooklyn, Buffalo, Chicago, and Cincinnati. For three days in April 1863, Irish dockworkers had rioted against and beaten up black workers in Gotham. Just a week before the riot, the city's police superintendent had requested that the Massachusetts Fifty-Fourth, the famous black regiment, not be routed through Manhattan in order to "save us from riot." The racial aspect of the 1863 riot did not exist in a vacuum.[74]

Despite all the odds against them, blacks had persistently pursued equality, further angering whites in the process. There were several stable African American communities such as those in Manhattan's Greenwich Village (around Sullivan, Roosevelt, Bleeker, and Carmine Streets) and Brooklyn's Weeksville. Blacks also supported numerous churches and petitioned for equal facilities in public schools. In 1855, a century before Rosa Parks, an African American teacher named Elizabeth Jennings sued successfully for the right to ride on city streetcars. (Her lawyer was the future president, Chester A. Arthur.) However, when Civil War was declared, New York State refused to commission African American regiments, which were forced to serve with other states' units and, after the war, the city's streetcars were resegregated.[75]

Gotham's racial tensions were exacerbated by the existence of a vocal, well-organized, aggressive movement of black and white abolitionists. Long Island, Brooklyn, and Manhattan were stops on the Underground Railroad and The New York Vigilance Committee regularly rescued blacks from reenslavement after the 1850 Fugitive Slave Act. A dramatic version of Harriet Beecher Stowe's *Uncle Tom's Cabin* played to packed crowds from 1852 to 1854 when it caused a riot after moving to an integrated theater. Stowe's brother, the Reverend Henry Ward Beecher, preached abolition and mesmerized the city with mock sales of slave girls at his Plymouth Church on Orange Street in Brooklyn Heights. All of these factors made the racial aspect of the 1863 riots especially volatile.[76]

Except for the first morning of the riot, the mob was never a unified whole. Rather, it encompassed different groups with different priorities. The initial issue that joined them was the draft, but they divided after Monday morning, with German skilled workers taking a less active role and Irish unskilled workers dominating the crowd. Nonetheless, it must be noted that Irish workers served valiantly in the much-lauded Fighting Sixty-Ninth Regiment. Moreover, the violence of the riot did not include some heavily Irish neighborhoods. It did, however, include some women and children, whose fate was tied directly to that of their fathers, husbands, sons, and brothers. In fact, soldiers' wives had already waged several protests against the city for not helping them survive while their husbands were at war.[77]

Controlling the riot was complicated by the large numbers of rioters who were active in different parts of the city, from the Battery up to Westchester. Starting from their headquarters at Mulberry and Bleecker Streets, the police took time to get organized, thereby allowing the riot to rage unhampered for a day. Once the telegraph lines had been pulled down and the train tracks ripped up, both communication and transportation were impeded. Consequently, the police were always behind events, struggling to walk from crisis to crisis.[78]

The riot alternated between mob action and guerilla warfare. Police captain George Walling recounted a confrontation on Tuesday at 45th Street and Fifth Avenue between the police and two thousand "howling . . . men and women" during which he gave orders to "kill every man who has a club." On the next day, his forces fought what he called "the Battle of the Barricades." Rioters volleyed bricks and bullets at police from behind clusters of carts and wagons positioned strategically along Ninth Avenue from 26th to 42nd Streets. Moving from barricade to barricade, the police worked with a company of volunteer firemen to disperse their opponents, shooting them if necessary. The operating principle was that they "took no prisoners, but left the rioters where they fell."[79]

Such strategies notwithstanding, the police needed outside reinforcements. However, all local troops were fighting at Gettysburg and were unavailable for riot duty until Wednesday evening. At that point, the situation changed. Although the fighting continued during Wednesday night and Thursday, the troops finally prevailed by Thursday night. The ordeal was over, but it had so devastated the city that the lawyer and diarist George Templeton Strong commented ruefully, "This is a nice town to call itself a centre of civilization."[80]

Throughout the riots, the city suffered from a lack of leadership. Republican newspapers blamed Democratic Governor Horatio Seymour for aiding and abetting the violence by publicly declaring conscription illegal, by dawdling in New Jersey while riot raged in New York, and by addressing the rioters as "my friends." Republican Mayor George Opdyke fared no better when he did nothing for the first two days of the riots and then announced that they were over when they were really accelerating. Another potential leader, Archbishop Hughes, waited until the fourth day of the riot to appeal for peace.[81]

Consequences

The riot had a variety of immediate results. Republican politicians convinced President Lincoln to halve New York State's draft quota, significantly reducing its impact. Henry J. Raymond and other prominent citizens formed a private charity that still assists the families of police and firemen. War Democrats, led by Tammany's William M. Tweed, set up an emergency fund to pay the three hundred dollars exemption fee for firemen, policemen, and poor men whose families depended on their income. Despite its large allocation of money to pay the substitution fee for white draftees, the city offered no aid to African American victims of the riot. In fact, blacks fled the city in droves and those who remained found themselves barred from work on the waterfront, banned from public conveyances, and beaten up by gangs throughout the summer.[82]

Meanwhile, some whites tried to make amends. The Union League Club was formed in February 1863 as an organization of prestigious, old-line merchants, lawyers, and businessmen who supported the Republican Party and the war. They included Central Park's Frederick Law Olmstead, Minister Henry Bellows, the lawyer (and grandson of the founding father) John Jay, the merchants Robert B. Minturn, Moses Grinnell, and William E. Dodge Jr., and the editors Henry Raymond, George William Curtis, and E. L. Godkin.

Their Committee of Merchants for the Relief of Colored People Suffering from the Late Riots provided forty thousand dollars worth of clothing and food to twenty-five hundred applicants. They also organized a regiment of a thousand African American men who were honored in 1864 in Union Square. Club members' wives participated prominently in the event, roundly offending those who resented the arming of blacks, their endorsement by the rich, and their affiliation with white women. On the surface, all was quiet, but many of the old tensions remained unresolved.[83]

The Draft Riots were the most brutal riots the nation had ever experienced and remain so to this day. Considered horrifying in themselves, they became even more ominous when they inspired similar uprisings in Boston, Troy, Jamaica, Jersey City, and Staten Island. Near riots were reported in Brooklyn, Harlem, Yorkville, and Westchester. Conversely, the daily press carried anxious assurances that there was no rioting in Albany, Buffalo, Hartford, Newark, Philadelphia, Springfield, and Portsmouth.[84]

New York City's Draft Riots amounted to a crisis layered on a crisis. President Lincoln and Secretary of War Edwin Stanton worried that the riots might strengthen Gotham's resolve to secede from the nation. The South hoped it would and relished the thought of disorder within the enemy camp. Indeed, Washington, D.C. was abuzz with the danger of "a revolt springing up among those who are putting down revolt." Even worse, wrote the *Albany Evening Journal*, the enemies of democracy abroad might use the violence as "a fresh illustration of the failure of free institutions."[85]

The *New York Commercial Advertiser* drew yet another message of national significance from the Draft Riots and their racial subtext. After all, job discrimination in the North kept blacks in a permanent state of economic oppression much akin to slavery in the South. Moreover, the "fiendish atrocity" of burning the Colored Orphan Asylum echoed the cruelty of the peculiar institution. Southerner and Northerner alike, it seemed, were determined "that the hated negro should not be permitted to walk the streets as a free man." The New York Draft Riots exposed the fault line of the national creed.[86]

Responding to widespread condemnation of the Draft Riots, the *New York Times* insisted that the rioters represented not the whole city but only its "very vilest elements." For others, that was precisely the point. The city itself was vile, wrote the *Philadelphia North American*. It consisted of a "foul and pestilential mass" of humanity that "seethes and boils" until it ultimately explodes. Awful as they were, the Draft Riots could not be laid at America's doorsteps because "New York has ceased to be an American city, typifying in any degree the order, industry, and good habits of the American people." The riots were so devastating as to demand disassociation; New York City was the nation's pariah.[87]

Because they were so central to America, New York City's agonies always had broad significance. The Astor Place Riots, the ethnic controversies, the labor struggles of the 1850s, the three riots of 1857, and the Draft Riot of 1863 all highlighted tensions and dilemmas that crystallized on the Hudson, but reverberated across the land. Divisions between native-born and foreign-born, Protestant and Catholic, rural and urban, Republican and Democrat, white and black, rich and poor, worker and employer, police and citizen captured current national trends and anticipated future national challenges.

For Whitman, the 1863 riots were "a terrible fury." In 1865, after tending to wounded soldiers and losing his brother in battle, he lamented that "War, red war is my song through your streets, O city." A few years later, however, Whitman supplanted his "doubt and gloom" with pride in the fact that "the land which could raise such as the late rebellion, could also put it down." Like the city, the country was resilient. Indeed, Whitman viewed urban dynamism as the perfect model for the nation. Aware that passivity and contentment could breed stagnation, he understood that "rage, fury, discussion" brought renewal. As he put it, "Vive, the attack—the perennial assault! Vive, the unpopular cause—the spirit that audaciously aims—the never-abandoned efforts. . . ." In his conflict-ridden city lay the true promise of democracy.[88]

5
The Empire City
Questioning the Gilded Age, 1865–1899

"I hope, my lad, you will prosper and rise in the world. You know in this free country poverty in early life is no bar to a man's advancement. . . .Save your money, my lad, buy books, and determine to be somebody, and you may yet fill an honorable position."

Horatio Alger, *Ragged Dick*

With these words of advice to a street urchin, Horatio Alger enshrined the rags-to-riches myth as an American article of faith. Many dismissed Alger's story as silly, but others proclaimed *Ragged Dick* the most influential American novel published before 1900. It was odd that Alger's benign, simplistic, preindustrial formula for success should have been so popular in the ruthless, complex, industrial world of late-nineteenth-century America. Yet, Alger's significance derives from this incongruity. *Ragged Dick* reassured readers that individuals still mattered and old values were still relevant in an increasingly impersonal and immoral world. Alger muted what the historian Samuel P. Hays called "the shock of change."[1]

Appropriately enough, Alger's book was set in New York City—the center of America's late-nineteenth-century modernization. As the home of robber barons, urban bosses, labor leaders, and social reformers, Gotham was simultaneously the symbol of excess and exploitation, reassessment and promise. *Ragged Dick* was the first American book to depict the city in positive terms as a source of fascination and opportunity as well as, but not solely, a place of suffering and sin. Its poor could prosper if frugal, hard-working, honest, and lucky. Because its elite had a social conscience, the gap between rich and poor was bridgeable. Social conflicts could be negotiated.

Like the accessible, engaging, inexpensive newspapers of Joseph Pulitzer and William Randolph Hearst, Horatio Alger's dime novels demystified the increasingly complex, anonymous metropolis. Guiding readers through the city's streets and snares, Dick became the friendly face of social Darwinism, proof that competition was not rudely ruthless and that one could be decent and still survive. He reinforced the optimism of the age and the belief that all was well with laissez-faire capitalism. In the process, Dick provided a new model for the American character—an urban hero who built upon but rose above the fact that, as he put it, "I ain't knocked about the city streets all my life for nothin.'"[2]

The writer Stephen Crane had a different perspective on the urban child and the urban environment. The heroine of *Maggie: A Girl of the Streets* (1893) was distinctly unlucky and unable to handle the seductions of the city. Social Darwinism's pessimistic, fatalistic side was captured by Maggie's brother's poignant question, "What's de use?" Crane's answer was that, given sober parents and a little help, Maggie might have flourished. Instead, the sweet little girl who briefly "blossomed in a mud-puddle" was dragged into the mire of prostitution, despair, and death. Reality ridiculed the play she once saw where "the poor and virtuous eventually overcame the wealthy and wicked." Depicting the tragic consequences of social Darwinism run amok, Crane interrogated society's priorities.[3]

In the late nineteenth century, New York seemed to encompass the best and worst of the industrial revolution. It earned the label the Empire City by becoming the nation's largest and grandest metropolis—a master of finance, trade, and industry; a mecca for the rich; a magnet for immigrants; and a market for the world, albeit a morass of political corruption. For the *New York Commercial Advertiser,* the "Empire City" was a truly "Cosmopolitan City," serving as the nation's "crucible in which the jarring and jangling elements are brought together." Gotham's challenge was to orchestrate that jarring and jangling during what the historian Alan Trachtenberg reminds us was a "watershed" period in American history, a true "age of conflict."[4]

More than ever, Gotham was the center for power, prosperity, patronage, pilfering, and protest. It astonished the nation with its infamous Tweed Ring and the 1871 riots, its unparalleled wealth and the "discovery of poverty," its labor strife, and its acrimonious 1886 mayoral contest. Old dilemmas acquired new dimensions as businessmen, labor organizers, politicians, and reformers tried to bring order to the painfully "distended society" described by the historian Robert Wiebe. According to Abram Hewitt, respected industrialist, philanthropist, congressman, and mayor, New York's "imperial destiny as the greatest city in the world is assured by natural causes." The question was whether its aspirations would be realized or "thwarted. . .by the folly and neglect of its inhabitants."[5]

Although Hewitt was confident about the future, the philosopher Henry George was skeptical. Hewitt's major opponent in the 1886 mayoral election, George was an internationally renowned reformer whose 1879 book, *Progress and Poverty*, was read by over six million people by 1906. In it, George posed the fundamental enigma of the era—the juxtaposition of increased material progress with "the deepest poverty, the sharpest struggle for existence, and the most of enforced idleness." As if in response to Alger, George predicted that, unless addressed, the problems that beset New York would spread across the country bringing with them the "ragged and barefooted children on her streets." Under these conditions, he warned, "progress is not real and cannot be permanent. The reaction must come."[6]

Late-nineteenth-century New York provided the perfect forum for the nation's debate over the meaning of progress. It exemplified what Mark Twain dubbed *The Gilded Age* (1873), an era when greed was the coin of the realm and all that glittered was not gold. The social contract was defined in terms of social Darwinian faith in material values, the survival of the fittest, the inevitability of progress, and the futility of reform. However, it also was a period in which many people, especially (but not exclusively) New Yorkers, were reexamining those values.[7]

To emphasize the point, Twain wrote a short story about an industrious but impoverished boy who followed Alger's prescriptions for success only to discover that the rich were mean and miserly instead of kind and generous. "Such is life as I find it," Twain wryly remarked. His parody of Alger challenged prevailing assumptions that the rich were deserving and superior, whereas the poor were undeserving and inferior. Like Crane and George, Twain questioned the relationship between myth and reality.[8]

Much of reality fed the myth. Befitting its imperial prowess, New York's accomplishments in this period were grandiose. The economic city was energized by robber barons, so called for the unprecedented and unsavory methods they used to dominate their businesses. John D. Rockefeller's Standard Oil Trust, Cornelius Vanderbilt's New York Central Railroad, Andrew Carnegie's steel trust, Jay Gould's brokerage firm, and J. P. Morgan's banking house made Wall Street the symbolic and actual home for new companies of phenomenal wealth controlled by a few men. Aggressive businessmen, notes the historian Thomas Kessner, were always "New York's heroes." In the Gilded Age, they made Gotham the crown jewel of America's economic empire—the nexus for national and international business.[9]

Rockefeller was the archetypal robber baron of the era. A pious farm boy from western New York, Rockefeller's frugality, shrewdness, and hard work led to big city success and stupendous wealth. He personified the rags to riches myth, minus Ragged Dick's cheerful charm. Although a generous philanthropist in his later years, Rockefeller's austere manner, ruthless business techniques, and "a mouth that was a slit, like a shark's" confirmed widespread opinion that he was "the greatest villain" of the Gilded Age. To many, however, he remains a brilliant innovator who modernized the American economy.[10]

After cornering 90 percent of America's petroleum refining business, Rockefeller moved his Standard Oil Company from Cleveland to New York in 1882 in order to be closer to the international market. Significantly, the country's first trust was headquartered near Wall Street at 26 Broadway, which, writes his biographer Ron Chernow, "soon became the world's most famous business address." From there, Rockefeller expanded his monopoly over oil refining to include pricing, shipping, and distributing. He created not merely a national but also a global empire. In his opinion, eliminating competitors was "a natural and absolutely normal" process through which efficiency prevailed and the fittest businesses survived. "As for the others," he declared, "unfortunately they will have to die."[11]

Rockefeller's social Darwinian model of cutthroat competition and systematic consolidation soon engendered trusts in steel, lead, sugar, salt, tobacco, and whiskey, among others. The Great Merger Wave inundated the American economy and overflowed onto foreign shores. Rockefeller understood the importance of this development. Consolidation, he said, had "revolutionized the way of doing business all over the world." Consequently, capitalism had been permanently altered because "the day of combination is here to stay. Individualism has gone, never to return."[12]

The result was twofold. On the one hand, trusts (particularly Standard Oil) horrified so many people that state and federal governments began reassessing the social contract and regulating business practices. In what the journalist Henry Demarest Lloyd considered a war of *Wealth against Commonwealth* (1894), the role of government in the economy was being redefined. Investigative commissions that collected data, established standards, and inspired laws represented, says the historian John Garraty, a shift "of epochal significance" in the relationship between public and private interests.[13]

On the other hand, because the initial regulations were weak, trusts multiplied anyway, and Gotham became increasingly pivotal to the new, corporate-based economy. By 1892, almost a third of America's millionaires lived in the New York metropolitan area; by 1900, it harbored over two-thirds of the nation's biggest businesses. Unlike other cities that waxed and waned over time, New York's flexibility enabled it to continually strengthen its mastery over the American economy. As Kessner points out, whereas Chicago may have dominated the Midwest, New York "was the center around which other regional metropolises orbited, the great organizer of American commerce."[14]

In order to keep pace with and serve the economic city, the physical city was transformed by gas, electricity, the telephone, elevated railroads, mansions, and brownstone buildings. Answering the poet William Cullen Bryant's question, "Can a city be planned?" the new rich shaped New York in their own image. A perfect example was the Brooklyn Bridge. When it opened in 1883 after sixteen years of work costing twenty lives, it instantly became an urban icon. The nation's longest suspension bridge, it blended art with technology in testimony to Gotham's innovative, soaring spirit. The majesty of the Brooklyn Bridge, said Hewitt, symbolized not just the preeminence of the city in the nation and the world, but also the potential for "harmony" between capital and labor in the pursuit of progress.[15]

Another urban icon of this period was the Statue of Liberty that, observes Kessner, replaced the Liberty Bell as America's key symbol of freedom when it was completed in 1886. In the words of poet Emma Lazarus, daughter of a Portuguese-Jewish sugar manufacturer, the grand lady in the harbor heralded Gotham's role as the "golden door" to America for the "huddled masses yearning to breathe free." However, unlike the "old" western and northern European immigrants, the "new" immigrants of the late nineteenth and early twentieth centuries came from eastern and southern Europe. After passing through Ellis Island, which opened in 1892, many of these Italians and Jews settled on the Lower East Side. Although often scorned as Europe's "wretched refuse" in the worst sense of the term, they also aroused social conscience, became social activists, and stimulated social reform. They changed the social city.[16]

The political city of the late nineteenth century is best known for the rise of urban bossism, replete with unprecedented corruption. Being "a City which, figuratively at least, is set upon a hill and cannot be hid," remarked the *Detroit Post* in 1871, what happened in New York was never inconsequential. "As it is the great metropolis of the country, and boasts of its wealth and its influence," the *Post* claimed that "its responsibilities are proportionately increased." Unfortunately, the Tweed Ring made New York the symbol of urban irresponsibility and won it universal condemnation as "the worst governed city in the world." In the Gilded Age, Gotham was the model of what municipal government should not be.[17]

Nonetheless, when five boroughs were combined to create Greater New York in 1898, it became the biggest city in America, second only to London in the world. After much controversy and several failed attempts, Gotham's population instantly leaped from 2 to 3.4 million, definitively outstripping its rival, Chicago. Mock funeral services were held in parts of Brooklyn and Queens where Consolidation threatened to bring more taxes, immigrants, crime and corruption. By contrast, fireworks and a grand parade in Manhattan hailed Consolidation as a milestone akin to the Erie Canal and the Brooklyn Bridge. In keeping with the era's economic ethos, the *New York Tribune* proudly announced that "the new firm invites the business of the world, and upon it the eyes of the world are turned."[18]

New York had become its own empire. The Gilded Age seemed glorious indeed and Horatio Alger's optimism seemed justified after all. Still, some people questioned the implications of prosperity and preeminence. As England's Darwinian scientist Thomas Huxley remarked when he visited America in 1877, "Size is not grandeur and territory does not make a nation. The great issue. . .is what are you going to do with all these things?"[19]

THE POLITICAL QUESTION: TAMMANY'S EMPIRE

> Among the downtown bootblacks was one hailing from the Five Points—a stout, red-haired freckled-faced boy of fourteen, bearing the name of Mickey Maguire. This boy. . .had a gang of subservient followers, whom he led on to acts of ruffianism. . . .If he had been fifteen years older, and had a trifle more education, he would have interested himself in politics, and been prominent in ward meetings, and a terror to respectable voters on election day.
>
> —**Horatio Alger,** *Ragged Dick*

Writing in 1868, Horatio Alger was aware of the rise of a new political system emerging in the city and epitomized by New York's Tammany Hall. Mickey Maguire was the prototype of the urban boss who became rich and powerful by providing jobs and other services to city dwellers in return for votes and kickbacks. Across the nation, urban politicians were taking advantage of the needs and opportunities of the industrial city. Although the journalist Lincoln Steffens considered this system *The Shame of the Cities* (1904), bossism paralleled the expansive capitalism of the Gilded Age. As Tammany leader Richard Croker once explained, "politics is business."[20]

No one understood that concept better than New York's William M. Tweed who, at six feet tall and three hundred pounds, has always loomed larger than life over New York City history. The author Oliver Allen branded him "the ultimate manifestation of predatory machine politics." To this day, we do not know whether Tweed stole twenty or two hundred million dollars from the city. We do know that, between 1865 and 1871, he was the city's master—the first person to harness its conflicting interests into a functioning, if corrupt, political system. Significantly, the cartoonist Thomas Nast depicted Tweed with New York City under his thumb.[21]

Tweed was a working-class Protestant of Scottish descent who entered politics in 1848 after organizing a volunteer fire company identified by the tiger, which later became the symbol of Tammany Hall. Never mayor himself, he held various elected and appointed positions—alderman, congressman, state senator, school commissioner, member of the Board of Supervisors, president of the Department of Public Works, and deputy street commissioner. With access to jobs, contracts, franchises, and licenses, not to mention gifts and bribes, Tweed came to dominate both the Democratic Party and Tammany Hall, a feat that escaped his rival, Fernando Wood, and made Tweed the nation's first true political boss.[22]

Tweed's success represented a shift of political power away from the old formal party structure dominated by patrician politicians to a new grassroots system, open to middle- and working-class power seekers. While promoting democracy by reaching out to the masses, Tammany subverted democracy by having friendly judges naturalize new immigrants (sometimes as many as three a minute) right before election time. The machine also used repeaters (men who voted often under different names) and dispatched gangs to keep opposition voters away from the polls and rough them up if necessary. As a last resort, Tweed would hold up the downstate returns until the upstate returns were in and then fix the final tally to insure victory. In response to his critics, he asked the key question of the era: "As long as I count the votes, what are you going to do about it?"[23]

By 1868, Tweed ruled both city and state. His cronies served as governor, mayor, city comptroller, and city commissioners in a solid circle of intrigue called the Tweed ring. Serving in the State Senate, he spread graft liberally to get pro-city bills passed. The 1870 City Charter reversed the 1857 charter by restoring the city's control over its own departments, including the police. Of course, home rule also meant more patronage jobs available for Tweed's use. Other bills facilitated annexing the Bronx, completing Central Park, constructing the Brooklyn Bridge, and building the Metropolitan Museum of Art. In addition, he secured allocations for orphans, schools, public baths, hospitals, public transit, a paid fire department, dock improvements, and the expansion of Broadway. Despite the disreputable methods employed, even Tweed's enemies admitted that he helped the city.[24]

Tweed's brand of governmental activism benefited businessmen who got contracts to provide city services or build city projects. Real estate owners and speculators profited as development enhanced the value of their properties. Railroad magnates Jim Fisk and Jay Gould learned the benefits of working with the Tweed Ring by getting favorable bills through Albany in return for bribes to legislators. These techniques gave conflicting interest groups a stake in Tammany's success. The only people to whom Tweed did not appeal were blacks and well-to-do Protestant reformers. Indeed, he used race to solidify his support among the white working classes and he angered the reformers by centralizing power with his ill-gotten wealth.[25]

At his peak, Tweed's patronage empire encompassed at least twelve thousand jobs. He became one of the city's largest landholders and amassed so much money that he set up a bank just to manage his own affairs. In the words of a later Tammany ward boss, George Washington Plunkitt, "He seen his opportunities, and he took 'em." However, the emperor was too ostentatious for his own good. His shiny diamond stick pin, his daughter's extravagant wedding, his lavish mansion at Fifth Avenue and 43rd Street, and his fancy estate and country club in Greenwich, Connecticut offended respectable New York.[26]

In 1869, Nast published his first cartoons identifying the members of the Tweed Ring and criticizing them for robbing the public coffers. Soon after, the *New York Times* joined the crusade but, as historian Alexander B. Callow Jr. remarked, "it was long on denunciation, short on documentation." Consequently, the public was slow to react and Tweed still seemed invulnerable. However, the cracks in his armor began to show when an insurgent movement developed within Tammany and when violence erupted in the streets, seemingly aligned with Tammany.[27]

The 1871 Orange Riot was particularly disturbing within and beyond New York. The riot pitted Irish Protestants against Irish Catholics, native-born against foreign-born, the middle and upper classes against the working classes. It resurrected the nativist tensions of the 1840s and 1850s while reviving horrific memories of the 1863 Draft Riots. The Orange Riot seemed to show that, despite the jobs Tweed gave them and the money he diverted to their schools, he could not tame his working class, Irish Catholic supporters. Tweed and his city were out of control.[28] (See Figure 11 following page 150)

Steeped in historic Old World conflicts between Irish Protestants and Irish Catholics, New York's tensions erupted every July during celebrations of the Battle of the Boyne when, in 1690, the Protestant Prince William of Orange had defeated the Catholic King James II. In 1870, New York's Irish Protestant Orangemen commemorated Boyne Day with a parade and picnic at Elm Park, located at Eighth Avenue and 92nd Street. Marching up Broadway, they sang anti-Irish Catholic songs. The result was a bloody battle in the park. After two days of fighting on the streets, eight people lay dead with scores more injured. Thousands of Catholics attended the funeral processions. Protestants condemned them as the same kind of "ruffian" who "under the leadership of William Marcy Tweed has taken possession of this City and State."[29]

A year later found Tweed under fire and wary of another July riot. At first, Tweed's puppet, Mayor A. Oakey Hall, banned the Boyne Day parade, but he reversed himself when pressured by prominent Protestants and another Tweed puppet, Governor John T. Hoffman. With fifteen hundred policemen fortified by over five thousand infantry and cavalry, the city braced for combat. As soon as the troops assembled at 6:00 a.m., the skirmishes started. At 2:30 p.m., one hundred Orangemen set off from 29th Street and Eighth Avenue flanked on all sides by policemen and militiamen. Irish Catholic crowds threw stones, bottles, shoes, and food at the marchers. Rocks were hurled from the rooftops; sniper shots rang out from tenements and alleys.[30]

The soldiers, mainly Protestants sympathetic to the Orangemen, fought back. In what an Irish Catholic newspaper called the "Slaughter on Eighth Avenue," troops fired directly into the crowd at point-blank range. Police used their clubs freely; cavalrymen charged spectators; heads were literally blown off. Six bodies lay on 25th Street, sixteen on 26th Street, six more on 27th Street. In all, sixty-two civilians (predominantly Irish), two policemen, and three soldiers were killed; at least one hundred people were wounded. The *Times* described the scene as "a panorama of blood, a vista of gore, an arena of agony." The event, says the historian Mary Ryan, was so brutal that it forever tarnished public ceremony in the American mind.[31]

Contemporary assessments were as charged as the riot itself. To Irish Catholics, it was not a riot but a "massacre." To native-born Protestants, it "was a mob of brutalized foreigners" demonstrating "their incapacity for self-government." Newspapers across the nation condemned the Catholic rioters and defended the Constitutional right of the Orangemen to march. In Albany, Cincinnati, Philadelphia, San Francisco, and Washington, D.C., the riots caused "a sensation." Indignation prevailed in Boston, Buffalo, Hartford, Pittsburg, Providence, Troy, and Utica, where the *Herald* quipped "And this is our much boasted City of Democratic rule?"[32]

Labeling the violence "the Tammany Riot," The *Times* used the event to accelerate its campaign against Tweed and to blame the Democrats for "suffering the Irish to usurp power in this City." Nast's cartoon war lampooning Tweed as corpulent and corrupt started to have an impact because, as Tweed himself remarked, even people who did not read "can't help seeing them damned pictures." Nevertheless, the *Times* still needed hard evidence.[33]

Finally, they got it when the Tammany Ring's bookkeeper died and was replaced by a Tweed opponent who copied the Ring's account books and gave them to the *Times*. The damning data became front-page news on July 22, 1871, a mere ten days after the Orange Riot. Within months, Tweed faced disaster. One building was most responsible for his downfall. Begun in 1862, the new County Courthouse, located behind City Hall, was supposed to cost no more than $250,000. By 1871, over $13 million had already been spent on the still unfinished structure. Questions had been raised since 1866, but it took until 1871 to get the answers.[34]

The facts were an astounding violation of the social contract. "Plunder of the city treasury ... was no new thing in New York," noted the British observer Lord James Bryce, "but it had never before reached such colossal dimensions." All bills for work on the courthouse had been processed through the Ring's contractor in a kickback scheme whereby companies would charge the city astronomical prices and return 65 percent of their fee back to the Ring. As a result, the city paid $1.5 million for carpets, $178,000 for three tables and four chairs, $75,000 for eleven thermometers and $41,000 for brooms.[35]

Nast depicted each member of the Ring blaming the other in answer to the question "Who Stole the People's Money?" The Ring employed its usual strategies to solve the problem. It offered to buy the *Times* and to send Nast to Europe; failing that, it threatened to evict the *Times* from its building. At this point, however, nothing could abate the fury of respectable New York.[36]

At a major rally at Cooper Union on September 4, the city's prominent men gathered to address the crisis and reestablish their dominance over the city's affairs. They took on the challenge, they said, not only as a measure of civic duty but also as a function of the Empire City's responsibility to set an example for the nation. In Springfield, Massachusetts, the anti-Tweed meeting was considered "the most momentous political event of the century." After numerous impassioned speeches, a Committee of Seventy was set up to rescue the city from Tammany by conducting investigations, pursuing the Ring in court, and stabilizing the city's finances. Answering Tweed's question, they proclaimed, "This is what we are going to do about it."[37]

Among the "best men" who joined the crusade against Tweed were Abram Hewitt and Samuel J. Tilden. The latter was a prominent lawyer and leader of the state Democratic Party who had previously condoned Tweed but now changed his mind. Tilden seized control of the legal and political strategy against Tweed in order to rescue his party while positioning himself to become governor in 1874 and presidential candidate in 1876. Andrew Haswell Green, Tilden's law partner and later the architect of Consolidation, was installed as acting New York City comptroller and, with access to the records, obtained ample evidence for Tweed's arrest.[38]

Although all of his cohorts managed to avoid punishment, Tweed underwent several trials. He escaped once to New Jersey and a second time to Spain where, recognized from Nast's cartoons, he was sent back to the United States and reincarcerated. Ever manipulative, he offered to write a full confession in exchange for early release. Apparently, he did his job too well because the confession implicated so many men, including Tilden, that Tweed was never pardoned. He died in the Ludlow Street jail at age fifty-five in 1878, doomed to everlasting infamy.[39]

In the struggle over who would dominate New York City, reformers managed to topple Tweed himself, but Tammany learned from Tweed's experience and bounced back. The first of six Irish bosses, "Honest" John Kelly controlled Tammany from 1872 to 1886 by centralizing power through an efficient organization that made Tammany respectable and even won support from Tilden and Hewitt. Kelly eschewed outright graft, but continued to use patronage and government favors in a system that Plunkitt labeled "honest graft." As a result, Tammany ruled the city until 1933 and remained powerful until 1961. In a sense, history vindicated Tweed by proving, as the *Times* had predicted, that "Tweedism will long survive Tweed."[40]

Tweed forced Americans to admit what they already knew—that Gilded Age bosses were corrupt and that greed could pervert democracy. Newspapers in Philadelphia, Milwaukee, Chicago, and London concluded that "unmasking the official villains of the Empire City" was essential lest the "poison" of bossism infect cities everywhere. In Bryce's opinion, New York had established an "especially notorious" paradigm of "plunder and misgovernment." Tweed's empire was so egregious that it shamed America into making good government a national priority. At the same time, Tammany forever changed urban politics by ensuring that the masses were attended to. Tammany's legacy both promoted and demoted democracy.[41]

THE SOCIAL QUESTION: THE DISCOVERY OF POVERTY

"I don't see why rich folks should be so hard upon a poor boy that wants to make a livin.' ... If everybody was like you and your uncle," said Dick, "there would be some chance for poor people. If I was rich, I'd try to help 'em along."

—**Horatio Alger,** *Ragged Dick*

Fortunately, the reputation of Gilded Age New Yorkers as totally consumed by greed and utterly disinterested in human suffering is inaccurate. In fact, the kindness shown to Ragged Dick was replicated by many people who were concerned about what they called "the Social Question." Their motivations were complex. Some patronized the poor as inferiors needing correction and control; others acted out of sincere social conscience. Both groups feared that misery could breed social instability or violence. This concept was captured by Charles Loring Brace, founder of the Children's Aid Society, in his book about *The Dangerous Classes of New York* (1872). Shaken by slums and strikes, a small but influential group of well-to-do New Yorkers decided that it was in their own self-interest to act on behalf of the social interest, that is, to "try to help 'em along."[42]

The huge mansions on upper Fifth Avenue, the grand Metropolitan Opera House at 39th Street and Broadway, and the luxurious Metropolitan Club at 60th Street and Fifth Avenue documented the advent of vast new wealth that contrasted sharply with the fetid slums. In New York City, the extremes of wealth and want were disturbingly conspicuous. That juxtaposition qualified the optimism of the age, posed the potential for conflict, and made people question their assumptions about the origins of poverty. By reaffirming old notions of the social contract, the social reform movement provided one of several "metropolitan filters," which, says Kessner, muted the worst abuses of the Gilded Age.[43]

The journalist Jacob Riis played a central role in the debate over the causes and consequences of urban problems in late-nineteenth-century New York. His influence spread beyond New York to undermine social Darwinism and alter concepts of poverty nationwide. As he put it, "conscience [was] not a local issue in our day." In assessing Riis' work, photographer Ansel Adams explained that the "intensity. . .[and] intimacy" of Riis' pictures created a "humanistic photography" that was widely influential. Imprinting New York's liberal traditions on America's consciousness enabled Riis to provoke many people to address the most disturbing social questions of the day.[44]

After emigrating from Denmark in 1870 at age twenty-one, Riis spent seven hard years at low-wage, menial jobs punctuated by unemployment and homelessness. He sought success in New York, Buffalo, Philadelphia, Pittsburgh, and Chicago, but failed repeatedly until, like Ragged Dick, he was helped by a sympathetic man who got him his first newspaper job. Having found his calling, Riis became police reporter for the *New York Tribune,* a job that took him into the Five Points daily. He was appalled by the suffering he saw and, in graphic prose, portrayed its realities to his middle-class readers.[45]

Determined to be yet more graphic, Riis started using magnesium powder to create a flash that would make the camera literally illuminate the darkest recesses of the slums. On the lecture circuit, he showed his pictures to church groups in New York, Brooklyn, Buffalo, and other eastern cities where he invoked Christianity to arouse sympathy for the poor. Just at the dawn of the new field of photography, the pictures were particularly powerful. Their stark, heart-wrenching quality inspired a widespread reconsideration of urban poverty.[46]

In 1890, Riis published his path-breaking book, *How the Other Half Lives: Studies Among the Tenements of New York,* that stimulated a nationwide "discovery of poverty." From California to Massachussetts, the book opened people's eyes and penetrated their hearts. The *Chicago Times* found it "of immense shuddering interest." Its statistics, images, and sympathetic descriptions of social conditions combined the new fields of photography, social science, and critical realism. Riis' pictures captured whole families rolling cigars in their tenements, men toiling in sweatshops, women sewing while starving in attics, and little orphans huddling together for warmth on street gratings. The book influenced Stephen Crane's writing and shaped Theodore Roosevelt's career as a political reformer. It touched poet James Russell Lowell whose words Riis used to ask: "Think ye that building shall endure which shelters the noble and crushes the poor?"[47]

How the Other Half Lives did for poverty what Harriet Beecher Stowe's *Uncle Tom's Cabin* did for slavery—exposed inequity, humanized suffering, elucidated ethical dilemmas, aroused guilt, awakened social conscience, and provoked social reform. Like Alger, Riis appreciated people's fascination with New York and ushered his readers through crowded streets, filthy alleys, sweltering apartments, stench-filled cellars, and sinful dives. He introduced them not only to tramps, prostitutes, pawnbrokers, thieves, alcoholics, drug addicts, and gamblers but also to decent men and women valiantly struggling to survive under what were "shocking conditions."[48]

Most of all, Riis discussed the children of the slums whom he considered "the key to the problem of city poverty." For him, the Ragged Dicks and the Maggies of New York were a scandal and a warning. He contrasted their cheerless lives stunted by work, hunger, violence, dirt, and disease with their innocent joy at seeing a flower for the first time. Suddenly, it was not mere fiction that thousands of children wore rags, slept in the streets, subsisted on beer, and descended into crime or prostitution. The lack of light, air, space, and sanitation doomed Gotham's youth to degradation and despair. They were a social time bomb fueled by a rich city that neglected the need for schools, parks, playgrounds, and housing. Advocating for the children's "right to play," Riis borrowed Tweed's question and asked New York, "What are you going to do about it?"[49]

New York was not sure. Prevailing notions of social Darwinism blamed the poor for their own suffering, and scorn for the new immigrants revived old strains of nativism. One strategy was to strengthen the police force and wage a war on vice. In 1892, the Reverend Charles Parkhurst ventured into the slums to document crime and police corruption. He concluded that New York was "hell with the lid off," but failed to get real change. Two years later, the Lexow Committee issued a scathing report on police protection rackets and police brutality. All of these horrors quickly became national news and reinforced existing negative images of Gotham in the Gilded Age.[50]

Spurred by the Parkhurst and Lexow investigations, New York reformers organized once more to unseat Tammany and temporarily regain control of the city. Creating a new Committee of Seventy, they elected reformer William L. Strong as mayor from 1894 to 1896. Strong used his powers to inaugurate scientific campaigns to fight disease, construct public baths, and set up the city's first effective street cleaning and sanitation removal systems. Commissioner Theodore Roosevelt made some improvements in the police department and kept himself in the news by inviting the journalists Jacob Riis and Lincoln Steffens to witness his investigations. Hewitt and Riis led efforts to build parks in the slums, later earning Riis the title "the Father of the Small Parks Movement." Riis also promoted slum clearance and tenement house reform.[51]

The struggle against Tammany carried over into the continuing controversy over children and public education. Reformers wanted to abolish community control of the schools, which made them vast sources of political patronage for Tammany. They hoped that improved schools would teach children the proper civic attitudes for resisting Tammany and the proper skills for working in the new industrial economy. In essence, schools were to become agents of assimilation, or what the playwright Israel Zangwill called "the melting pot." For many reformers, the subtext was, in the words of the *New York Tribune*, to uplift "pupils who are offensively dirty and densely ignorant, both by inheritance and by force of circumstance."[52]

In indignant response, the new immigrants, who valued education as a ladder of social mobility, joined Tammany and the teachers under the slogans "Public schools in danger!! Aristocracy versus the People." During the 1890s the situation was hotly debated, reports were issued, hearings held, and bills proposed. Finally in 1896, the reformers prevailed when the state reorganized New York City's schools under a centralized system. In 1901, New York became the nation's first city to require schooling for all children under twelve. The "school wars" conflated political with cultural and class issues.[53]

An even thornier controversy over public education revolved around racial segregation, a state policy from 1864. For all his ethnic prejudices, Riis recognized the evils of "the color line in New York" and deplored the fact that "the name of the negro, alone among the world's races, is spelled with a small n." Given this reality, African Americans knew that they had to advocate for themselves if they wanted change. Accordingly, in the town of Jamaica, they waged a five-year fight against the policy of relegating black children to a one-room schoolhouse with a single teacher for seventy-five students. Although aided by black lawyers, the activists were working-class men and women who organized, went to jail, and risked being fired for their cause. Victory came in 1900 when Governor Theodore Roosevelt signed a law desegregating schools in the state.[54]

Meanwhile, many upper- and middle-class New Yorkers were being reeducated about the nature of urban problems. As Riis observed, the difficulty was not just "ignorant poverty," but also "ignorant wealth." Josephine Shaw Lowell was a good example. Member of a prominent abolitionist family, she dedicated her life to charity after being widowed by the Civil War at age twenty. Lowell became the first female commissioner of the State Board of Charities and head of the New York Charity Organization Society (COS). In keeping with social Darwinism, her initial goals were to reduce assistance and discourage dependence. Accordingly, she improved prisons, workhouses, and reformatories, but vetoed public works jobs programs and refused to give out free coal in winter lest it encourage "idleness and vice."[55]

By the late 1880s, however, Lowell modified her position, especially after the COS was labeled "the meanest humbug in the city of New York." She was touched by the humanism of Henry George (whom her father had admired and befriended) and startled by information about the precarious lives of workers. When she discovered that low wages kept virtuous, hard-working people poor, she realized that poverty was not just a function of individual morality and decided that society had a responsibility to promote "just and humane conditions" of work. Consequently, she advocated a "living wage," that is, one that would sustain a decent life.[56]

Over forty years of public service, Lowell was an indefatigable crusader. She joined the Social Reform Club that emerged from George's mayoral campaign, backed Parkhurst's anti-vice campaign, supported Samuel Gompers' labor movement, and helped Riis with a variety of reform projects, including aid for children. During the Depression of 1893, Lowell established a jobs program for the unemployed. Then she organized women to help elect reformers and rose to leadership in the women's suffrage movement. Her ever-expanding role made Lowell one of the most important, most influential women in the history of American reform.[57]

In 1891, Lowell became president of the New York City Consumers' League, which mobilized upper- and middle-class women (including the young Eleanor Roosevelt) to boycott stores that exploited female workers. It was a clever model of cross-class collaboration that capitalized on the fact that the department store was a new forum for female consumption and employment. The League focused on department store clerks who worked ten to twelve hours a day with only a half-hour break for meals. The women were forbidden to sit on the job and were harassed if they dared use the sanitary facilities. Wages were absurdly low and did not cover overtime, which was considerable during the holidays. They lived in fear of fainting from fatigue or famine, being fined for minor transgressions, or being fired without cause and without redress.[58]

The Consumers' League drew up a list of acceptable working conditions for a "fair house," asked stores to subscribe to them, and then published a "White List" of establishments that met their standards. Only eight qualified in the first year, but twenty-four qualified in the second year, including Bloomingdales, Lord and Taylor, and F.A.O. Schwartz. Patronizing only stores on the "White List," Consumers' League members found that pocketbook pressure was effective. By 1896, they got New York State to set minimum standards for working conditions.[59]

The New York City group was replicated in twenty states and seven European countries. A National Consumers' League was formed in 1899 led by Chicago's Florence Kelley, who became the nation's foremost crusader for improving women's working conditions and eliminating child labor. She asked, "Why have newsboys" when men were unemployed? Her answer was to promote laws to ban the labor of children under sixteen so that they could "go to school, as our own children do." Perceptions of the poor were changing.[60]

Similar discoveries were being made throughout the city. The Settlement House movement, which came to Chicago and New York via London, spread throughout Gotham's slums, including the Henry Street Settlement, Greenwich House, and the University Settlement (called the Neighborhood Guild when it opened as the nation's first settlement house in 1886). The initial sponsors were idealistic upper- and middle-class young men who were joined by the first generation of college-educated young women for whom few employment opportunities existed. By working and sometimes living in the settlement houses themselves, they acquired an understanding of the people they helped and developed programs to meet their needs. The settlement houses offered inexpensive meals, free kindergartens, and health clinics, plus classes in language and job skills. Out of these efforts emerged a professionalizing of social concern through the new field of social work.[61]

So many private organizations contributed to the crusade against poverty that Riis proclaimed New York "the most charitable city in the world." The Salvation Army, the Young Men's Christian Association, the Ethical Culture Society, and numerous other groups reached out to the poor. The Society for the Prevention of Cruelty to Children used lawsuits to stem child abuse. The Working Women's Protective Union offered free legal services to women cheated out of their pay. Wealthy individuals sponsored model tenements, trade schools, and Working Girls Clubs. In 1891, German Jews established the Educational Alliance to help Eastern European Jews assimilate.

Meanwhile, the Children's Aid Society continued to place children in country homes and to maintain the five newsboys' lodging houses (plus one for girls) that both Alger and Riis praised for saving thousands of waifs yearly. Although these organizations were sustained wholly or in part by the well-to-do, they were supplemented by mutual benefit associations created by the poor who pooled their own meager resources to cover funerals, medical costs, and other emergencies. For the historian Alan Nevins, this spirit of philanthropy and civic activism comprised a "truly golden thread in the history of New York ... that no other city can quite match."[62]

By the same token, Riis concluded that all of these private efforts proved how much the public needed to reassess urban problems. The realities of life in the Gilded Age city clarified the limits of competitive individualism and the consequences of unrestrained greed. Riis contended that the "Dangerous Classes" only become a threat when reduced to despair and they only succumbed to despair when driven there by the "avarice" of employers and landlords. Industrialism was creating problems "yet unsolved, more perplexing than ever." Nonetheless, Riis believed that if people understood that "we are all creatures of the conditions that surround us," they would see the wisdom of improving those conditions.[63]

According to the historian Tyler Anbinder, Riis' pictures "transformed Mulberry Bend and its wretched tenements into a national issue." By adding a compelling visual dimension to the dilemmas of the age, they reached many more people than the printed word alone. They stimulated what Riis called an "awakening." Images of the nation's first slum in the city of the nation's first trust challenged the stranglehold of Social Darwinism on the American mind. A new model of the social contract was emerging.[64]

THE LABOR QUESTION

> Dick was willing to work. . . . His street education had sharpened his faculties, and taught him to rely upon himself. . . . He knew that he had only himself to depend upon, and he determined to make the most of himself—a resolution which is the secret of success in nine cases out of ten.
>
> **—Horatio Alger,** *Ragged Dick*

The central lesson of the Gilded Age was that Alger's "secret of success" no longer applied to the majority of people. Instead of relying on themselves, they learned to rely on each other. Groups as different as farmers, manufacturers, factory workers, and middle-class professionals organized to offset the depersonalization of life in industrial society. This shift from individual to collective action represented what the historian Robert H. Wiebe called "a revolution in values." It was particularly evident in Gotham, which led in the development of workers' organizations during one of the nation's most contentious periods of labor history. As a result, declared Samuel Gompers, "New York City was the cradle of the modern American labor movement."[65]

The "Labor Question" provoked the Gilded Age to ask why there was so much strife in a booming capitalist economy. Increasing evidence of economic conflict, says Hays, "deeply stunned Americans who had cherished views that classes did not exist in their country." Modernization challenged assumptions about equality of opportunity, social mobility, hard work, individual initiative, fair play, and personal morality. Adam Smith's labor theory of value, a core component of traditional capitalism, seemed irrelevant when labor was underpaid and overworked. Both the trusts and the tenements threatened the American Dream. As a result, more and more people shared Josephine Shaw Lowell's conclusion that "the Labor Question is, after all, only another phase of the Liberty Question."[66]

Getting Organized

New York City's unions grew by fits and starts during the 1860s and 1870s. An eight-week strike in 1872 involving one hundred thousand workers, the largest yet in the city, was crushed by the united front of an employers' association that reflected a hardening of class lines. Labor's efforts were further undermined by a financial panic in 1873, which begat a five-year depression. 1874 brought wage reductions and unemployment for almost a quarter of New York City's workforce. During that winter, the poor appealed to the city government for relief, but their requests for "Work or Bread" were dismissed as communistic. Instead, the police were sent out to patrol the streets under orders to "quell any disturbance within thirty minutes."[67]

Concluding that "nobody will attempt to help if we don't do something ourselves," a coalition of laborites and socialists called a mass meeting for January 13, 1874, in Tompkins Square Park. Despite the frigid weather, seven thousand people assembled. They did not know that the police had revoked permission for the rally at the last minute and that sixteen hundred policemen peppered the vicinity. They were unprepared for a sudden assault by police wielding clubs, cracking heads, and arresting many. Mounted police charged the crowd to clear the square and then chased people at top speed through the streets while beating them with their batons. Men fell under the horses' hooves and into the gutters. The violence continued for hours in what Gompers denounced as "an orgy of brutality."[68]

Prominent New Yorkers praised the police for saving the city from "riot and terror." The mayor rejoiced that Gotham's "vagabonds" had received "a sound flogging." The police commissioner bragged that his men "broke and drove that crowd." Nonetheless, some citizens were upset. Workers filed complaints, held protest meetings, and petitioned Albany. Thomas Nast drew a scathing cartoon of the police as vicious dogs that should be muzzled or sent to the pound. The *New York Tribune*'s editor, Whitlaw Reid, called for the police to exercise more self-control. Others simply saw the affair as part of a larger crusade to "utterly crush the people."[69]

Three years later, the scene was replayed. Plans for a July meeting in Tompkins Square Park supporting the 1877 national railroad strike inspired the city fathers (over Hewitt's opposition) to call out the National Guard and import a thousand men from the Navy in anticipation of a "Communist riot." Despite the fact that twenty thousand spectators did nothing for two hours but peacefully listen to speeches (albeit some quite radical), again the rally ended with a sudden attack by club-wielding policemen.[70]

In the spirit of mainstream social Darwinism, Brooklyn's preacher, Henry Ward Beecher, castigated labor activists for seeking better pay. Insisting that men should be able "to live under the conditions which exist," he asked rhetorically, "But is not a dollar a day enough to buy bread with?" His answer was clear: "Water costs nothing and a man who cannot live on bread is not fit to live." Such lack of sympathy for labor was accompanied by so much fear of a labor uprising that the wealthy themselves paid for the construction of a formidable new armory at 66th Street and Lexington Avenue. Class antagonism had acquired a very physical presence.[71]

Meanwhile, the workers were bolstering their own defenses. An 1877 cigarmakers' strike mobilized more workers than any previous labor action in New York City history, even though it occurred during a depression. The strike trained Samuel Gompers for his role as the nation's premier labor organizer. Actually, he had been preparing since age ten when he learned cigarmaking from his Dutch Jewish father then living in the London slums. Gompers came to the United States with his family three years later, in 1863, and soon started working in the Lower East Side cigarmaking factories. He also attended lectures on political economy at Cooper Union and studied economic theory (including Marx) with his coworkers. Although Gompers believed that harmony between employers and employees was impossible in a profit-driven economy, the Tompkins Square episodes convinced him that radical rhetoric made the workers vulnerable to division from within and attack from without.[72]

Given the realities of industrialism, Gompers concluded that the strike was a crucial weapon in labor's limited arsenal for self-advancement. Only coordinated protest would be effective against concentrated wealth. Only organization of, by, and for the workers themselves would consistently and persistently focus on improving their lives. This position contrasted sharply with that of the Knights of Labor, which pursued cooperation between workers and employers and had been organizing skilled, semiskilled, and unskilled workers from its Pennsylvania base since 1869. Seeking social harmony, the Knights repudiated the strike as a perpetrator of social conflict.[73]

In 1877, the Cigarmakers' Union, led by Gompers, confronted the full complexities of striking. One problem was the internal division between the skilled "American" men working in the small shops and large factories as opposed to the less-skilled immigrant women working in the tenements. The former looked down on the latter, but changed their position when the tenement workers backed the factory workers' strike over a 20 percent pay cut in August. By late October, Gompers had to find ways to support fifteen thousand strikers and their families. With funds raised in the city, across the country, and in Europe, the union gave out food, paid rents, found alternative housing for evicted families, and opened a cooperatively owned cigar factory. Nonetheless, as they struggled into December, their resources dwindled.[74]

On the other side, large and small cigar manufacturers were initially hampered by their own internal divisions, but soon they too began working together. Not to be outdone by labor, management used strikebreakers, black-lists, lockouts, and evictions to wear down the strikers. Violence mounted between the police and the pickets, the pickets and the strikebreakers. Winter took its toll and, finally, the strike collapsed by the end of January. Failure was devastating, but it taught Gompers how hard it was to strike and how vital it was to make the union economically stable before striking. At the same time, the experience underlined the importance of striking in order to create the "opportunity to be heard in our own interests."[75]

Gompers learned more lessons from the short-lived Central Labor Union (CLU), which was formed by twelve unions in New York City in 1882, reached its peak in 1886 with two hundred member organizations, but died by 1888. Like the Knights of Labor, the CLU brought together a variety of workers' groups with socialists and radicals, but, unlike the Knights, it endorsed a wide range of strategies including strikes, boycotts, and political activism. Atypical for its day, the CLU embraced black and white, native and foreign-born. The CLU's broad appeal was evident in 1882 when it sponsored America's first Labor Day parade with twenty thousand people marching from City Hall to Union Square. For the next few years, the CLU was central to the nation's militant labor struggles.[76]

In 1886, labor activism peaked across the country, with twelve hundred strikes in New York City alone. A particularly significant battle was waged from winter through summer by horsecar drivers trying to reduce their sixteen-hour shifts. During that struggle, the strikers and their community supporters mobbed the streets, threw food at the police, piled wood and stones on the tracks, and pushed over the horse cars. Employers, like William Steinway at his Astoria, Queens piano factory, responded to the strikes by calling in the police and paying them extra for their help. In return, the police protected the scabs, dispersed the picketers, and disrupted all labor meetings, clubs in hand. Indeed, police brutality was so prevalent that one captain earned the nickname "Clubber" Williams.[77] (See Figure 9 following page 150)

The strikes of 1886 culminated when the CLU organized a walkout of sixteen thousand horse car drivers, conductors, and stable hands. By closing down every streetcar line in the city, they demonstrated the power of labor solidarity. Ultimately, however, the strike was settled by force at the expense of labor. The horse car companies' reliance on violence revealed not just their own influence but also the strength of popular resistance and the depth of social conflict. The labor crisis moved the genteel author, William Dean Howells, closer toward critical realism and an understanding of urban complexity. As he depicted it in *A Hazard of New Fortunes* (1890), the 1886 strike was part of "a great social convulsion" gripping the city and the country.[78]

The CLU's second major strategy for promoting labor's cause was the boycott that, when coordinated with strikes, delivered a double blow to recalcitrant employers while being less dangerous and costly for workers than strikes. In 1886 there were 165 boycotts in New York State, 119 of which were tied to strikes. Labor pickets targeted small employers who could not withstand the economic pressure and capitulated quickly. As successful boycotts spread from bakers to shoemakers, they upset businessmen and the mainstream press. Despite its use in the American Revolution, the boycott was widely disparaged as a "foreign" tactic, a form of "blackmail" and "terrorism" that undermined American institutions.[79]

Consequently, the powers of the state were marshaled to arrest the pickets and their leaders on the grounds of "conspiracy against trade." After the boycott was declared illegal and a judge issued severe prison sentences, the workers found themselves circumscribed. Another major setback occurred when a bomb killed seven policemen at a demonstration for the eight-hour day in Chicago's Haymarket Square on May 1, 1886. Now all labor protesters were stereotyped as dangerous anarchists, and the repression of unions intensified nationwide. As Gompers observed, the combined effect of management resistance, police brutality, and judicial restraints on protest pushed labor to "the breaking point."[80]

Raising Hell

Anger fostered activism and the CLU turned to politics as a third way to demonstrate the power of labor. Backed by over two hundred labor unions accounting for over fifty thousand workers, the CLU nominated the popular reformer, Henry George, to run for mayor in 1886. It was a thoroughly unconventional choice. Full of infectious energy and inspiring idealism but lacking political experience, a party structure, and money, George's nomination could easily have been a disaster. Instead, it unified moderate and radical laborites, middle-class reformers and socialists, Irish nationalists and Eastern European immigrants, and blacks and whites.[81]

Tammany took George's candidacy seriously enough to offer him election to Congress if he pulled out of the race. Although the politicians did not believe he could win, they feared that his candidacy would "raise hell." Enticed by that prospect, George jumped into the fray. The Republicans chose a young, Harvard-educated State Assemblyman of Knickerbocker origins named Theodore Roosevelt who would later become police commissioner, governor of New York, and president of the United States. In 1886, however, he was eclipsed by his rivals.[82]

Tammany and the Democrats joined behind the most respectable, most liberal candidate they could find. A five-term congressman, Abram Hewitt, was an industrialist acclaimed as a humane employer because he paid decent wages and supported labor's right to strike. The partner and son-in-law of industrialist Peter Cooper, Hewitt was a trustee and major financial supporter of Cooper Union. In addition, he was an alumni trustee of Columbia College, a noted philanthropist and a prominent member of numerous reform groups, including those that brought down Tweed. In 1880, he had briefly hired a struggling journalist named Henry George to be his researcher. They did not get along.[83]

The campaign was electrifying. George worked around the clock speaking at union meetings, neighborhood rallies, factories, church fairs, local clubs, and on street corners. Thousands of workers contributed nickels and dimes to finance his independent third-party effort. The campaign distributed its own newspaper to over forty thousand readers. Despite preferring that labor be apolitical, Gompers ran the speakers' bureau, gave many speeches himself and coordinated Henry George Clubs all over the city. Ever the opportunist and pragmatist, he seized the moment to promote trade union interests. In the process, Gompers helped George democratize politics by involving ordinary people directly in the political dialogue.[84]

Hewitt's campaign was more formal and sedate. Accepting the prevailing notion that campaigning was undignified, he only gave a few speeches at dinners and political meetings. When challenged by George to a verbal debate, Hewitt refused, but the candidates' differences were made clear in their acceptance speeches and in letters published by the local and national press. George asked two key questions: "Why should there be such abject poverty in this city?" and "What do we propose to do about it?" His answers were partly a function of his ideas about taxing the land, partly a call for better government, but mainly a cry for "social justice" and the "abolition of industrial slavery." In addition, he was the first mayoral candidate to excoriate police brutality.[85]

Hewitt saw George as a dangerous man intent on fomenting social disorder much like "Anarchists, Nihilists, Communists." To Hewitt, capital and labor should be "allies ... [not] antagonists." Like Alger, Hewitt declared that there was no better haven for "honest working people" than the city of New York, where opportunity abounded to earn, save, and succeed. Proclaiming himself the best friend of the poor, Hewitt branded George "the demon of discord." The press attacked him at every turn, and the cartoonist Joseph Keppler depicted him duping the workers into selling their souls to the Devil of anarchy.[86]

George was visionary but not revolutionary and he insisted that he represented "not a class but the mass." More favorable cartoonists represented him as a hero strangling the serpent of want, corruption, and monopoly. (See Figure 10 following page 150) However, George's criticisms of the unearned wealth reaped by landlords through rent upset the city's landowners and real estate interests. So, too, did a spectacular pro-George parade in late October during which thirty thousand people marched from Cooper Union to Tompkins

Square in the pouring rain with thousands more lining the streets to watch. It embodied, says the historian David Scobey, not an actual revolution, but a cultural one—an expression of protest against the demise of equal opportunity under industrial capitalism. As a "ritual of class resistance," the parade captured the campaign's larger significance.[87]

Hewitt won in November. However, there were accusations of manipulation at the polls by Tammany men who assiduously counted George votes for Hewitt. Under its new leader, Richard Croker, Tammany also pressured the Catholic hierarchy to issue a statement of opposition to George's candidacy and to suspend the popular George supporter, Father Edward McGlynn. Some employers fired George activists; others (including the streetcar companies) warned that their workers' jobs hinged on George's defeat. Despite these deterrents, George did remarkably well, garnering almost a third of the vote for an official tally of sixty-eight thousand.[88]

New York and the nation were taken by surprise. "The size of the George vote," admitted numerous politicians and mainstream newspapers, "has startled a good many people." Upholding the validity of the social contract, Hewitt himself recognized "that 68,000 people have deliberately declared that they have grievances which ought to be redressed." According to the *New York Evening Post,* the situation was more serious "than in Tweed's time. Tweed and his Ring were passing phenomena," said the *Post,* but the George movement exposed a deep well-spring of "discontent." In this sense, conclude the historians Edwin Burrows and Mike Wallace, the Henry George campaign was the most serious "challenge to the established order since the Sons of Liberty contested merchant control of the city in colonial days."[89]

New York City's mayoralty contest had a widespread impact. It was particularly interesting in Ireland and England, where land reformers, Irish nationalists, and English Socialists greatly admired Henry George. Frederich Engels, Karl Marx's collaborator, considered the election "an epoch making day" in the development of working-class politics. Indeed, it was the first time that labor dominated a New York City campaign and, said labor leaders in St. Louis, it would become "the battle cry for all the enslaved toilers from the Atlantic to the Pacific."[90]

After the election, other labor candidates entered politics in unprecedented numbers across the country. They ran for municipal, state, and national offices winning elections in New Jersey, Virginia, Colorado, Florida, Illinois, Connecticut, Wisconsin, Massachusetts, and Texas. Significantly, both the Democrats and the Republicans rushed to run their own pro-labor candidates and Father McGlynn accurately anticipated that "in the future no political party in the United States can afford to leave [labor] out of its calculations." Not surprisingly, Tammany quickly shifted its position by reaching out to labor, backing pro-labor laws, and restraining police during strikes.[91]

Labor's success was brief. The hostile tone set by the courts, the police, the business community, the regular parties, and the press effectively undercut labor activism. In addition, the labor coalition itself began to dissolve as different segments vied for control of the postelection movement. In New York City, the struggle was intense between different types of socialists, between socialists and moderates, between the Knights of Labor and the trade unionists. This internal division was exactly what Gompers had feared and he left the 1886 campaign determined to separate unions from politics.[92]

The result was the creation of the most important labor organization in American history. Formed in 1886 under Gompers' leadership, the American Federation of Labor embraced a "business unionism" well suited to the Gilded Age. The answer to Gompers' own question, "What does labor want?" was simple. Labor wanted "to obtain a better life every day" as defined by hours, wages, benefits, and working conditions. This "bread and butter" pragmatism made Gompers seem as conservative, materialistic, and optimistic as Alger, but it worked. Over time, he used what Kessner calls a "New York model" to build a powerful national labor movement that, for all its limitations, may have been the most lasting legacy of the Henry George campaign. George got labor on the nation's political agenda, but Gompers got labor its seat at the nation's economic table.[93]

In the 1890s, however, the struggle was still formidable, as proven by the Brooklyn Trolley Strike of 1895. Responding to wage cuts, the workers took on Brooklyn's three biggest trolley companies. They faced serious disadvantages, especially during a depression when many men were so desperate for work that they could easily be hired as scabs. Of course, Theodore Dreiser explained in *Sister Carrie* (1900) that scabs suffered, too. They were reluctant to undermine their fellow workmen and were frightened by the violence of strikes but were even more frightened by hunger. As one of Dreiser's scabs pointed out, "You could starve, by God, right in the streets, and there ain't most no one would help you."[94]

Defying extensive community support for the strikers, Brooklyn's mayor put policemen on every trolley car and, for the first time in that city's history, summoned the Brooklyn militia for riot duty, soon to be reinforced by New York's own militia. The seventy-five hundred soldiers did not find a riot but, as in earlier conflicts, their mere presence created one. After several days of escalating tensions, the troops started shooting and two men were killed. Brooklyn remained an armed camp throughout January and the trolley owners refused to give in. Ultimately undone by hunger, scabs, the cold, and the military, the strike collapsed after five weeks. Bitterness lingered in the strikers' song:

The soldiers and policemen were called to take a hand

To terrorize the motormen in this our own free land
The mayor who called for troops should ever bear in mind
That capital is never right when it attempts to grind.[95]

The newsboys agreed. In the late nineteenth century, child labor was common because adult wages were pitiful and orphans were plentiful. One of the better jobs for children was selling newspapers in the street, an expanding business during the era of yellow journalism in the nation's newspaper hub. Called "newsies," they made a very small margin of profit. When Gotham's two largest papers, William Randolph Hearst's *New York Journal* and Joseph Pulitzer's *New York World,* raised their wholesale prices in 1898, the newsies took note.[96]

In 1899, the year of Horatio Alger's death, the newsies met in City Hall Park to form a union and call a strike. Their assertiveness paralleled the hawking street style associated with their job since the emergence of the penny press in the 1830s. "We're here for our rights," insisted one eleven-year-old, "an' we will die defendin' 'em." They did not die, but they did prevent the sale of papers by stopping delivery trucks and assaulting scabs. Within a few days, the *World* suffered a 66 percent decrease in sales. After two weeks, the papers settled with the newsboys.[97]

Although their organizations did not last, the newsies' strike succeeded for a number of reasons. First, the boys were able to cooperate because they had an established community built up after so much time spent together on the streets. Second, they won the sympathy of adults with their parades, placards, songs, circulars, rallies, and appeals to "Help the Newsboys" because "Our Cause is Just." Businessmen gave them tips and Bowery bums refused to scab. Even the police were less vigilant than usual, perhaps partly because they were distracted by another Brooklyn trolley strike.[98]

Third, the newsboys' strike spread throughout the area starting in Long Island City and moving rapidly through Manhattan, into Brooklyn, Jersey City, Newark, and Yonkers. Secondary children's boycotts by messengers and bootblacks strengthened the newsies' position. Fourth, and quite appropriately, newspapers spread word of the strike across the country. Sympathetic strikes erupted in Boston, Cincinnati, Philadelphia, Pittsburgh, Lexington, Kentucky, and Providence, Rhode Island. As the historian David Nasaw observed, labor protest had become an inherent "part of the urban environment," even among its youngest workers.[99]

The newsies' strike attested to the complexities of economic change. Like their elders, the newsies maintained their faith in capitalism even as they modified individualism through collective action and used the public domain to counteract powerful private interests. They employed the city's central position in the region and the nation to magnify their impact. They appealed to social conscience. Rejecting the desperation of Maggie, the newsies adapted the optimism of Ragged Dick to modern conditions proving that they, too, "ain't knocked about the city streets all their lives for nothin.'"

Riis had always contended that "the problem of the children is the problem of the State." It mirrored the current character of society and foretold its future. Because children became adults who determined social values and shaped social organization, improving their lives was a wise social investment in a better life for all. The challenge was clear, the need critical. As he explained in 1900:

> New York is the youngest of the world's great cities, barely yet out of its knickerbockers. It may be that the dawning century will see it as the greatest of them all. The task that is set to it, the problem it has to solve, and which it may not shirk, is the problem of civilization, of human progress, of a people's fitness for self-government. . . .We shall solve it by the world-old formula of human sympathy, of humane touch. . . .When we have learned to smile and weep with the poor, we shall have mastered our problem. Then the slum will have lost its grip and the boss his job.

To Riis, such an awakening would be the true measure of "metropolitan greatness," a sentiment suitable for an Empire City in a Gilded Age.[100]

6

The City of Ambition

Progressivism on Trial, 1900–1919

In 1910, Alfred Stieglitz used the title "The City of Ambition" to describe his photograph of New York's busy harbor set against smoking factories and towering office buildings. Human invention reigned supreme; technology had conquered nature. Although the picture conveyed modernity and economic prowess, it was dark. The gray clouds above reflected the swirling waters below in ominous commentary on perils of prosperity. Yet, the title effectively captured Gotham's aggressive, optimistic commitment to progress. From 1900 to 1919, that quest would repeatedly roil New York as ambition pervaded the city, challenged convention, and stimulated conflict.[1]

Another somber photograph, another image of ambition depicted a man, not a place. He was a figure as formidable as his city and, to many people, more so. In early-twentieth-century New York, the only thing that J. Pierpont Morgan could not control was the camera. Taken by Stieglitz's friend, Edward Steichen, the famous 1903 portrait of Morgan captured the essence of a man called Jupiter because he was as omnipotent as an ancient Roman god. Reflecting the searing power of his influence, Morgan stared sternly out from the dark recesses of the picture elegantly attired with stiff collar, silk ascot, golden watch, and chain. His left hand tightly clutched the arm of his chair as if symbolizing the intensity of his grip on the American economy. Morgan so hated the picture that he tore the first print to shreds.[2]

Son of a prominent London banker, Morgan built the family firm into the predominant financial powerhouse of the world located at 23 Wall Street across from both Federal Hall and the Stock Exchange. With vast monetary resources at his command, he engineered major mergers in the fields of electricity, communications, farm machinery, insurance, and banking. After systematically seizing control of small railroads, Morgan organized the nation's remaining major railroads (including Rockefeller holdings) into one vast Northern Securities Company in 1901. His restructuring of the economy was so momentous that it necessitated a new noun, "morganization," accompanied by a new verb, to be "morganized." When criticized, he declared, "I owe the public nothing."[3]

Morgan's most spectacular maneuver came in 1901 with the combination of seventeen steel companies (including Andrew Carnegie's) into a massive steel trust, the first corporation in the world to be worth a billion dollars. Later that year, Morgan built a North Atlantic shipping trust with England and Germany. Not only had Morgan's mergers magnified Rockefeller's monopoly manyfold, but they also ushered in a new era of economic centralization through which the investment banker replaced the industrialist as the engine of capitalist development.[4]

While he was reorganizing private enterprise, Morgan also was rescuing the public sector, always for a profit. In 1895, he used his British connections to float $60 million worth of bonds that bolstered the federal government's gold reserve and prevented fiscal collapse. During the Panic of 1907, he secured a $25 million federal loan and raised an additional $16 million in private money to shore up key banks, trusts, and the New York Stock Exchange. It was a remarkable feat that stabilized Wall Street and saved the nation from economic disaster. Morgan had become America's banker, or as journalist Lincoln Steffens put it, "the boss of the United States."[5]

That was the problem. Morgan was the most powerful man on America's most powerful street. In fact, "Wall Street is not merely a street," wrote Steffens. "Wall Street is a national institution. It is to American business what Washington, D.C. is to national politics. . .[and] it ramifies all over the United States." The truth was that Steffens and others feared that Wall Street was more potent than the federal government and they decided that it was time to correct the balance. The seeds of reform planted in the Gilded Age now flowered in a Progressive movement that used government to begin rectifying the worst abuses of capitalism in order to prevent the most extreme reactions against those abuses by workers, farmers, socialists, and radicals.[6]

Tragedy provided Progressivism with a champion when, in 1901, Vice President Theodore Roosevelt (TR) became President of the United States after William McKinley was assassinated by an anarchist. Ambition personified, Roosevelt was the only Gothamite ever to occupy the White House. This Harvard graduate of Knickerbocker stock assumed power equipped with ideas developed during his career as state assemblyman, police commissioner, governor of New York, and assistant secretary of the navy. Roosevelt's association with Jacob Riis, Lincoln Steffens, and Samuel Gompers, plus his exposure to New York City's sweatshops and slums, convinced him that government should address economic inequities. Accordingly, as governor, he endorsed reforms in the areas of education, housing, and labor.[7]

In 1902, President Roosevelt initiated a federal suit to break up the Northern Securities Company. News of the case sent the stock market into a panic, infuriating Morgan and forcing him to buy frantically in order to avoid a crash. More important, it marked a bold break with the federal government's historic support for private enterprise and a new commitment to the social contract. Despite the risk entailed in confronting corporate wealth, the president had decided that no one should "combine to the public injury."[8]

The country cheered Roosevelt's assault on the money moguls of Wall Street and dubbed him a trustbuster, even though he only wanted to control (not eliminate) corporate growth. The nation was further elated when the Supreme Court ruled in 1904 that the Northern Securities Company was an illegal monopoly and when it dismantled the Standard Oil trust in 1911. The following year found Congress investigating Morgan and the "money trust." Four months later, the seventy-five-year-old financier passed away, leaving a surprisingly small monetary legacy (compared to Carnegie and Rockefeller) but an outstanding art collection and a long-standing impact on the American economy.[9]

Negotiations during the 1907 Panic took place in the lavish Morgan Library on 36th Street and Madison Avenue where bankers and industrialists haggling over cold cash were surrounded by rare books, paintings, sculpture, and tapestries. The lavish marble building reflected the Beaux Arts style of the City Beautiful movement. As evidence of Gotham's wealth, its established prominence, and its civic pride, New York was transformed with monumental signature structures during the first decade of the twentieth century. They included the Plaza Hotel, the U.S. Customs House, Pennsylvania Railroad Station, the New York Public Library, the New York Stock Exchange, Grand Central Station, the Municipal Building, and the Brooklyn Museum. In addition, there was the massive Metropolitan Museum of Art where Morgan was president and benefactor. Such grand buildings, wrote novelist Henry James, reflected "the power of the most extravagant of cities."[10]

At the same time, tall buildings were beginning to dominate the skyline, as in Stieglitz's photograph. The elevator combined with steel-frame construction facilitated building up to ten stories by the 1870s and thirty stories by 1900. Completed in 1902, the twenty-one-story Flatiron building was one of Stieglitz's favorite photographic subjects. Skyscrapers continued to climb with the sixty-story Woolworth building (called a Cathedral to Commerce) reigning as the tallest building in the world from 1913 to 1930. In contrast to the massive, horizontal Beaux Arts buildings, the sleek, vertical skyscrapers heralded the new, more modern city.

However, there were some limits. In 1915, the forty-one-story Equitable building filled up an entire block on Broadway at Pine Street. It threw shadows over so many surrounding buildings that, in order to avoid being doomed to darkness, the city decided to regulate future construction. Creating a national model, Gotham adopted America's first zoning law in 1916. It reduced the percentage of the lot that a building could fill and required that tall buildings have stepped setbacks to let light onto the street. The new codes reflected the Progressives' desire to ensure that the social contract balanced private with public interests.[11]

Similarly, the 1901 New York Tenement House Law had established socially responsible guidelines for urban development regarding the poor. Sponsored by Josephine Shaw Lowell's Charity Organization Society and supported by Roosevelt, it too was a national model, replicated in eleven states and forty cities. Now there would have to be more space between tenements, with all apartments required to have toilets and a window in every room. These standards, which Jacob Riis had promoted, were timely because the early 1900s were America's peak period of immigration. With over 70 percent of the newcomers settling in the Gateway City, the Lower East Side became denser than Bombay, India. Using public policy to address modern problems, wrote the historian Richard Hofstadter, concretized the Progressives' belief that "industrial society was to be humanized through law."[12]

In 1904 William Randolph Hearst, ambitious publisher of the *New York Journal,* decided that society should be humanized through politics. Already a U.S. congressman, Hearst ran for mayor as an independent on an antitrust, anti-Tammany platform. He contended that if the city took over the management and distribution of transportation, gas, ice, and electricity, the trusts controlling those services would die. In turn, their demise would deprive Tammany of a major source of graft revenues, thereby crippling it and returning city government to the people. Democracy would be restored.

Although condemned by Tammany and the Republicans as a dangerous radical, Hearst's program was so popular that he nearly won the 1905 election. Much to everyone's surprise, he got almost twice as many votes as the Republicans and only 1.5 percent fewer votes than the victorious Tammany candidate (George B. McClellan), whose majority was attributed to violence and fraud at the polls. Hearst's support came from immigrants and the working classes in Tammany's heartland on the Lower East Side as well as from Brooklyn and Queens. His success, says the historian David Nasaw, forever changed Gotham's political landscape by forcing Tammany to back reform candidates and reform legislation from then on. Popular pressure could bring change after all.[13]

Meanwhile, a different facet of change was emerging in a different area of the city. As part of Gotham's perpetual movement uptown, the *New York*

Times abandoned Park Row in favor of 42nd Street and Broadway above the city's first subway line, completed in 1904. Rising twenty-five stories to become the city's second tallest structure, the *Times* building symbolized the development of a unique center of city life and created a bustling new "crossroads of the world." When the *Times* sponsored the first New Year's Eve fireworks in 1904, it signaled exploding new possibilities for Gotham in the twentieth century. In 1913, Grand Central Station solidified 42nd Street's role as the nexus of the modern city.[14]

Departing from the traditional city square dedicated to political, religious, or economic functions, Times Square celebrated activities that challenged mainstream mores and were usually kept away from the center. The entertainment industry and commercial sex were already settling around 42nd Street by the turn of the century and drawing large numbers of people to what was rapidly becoming a major tourist attraction. Huge, illuminated billboards harnessed electricity to advertising, creating the Great White Way and rendering Gotham "the city that never sleeps." Popular culture trumped formal culture. Theaters, movie houses, restaurants, dance halls, and hotels spelled the demise of Victorian restraint. As Times Square became the national symbol of entertainment, commercialism, and vice, New York seemed more ambitious, more exciting, and more threatening than ever.[15]

During the Progressive era, New York played a special role in helping the nation modernize. Although it symbolized economic power, it nurtured reform. Although it exuded confidence, it generated conflict. Most provocatively, the agents of change in Gotham were often from nontraditional groups such as artists, blacks, women, the poor, and radicals. As in the Jacksonian era, New York pushed the prevailing ideology of reform to its limits. Through the arts, on the streets, and in the courts, New York was a testing ground for Progressivism.

THE BOHEMIAN REVOLT

A striking example of the Progressive spirit was the early-twentieth-century Bohemian rebellion that emerged from Greenwich Village and horrified the nation's proponents of bourgeois Victorian values. Young middle-class intellectuals from across the nation gathered at the Liberal Club on MacDougal Street and the salon of wealthy patron Mabel Dodge at 23 Fifth Avenue. They reveled in the uninhibited dance of Isadora Duncan, the experimental plays of Eugene O'Neill, the innovative music of Scott Joplin, and the psychoanalytic theories of Sigmund Freud. Social control gave way to a culture of youth, liberation, paganism, socialism, birth control, free speech, and creativity. Their "ambition," says the historian Christine Stansell, was "to matter," to be different and to make a difference in the emerging century.[16]

For the Bohemians, Greenwich Village was a cultural "Free City." As if to parody Fernando Wood's mid-nineteenth-century free city proposal, they declared that Greenwich Village should become an independent republic. The radical poet John Reed put it best when he wrote:

Yet we are free who live in Washington Square,
We dare to think as Uptown wouldn't dare,
Blazing our nights with arguments uproarious;
What care we for a dull, old world censorious
When each of us is sure he'll fashion something glorious?
Blessed are thou, Anarchic Liberty
Who asketh nought but joy of such as we!

The Bohemian Revolt hit such a responsive chord across America that, within a decade, what had once been daring became commonplace, making Greenwich Village less a site of revolt than a fashionable tourist destination. Plays, poems, paintings, magazines, newspapers, books, music, dance, and protest movements spread the new spirit widely. Like Times Square, the Bohemian Revolt confirmed Gotham's dual role as cultural cesspool and cultural model for the nation.[17]

The impact of the Greenwich Village rebellion was particularly great for women. The demure, domestic, dependent traditional woman was being displaced by an independent, educated, employed, sexual, and very urban "New Woman." Even the Bohemian writer Randolph Bourne admitted that the "audacious" Greenwich Village women "shock you constantly." Their simple shirtwaist dresses (without corsets), short hair, makeup, cigarette smoking, and drinking in public were considered outrageous in the early twentieth century. However, by the 1920s they defined a new norm, "the Flapper." To be sure, women's roles remained circumscribed. However, it was the defiance of the Greenwich Village rebels in the 1910s that made possible the nationwide "Revolution in Manners and Morals" of the 1920s.[18]

Alfred Stieglitz reflected the spirit of reassessment that suffused the Bohemian revolt. Son of a prosperous wool merchant, he graduated from the City College and then spent time in Berlin absorbing European culture while studying photography. On returning to New York, he came to appreciate the city as an artistic subject and decided to promote photography as art for its own sake rather than just as an adjunct to journalism. In 1902, Stieglitz started the Photo-Secession movement that, by its very name, announced its rebellion against convention. His photography journal and independent art gallery at 291 Fifth Avenue (right across from Steichen's studio) were, he said, dedicated to the proposition that each artist should have "the right to work out his own. . .vision."[19]

Similarly, a small group of painters insisted that art should portray reality rather than sentimentalize it. Inspired by Stephen Crane and Walt Whitman, they depicted life as it was—finding beauty in the mundane, fascination in urban types, and drama in city streets. They wanted to free art from the formal, static ideals defined by upper-class monitors of artistic standards. Their leader, Robert Henri, was a friend of Stieglitz who had migrated from Philadelphia to New York in 1899 to teach painting. He urged his students to "stop studying water pitchers and bananas and paint everyday New York." For him, "a Hester Street pushcart [was] a better subject than a Dutch windmill." Because critics considered this focus on the commonplace ridiculous, they derided its advocates as the Ashcan school.[20]

Two exhibitions defined New York's Progressive era artistic rebellion. The first was held by "The Eight" independent artists in February 1908 to show works rejected for exhibition by the prestigious National Academy of Design, from which Henri had just resigned in protest. One of the eight artists was John Sloan. who studied painting with Henri in Philadelphia and followed him to New York in 1904. Their friendship was fed by Whitman's poetry, which was popular among Bohemians. In 1908, Sloan exhibited two New York scenes of ordinary people on ordinary streets engaged in ordinary activities. To critics, the paintings evoked not admiration, but "nausea." Widely advertised as "New York's Art War," the exhibit drew so many visitors that it was extended and then traveled in triumph to nine cities on the East Coast and in the Midwest. It inaugurated a new era in American art, one born in and of New York City.[21]

The second pathbreaking exhibit, which Sloan described as "dynamite," was held in February 1913 at the Armory on Lexington Avenue and 25th Street. In defiance of the National Academy's resistance to progressive art, the Armory Show displayed new European works by Picasso, Rodin, Matisse, and Van Gogh, as well as American works by Stieglitz and "The Eight." After New York, the show traveled to Chicago and Boston, commanding national and international press attention for three months. Its significance, explained the *New York Evening Mail,* was in freeing the public mind from "the artistic strait jacket" of convention. "American art will never be the same again," declared the *Boston Globe.* Ashcan art was no longer trash.[22]

The struggle over creative freedom found expression in New York City's radical magazine called *The Masses.* From 1911 to 1917, *The Masses* provided an outlet for Ashcan art as well as for innovative poetry, short stories, and social satire. With typical New York attitude, it proclaimed itself "A Magazine with a Sense of Humor and no Respect for the Respectable; Frank; Arrogant; Impertinent. . . ." Its goal was to assail "rigidity and dogma wherever it is found." As such, it embodied the overall spirit of the Greenwich Village rebellion which, wrote the author Malcolm Cowley, was the first American cultural movement to question middle-class values, to pit "bohemian against bourgeois, poetry against propriety."[23]

The Masses attacked capitalism and religion, explored taboo subjects such as birth control, and supported the controversial free speech movement. It outdid what Roosevelt labeled the "muckraking" magazines of exposure with powerful print and even more powerful images, many by the art editor John Sloan. As the historian Henry F. May explained, "the magazine's main weapon was shock." Accordingly, proper Americans viewed it as "nasty, dirty, smutty, harmful, immoral, blasphemous and destructive." Such attacks revealed how effectively *The Masses* challenged existing orthodoxies and, said the writer Irving Howe, provided "the rallying center. . .for almost anything that was then alive and irreverent in American culture."[24]

The Masses was embroiled in numerous trials, each of which increased its national visibility and influence. In 1913, *the Masses'* editor, Max Eastman, was sued for libel after calling the Associated Press (AP) a "truth trust" that was antithetical to freedom of the press because it failed to report the use of armed thugs against strikers. Ultimately, the case was dropped when a massive rally at Cooper Union and a protest by nationally prominent figures embarrassed the AP. However, not even testimony by Columbia professor John Dewey and the educator Helen Keller was enough to win a 1916 case against distributors who banned *The Masses* from subway news stands because of material considered impious. In fact, the magazine was deemed so obnoxious that it was subsequently prohibited in Boston, Philadelphia, and Canada.[25]

Committed, declared Eastman, to both "revolt and regeneration," *The Masses* was particularly attuned to labor conflict. In 1913, its staff helped organize a spectacular Madison Square Garden pageant that dramatized a Paterson, New Jersey silk workers' strike in which a man had recently been killed. Sloan created a banner one hundred feet long and Reed wrote a play for one thousand participants. As a blend of art, drama, and politics bringing together the middle and working classes, this event was hailed as the high point of the Bohemian revolt.[26]

Nonetheless, in 1916 *The Masses* had to deal with its own labor strife when some of its artists, led by Sloan, went on strike to protest editorial policies that were making the magazine too rigid and too political. Other inconsistencies existed. Although *The Masses* was adamant about women's rights, concerned about poverty, and respectful of diverse immigrant cultures, it often stereotyped African Americans. Moreover, the magazine's radical commitments were contradicted by the fact that it depended on the financial support of the well-to-do. Ironically, its audience was less the actual masses than middle-class intellectuals.[27]

The Masses, like Progressivism itself, fell victim to World War I. As militarism mounted, the pressure for conformity increased and all criticism became suspect. *The Masses'* staff vigorously opposed the war through articles, cartoons, speeches, and demonstrations. When they protested against the draft and the arrest of "Red" Emma Goldman, the federal government restricted distribution of the magazine and accused its editors of treason under the Espionage Act of 1917. During two trials, the defendants used the courtroom as a platform for dissent, socialism, and pacifism. Despite a split jury in both cases, the government revoked *The Masses'* mailing privileges.[28]

Still seeking victory in the courts, the government initiated another suit in 1918 charging *The Masses* with conspiracy to obstruct conscription. Morris Hillquit, the Jewish, Lower East Side, socialist politician and labor lawyer, was the main defense attorney. No conspiracy was proven, but the three trials killed *The Masses*. Although resurrected as *The Liberator* (after the nineteenth-century abolitionist paper) in 1918 and as *The New Masses* (allied with the Communist party) in 1926, it never regained its original free-form spirit. Nonetheless, in its day, *The Masses* had been influential enough to be the first significant journal targeted by the federal government. The magazine pushed Progressivism to its cultural limits and broadened the national discourse about freedom of expression. According to one of its admirers, it covered "all the shocking realities, not because they are shocking but because they are realities."[29]

Together with the Bohemian Revolt, the Photo-Secession movement, and the Ashcan school, *The Masses* confirmed Gotham's status as the nation's fountainhead for cultural ferment. Ever a historic haven for diversity and tolerance, New York City was a logical locus for new ideas and behavior patterns. During the Progressive era, it provoked Americans to reassess some of their most fundamental cultural and social assumptions. The result, says Stansell, was the development of a "democratic curiosity" that invigorated New York City and enriched the American mind in the twentieth century.[30]

THE COLOR LINE

The complexity of Progressivism was apparent in the area of race relations. Emerging as the center of African American protest, Gotham guaranteed that Progressivism would not be exclusively white. Race riots in 1900, 1905, and 1910 highlighted the problem but also strengthened the determination to solve it. For example, the National Association for the Advancement of Colored People (NAACP) and the National Urban League were created with interracial support in 1910 and 1911, respectively. As the African American scholar and activist W. E. B. Du Bois explained in 1903, the objective was "simply. . .to make it possible for a man to be both a Negro and an American without being cursed and spit upon by his fellows, without having the doors of Opportunity closed roughly in his face."[31]

Since Reconstruction, America had been systematically closing those doors. The "negro problem" was resolved by taking away the freedmen's newly acquired right to vote, severely limiting their economic opportunities, and legalizing segregation. The virulence of prejudice was evident when President Roosevelt was vilified for inviting Booker T. Washington, former slave, self-made man, and educator, to dine at the White House in 1901. Most horrific was the sharp increase in lynchings after 1885, with 241 recorded for 1892 alone, an average of four a week. When the Memphis journalist Ida B. Wells-Barnett received death threats for criticizing lynching as a "mockery of law and justice," she took refuge in New York City as a writer for the *New York Age,* the nation's foremost African American newspaper.[32]

Its editor, T. Thomas Fortune, a former slave, was one of the era's most prominent and most vocal critics. He was labeled a dangerous "agitator" because he urged blacks to fight lynching, resist segregation, and affirm their rights as citizens, especially the right to vote (even for women). His National Afro-American Council was designed to coordinate these efforts. Fortune himself filed suit twice—first, when a hotel bar refused to serve him and, second, when a theater would not sell him tickets. An early advocate of using the term "Afro-American" rather than "colored" or "negro" with a small "n," Fortune supported the reformer Henry George, the gradualist Booker T. Washington, and the radical pan-Africanist Marcus Garvey at different points in his life. Through it all, Fortune contended that blacks had to make a lot of "noise" in order to combat the "unjust, grinding, and. . .inhuman" realities of American race relations.[33]

The Riot of 1900 showed how great that challenge was. On a hot August night, an African American woman waited for her boyfriend, Arthur Harris, at 41st Street and Eighth Avenue, in a racially mixed, rough neighborhood called the Tenderloin. When a plainclothes policeman accused her of soliciting, Harris, unaware that the white man was a cop, rushed to her defense. In the ensuing fight, the policeman was mortally wounded with Harris' penknife. Word quickly spread that a black man, newly arrived from the South, had killed a white cop.

Mayhem sparked a few days after the policeman's funeral and another fight between a black man and a white man. Mobs of whites, some numbering ten thousand, surged through the streets of the West Side, from the 20s to the 30s, attacking any blacks in sight, dragging them off streetcars and pulling them out of their homes. Blacks were brutally beaten by gangs of white males shouting "Lynch the niggers." Policemen not only chased blacks and threw them to the mob but also clubbed them mercilessly both outside and inside the station houses. Moreover, many blacks were arrested by the very policemen who beat them. Only one white youth was arrested. Harris, who had fled to Washington, D.C., was brought back to New York, tried, convicted, and given a life sentence.[34]

Some whites tried to defend or shelter blacks during the riot and others held a well-attended fund-raiser to help the victims. Mainstream newspapers assailed the police brutality and admited that "colored people have been harshly and unfairly used by the force in this city for many years." Now they feared that police misconduct could harm whites, too, if the city was abandoned to "thugs." Echoing reactions to the 1871 Orange Riot, Tammany was blamed for putting so many violence-prone Irishmen on the force in the first place. In a *New York Daily Tribune* cartoon, an Irish policeman was depicted as a Tammany Tiger arrogantly swinging his club while a bloody, battered African American man slumped in the street. The riot was widely considered a "disgrace" to New York City, especially since it so pleased the South to see that racial violence was not just a sectional affair.[35] (See Figure 12 following page 150)

Requests from white and black alike that the police should be punished fell on deaf ears. All charges against the police were declared unsubstantiated and, after a sham hearing, the official case was closed. Damage suits filed in court were summarily dismissed. Ironically, people who wanted a trial could not get one. Lacking legal redress, prominent black leaders sponsored a rally at Carnegie Hall attended by thirty-five hundred people. A Citizen's Protective League was formed, with T. Thomas Fortune as chairman. In essence, they conducted their own trial by soliciting eighty witnesses and victims whose sworn statements were sent to the mayor with a request for official action. The city's unresponsiveness left the situation unresolved and racial conflict in the Tenderloin continued for a month, resulting in two known deaths.[36]

As the city's worst racial confrontation since the 1863 Draft Riots, the Riot of 1900 dismayed New York's African American community because it showed, said Du Bois, that "the black man is in continual danger of mob violence in New York as in New Orleans." That reality was confirmed in 1905 by another riot in San Juan Hill, an old Irish neighborhood in the West 50s and 60s now increasingly inhabited by blacks, including veterans of the battle of San Juan Hill during the 1898 Spanish-American War. The riot was sparked by the rare conviction of an Irish policeman for killing a black night-watchman. Two nights of violent attacks on blacks by Irish residents and Irish policemen resulted in sixty arrests and one death, all black. In response, the African American community formed another Colored Citizens' Protective League led by T. Thomas Fortune and the realtor Phillip A. Payton Jr. Their emphasis on the racial context of police brutality sounded a new tone of protest and resulted in the appointment of the city's first black police officer in 1911.[37]

The reform impulse was strengthened by crisis. Although there were two Negro Young Men's Christian Associations plus a few settlement houses and trade schools for blacks, efforts were now made to better serve the community and to forge the first concerted interracial alliances since abolitionism. Building on its long history of liberalism and philanthropy, its large black population, its solid (albeit small) black middle class, and its activist Progressive movement, New York now became the national center for African American reform efforts.[38]

In 1906, white and black progressives created the National League for the Protection of Colored Women (NLPCW) to help female migrants from the South settle in the city and avoid prostitution. A Committee for Improving the Industrial Condition of Negroes in New York (CIICN) also was created in 1906 with interracial support. Led by William L. Bulkley, the first black principal of a largely white public school, the group tried to expand access to skilled vocational jobs for African Americans. In 1910, the Committee on Urban Conditions Among Negroes was formed, which merged with the NLPCW and the CIICN to create the National Urban League in 1911. Linked to Booker T. Washington, the organization focused on providing social services and securing jobs for blacks. Bulkley, its vice chairman, authored the motto, "Not Alms, but Opportunity."[39]

A separate organization allied with Washington's nemesis, Du Bois, emerged at the same time. Inspired by the Niagara Movement that Du Bois initiated in 1905 and incensed by a 1908 race riot in Lincoln's hometown of Springfield, Illinois, an interracial group of prominent Progressives established the National Association for the Advancement of Colored People (NAACP) in 1910. Rejecting, as Du Bois put it, Washington's "silent submission to civic inferiority," the NAACP advocated full economic, political, and social equality. This platform was promoted in *The Crisis: A Record of the Darker Races*, a journal edited by Du Bois. Over time, the NAACP's major contribution was dismantling segregation through legal cases addressing voting rights, criminal rights, housing, access to public facilities, and education.[40]

The need for the NAACP was underlined in the year after its founding when Jack Johnson, a black boxer, defeated the reigning champion, Jim Jeffries, nicknamed "the Great White Hope." Immediately, race riots erupted across the country in a national sweep unparalleled until Martin Luther King Jr.'s assassination in 1967. The boxing bout was seen as a symbolic test of racial superiority. A painting of an earlier Johnson fight by the Ashcan artist George Bellows captured the distress of white spectators observing a fit, supple Johnson overpowering his withering white opponent, Tommy Burns. Originally called "A Nigger and a White Man," the painting was later renamed "Both Members of the Club." It marked a significant shift.[41]

In the moment, however, less generous sentiments prevailed. On July 4, 1910, a predominantly white crowd of thirty thousand gathered at the *Times* building to await news bulletins arriving from Nevada. Immediately after Johnson won the fight against Jeffries, angry white gangs roamed the city streets seeking revenge. All along the West Side, blacks were assaulted and their homes set afire amidst efforts to lock the inhabitants inside. Calls went out for a lynching. Black men were pulled off trolleys and beaten to a pulp. One gang even made its way to a small black enclave on Barren Island in Jamaica Bay to attack its residents and burn down their huts. Rushing from incident to incident, the police never seemed to arrive before the gangs scattered. Several blacks found unconscious in the street were taken to nearby hospitals and one died from a fractured skull.[42]

In the aftermath of these riots, New York's liberal traditions resurfaced. Unlike his colleagues in other cities, Mayor William Gaynor refused to ban pictures of the fight from local movie houses, saying that he was not a censor. In a strikingly progressive editorial, the *Times* pointed out that Johnson had legitimately earned his title according to standards set by whites in the sport and, therefore, deserved due respect. It further noted that, if there were less job discrimination generally, blacks might rise in other professions as well. Most important, it called upon the public to address "the negro problem" by more consistently pursuing "the rule of the ring" outside of the ring, that is, by practicing "equality and fairness."[43]

At the same time, the Progressive movement completely bypassed another group beset by discrimination. Since the mid-nineteenth century, a small Chinese community had developed in lower Manhattan. It grew after the transcontinental railroad was completed and Chinese laborers were chased out of the West for fear they would compete with white men for jobs. Resentment bred vicious stereotyping, violence, and riots. Anti-Chinese sentiment was so strong that Chinese immigration was banned starting in 1882, marking the nation's first ethnically based immigration restriction policy. In New York City, as elsewhere, the Chinese faced severe job discrimination and were segregated in a narrow residential district. However, unlike elsewhere, they also had to make constant payoffs to Tammany for protection from police harassment and noninterference by the city government.

Although the restaurant, laundry, and tourist trades provided small ethnic economic niches, poverty persisted. The repressive conditions bred an underground economy based on drugs, gambling, and prostitution, which in turn fostered competition and violence within Chinatown. Organized groups known as Tongs waged three lethal wars against each other in New York City from 1900 to 1918. Unknown numbers of men were killed in shoot-outs on the streets, in movie houses, theaters, and restaurants, and at home and work. To outsiders, the Tong Wars offered spectacular confirmation of Chinese venality. To the Chinese, they embodied a desperate struggle for survival within a community that was isolated by prejudice in a hostile city. Their plight documented Du Bois's lifelong conviction that "the problem of the Twentieth Century is the problem of the color-line."[44]

Du Bois saw the similarities between the struggles of various peoples of color, but he also knew that the situation of African Americans in New York City was unique. Despite discrimination, they were not as isolated as the Chinese. Moreover, they had a long tradition of protest, a strong community, and a ready source of articulate leadership. These assets were particularly apparent in 1917 when the NAACP orchestrated the Silent Protest Parade on Fifth Avenue. In the nation's first major African American protest march, ten thousand hushed men, women, and children dressed in mourning registered their opposition to lynching and their horror at the deaths of thirty-nine blacks in recent East St. Louis riots. With muffled drums and signs asking "Why Not Make America Safe for Democracy?" leaders like Du Bois hoped to awaken not only the city but also the nation and the world. "Nothing," it was felt, "could better convince America of the new spirit of the New Negro."[45]

In 1919, when World War I veterans returned home through the port of New York, the Harlem Hellfighters marched proudly down Fifth Avenue in the front of the ranks accompanied by James Reese Europe's widely acclaimed ragtime band. They had not always been so well received. In fact, they were segregated in the United States army, assaulted by white units, and remanded to the French army where they amassed an outstanding record of valor. It had been a special experience to be treated as equals by Europeans. After risking their lives for democracy abroad, African Americans were determined to secure equality at home. As Du Bois declared, "We return. We return from fighting. We return fighting."[46]

TO EAT, TO WORK, TO VOTE
To Eat

During the Progressive era, women consciously created conflict in order to address issues of hunger, working conditions, and the vote. Paralleling the Bohemian concept of the "New Woman," they challenged and ultimately redefined female stereotypes by adopting aggressive strategies that cut across class and ethnic (but rarely racial) barriers. For example, food was typically a woman's concern, but public protest was not typically within a woman's province. Yet, hunger was a powerful motivator and women's traditional homemaker role justified activism. "We're not rioting," one woman explained to a judge. "Only see how thin our children are; our husbands have no more strength to work harder. . . . If we stay at home and cry, what good will that do us?"[47]

Women understood that defiant and dramatic collective action was needed to offset the powerful forces that controlled their lives. To them, the local butcher was a cog in the vast machinery of production and distribution represented by the national Beef Trust. Change required boldness, an attribute they demonstrated on the streets and in the courts. When a judge contemptuously asked an arrested woman, "What do you know of a trust? It's no business of yours," she shot back, "Whose business is it, then, that our pockets are empty?" The struggle over food, noted a contemporary flier, was a "women's war," but hunger crossed gender lines.[48]

In 1902, facing steadily increasing kosher meat prices, Orthodox Jewish women on the Lower East Side protested for over three weeks, inspiring spin-off protests uptown, in the Bronx, and in Brooklyn. They were not polite. On Wednesday, May 14, an organizing committee of residents from Monroe and Pike Streets went door-to-door explaining to their neighbors what they were planning and why. On Thursday, women took to the streets invading butcher shops and throwing meat on the curb. Quickly the food riot spread from street to street until it encompassed the Lower East Side and involved twenty thousand protesters. Police who were trying to rescue the butchers were assaulted by slabs of liver. Angered, they pummeled the women and arrested seventy of them.[49]

On Friday, the women held a rally, resumed their house-to-house appeals, placed pickets in front of every butcher's store, and, at great personal sacrifice, raised money to pay for court costs. Again they surged into the streets, broke butcher shop windows, and destroyed meat. Violent confrontations with the police resulted in a hundred more arrests. The rioting stopped for the Sabbath, but, using the tradition of raising matters of social justice during the service, women appealed to men for support. By Sunday, all the butcher shops were closed, restaurants had taken meat off the menu, and, at a rally of five hundred, a Ladies' Anti-Beef Trust Association was born.[50]

The new group was effective. It distributed fliers targeted to men, reached out to Christians, organized committees to coordinate boycotts in Brooklyn and the Bronx, sent delegations to labor unions, and formed meat cooperatives, some of which outlasted the boycott. Equipped with their religion's emphasis on social responsibility and supported by a tightly knit community, the women considered disorderly conduct necessary and legitimate. Their sense of mission was strong. "They think women aren't people. . .," proclaimed one protester. "We'll show them that we are more people than the fat millionaires who suck our blood."[51]

Taken aback by the women's aggressiveness, the *Times* dismissed them as "a swarm of ignorant" foreigners who "do not understand the duties or rights of Americans." Therefore, the best strategy would be to "let the blows fall." Supporting the boycott but fearing more violence, the popular Yiddish newspaper, the *Jewish Daily Forward*, urged the women to "agitate quietly in your homes." Some men formed a competing organization for cheap kosher meat, and a few openly disparaged the protests. However, many rabbis called for cooperation, and most men stood by their wives. After a month, kosher meat prices went down. For the moment, the women had won.[52]

The May 1902 kosher meat riots were followed in July by America's most extensive episode of anti-Semitic violence. It occurred during a chief rabbi's funeral procession attended by fifty to one hundred thousand people. As they moved slowly across Grand Street, they passed the Hoe factory where Irish workers, already known for harassing neighborhood Jews, started throwing water, wood, nails, and iron bolts from the windows. Mourners' protests resulted in fire hoses being used against them. After one contingent of police managed to stop the assault, another, larger contingent arrived and suddenly began their own assault with some of the factory employees joining in. For a half hour, mourners were clubbed and beaten; hundreds were seriously injured; several were arrested.

Likening the attack to a Russian pogrom, the Jewish community held protest meetings and, as in the race riots of 1900 and 1905, created defense organizations that appealed to the city for redress. In August, Mayor Seth Low formed a special investigatory committee that held public hearings at the University Settlement House on Rivington Street. Testimony on testimony documented long-standing patterns of police brutality against Jews. For the first time in the city's history, the ethnic context of police brutality was officially acknowledged by the committee's report. Although several officers were brought to trial, none were convicted. However, the police commissioner did resign and the Jewish community felt that it had successfully drawn attention to its grievances.[53]

During the next decade, there were rent strikes, bakery riots, and factory strikes on the Lower East Side. Then, in February of 1917, food shortages and high prices spurred another set of riots dominated by working-class Jewish women. Hunger stalked the streets and radical protester Marie Ganz reported that she had "never. . .seen mothers brooding over their wan babies with such anxious eyes." When a woman shopping in Brownsville, Brooklyn did not have enough money to pay a vendor, she angrily pushed over his cart. Instantly, women descended on other pushcarts, throwing food, assaulting vendors with their shopping bags, and setting some pushcarts afire. A thousand rioters rampaged for two hours and a similar protest in Williamsburg, Brooklyn, lasted forty minutes. The police tried to control the fracas, but made no arrests out of pity for the women who, as one cop explained, "were just crazy with hunger."[54]

In subsequent days, hundreds marched to City Hall and thousands attended a rally at the *Jewish Daily Forward* building on East Broadway. When the city proved unresponsive, the women continued to picket markets, confiscate chickens, and harass consumers buying boycotted goods. On one day, five thousand people, mainly women and children, rallied in Madison Square Park at Fifth Avenue and 23rd Street. Then a large contingent proceeded to the Waldorf-Astoria Hotel at Fifth Avenue and 34th Street. Clamoring for food for two hours, the protesters assaulted several wealthy patrons and threatened to storm the building. Many were injured when police on horseback charged the crowd and a terrified driver plowed his car into them.[55]

Because the 1917 food riots spread from New York to several other states, they became a national issue and a Congressional agenda item. The Lower East Side's Meyer London, Congress's sole Socialist representative, proposed creating a Federal Food Commission to regulate food distribution and pricing. However, the government did not act, so food riots and boycotts continued until America entered World War I and price controls were imposed. For London, the protests proved that Progressivism was a farce because it left the trusts in control of the economy and tolerated a "shortage of food in our richest cities." How absurd it seemed that America should be "rich as never before—and [have] bread riots!"[56]

The food crises of 1902 and 1917 framed the Progressive era, displaying its strengths and weaknesses. On the one hand, the impact of reform was clearly limited. Trustbusting cases were nice, but failed to bust many trusts or solve ordinary people's most pressing problems. On the other hand, the activism of ordinary people promoted civic engagement in keeping with the Progressive spirit while extending that spirit beyond the middle classes. So, too, immigrants and women invaded the domain of public conflict. Using their traditional roles as homemakers and consumers, they transcended those roles and began breaking down the boundaries between public and private, male and female, native-born and immigrant spheres of life.[57]

To Work

The most spectacular example of how ordinary people challenged and changed America during the Progressive era occurred in the New York City needle trades from 1909 to 1911. The agents of change were young Jewish and Italian women earning as little as three dollars for toiling as much as sixty hours a week. Commonly considered unorganizable, they defied gender stereotypes with courage and solidarity against great odds. According to the historian Philip Foner, their actions not only revolutionized women's roles in the union movement but also inspired all workers everywhere.[58]

The Triangle Shirtwaist Company strike of 1909 and fire of 1911 catapulted the problems of female industrial workers to the forefront of the nation's agenda and, said Socialist leader Morris Hillquit, "helped awaken our dormant social conscience." Never before had the inhumane implications of greed and the humane necessity for reform seemed so compelling. The long-range effect was the passage of progressive labor legislation in New York State that provided a model for other states and foreshadowed the New Deal.[59]

It began unofficially in late September 1909 when the Triangle Shirtwaist factory locked out workers who were trying to organize a union. In response, the fledgling International Ladies Garment Workers Union (ILGWU) called a strike that quickly spread to other shops and was supported by some of the male-dominated unions, socialists, and suffragists. Crucial help was provided by the Women's Trade Union League (WTUL), a unique organization of well-to-do and working-class females jointly promoting unionization for women.[60]

On November 22, a rally at Cooper Union marked the official start of the nation's first major women's strike. After endless speeches by men (among them Samuel Gompers) urging caution, a sixteen-year-old female striker pushed her way to the podium. In Yiddish, she called for action and when the crowd shouted approval, she asked them to take an ancient Hebrew oath pledging to stand together come what may. The three thousand women who packed the hall responded as one and the "Uprising of the 20,000" began.[61]

Actually, about thirty thousand women turned out on the next day, but within a week many small companies settled and the number of strikers diminished. Nonetheless, twenty thousand represented a significant presence and their persistence over time proved remarkable—especially as winter and hunger set in. Picketing was dangerous. The police arrested the girls on any pretext and were supplemented by hired thugs who beat them up. Over seven hundred strikers were arrested and nineteen were sent to the workhouse. Members of the WTUL joined the picket lines to offer protection and bear witness. When the WTUL's president was hauled into court, the policeman apologized, saying that if he had only known she "was a rich lady," he would "never have arrested" her.[62]

The WTUL raised funds to bail strikers out of jail, set up soup kitchens, and recruited female college students as picketers. Newspaper reports of frail young girls being clubbed, thrown down, trampled on, and arrested while shivering and starving for their cause created widespread sympathy akin to the support for the newsboys' strike of 1899. In Philadelphia, garment workers also struck in order to keep New York manufacturers from sending goods to be finished there. Despite some tensions between male union leaders and female strikers, Italian and Jewish workers, and upper- and lower-class allies, the women stood fast. Even the usually scornful *Times* printed the strikers' protest against police "insults, intimidations and. . .abuses."[63]

Although most employers were willing to sign agreements to improve working conditions, they refused to recognize the union itself and, on this key issue, the strike ultimately ran aground in February 1910. Victory was partial but historic because it demonstrated the power of women as workers, protesters, and organizers. The significance of the strike was expressed in song:

Hail the waistmakers of 1909
Making their stand on the picket line...
Breaking the power of those who reign
Pointing the way and smashing the chain
In the bleak winter of 1909
When we froze and bled on the picket line
We showed the world that women could fight
And we rose and we won with women's might[64]

Unfortunately, employers who signed the agreements often did not keep them and some of the biggest employers refused to sign at all. One of the worst offenders was the Triangle Shirtwaist Company, where the strike had begun. If the owners had cooperated with labor, no one would have been working in the factory at Waverly Place and Greene Street, near Washington Square Park, on Saturday afternoon, March 25, 1911. As it was, seven hundred people, mainly young Jewish and Italian girls, were in the factory when fire broke out.[65]

Amidst all the flammable cloth, wooden tables, and machine oil, the fire spread quickly. The owners and a few workers escaped to the roof; some girls took stairs or elevators to the street, but fire and smoke quickly closed off these options. Other exit doors were locked. Now the danger of tall buildings became apparent as fire hoses and ladders failed to reach the eighth, ninth, and tenth floors where the factory was located. Workers started jumping out of the windows. Singly or holding hands with hair and clothing ablaze, they plunged to the street crashing through the life nets intended to catch them.[66]

As mangled bodies accumulated on the concrete, horror swept the city and the nation. Thousands converged on the scene; thousands more filed through a temporary morgue desperately trying to identify the pitifully charred human remains. The Red Cross provided aid and the WTUL started collecting testimony on factory conditions. Money poured in. Muckraking journalists wrote heart-wrenching accounts of the lives of factory workers. Days of funerals culminated in a memorial parade of 120,000 silent marchers with 300,000 spectators along the route. Eight days after the fire, the union held a protest meeting for two thousand people, most of them women. Tears were mixed with angry cries for blowing up City Hall and fervent appeals for stronger labor organization.[67]

The WTUL sponsored a major rally at the Metropolitan Opera House, which was rented for the occasion by J. P. Morgan's daughter. The rich paid for seats in reserved boxes while the poor occupied the orchestra and galleries for free. Resolutions called for the enforcement of existing fire protection laws and for the creation of stronger new laws. It was a rare moment of cooperation across class, gender, and ethnic lines.

Nonetheless, some were skeptical of gradual methods and grandiose promises. In particular, the labor organizer Rose Schneiderman castigated the public for tolerating the murder of workers, not just by occasional fires, but daily by industrialism's "instruments of torture," which were always protected by "the strong hand of the law." To her, the sad lesson was that "the life of men and women is so cheap and property is so sacred."[68]

The manslaughter trial of the two Triangle factory owners proved her point. The case revolved around the fact that the bosses customarily locked all but one of the factory doors in order to better monitor their workers' activities and to check them for theft as they left each day. Consequently, many women were unable to escape and piles of bodies burned to the bone were found behind the locked exits. However, without witnesses who actually saw the men locking the doors, the case collapsed seven months after the fire. Meanwhile, the owners collected their insurance money and went right back into business. New York and the nation were appalled by the clear miscarriage of justice.[69]

It took three more years of litigation until the Triangle Shirtwaist Company was required to pay a mere seventy-five dollar compensation for each victim. A cartoon by Sloan summarized the situation. In the center lay a burned girl surrounded by a triangle representing rent, profit, and interest. Two figures held up the triangle—a rich man and a skeleton. A dagger labeled "Courts" pierced a labor agreement that had been discarded on the floor out of reach of the working girl. Sloan put the tragedy into its broader context. To this day, the Triangle fire remains one of the most solemn and significant events in American labor history.[70] (See Figure 13 following page 150)

Other cities were thoroughly alarmed. Chicago, Milwaukee, Newark, Toledo, and Washington, D.C. immediately called for reports on the fire safety of their own buildings and for enforcement of existing fire laws. Suddenly everyone seemed to understand that, as the New York Tribune commented, the fire was a case of "manslaughter through contributory negligence." Something had to be done to prevent similar urban catastrophes in factories as well as in hotels, apartment houses, schools, asylums, and hospitals. Otherwise, said the Philadelphia North American, ours would be nothing but a "careless, selfish, or cowardly society."[71]

In Albany, State Senator Robert F. Wagner Sr. and State Assemblyman Alfred E. Smith led the New York State Factory Investigating Commission consisting of Progressive politicians, labor leaders, social workers, and reformers. Poignant testimony from survivors and visits to factories all over the state resulted in fifty-four new bills put forward in the Assembly by Smith and engineered through the Senate by Wagner from 1911 to 1914. Tammany leaders Charles F. Murphy and Big Tim Sullivan lent their support partly out of genuine sympathy for the workers and partly in the interest of winning more Jewish and Italian votes.[72]

The new legislation set "epoch-making" standards for factory fire prevention, sanitation, ventilation, lighting, and crowding, as well as for child labor and women's labor. A State Industrial Board was established to enforce the new codes, and the powers of the State Labor Department were strengthened. Although enforcement was uneven and the reform coalition soon dissolved, New York acquired the most advanced factory legislation in the nation, making it the model for other states.[73]

Frances Perkins was a social worker who witnessed the fire, sat on the State Factory Investigating Commission, and later became the nation's first female cabinet member under the New Deal. In her opinion, these laws were "a turning point" in the nation's history. They represented the most ambitious, most idealistic, most humanistic side of Progressivism—the assertion that the government should pursue social and economic justice. One hundred and forty-six corpses had penetrated the collective consciousness and redefined the social contract.[74]

To Vote

Another instance in which New York City reform efforts marked a national turning point was the women's campaign for the vote. The New York City suffrage movement turned the tide in the larger national effort to secure passage of the Nineteenth Amendment to the U.S. Constitution, granting women the franchise. Women active in the Bohemian Revolt, the settlement houses, the Consumers League, the WTUL, the woman's club movement, the temperance movement, and labor unions supported the suffrage crusade giving it a uniquely rich and diverse base while also making it a nucleus for the national movement.[75]

By definition, the campaign challenged the existing structure of society and the exclusive control of the political process by men. To be sure, some men were supportive, such as The Masses' editor Max Eastman, who formed a Men's League for Woman Suffrage, and W. E. B. Du Bois, for whom woman's suffrage was part of the larger struggle for freedom. However, white suffragists themselves discriminated against black suffragists. Not until 1917 were the two groups bridged when the president of New York City's Colored Woman Suffrage Club became the vice president of New York State's Woman Suffrage Party.[76]

Gotham's women's suffrage movement was invigorated by Harriet Stanton Blatch, daughter of Elizabeth Cady Stanton, America's suffrage pioneer. Finding the existing suffrage organizations too timid, in 1907 she organized a new group with more aggressive techniques that were then adopted by suffragists throughout the country. Following the example of Tammany, Blatch set up city-wide, borough-wide, and district committees complete with election district captains. Borrowing from the food boycotters and the labor movement, the suffragists printed literature and gave speeches in several languages, reached out to people of different religions, and went door-to-door with petitions. Sporting yellow hats, banners, and signs, they paraded down Fifth Avenue, staged outdoor pageants, and held hundreds of meetings and one twenty-six-hour speaking marathon. These public, dramatic tactics were supplemented by countless personal telephone calls to solicit support.[77]

The suffragists' aggressiveness offended many and, in 1912, a mob disrupted their parade, much to the amusement of the police. However, their persistence ultimately bore fruit. After six failed attempts, New York State finally passed an amendment to the State constitution granting women full suffrage in 1917. Significantly, New York City itself, especially its working-class Jewish districts, provided the key to victory, enabling the positive downstate votes to offset the negative upstate votes. At last there would be a sufficient number of states to support a federal amendment granting women the vote, which passed in 1919. New York City's role in this major extension of American democracy had been critical.[78]

Many people, both male and female, feared that woman's suffrage would destroy the family, but the suffragists insisted that women needed the vote to protect the family against political indifference, marketplace monopolies, and workplace exploitation. Like other Progressives, they wanted to reform child labor, education, housing, crime, and prostitution. As they explained, "We prepare children for the world. We ask to prepare the world for children." Once again, women were using traditional roles to expand those roles.[79] (See Figure 14 following page 150)

Through the food riots, the campaign to improve working conditions, and the suffrage movement, New York City's women repeatedly challenged convention and tested Progressivism. Although not entirely successful, they were much more successful than expected because their causes inspired both determination and sympathy. By cooperating across lines of class and ethnicity, adopting innovative methodologies, and, above all, resolving to "not be silent," they gave voice to the grievances and ambitions of one half of the population. Their aggressive tactics reflected their understanding, as one suffragist journal put it, that the public "demands to be shocked before it will listen."[80]

"RED EMMA"

Emma Goldman was not impressed by the women's suffrage movement, which she dismissed as "a parlor affair." In her opinion, obtaining the vote would simply make women part of a repressive political system without liberating them from their social and economic bonds. Anarchist and radical feminist, Goldman disparaged the genteel, moderate reforms of Progressivism, its reliance on the goodwill of the state, and its assumption that capitalism could be fixed. She particularly deplored Roosevelt's authoritarianism and the Darwinian ruthlessness of his "rugged individualism." Extolling full freedom for the individual, she supported free speech, free love, birth control, and homosexuality. Goldman courted controversy and became the most controversial woman of the Progressive era.[81]

Like Fanny Wright, "Red Emma" was a symbol of the independent (and therefore dangerous) urban woman whose rebellion transcended women's issues to encompass society's most fundamental dilemmas. Like Wright, Goldman was closely identified with Gotham, her "beloved city," even though she was also a national and international celebrity. Like the "Red Harlot," "Red Emma" was widely condemned as a loose woman. However, unlike Wright's upper-class, British ancestry, Goldman's Eastern European, lower-middle-class, Jewish origins made her particularly suspect. Her name became a code word for evil and her mere arrival in town could foment a riot. To most Americans, she was the rebel's rebel, the devil's devil.[82]

As compassionate as she was defiant, Goldman's personality had been shaped by conflict with an oppressive father and experience with violent Russian anti-Semitism. These negative factors were offset by the Jewish tradition of social justice, stories of Russian revolutionists, and support from a caring teacher. After immigrating to Rochester, New York in 1885 at age sixteen, she became trapped in a disastrous marriage and a demeaning factory job but started life anew by fleeing to New York City in 1889.

Gotham was the perfect place for such an unconventional person. There she befriended anarchists to whom she was drawn by outrage over the execution of the men blamed for the 1886 Haymarket Square bombing in Chicago. Her charisma and eloquence soon made her a popular speaker, the first immigrant Jewish woman not just to lecture and publish in English but also to acquire a national following.[83]

Throughout her career as an agitator, Goldman tangled with the legal system. It began in 1892 when her lover, Alexander Berkman, tried to assassinate Henry Clay Frick, the antilabor manager of Andrew Carnegie's Homestead steel mill near Pittsburgh. Goldman was implicated as an accomplice but, being in New York at the time, avoided arrest. She was less lucky at a Union Square rally during the cold depression winter of 1893 when she advised the hungry to insist on "work or bread." Although no riot ensued, she was arrested for inciting one. Hoping to revive his career, former Tammany Mayor A. Oakey Hall defended her pro bono, but she was convicted and incarcerated on Blackwell's Island for a year.[84]

In 1901, she was blamed for inspiring the anarchist who assassinated President William McKinley. Despite the perpetrator's denials, Goldman was jailed for fifteen days and lost a tooth when punched by a policeman. Since 1892, she had been relentlessly pilloried by the sensational press as a monster, a terrorist, a revolutionist, and a bloodthirsty vampire. Hence "Red Emma." In the post-assassination hysteria, she was so reviled that she had to assume a false identity in order find a job and a place to live in Gotham. For the rest of her life, she was targeted as an enemy of the state and federal immigration officials never stopped trying to revoke her citizenship until they finally deported her in 1919.[85]

By the same token, the 1903 federal Anti-Anarchist law (supported by Roosevelt and based on a 1902 New York State law aimed at Goldman) made Progressives, Bohemians, laborites, socialists, and radicals more aware of the importance of protecting free speech, which Goldman now made a national issue. When she resumed lecturing, Goldman found herself harassed by local police everywhere she went. In 1909, she was arrested for "unlawful assemblage ... and preaching Anarchist doctrines," but was acquitted. Several of her lectures were prohibited and some were disrupted by the police, including one in New York City. The result was a free speech rally at Cooper Union attended by two thousand people who formed a Free Speech League, which later became the American Civil Liberties Union.[86]

Goldman did not advocate violence, but her powers of persuasion engendered fear. The mere label of anarchist was terrifying enough until Goldman explained that she opposed the state because she believed that everyone should be able to develop his or her full potential free from restraint. She considered all social norms and institutions repressive. Marriage enslaved women; schools stifled children; prisons bred crime; private property perpetuated inequality; patriotism produced wars; and religion lulled people into passivity. Although she later condemned the tyrannies of communist Russia, she always believed in an idealistic form of communism defined by "the sovereignty of the individual" and social harmony. To her, these ideals infused Walt Whitman's poetry about which she often wrote and lectured.[87]

Goldman considered socialists, who were then prominent in Gotham, too moderate, but she consistently supported their right to be heard and publicly defended anyone arrested for radical behavior or speech. Likewise, she found Samuel Gompers' labor movement too conservative, but she rushed around the country speaking at strikers' rallies and leading labor demonstrations. She preferred the radical International Workers of the World (IWW) and its efforts to organize all of labor into "one great industrial union." During the harsh winter of 1913–1914, Goldman supported the IWW's peaceful meetings in Union Square coupled with its strategy of bringing homeless men directly to churches for shelter and food.[88]

Most clerics simply refused, but one priest called the police, who arrived in force and, with clubs swinging, arrested 190 men as they were quietly leaving the church. Sloan recorded the event in a drawing entitled "Calling the Christian Bluff." Instead of being sympathetic, mainstream New York (including Gompers) branded the tactic as "riotous," dismissed the supplicants as "bums and toughs," and recommended that the police "club and shoot" any future protesters. The IWW organizer, Frank Tannenbaum (later a Columbia College history professor) was arrested, convicted for inciting a riot, levied a large fine, and sentenced to one year on Blackwell's Island.[89]

Tannenbaum's harsh punishment inspired numerous protest rallies in Union Square and Astor Place that were met with more police brutality, thereby inciting more protests. Frequent labor strikes compounded the chaos. Lower Manhattan seethed with tension and violence unlike anything seen since Chicago's Haymarket affair in 1886. Despite having witnessed similar incidents for two decades, Lincoln Steffens was still sickened to "see a policeman take his nightstick in both his hands and bring it down with all his might on a human being's skull." Such events confirmed Emma Goldman's lack of faith in "the law and its machinery," a system from which she learned to "expect no justice."[90]

Accordingly, she was surprised when an Oregon appellate judge reversed her 1915 conviction for disseminating birth control information. However, in 1916, when she was deemed guilty of the same crime in New York, she chose to serve time in the Queens County Jail rather than pay a fine. Using the court as a stage, Goldman delivered an eloquent soliloquy on birth control. She was backed by New York's intellectual, professional, and artistic communities with Ashcan artists and *The Masses* staff playing key roles. Her third arrest on a similar charge resulted in acquittal, thanks to the skills of her lawyer, a dedicated follower of Henry George.[91]

Sympathetic to (but more radical than) the birth control advocate Margaret Sanger, Goldman believed that being able to choose or refuse motherhood would free women from subjection to men, marriage, and sexual exploitation. Birth control was essential to free women from "external" as well as "internal tyrants," that is, from political, legal, and economic as well as social, cultural, and psychological limits. In this context, Goldman also advocated free love, which she defined as mutually chosen, mutually pleasurable, deeply felt relationships, not casual sex. For the early twentieth century, these ideas were so radical that, she observed, they thoroughly upset her audiences, male and female alike.[92]

Emma Goldman's concern with women's issues was part of her larger commitment to social justice and freedom for everyone. Throughout her life, she saw the arts as a key vehicle for awakening social conscience. Her monthly magazine, *Mother Earth,* disseminated new trends in radical poetry and literature across the country until it, like *The Masses*, was repressed during World War I. Her lectures on the social relevance of George Bernard Shaw, Eugene O'Neill, August Strindberg, and Henrick Ibsen brought the New Drama to countless listeners. Sometimes speaking as often as three hundred times a year, she reached thousands of people of all classes and had a huge impact.[93]

Whatever the medium, individual freedom dominated Goldman's agenda and, after defending conscientious objectors during World War I, she was arrested for conspiracy against the draft. Despite widespread support and testimony from John Reed and Lincoln Steffens, complemented by her own riveting defense of free speech, Goldman was convicted, sent to prison for two years, and then deported to Russia during the 1919 Red Scare. According to J. Edgar Hoover, who was just starting his career in the Justice Department, Goldman was one "of the most dangerous anarchists in this country."[94]

Homesick and disillusioned by developments abroad, but prohibited from resettling in the United States, she made one American speaking tour in 1934 and then reluctantly returned to Europe. When she died in Toronto in 1940 at age seventy, she was still organizing and speaking out against wartime repression of dissent. Posthumously, Goldman was granted the right to reenter the United States and, appropriately enough, was buried near the graves of the Haymarket martyrs whose executions had so horrified her as a young woman. In death, as in life, she remained a radical.[95]

Although Goldman disparaged Progressivism, she benefited from, intersected with, and intensified it. The spirit of reform, activism, and rebelliousness made people receptive to her various crusades and swelled her audiences. Several of the Ashcan artists and *The Masses* staff, especially Sloan and Henri, supported her causes and contributed to her monthly magazine. She became a national symbol of the free speech movement and a prototype (albeit extreme) of the New Woman. Although race relations were not her primary focus, she assailed mob rule, deplored lynchings, and declared that the "anti-Asiatic and Negro questions" deserved more attention.[96]

Goldman's whole life was dedicated to defending freedom and individual rights, to opposing oppression and orthodoxy. As such, she perpetuated Gotham's long-standing commitment to tolerance. Goldman fervently believed that the spoken and written word combined with protests, marches, the arts, and court cases would stimulate constructive controversy, convert skeptics, and change the world. As a woman, a Jew, an immigrant, an urbanite, and an activist, "Red Emma" was profoundly provocative. Her impact was at once startling and subtle because, contends her biographer Richard Drinnon, she "made them think." The more idealistic and iconoclastic, aggressive and ambitious Emma Goldman was, the more she personified New York in the Progressive era.[97]

7

The Big Apple

Pursuing the Dream, 1920–1945

There is no thrill in all the world like entering, for the first time, New York harbor, coming in from the flat monotony of the sea to this rise of dreams and beauty. New York is truly the dream city, city of the towers near God, city of hopes and visions. . . ."

—Langston Hughes, 1925[1]

The name, the Big Apple, was originally popularized by jazz musicians of the 1920s and 1930s who considered New York City the best place to create, to succeed, and, said the poet Langston Hughes, to have fun. New York was the dream city of excitement and opportunity. However, the Big Apple label had contradictory connotations. Although the city was glamorous and inspiring, it was often considered too shiny on the outside and too rotten on the inside. Significantly, the name was abandoned after the 1940s and was not revived again until the 1970s. Thus, it captured a unique moment in time, an optimistic but anxious period when New York represented different, sometimes disparate, dreams for the future.[2]

In Gotham, the period between the end of World War I and the end of World War II was shaped by both dream and nightmare. The threadbare thirties negated the Roaring Twenties. The desperation of the Harlem riots shattered the optimism of the Harlem Renaissance. The superficiality of Jimmy Walker parodied the social conscience of Al Smith. The protests of Adam Clayton Powell Jr. strained the reform efforts of Fiorello H. LaGuardia. If foreigners were awed by the "gigantic chaos" of New York City, Americans were dismayed by the riots of 1935 and 1943. Gotham's glitter was irrevocably tarnished by anger so profound that it exploded twice in seven years. Indeed, conflict was such a powerful undercurrent of city life that, to one French visitor, New York was not a whirlpool but "a perpetual thunderstorm."[3]

Prohibition exposed conflicting concepts of the city. When a Constitutional amendment made it illegal to sell alcohol after January 1920, Gotham was offended. Federal support for Prohibition reflected a long-standing belief that alcohol was the source of urban poverty, disorder, and vice. This conviction was part of an underlying prejudice against Irish, German, Italian, and Jewish immigrants for whom drinking was culturally legitimate. Native-born, Protestant temperance reformers thought that banning alcohol would solve all the problems associated with cities.[4]

Instead, Prohibition caused more problems, especially among New Yorkers who disliked being told how to behave and who cheerfully defied the law. Alcoholic beverages were smuggled in from Canada and the Caribbean or manufactured on rooftops, in backyards, basements, and bathtubs. Over thirty-two thousand illegal drinking establishments called speakeasies sprang up overnight—many of them in Greenwich Village, where rebellion was almost a religion. Important New York politicians like Governor Alfred E. Smith and Congressman Fiorello H. LaGuardia opposed Prohibition. In Washington, D.C. and East Harlem, LaGuardia ridiculed the law by demonstrating how easy it was to make illegal beer with legal ingredients readily available in drugstores. The press obligingly publicized his antics and his recipe. New Yorkers seemed increasingly at odds with the nation.[5]

The demand for alcohol fostered organized crime, which predated Prohibition but reached new heights during it. The most infamous gangsters of this era included Gotham's Dutch Schultz, Frank Costello, Louis Lepke, Lucky Luciano, and a former member of the Five Points gang, Chicago's Al Capone. On the other side were the Prohibition enforcers. Two New York City agents, Izzy Einstein and Moe Smith, gained national notoriety by using clever disguises and tricks to confiscate five million bottles of liquor and make four thousand arrests. Although amused by Izzie and Moe, New Yorkers disobeyed Prohibition until it was repealed in 1933. Social conformity violated the urban ethos.[6]

New York City's rebellious reputation, compounded by its polyglot population, earned it widespread contempt. Gotham was so swamped by "immigrant trash," said the *Denver Post*, "that it can scarcely be considered American anymore." Similarly, the author Madison Grant warned that real Americans were "being literally driven off the streets of New York City by the swarms of Polish Jews" whom another writer of the period called "human parasites."[7]

These anti–New York sentiments were strengthened in 1920 when a cartload of dynamite exploded in front of J. P. Morgan's office at Broad and Wall Streets (opposite the Stock Exchange), killing thirty-eight and injuring hundreds. Although the perpetrator remained forever unknown, public opinion blamed anarchists and foreigners. Consequently, the event solidified support for the immigration restriction laws of 1921 and 1924, which favored Northern European over Southern and Eastern European immigrants. In essence, Congress declared New York's diversity a national disaster.[8]

Much of the anxiety about Gotham derived from its image as what the writer Ford Maddox Ford called "the city of the good time." The Big Apple meant novelty, not only in terms of jazz but also in drama, literature, architecture, photography, poetry, the Broadway musical, the Ziegfeld Follies, the Lindy Hop, burlesque, swing, modern dance, movies, radio, and television. Speaking of his new music in terms that applied across the arts and sounded much like Walt Whitman, the composer George Gershwin extolled the creative "kaleidoscope of our vast melting pot. . .of our metropolitan madness." He celebrated what Prohibitionists and immigration restrictionists condemned.[9]

Critics notwithstanding, New York was still America's "Wonder City," its exemplar of "wealth, culture and achievement." It was truly remarkable that, in the midst of the nation's worst depression, New York produced two architectural icons—the Chrysler Building (1930) and the Empire State Building (1931), where Al Smith was corporate president. These structures symbolized change and defined what the historian William R. Taylor calls "the city as silhouette," replete with its assertions of prosperity and power. New York's new skyline became the model urban skyline.[10]

At almost seven million strong, New York's population more than doubled that of its nearest competitor, Chicago. Always in motion, the rich were abandoning their Fifth Avenue mansions in favor of elegant apartments on Park Avenue. Meanwhile, an expanded transit system enabled the working classes to leave Manhattan's slums for new neighborhoods in the Bronx, Queens, and Brooklyn, which now became the city's most populous borough. It was the American Dream come true for over a million people seeking social mobility.[11]

By far the most spectacular private project of this era was Rockefeller Center, constructed from 1932 to 1940 on six midtown blocks with soaring art deco towers studded with murals, sculptures, and containerized gardens. It advanced a new corporate vision of urban planning that integrated office space with entertainment space (Radio City Music Hall, the ice-skating rink, the Rainbow Room) and retail space (America's first shopping mall). Occupancy by major radio, film, and journalism companies confirmed New York's role as the nation's communications nexus. Like the World Trade Center thirty years later, Rockefeller Center symbolized the prominence, not only of New York but also of the nation's richest family. Rockefeller Center was as massive, multifaceted, innovative, and truly central as the city itself.[12]

The dream imagery of New York between the wars was epitomized by the 1939 World's Fair. Built not in Manhattan, as in 1853, but in the newly developed borough of Queens, the World's Fair was a statement of faith in a future defined by commercialism, consumption, and technology. It treated twenty-five million people to a glimpse of "The World of Tomorrow" through "futurama" visions of a modern "Democracity" characterized by immense skyscrapers, fourteen-lane highways, and sparkling new suburbs. At night, when colored lights played on the otherwise bland buildings, wrote Lewis Mumford, "a dream world becomes a reality." In the words of Ira and George Gershwin's official World's Fair song, it promised the "Dawn of a New Day" predicated on opportunity, peace, and prosperity.[13]

Nonetheless, the fair was marred by pickets protesting racially discriminatory hiring practices and by the prospect of impending war. It was not even a financial success. Undaunted, Mayor LaGuardia declared that the prime exhibit was really "the city of New York itself." Always the showman, he saw Gotham as a showcase for "the greatest, most daring experiment in social and political democracy." From 1920 to 1945, racial protest and economic disaster would threaten to derail that dream. Yet, New York emerged from these crises with an honest government that offset the legacy of Tammany corruption and an expanded social contract that institutionalized a commitment to the general welfare. The major contribution of the restless, ambitious mayor, said the historian Thomas Kessner, was to harness "personal rule in the service of transcendent public purpose" and forever change New York in the process.[14]

THE NEW NEGRO

"We younger Negro artists, who create now, intend to express our individual dark-skinned selves without fear or shame. . . .We build our temples for tomorrow, strong as we know how, and we stand on top of the mountain, free within ourselves."

—Langston Hughes, 1926[15]

The attitude of defiant racial pride "without fear or shame" that the poet Langston Hughes expressed in 1926 challenged a nation that assumed black inferiority and feared African American aggressiveness. It was significant, then, that in the Twenties, New York nurtured two major nonviolent African American movements of self-assertion, both of which reverberated nationally and internationally. Of course, there was a long tradition of African American activism, but the Harlem Renaissance and Garveyism represented what Howard University professor Alain Locke labeled "The New Negro." This time, neither the music nor the message could be ignored.[16]

The Harlem Renaissance

Hughes enrolled at Columbia College in 1921 in order to escape from his domineering father and to see Harlem, which, despite extensive travel, always remained his home base. Hughes' father was an educated, financially successful mulatto who disparaged poor blacks. Nor did he think much of his son's penchant for poetry. By age nineteen, however, Hughes was already publishing in W. E. B. Du Bois' *The Crisis* and earning the fame that lasted until his death in 1967. Hughes was deeply influenced by an abolitionist tradition on his mother's side and by the democratic themes of Walt Whitman. Indeed, says his biographer Arnold Rampersad, Hughes was so sensitive to human suffering that his life became "an interplay between art and social conscience." Through it all, Hughes contended that "if dreams die, life is a broken-winged bird that cannot fly."[17]

Dismayed by Columbia's stifling, segregated climate, Hughes left after a year and gravitated to Harlem. So did thousands of other African Americans and Afro-Caribbeans. Blacks had steadily migrated northward on Manhattan Island from the 1600s, pushed out of each successive neighborhood by European immigrants. In Harlem, the pattern was reversed as Irish, Jewish, and Italian residents fled their middle-class suburb rather than see it integrated once the subway made uptown accessible, and when the black realtor Philip A. Payton Jr. broke through the color barrier. By 1914, fully two-thirds of Manhattan's African American population lived in Harlem. For the first time in New York City's history, blacks dominated an entire neighborhood and had access to good housing, albeit at exorbitant rents.[18]

Quickly, Harlem became the Negro Mecca or, as Hughes put it, "a great magnet for the Negro intellectual, pulling him from everywhere." Black professionals, scholars, and artists flocked to Harlem. They included, among others, the poets Claude McKay, Countee Cullen, and Arna Bontemps, the historians Arthur Schomburg and James Weldon Johnson, the actress Florence Mills, the actor Charles Gilpin, the painter Aaron Douglas, the tap dancer Bill "Bojangles" Robinson, the blues singer Bessie Smith, the jazz pianist James P. Johnson, the writers Zora Neale Hurston and Jean Toomer, the band leader Duke Ellington, and the actor, singer, and political activist Paul Robeson. The concentrated cultural flowering astonished America and the world, making New York the undisputed center of black culture and leadership.[19]

Much of the new literature and poetry was published in the black press that flourished in New York during the twenties. In addition to *The Crisis*, there were several more radical African American magazines with revealing names such as *Opportunity, Challenge, The Crusader,* and *The Emancipator.* Best known was *The Messenger,* a monthly edited by A. Phillip Randolph. After migrating from Florida, Randolph studied socialism at the City College and dreamed of economic democracy based on cooperation, not competition. He considered racial tension the inevitable product of economic exploitation and believed that "when no profits are to be made from race friction, no one will longer be interested in stirring up race prejudice."[20]

Such sentiments convinced Assistant Attorney General J. Edgar Hoover that *The Messenger* was "the most able and most dangerous of all the Negro publications." Despite Hoover's constant surveillance, Randolph organized the Brotherhood of Sleeping Car Porters that, after much struggle, became the first African American union to be granted equality with white unions in the American Federation of Labor. Known as "Mr. Black Labor," Randolph was the first major African American labor leader and one of America's most important civil rights figures. Until his death at ninety in 1979, Randolph persistently pursued his 1920s vision of a New Negro who aggressively challenged inequality wherever it existed.[21]

The less serious side of the Harlem Renaissance was evident at the Savoy Ballroom, a colorful counterpoint to Rockefeller Center. Capable of hosting four thousand people in a block-long club on Lenox Avenue between 140th and 141st Streets, the Savoy was the biggest, most exciting haven in what was now the "nightclub capital of the world." Unlike Dutch Schultz's expensive Cotton Club, where blacks were performers but not patrons, the Savoy's moderate prices and open door policy drew black and white, rich and poor together in America's first truly integrated major nightclub. The fast, free, seductive movements of the Charleston and the Lindy Hop took America by storm. One dance was called the Big Apple. "Stompin at the Savoy" became legendary and the club was nicknamed "Home of the Happy Feet."[22]

Above all, the Savoy meant stirring music in a period when New York became the nation's music capital. According to the historian Nathan Huggins, jazz provided a form of "soft rebellion" against cultural conventions and social constraints. Chick Webb's "hot" jazz band and Fletcher Henderson's "cool" jazz band set the tone for both the Jazz Age of the Twenties and the Era of Swing that followed. Thanks to radio and records, Ella Fitzgerald, Ethel Waters, and Louis Armstrong (whose Queens home is a museum) became national and international household names. As an agent of cultural change, concludes the historian David Levering Lewis, the Savoy "shook America as profoundly... as the 1913 Armory Show had turned the world of mainstream art inside out."[23]

The Harlem Renaissance marked a rare moment of acceptance and admiration for a people accustomed to rejection and disdain. Among whites, it forced a reassessment of black stereotypes and a recognition of black artistry. Among African Americans, it strengthened black pride and fostered the hope that creativity could overpower prejudice. Hughes later recalled that "Harlemites thought the race problem had at last been solved through Art." In that sense, notes Lewis, the Harlem Renaissance was an "arts-cum-civil rights initiative."[24]

Garveyism

During this same period, another nonviolent protest with a different message directed toward a different audience emerged from Harlem. Historians agree that Garveyism was the nation's most extensive and most significant African American mass movement—the first to mobilize ordinary people, to include Caribbean immigrants, to promote black nationalism, and, most important, to emphasize racial pride. Whereas the Harlem Renaissance sought equality within an integrated American context, Marcus Garvey's racial renaissance assumed that blacks would never be treated equally in the United States. Consequently, he recommended economic self-sufficiency in America and resistance to racial oppression worldwide. Eloquent and charismatic, Garvey upset mainstream society by urging his followers to rise "up, you mighty race" and by advocating "Africa for Africans."[25]

Born in Jamaica, West Indies, Garvey came to the United States in 1916 and established the New York chapter of the United Negro Improvement Association (UNIA) in 1918. The organization quickly spread to seven major American cities and soon there were seven hundred branches across the United States plus two hundred more around the globe. Garvey's magazine, appropriately called *Negro World*, celebrated African history, African American rebellions, and black resistance to European domination. In promoting race pride (an early version of "black is beautiful"), it rejected all advertisements that connoted racial inferiority, such as chemicals for straightening hair or lightening skin. *Negro World* was printed in several languages and had an international audience of two hundred thousand readers.[26]

In Harlem, the UNIA caught on like fire, ignited by the experience of military segregation during World War I, the resurgence of the Ku Klux Klan, and the rise of lynching. Nationwide, seventy-six blacks, including soldiers, were lynched in 1919 and, of fourteen others set afire, eleven died. To make matters worse, during the "Red Summer" of 1919, twenty-six cities from Texas to Nebraska exploded in racial violence when white mobs attacked black communities. In Chicago, five days of rioting resulted in thirty-eight deaths, hundreds of injuries, and thousands of blacks rendered homeless.[27]

Such circumstances made Garvey's philosophy of racial dignity and self-determination particularly powerful. It touched sensitive, if opposite, nerves in both black and white America because it challenged white supremacy. Bolstered by strong African American religious traditions, Garvey insisted that blacks should worship a black god and started an African Orthodox Church that was replicated in other states and countries. His audacious movement was enriched by ceremony, uniforms, music, honorific titles, spectacle, and religious reference. Garvey himself dressed in military regalia and was dubbed the Black Moses.[28]

Understanding the dire economic situation of African Americans, Garvey promised sickness and death benefits for all dues-paying members even though he never had adequate funds to support such programs. He promoted economic independence through black-owned businesses including a restaurant, a laundry, a tailor, a publisher, and several grocery cooperatives. His most ambitious business venture was the Black Star Steamship Line, designed to take blacks back to Africa. Thousands of ordinary people signed up, but Garvey's own mismanagement, compounded by the deception of others, doomed this project and his career.[29]

Nonetheless, at his peak, Garvey was so successful that he was deemed dangerous, not only by New York State and the United States but also by foreign governments anxious to keep his message out of their African colonies. Garvey's popularity was evident at the first UNIA international convention held in 1920. For the entire month of August, twenty-five thousand people representing every American state, plus twenty-four countries in Africa, Central America, South America, and the Caribbean, met at Madison Square Garden and at Garvey's Liberty Hall on 138th Street near Lenox Avenue. In a massive parade through Harlem, uniformed men, women, and children were cheered by thousands. One sign proclaimed "The New Negro HAS NO FEAR." Observers were taken aback by the discipline, extensive organization, and wide support the parade revealed.[230]

They were equally disconcerted by the convention's aggressive tone. Declaring that "we are the descendants of a suffering people. . .determined to suffer no longer," Garvey pledged to "organize the 400 million Negroes of the world" and to free Africa from white domination. The convention drew up a "Declaration of the Rights of the Negro Peoples of the World" and adopted official colors—red for the blood spilled over the centuries, black for race pride, and green for a better future. The members also demanded that a capital "N" be used for the word Negro. In 1929, this spelling revision was accepted by New York City's Board of Education and the New York Times "in recognition of racial self-respect for those who have been for generations in 'the lower case.'"[31]

Garvey provoked controversy among blacks as well as whites. Prominent African Americans, such as Du Bois and Randolph, attacked Garvey's pomposity and demagoguery, his impractical shipping venture, and his self-anointed title as provisional president of Africa. They were incensed when he labeled them "part-white Negroes" and applauded the Klan for being honestly racist. In response, Du Bois lambasted Garvey as "the most dangerous threat to the Negro race," and Randolph dismissed him as an "imperial buffoon." Determined that "Garvey must go," his critics asked the federal government "to disband and extirpate this vicious movement."[32]

They need not have worried, because U.S. Attorney General A. Mitchell Palmer and his assistant, J. Edgar Hoover, had already begun prosecuting Garvey for mail fraud in connection with the Black Star Steamship Line. Although never found guilty of personal dishonesty, Garvey was convicted on a technicality in 1923, and, after losing an appeal, served two years in prison until he was deported to Jamaica in 1927. During this period, T. Thomas Fortune (an early advocate of spelling negro with a capital "N") kept the *Negro World* alive. Defiant until his death in London at age fifty-two in 1940, Garvey continued to work "for the real emancipation of my race," but he never regained his former stature.[33]

His critics contended that "Garvey defeated Garvey," but no one denied the impact he had on people of African descent in New York City, the United States, and the world. Even his enemies had to recognize Garvey's positive contribution in promoting racial dignity among thousands of ordinary people and creating one of American history's most potent protest movements. As a New York City journalist commented, "Thousands who merely dreamed dreams now see visions."[34]

Together the Harlem Renaissance and Garveyism demonstrated how effectively nonviolent protest could expose inequity and affirm racial pride. They assumed, as Hughes suggested, that if "every man is free," it should not matter "whatever race you be." To most whites, however, these movements were disturbing reminders of problems denied and even more disturbing evidence of the potential power of people considered powerless. The Harlem Renaissance and Garveyism were of national and international significance because they so boldly and so effectively advanced what cultural analyst Ann Douglas called "undoing dispossession."[35]

THE SIDEWALKS OF NEW YORK

East side, west side,
All around the town.
The tots sang Ring-o-Rosie,
London Bridge is falling down.
Boys and girls together.
Me and Mamie O'Rourke,
Tripped the light fantastic,
On the sidewalks of New York.

—James W. Blake and Charles B. Lawlor, 1894[36]

"The Sidewalks of New York" was one of the most popular songs of this period, with its bucolic image of cheerful Irish-American children playing together on city streets illuminated by dreams of "the light fantastic." Antiurban versions of the lyrics emphasized drinking and gambling "all around the town," but the original rendition persisted and was played widely at the 1939 World's Fair. Nonetheless, reality often differed from the song as New York grappled with the strains generated on its streets by an ever-changing, ever-contentious population.[37]

In Greenwich Village, competition between old Irish residents and new Italian migrants resulted in constant strife during the twenties. German Jews clashed with Irish Catholics in Washington Heights where tensions over territory were inflamed by anti-Semitic groups during the thirties. Furor erupted in Bedford, Brooklyn when black students at Girls High School petitioned to attend the senior prom in 1920 and when a white Episcopalian minister told his black parishioners to go to black churches in 1929. In both Harlem and Brooklyn, there was conflict among New York–born African Americans, Caribbean immigrants, and Southern migrants.[38]

Adding to this volatile urban mix were newcomers from Puerto Rico, which was occupied by the United States in 1898 and whose residents were granted U.S. citizenship in 1917. Their enhanced legal status dovetailed with a demand for unskilled labor during World War I when many men went abroad to fight, as well as in the twenties when immigration laws restricted the flow of cheap labor from Europe. With stagnant economic conditions on the island stimulating an exodus to the mainland, New York City became home away from home for over 60 percent of all Puerto Ricans living in the United States by 1920 and over 80 percent by 1930.[39]

Puerto Ricans developed a community called El Barrio that would soon extend from 96th to 112th Streets between Fifth and Third Avenues. Distinguished by their use of the Spanish language and their retention of close ties to Puerto Rico, the new settlers seemed very different from the established Jews and Italians who then dominated East Harlem and its economy. Some vendors learned enough Spanish to sell the items Puerto Ricans wanted. Others saw the newcomers as a threat, especially when they opened businesses to serve their own community.[40]

The precarious proximity of disparate groups exploded in the East Harlem Riot of 1926. The trouble started during July when a heat wave drove people out of their stifling apartments into the streets. Arguments arose, tempers flared, fights broke out, and bottles were thrown. For a week, gangs of old residents battled gangs of new residents. Pushcarts and stores were vandalized on both sides of the ethnic divide. Each group boycotted the other groups' businesses. Over fifty people were badly hurt and three Puerto Ricans were arrested.[41]

For the Puerto Rican community, the lesson was twofold. First, they recognized the need for buffers against and bridges to mainstream society. Accordingly, the Porto Rican Brotherhood began coordinating existing community groups into an omnibus advocacy organization. Second, they determined to resist assimilation and preserve their heritage through Spanish language music, media, cultural activities, and community programs. In the process, Puerto Ricans challenged prevailing assumptions about the melting pot and the American Dream. East Harlem was developing a new model of ethnic pride similar to West Harlem's racial pride.[42]

By contrast, Al Smith believed in the conventional melting pot and the classic American Dream because he exemplified them. His parents were of poor Irish immigrant stock; his Oliver Street home was on the Lower East Side; his favorite childhood author was Horatio Alger. As a boy, Smith sold newspapers on the streets and brought back copies of Henry George's *The Standard* for his parents to read. In 1886, his father, who had rescued several blacks during the 1863 riots, died. Twelve-year-old Al dropped out of school and went to work full time at the Fulton Fish Market, which he often called his college. He soon joined Tammany, rose through the system, and was elected a state assemblyman in 1903.[43]

Hardly hampered by his lack of formal education, Smith was a masterful debater and legislator, especially after the 1911 Triangle Factory Fire made him a champion of the working classes. In 1918, he became governor of New York State, the nation's first Irish Catholic to achieve such prominence. Reelected five times (with one break in 1920), Smith secured significant reforms in education, housing, working conditions, child labor, and public health. In 1928 he won the Democratic presidential nomination. His remarkable career proved, as he put it, that former newsboys could enter "the gateway of opportunity irrespective of race, creed or color, so that the most humble in the land may rise to greater things."[44]

Not exactly. Smith's candidacy was a moment of legitimacy for the Irish, for immigrants, for Catholics, for liberalism, and for the city, but the moment was short. Exhilarated, he immediately chose "The Sidewalks of New York" as his campaign song. The words were changed to reflect his progressive platform and to embrace "German, Frenchman/ Irishman or Swede/ Italian, Hebrew or Scotchman/ Makes no difference race or creed." Soon he discovered that it did make a difference and that the cosmopolitanism so endemic to his city appalled America. This conflict was not in Gotham but about it.[45]

In the first campaign to use radio, Smith's Lower East Side speech patterns grated the nation's ear. People derided the prospect of his wife as first lady and suggested that the Holland Tunnel really went straight to Rome.

Campaigning across the nation, Smith was stunned by burning crosses, open anti-Catholicism, and avid hatred of the city. Time and again, he was associated negatively with Wall Street, Tammany, alcohol, foreigners, socialism, Negroes, and Jews. Because so many people believed that "the whole Puritan civilization which has built a sturdy, orderly nation is threatened by Smith," he lost the election to Republican Herbert Hoover. Smith's defeat, wrote the editor Walter Lippman, was "inspired by the feeling that the clamorous life of the city should not be acknowledged as the American ideal." The nation heard but refused to sing New York's song.[46]

If Al Smith represented the gritty, unassuming, humanistic, and honest side of New York City's streets, Jimmy Walker represented the glamorous and corrupt side. Gotham's dashing "nightclub mayor" from 1926 to 1932, Walker epitomized the Roaring Twenties and the lavish lifestyle non–New Yorkers criticized. A former songwriter, he spent most of his time vacationing and entertaining women. His lax administration spurred an investigation greater than that of the Tweed era. Led by Judge Samuel Seabury, a disciple of Henry George, the two-year inquiry unveiled widespread graft, vice, and protection rackets. The good times were over and Governor Franklin D. Roosevelt (FDR) sent Walker's Tammany associate, Al Smith, to demand that the disgraced mayor resign.[47]

Walker's fate was tied to that of the nation. He was applauded during prosperity and abandoned during depression. The 1929 collapse of the Stock Market brought the international center of finance to its knees. Unemployment reached a million by 1932, and, without income, people could not pay the rent or buy food. Accordingly, they slept on subways or built makeshift huts in vacant lots. A large squatter settlement in Central Park was called Hoover Valley in homage to the President's failed recovery policies. Instead of the game "Monopoly," children played "eviction" and "going on relief." Apples became a somber symbol of despair as unemployed men sold them on street corners for a nickel a piece. Because soup kitchens could not meet the demand, people starved.[48]

The city faced disaster and the Walker administration's debt compelled it to cede control of municipal finance to the banks in 1932. Charitable organizations set up work relief programs using private funds, including significant donations from the Rockefellers and William Randolph Hearst. Nonetheless, the wages were too small, the jobs too few, and the situation too critical. New York State did not help defray the cost of relief until 1931 and the federal government's role was limited until FDR became president in 1933. These circumstances fostered radicalism and fomented conflict.[49]

During the late nineteenth and early twentieth centuries, socialism flourished in working-class New York, especially among Eastern European Jews. In 1920, the State Assembly refused to seat five duly elected New York City socialists despite protests from across the country as well as from the State Bar Association and Fiorello LaGuardia, then president of the city's Board of Aldermen. However, in 1929, Norman Thomas garnered more votes than any previous Socialist mayoral candidate in the city's history. Misery made people question the American Dream.[50]

Michael Gold pointed out that there were plenty of *Jews Without Money* (1930) whose already marginal existence became desperate during the Depression. With many people fearing eviction, Gotham's small but vocal Communist party organized rent strikes in neighborhoods dominated by Eastern European Jews on the Lower East Side, in Brooklyn, and in the Bronx. Large crowds battled the police and, at one point, Brownsville, Brooklyn was placed under semi-martial law. In retaliation, landlords organized themselves and pressured City Hall to "take the streets away from the strikers."[51]

In 1932, there was a rent riot in the Bronx and by 1933 there were rent strikes in over two hundred Bronx buildings. As in the earlier food riots, Jewish women played leadership roles, fought with the police, and got arrested. The LaGuardia administration responded by replacing some slum housing with public housing. The Communist party was active in Harlem where a major rent strike was waged in 1934. Success in winning rent reductions led to the formation of a Consolidated Tenants League and a strategy, designed by Garvey's former lawyer, of using court cases to challenge the pro-landlord bias of tenant law. New York's Depression-era anti-eviction movement was the nation's first significant tenant revolt. It educated city, state, and national politicians about urban conditions and won support for public housing, rent control, and tenants' rights.[52]

In 1930, the Communists held their largest New York City demonstration that turned into a riot as over thirty-five thousand people gathered at Union Square to ask for jobs and housing. When the Communist leaders refused to end the rally and began marching to City Hall, the police advanced in full force. Horses trampled the crowd. Police beat women, children, and old men with nightsticks. Seven cops attacked a group of young boys. One cop held onto a girl while another beat her face with a blackjack. It was over in fifteen violent minutes, but hundreds were injured and the city was distraught. Protests poured in from the press, prominent citizens, law professors, and the public. Only the Communists were pleased. To them, the riot was "a great success" because it showed how oppressive capitalist governments really were.[53]

Fiorello LaGuardia offered the city an alternative to violence and despair. "My answer to communism," he once said, is "to remove the cause of complaint, to take away the argument of the agitator and do something that will make life easier and better for the great masses of the working people of this country." Throughout his political career, LaGuardia's mission was always to "speak for Avenue A and 116th Street, instead of Broad and Wall." Although he grew up on an Arizona army base where his father was a bandleader, LaGuardia was New York to the core—a product of its diversity, a mirror of its humanity, a measure of its complexity, an example of its audacity, and a symbol of its vitality.[54]

Short, round, and swarthy, LaGuardia did not fit neatly into any categories except for being passionately progressive and anti-Tammany. He was Jewish on his mother's side and Catholic on his father's side, but he was raised as a Protestant. Speaking six languages served him well as interpreter at Ellis Island, lawyer, and master of melting pot politics. After losing his first wife and daughter to tuberculosis in 1921, LaGuardia embraced a life of public service that made him a national and international celebrity. He did so with a distinctive flair that was often as abrasive as it was entertaining and effective. When Yale honored him in 1937, they called him "an expert in nerves. He knows how to explode them to the public advantage [and] how to control them. . . . He rides in a whirlwind and directs the storm."[55]

LaGuardia proudly represented his East Harlem working-class, mainly Italian, immigrant district in the House of Representatives from 1922 to 1932. Persistently liberal in the conservative twenties, LaGuardia became a dynamic, if controversial, national champion of immigrants, workers, the poor, and the cities. His critics were outraged that a person of LaGuardia's ancestry and class could influence American government. Recommending that LaGuardia "go back to the country whence his ancestors came," the *Denver Post* declared that "No state but New York would disgrace itself by sending such a man as LaGuardia to Congress."[56]

As New York's first Italian American mayor and the first reformer elected three times (from 1934 to 1945), LaGuardia reenvisioned New York City. Despite the Depression, he promised "a vital new type of government. . .for the benefit of all the people. . .an administration, tender-hearted toward the weak and unfortunate and hard-hearted toward the wrongdoer and grafter." This philosophy, he said, perpetuated Henry George's fundamental precept that "in a land of plenty there should be no want." Invoking the ancient Athenian oath, LaGuardia pledged to "transmit this city. . .far greater and more beautiful than it was transmitted to us." His concept of the social contract was expansive.[57]

Many of LaGuardia's reforms were successful, but his effort to revive Fernando Wood's proposal for a free port failed and he never eradicated either corruption in government or the vice and gambling that he deplored. He did manage to hold down the cost of milk, utilities, and subway fares. While blocking the imposition of tuition at the municipal colleges, he built new campuses in Brooklyn and Queens. LaGuardia brought arts to the people through schools, museums, and public concerts. He unified the cumbersome, inefficient transit system. His love for children meant more parks, schools, and health centers, not to mention reading the comics over the radio during a newspaper strike. LaGuardia also opened up municipal jobs to Jews, Italians, and African Americans, thereby undercutting Tammany and the Irish but benefiting other segments of the city's populace.[58]

Sometimes LaGuardia's sympathy for the underdog backfired, as in the 1934 taxi strike. Earlier in his career, LaGuardia had been a labor lawyer and had marched with strikers. As congressman, he consistently spoke out on behalf of workers and against child labor. In 1932, he cosponsored landmark federal legislation that limited management's ability to suppress labor unions and to use injunctions against strikers. In February 1934, LaGuardia's pro-labor bias showed when he ordered the police not to restrain striking taxi drivers even when they were violent.

Struggling for a month with employers over money and the right to union-ize, a thousand drivers swooped through the streets around Times Square, the Pennsylvania Railroad terminal, and lower Broadway. They attacked scabs, vandalized their cabs, and set several vehicles afire. Five hundred young Communists staged a midnight sympathy march. After two days of escalating confrontations, LaGuardia finally let the police stop the riots. Widely criti-cized for condoning violence, he struggled to defend himself before a grand jury. For the moment, his ideology outweighed his concern for civic order. It was a startling example of how LaGuardia could be, just as his Tammany ene-mies charged, "rabble-rouser in chief."[59] (See Figure 15 following page 150)

In most other cases, LaGuardia's liberalism had positive results, espe-cially when he got unprecedented federal aid to build schools, parks, bridges, hospitals, housing, sewer systems, and airports. These projects created jobs and restored hope. They expanded the Progressive vision of active govern-ment and, says the historian Thomas Kessner, shaped the modern city. Albeit with crucial help from FDR, LaGuardia advanced his greatest ambition—to make New York not only the nation's leader in terms of wealth and size, but also "first. . .in wholesome housing,. . .in public health,. . .in happiness. . . ." He insisted that the American Dream include the cities.[60]

In 1938, LaGuardia translated that dream into an amendment to the New York State Constitution making "the aid, care and support of the needy" a public obligation. This humanitarian policy was unique in the nation at the time and remains so today. Like Al Smith, LaGuardia was controver-sial because of his plucky immigrant pride, his fervent social commitments, and his aggressive urban agenda. Although Smith's Tammany connections were anathema to LaGuardia, although the two men represented competing ethnic groups and opposite ends of Manhattan, they were fundamentally similar. Above all, they both believed in and left a legacy of what LaGuardia called "government with a soul." It was a dream derived from the sidewalks of New York.[61]

THE RIOTS OF 1935 AND 1943

Langston Hughes knew that sooner or later "a dream deferred" would "explode." Instead of joy "east side, west side/ all around the town," he saw the pain that prevailed "from river to river/ uptown and down" when opportunity is denied and "a dream gets kicked around." How right he was. Three hundred years of disappointment bore fruition in two major riots that rocked New York City in 1935 and 1943, both on Mayor LaGuardia's watch. These dramatic events were turning points in American history because they inaugurated a new form of urban conflict that documented the dimensions of desperation in the Northern city.[62]

Unlike the classic race riot in which whites attacked blacks on contested turf, these riots occurred within the black community and focused on expressing anger toward white society. They resembled racial rebellions. To his credit, after the first riot, LaGuardia did more to promote racial equality than any previous mayor, but he also faltered and failed to forestall the second riot. At the same time, the riots fed on a long tradition of discrimination against and protest by African Americans. They were the direct result of dreams long deferred.[63]

From colonial times, New York City's African Americans had protested against injustice and inequality, but those efforts now entered a new, more aggressive phase. The cumulative effect of the NAACP, the Urban League, the African American press, the Harlem Renaissance, and Garveyism highlighted grievances, created a more cohesive black community, and broadened the base for activism. Moreover, the 1929 Depression deepened the dilemmas of Harlem, where unemployment was always high and wages were always low. Now, with the city's unemployment rate reaching 30 percent, white workers pushed black workers out of the few jobs they had. The suffering was unparalleled.[64]

Churches, traditionally the anchors of the black community, tried to meet the crisis. In 1930, seventeen religious groups cooperated to provide emergency rent money, clothing, and referral services. Together they fed over twenty-four hundred people a day, mainly paid for by parishioners, but partly aided by the Rockefellers who often supported Harlem's charities. Starting in 1933, the charismatic evangelist Father Divine fed three thousand people a day at his fifteen "heavens" where white and black followers lived communally. In many ways Garvey's heir, Divine set up black-owned stores, restaurants, and laundries. However, his immense popularity threatened the black establishment and his interracial policies upset the white establishment. Several real estate suits finally drove Divine out of Harlem to Philadelphia in 1940.[65]

The nationally prominent Abyssinian Baptist Church, on 138th Street near Lenox Avenue, offered Harlemites a thousand meals a day plus clothing and coal. It sought jobs for the unemployed and offered shelter for the homeless. These efforts were organized by Adam Clayton Powell Jr., namesake and son of Abyssinian's renowned pastor. A recent graduate of Colgate College, Powell was moved by Harlem's problems. In 1930, at age twenty-two, he led six thousand people on his first protest march to City Hall demanding that African American doctors and nurses be hired at Harlem Hospital. From that moment on, Powell commented, "we stepped up the tempo of democracy in action in New York City."[66]

Job discrimination was particularly vexing in Harlem where blacks spent their money in stores owned and staffed by whites, many of them remaining from the period when Harlem was largely Jewish. A few blacks were hired as floor sweepers or janitors, but college graduates were lucky to become elevator operators. Previous efforts to expand employment opportunities for African Americans in Harlem had been made by the NAACP, the Urban League, local clerics, black businessmen, and a black women's league, but they had all failed.[67]

In 1934, a new coalition of radicals and moderates began a "Jobs for Negroes" campaign and Powell helped picket Blumstein's Department Store on 125th Street. After six weeks, Blumstein agreed to hire more black employees, but when he only hired light-skinned women, the coalition radicals demanded that dark-skinned women be included and accused the coalition moderates of supporting Blumstein. Splitting from the group, the radicals boycotted other stores along 125th Street, leading to a 1934 court injunction against nonunion picketing. The coalition died, but it had nourished protest in Harlem. Now activism, rather than art, held the key to change. As Hughes put it, "poems became placards."[68]

Set against the backdrop of the Depression and the 1934 boycotts, the riot of 1935 demonstrated how minor incidents mask major conflicts. In the afternoon of March 19, a guard at the S. H. Kress variety store on 125th Street caught a Puerto Rican boy stealing a ten-cent pocketknife. After a struggle, the boy was apprehended, taken to the rear of the store, questioned, and released through a back door. Rumors that the boy had been beaten were given credence when an ambulance arrived. Then, when a hearse driver stopped to make a purchase, people deduced that the boy had been killed. The police refused to give out any information.

By the time the store manager located the boy again and brought him forward to prove that he was alive, a riot of thousands was in full swing and that particular boy no longer mattered. Word spread quickly that a nonwhite child had been brutalized by white law enforcers in a white-owned store. Radical groups immediately distributed inflammatory leaflets, riled the crowds, and picketed Kress. It took little effort to unleash decades of repressed anger against white businesses and white police. As Alain Locke commented, the cause of the riot was less the specific events than "the state of mind on which they fell."[69]

The rioters first focused on the Kress store where windows were broken, counters were upset, and merchandise was looted. As evening fell, thousands rampaged across 125th Street from Fifth to Eighth Avenues. The police were pummeled with bricks and bottles; store windows were smashed and goods were seized; fires were set and shots rang out from rooftops. Order was not restored until the next afternoon. In the end, 3 African Americans were killed, 64 people were injured, 125 people were arrested, and 625 windows were broken. The press and the district attorney blamed the whole affair on Communists and aliens.[70]

Although condemning the riot itself, New York newspapers acknowledged that many factors made Harlemites "a volatile population." Powell clarified the matter. "It was not a riot," he said. "It was an open, unorganized protest against empty stomachs, overcrowded tenements, filthy sanitation, rotten foodstuffs, chiseling landlords and merchants, discrimination on relief, disfranchisement, and against a disinterested administration. It was not caused by Communists." Emphasizing the point, an *Amsterdam News* cartoon depicted death, draped in a cloak of economic evils, carrying the flame of riot while trampling over the masses.[71] (See Figure 16 following page 150)

After the riot, LaGuardia tried to be responsive. He asked Randolph and the poet Countee Cullen to join a Commission on Conditions in Harlem led by the Howard University sociologist E. Franklin Frazier. One hundred sixty witnesses spoke at twenty-five hearings detailing the circumstances that had sowed the seeds of the riot, just as Powell had explained them. In addition, they assailed police brutality and reported being harassed, beaten, and shot without warning. Harlemites castigated the police department's refusal to admit any wrongdoing and its habit of exonerating abusive cops. The Commission concluded that resentment against policemen had been building up for so long that any "spark" could easily "set off an explosion."[72]

The Commission warned that increasing police presence in Harlem was hardly the solution. Instead it recommended addressing Harlem's "most fundamental problem," which was securing decent jobs at decent wages. Second, the report implored the city to control rents and provide blacks with schools equal to those provided for whites. Third, it urged that the staff of Harlem Hospital be fully integrated and that an additional hospital be built. Finally, it insisted that the police department stop condoning prejudice, that a citizens' committee be established to assess complaints about police behavior and that police be prosecuted if they violated the law.[73]

LaGuardia refused to release the scathing report, but he did steer substantial resources toward Harlem, including public housing, schools, a health center, and a woman's pavilion at Harlem Hospital. Moreover, he implemented integrated hiring in municipal hospitals and the civil service, appointed several blacks to upper-level city jobs and named the city's first African American male and female judges. LaGuardia's major omission was reforming the police department, which was deemed too politically risky. In fact, all efforts to address discrimination in the 1930s were inherently risky and attested to LaGuardia's good intentions. Within the context of the times, he felt that he was doing as much as he could and more than most others would.[74]

It was not enough. The Depression had worsened conditions in Harlem, making it, as the author Richard Wright said, "a poor man's land." Significant as they were, the programs of the Roosevelt and LaGuardia administrations did not solve Harlem's problems or eliminate discrimination. Accordingly, in 1938, a cross section of African Americans, West Indians, church leaders, Garveyites, and communists formed the Greater New York Coordinating Committee for Employment for Blacks (GNYCC), led by Powell. Although comprising groups "who dreamed different dreams," said Powell, "we all had but one objective: the full emancipation and equality of all peoples."[75]

Emboldened by a 1938 U.S. Supreme Court decision that legitimized picketing against discrimination, Powell's group carried signs saying "Don't Buy Where You Can't Work" and targeted all the stores on 125th Street, one by one. Soon enough, merchants began desegregating their workforces and signing employment agreements similar to those used by the earlier Consumers' League. Powell then took on Consolidated Edison Lighting by threatening to have all Harlemites turn off the electricity one night a week. Next his followers flooded the New York Telephone Company with phone calls that tied up all the lines. Both companies quickly capitulated and slowly started hiring blacks.

In 1939, Powell's group descended upon the World's Fair offices at the Empire State Building where Broadway chorus girls, Bill "Bojangles" Robinson, and other prominent figures joined the picket lines and won blacks six hundred World's Fair jobs. In 1941, the effort spread to the Silvercup Bread Company, Macy's, Gimbels, newspapers, movie theaters, and two of the city's bus companies. In 1942, when Powell became New York's first African American city councilman, he got a resolution passed to halt "obvious discrimination" in faculty hiring at the municipal colleges where not one of the two thousand tenured professors was black.[76]

Powell's equal employment campaigns exposed local discrimination, reinvigorated the black tradition of popular protest, and kept Mayor LaGuardia on the defensive. Deftly using his "flaming tongue" in sermons, speeches, interviews, and legislative combat, Powell heated up the discussion of racial injustice in New York City. He also drew attention to the national context of racism through his "Double V" campaign, which posited that war against prejudice abroad should be accompanied by war against prejudice at home. Abuse of African American soldiers, including the murder of several in the South, made it imperative "to know," said Hughes, "how long I got to fight both Hitler and Jim Crow." Only the threat of a massive march on Washington planned by A. Philip Randolph compelled FDR to issue a landmark 1941 executive order banning discrimination in defense industries. LaGuardia helped pressure FDR to make this change, but he exacerbated Gotham's racial conflicts in other ways.[77]

By allowing the Navy to use Hunter College and Walton High School to train women for an all-white unit, LaGuardia seemed to endorse racism. A protest resolution against using public buildings for such purposes was sponsored by Powell and passed the City Council unanimously. In addition, LaGuardia refused to investigate when, in 1942, a court closed the Savoy Ballroom for harboring prostitutes. Considering that no downtown dance halls with far worse reputations were closed, most people believed that the real issue was racial mixing in Harlem. A month later, when a black man was killed by a white policeman, Powell, by now LaGuardia's nemesis, led a loud protest rally over LaGuardia's strong objections.[78]

African Americans were further angered by a 1943 agreement, engineered by Parks Commissioner Robert Moses and condoned by LaGuardia, that the Metropolitan Life Insurance Company could build a segregated semipublic housing development called Stuyvesant Town. Located on eighteen square blocks from 14th to 20th Streets between First Avenue and Avenue C, it was the largest inner-city housing project yet built. According to the historian Joel Schwartz, Stuyvesant Town cemented "the New York approach" to urban development by which the city gave private builders advantages for projects deemed beneficial to the public. It was a new version of the old Tammany era "honest graft." In this case, the low-rent apartments were intended primarily for veterans, but only if they were white. LaGuardia's position seemed at best inconsistent, at worst hypocritical. Powell called for the mayor's impeachment and ordinary citizens asked, "Can it be, Mr. Mayor, that you of all people, are approving discrimination?"[79]

Although a broad spectrum of white and black liberal organizations mobilized against the Stuyvesant Town proposal, it proceeded with the support of the mayor and his parks commissioner. Not until 1950 would the first three black families be allowed to move in. Throughout Harlem there was a pervasive sense of bitterness that was only strengthened, rather than appeased, when Metropolitan Life said it would build a separate (i.e., segregated) housing development in Harlem. Not surprisingly, when participants were later asked why they rioted in 1943, most cited "racial injustice" as the key source of their anger.[80]

Matters were made worse by race riots in Alabama, New Jersey, California, and Texas during the spring of 1943. A three-day riot in June ravaged three-quarters of Detroit resulting in thirty-four fatalities, twenty-five of them blacks. Many people feared a national race war. Immediately, LaGuardia appealed for calm and commissioned two reports on Detroit, one by the police and the

Figure 1 Peach Tree War. The Manhattan Company, *Manna-hattin, The Story of New York*. Port Washington, L.I., N.Y.: Ira J. Friedman, Inc., 1929. Conflict was built into the settlement process. Two world views clashed when a Native American woman picked fruit from a Dutchman's orchard in 1655. For the former, nature's bounty was to be shared; for the latter, it was private property. The result was the Peach Tree War and a long struggle over land (real estate) in Gotham.

Figure 2 Stamp Act riots. Thomas Jefferson Wertenbarker, *Father Knickerbocker Rebels: New York City During the Revolution*. New York: Charles Scribner's Sons, 1948. The social complexity of the English colony during the 1765 Stamp Act crisis is revealed by the juxtaposition of rich merchants, a slave, and a poor boy. The merchants' attire, the stocks, and the sturdy building convey New York's prosperity, order, stability, and potential for self-sufficiency. The drawing omits the seamen who were active in the riots.

Figure 3 Hog Riot. Picture Collection, The Branch Libraries, The New York Public Library, Astor, Lenox and Tilden Foundations. Laws banning pigs from the streets on the premise that they were dirty caused much squealing and several early nineteenth century hog riots led by poor people who needed the animals for food and income. The new regulations reflected a growing polarization between rich and poor in the city. As depicted in *Leslie's Monthly Magazine*, the aggressive hog catchers contrast with the distressed residents whose dwellings seem to abut communal land on the outskirts of town.

A DOWNWRIGHT GABBLER,
or a goose that deserves to be hissed_

Figure 4 Fanny Wright. Collection of the New York Historical Society (43461). A. J. Akin caricatured radical Frances (Fanny) Wright by exploiting female stereotypes and depicting her as a silly goose who gabbles too much. Note the conscious misspelling of downright and the dark conventional dress rather than the simple spare white toga she wore at her speeches in the 1820s and 1830s. Is the man her colleague, the reformer Robert Dale Owen? Is Akin suggesting that such men were her servants? Is he carrying another goose, making him an object of ridicule too? The candles could symbolize the traditional homemaker role Wright rejected or the fires she ignited with her radical ideas (in the books) about race, gender, education, religion, and democracy.

Figure 5 Sunshine and Shadow. Picture Collection, The New York Public Library, Astor, Lenox and Tilden Foundations. New York City's increasing economic disparities are evident in this mid-nineteenth century contrast between the homes, streets, vehicles, clothing, and behavior of rich and poor. The Old Brewery, a tenement that symbolized the depravity of American's first slum, became the Five Points Mission in 1853. Is it implied that the future may bring more sunshine than shadow if poor Irish Catholics can be converted to Protestantism?

ASTOR PLACE OPERA-HOUSE RIOTS.

Figure 6 1849 Astor Place Riot. Picture Collection, The Branch Libraries, The New York Public Library, Astor, Lenox and Tilden Foundations. The class component of the 1849 Astor Place Riots is apparent in the size and grandeur of the opera House as compared to the people in this Currier and Ives lithograph. Controversy over the use of force to quell civil unrest is dramatized by the militia shooting directly into the mob. Indeed, the subsequent thirty-one deaths made a seemingly trivial controversy over two actors truly tragic.

Figure 7 1860 Politics. Maud Wilder Goodwin et al., editors, *Historic New York, Being the Second Series of the Half Moon Papers.* New York: G. P. Putnam's Sons, 1898. The positive and negative aspects of nineteenth century participatory politics are captured by this parade of partisans carrying their candidate's signs while a fight erupts between men of different parties as well as different classes. The use of gangs to pressure voters on election days compounded by the consumption of alcohol in the taverns that served as voting places caused many election riots.

THE RIOTS AT NEW YORK. – [SEE PAGE 494.]

RUINS OF THE PROVOST-MARSHAL'S OFFICE.   FIGHT BETWEEN RIOTERS AND MILITARY.

CHARGE OF THE POLICE ON THE RIOTERS AT THE "TRIBUNE" OFFICE.

SACKING A DRUG STORE IN SECOND AVENUE.   HANGING A NEGRO IN CLARKSON STREET.

Figure 8 1863 Riots. Picture Collection, The Branch Libraries, The New York Public Library, Astor, Lenox and Tilden Foundations. Because the 1863 Draft Riots caused at least one hundred deaths, they remain the worst riots in American history. For four days mobs raged through the city. *Harper's Weekly* chronicled the events beginning with an attack on the provost-marshal's office where the draft was held. The bitter fighting spanned day and night. Failed attempts to kidnap Horace Greeley, a draft supporter and the Republican editor of the *New York Tribune*, resulted in a general melee. Note the animalistic depiction of the rioters as compared with the police and the gentleman kneeling in the foreground. Was the woman on the ground an observer or a participant? As in many riots, looters took advantage of the breakdown of law and order. The racist dimension of the riot was evident in the brutal assaults, the destruction of the Colored Orphan Asylum, and four known lynchings.

A RIOT ON FORTY-SECOND STREET, NEAR BROADWAY. Drawn by Graham & Durkin.

Figure 9 Streetcar strike, 1889. Picture Collection, The Branch Libraries, The New York Public Library, Astor, Lenox and Tilden Foundations. *Harper's Weekly* documented the violence of the streetcar strike of 1889 when the police assaulted strikers who had obstructed the tracks by overturning and setting fire to a streetcar. Police often received extra compensation from employers for such assistance. Ordinary citizens, like those on the sidewalk, often supported the strikers, as in the 1895 Brooklyn Trolley Strike.

Figure 10 Henry George. Print Collection, Miriam and Ira D. Wallach Division of Art, Prints and Photographs, The New York Public Library, Astor, Lenox and Tilden Foundations. Condemned as a dangerous radical by mainstream politicians, Henry George ran for mayor in 1886 to speak for the working classes. His supporters saw him as a David struggling against a Goliath snake of rings, corruption, monopoly, and want whose tail wraps around (controls) City Hall. George's only weapons were courage and, in the bottom right corner, the reform spirit of his book, *Progress and Poverty*.

Figure 11 1871 Orange Riot. Collection of the New York Historical Society (77959d). Cartoonist Thomas Nast linked the 1871 Orange Riot to the 1863 Draft riots through the burned Colored Orphan Asylum and the lynched black man hanging from a lamppost labeled 1863. The words in the arch parody the 1857 Dred Scott case when the U.S. Supreme Court held that slaves "had no rights which the white man was bound to respect." The dead bodies parody New York's historic commitment to Live and Let Live.

Figure 11 (continued) 1871 Orange Riot. Collection of the New York Historical Society (77959d). Nast's villains are the Irish Catholics whom he stereotypes as primitive creatures chasing people of other ethnicities out of The Promised Land (top). He holds Tammany and the Catholic Church (erect flag and steeples) responsible for destroying public schools and freedom (inverted flag). As the city goes up in smoke, riots render democracy a distant dream (tiny Washington, D.C. on top).

HE'S ON THE POLICE FORCE NOW.

Figure 12 1900 cartoon. *New York Daily Tribune*, August 19, 1900. This cartoon, which criticizes police brutality and shows rare sympathy for African Americans, was inspired by the Race Riot of 1900. Tammany, as symbolized by the tiger, is held responsible for packing the police force with political supporters, presumably Irish Catholics, who were often the target of nativist sentiment.

Figure 13 Triangle Fire cartoon. The city and the nation were horrified by the 1911 Triangle Shirtwaist Company Fire in which 146 immigrant workers, mostly women, died. In the spirit of the *Masses* magazine, artist John Sloan attacked the greedy capitalist for putting profit ahead of human decency. As a comment on how labor was exploited and how private interests drove public policy, a labor contract speared by a dagger labeled courts lies on the floor out of reach.

Figure 14 1917 suffrage photo. Robert R. Wagner Labor Archives, New York University, Rose Schneiderman Collection. During the Progressive era, traditional female roles were used to call for a redefinition of those roles. While challenging men to treat them as equals (vertical sign), these suffragists assert that as women they were particularly well equipped to be the nation's housekeepers (horizontal sign and aprons). New York City's support for women' suffrage was critical to expanding the franchise in the state and the nation.

Figure 15 1934 LaGuardia cartoon. Unidentified image in the Mayor LaGuardia Photography Collection, NYC Municipal Archives. Mayor Fiorello H. LaGuardia was a solid supporter of labor. His reluctance to let the police control the violence during the 1934 Taxi Strike earned him praise from the working classes but a black eye from almost everyone else. He was even subpoenaed to testify before a Grand Jury to defend his actions. As the drawing suggests, LaGuardia was always pugnacious.

The Real Rioter

By CHASE

Figure 16 1935 cartoon (The Real Rioter). *New York Amsterdam News*, March 30, 1935. In contrast to allegations that the 1935 Harlem Riot was an isolated event instigated by radicals and ruffians, this cartoonist attributed communal anger to historic patterns of racial discrimination.

Bullseye

Figure 17 1964 cartoon (Bullseye). © 1964 by Bill Mauldin. Reprinted courtesy of the William Mauldin Estate. For cartoonist Bill Mauldin, the violence of the 1964 Harlem Riot was counterproductive because it undermined mainstream support for civil rights legislation and contributed to the white backlash. The national significance of local events is clear.

Figure 18 1967 Puerto Rican demonstration. Library of Congress Photographic Services. In the spirit of the sixties and as an alternative to the 1967 East Harlem Riots, Puerto Rican protesters demonstrated at City Hall for equal opportunity through public education, an issue that permeated New York City's history and was echoed in Ocean Hill-Brownsville a year later. The signs reflect an awareness of prejudice matched by an affirmation of ethnic identity and pride.

Figure 19 1969 CCNY demonstration. Photograph by Nancy Shia from the Collection of the Archives, The City College of New York, CUNY. In 1969 African American and Puerto Rican students took over academic buildings at the City College of New York (CCNY). Reflecting their demands that CCNY not only have more African American students, faculty, and courses, but also have better relations with its surrounding community, they renamed the college the University of Harlem. Their protests pushed the City University of New York to adopt open admissions. The white students and the ornate gates represent the old CCNY; the signs represent change. Two of the smaller signs proclaim Power to the People and The New Puerto Rican Struggle.

Figure 20 1980 TWU strike. Robert F. Wagner Labor Archives, New York University, New York Central Labor Council Photographs. The 1980 Transit Workers Union strike pitted Mayor Edward I. Koch against labor unions as well as old-line white labor leaders against an increasingly diverse union membership. Here the dissident members amass at City Hall early in the eleven-day strike. The sign captures the struggles of labor in a post-fiscal crisis world. It reads, "Why should our families suffer for bankers' profit?"

Figure 21 2000 Dorismond Funeral. Courtesy of Lawrence Rushing. The death of Patrick Dorismond, an unarmed Haitian immigrant shot by the police in 2000, exacerbated the crisis over police brutality that demonized Mayor Rudolph Giuliani (see the sign) and unified his opponents across lines of class, race, and ethnicity. The city's long debate over freedom and authority intensified. As always, conflict reflected the dynamic complexity of Gotham.

other by the secretary of the NAACP, Walter White, who was LaGuardia's key advisor on race matters.[81]

New York City residents were asked to sign a "unity pledge" committing them to reject violence, and five thousand people attended a "No Detroit Here" rally. LaGuardia pushed for the hiring of more African American policemen, opened a music school, and planned two more housing projects for Harlem. He lobbied the state and federal governments for rent controls but did not take White's advice to create a committee on race relations. As the summer wore on, the mayor mistakenly concluded that the crisis had passed.[82]

On August 1, 1943, a black soldier was shot and superficially wounded by a white policeman after the former tried to help a black woman being arrested for causing a disturbance at the Braddock Hotel on West 126th Street. Rumors spread that a black soldier defending his mother had been shot and killed by a white cop. The rumors were readily believed because they confirmed pre-existing indignation over discrimination, police brutality, historic victimization of black women, and recent assaults on black soldiers. All of these factors, wrote Hughes, gave Harlem "the urge to raise hell."[83]

Groups of angry people of all classes gathered at the hotel and at Sydenham Hospital while three thousand protested at the police precinct. In short order, tempers flared, windows were broken, fires were set, and stores were looted. The rioting continued for almost eleven hours encompassing over thirty blocks across 125th Street from Lenox to Eighth Avenues and along the avenues from 110th to 145th Streets. Chaos reigned and Harlem looked like a war zone. Six blacks were killed, 185 people (mainly black) were wounded, and over 500 blacks were arrested. Property damage of between $225,000 and $5 million was caused at 1,450 stores.[84]

As soon as LaGuardia heard about the riot, he rushed uptown and mobilized his resources. Policemen, firemen, doctors, and nurses were dispatched to Harlem, which was sealed off from the rest of the city. Bars and liquor stores were closed and a curfew was imposed. The mayor promised that Harlem's needs would be met, "particularly milk for the children." Walter White arranged for prominent blacks to call for calm from sound trucks and fifteen hundred residents volunteered to patrol the community. Ordered to avoid wanton brutality, the police were later praised for their restraint.[85]

LaGuardia initially blamed the 1943 riot on "hoodlums" and denied that it was racially based. Nonetheless, most commentators pointed out that it was a "civil disturbance along racial lines." Surely it was significant, they said, that white-owned stores were vandalized and black-owned stores were spared. As for the hoodlums, everyone criticized them, but the *Amsterdam News* claimed that they were "not as ignorant" as people thought. Instead, they were the people on the bottom, "the burden-bearers of the race." The rioters acted less out of "criminal tendencies," noted the paper, than out of "deep resentment against oppression and a sense of utter futility which Negroes everywhere feel with all their soul."[86]

LaGuardia's responses showed how well he really understood the causes of the riot. The mayor gave radio addresses to reduce racial tension and recommended that racially progressive curriculum materials be used in public schools. He officially opposed discriminatory rental policies like those used at Stuyvesant Town. (Although without effecting Stuyvesant Town directly, the City Council adopted the nation's first antidiscriminatory housing policy in 1944.) LaGuardia not only attended an Interracial Unity Conference at Hunter College where he supported the Double V campaign, but he also reopened the Savoy Ballroom. Addressing slum conditions, he planned several new public housing projects and moved to control rents and food prices. Finally, he established White's biracial committee on race relations. Soon thereafter, LaGuardia turned his attentions to the war effort which dominated his last year in office.[87]

The war also preoccupied President Roosevelt. Agreeing with J. Edgar Hoover, now director of the Federal Bureau of Investigation, that the riots were "a national disgrace," FDR appointed a special assistant on race relations during the summer of 1943. However, he rejected numerous appeals to speak out against racial tension, leaving his wife, Eleanor, to call for better understanding. Concerned about foreign affairs and afraid of losing southern support, the president dodged the race question and adopted what one African American contemptuously called the "Ostrich Policy." The issue of race relations remained so fundamental and so controversial that it had to be avoided.[88]

The riots revealed the persistence of what the Swedish scholar Gunnar Myrdal identified as the core American Dilemma, that is, advocating "freedom, justice, and... opportunity" for all, while denying it to some. Accordingly, Du Bois challenged the nation not only to "abolish Negro illiteracy by 1980," but to "ignore the color line and attack poverty, disease, ignorance and crime" generally. Harlem citizens' groups and newspapers called for more jobs, lower rents, and price controls on food. In addition, they demanded playgrounds and summer schools for black children kept out of white facilities. As the *Times* observed, "Harlem doesn't want special favors. It wants fair play." New York, the paper admitted, should be "everybody's city."[89]

The 1935 and 1943 Harlem riots marked a new era in the history of American rioting that set the pattern for the urban violence of the sixties. Unlike earlier "race riots" in which blacks were on the defensive, these were considered "ghetto riots" because residents of Harlem took the offensive and attacked symbols of racism in their own neighborhood, particularly white policemen and white-owned businesses. The events of 1935 and 1943 were also called "commodity riots" because of the emphasis on destroying property, not injuring people, as in race riots. The new vocabulary reflected the dramatic new dynamics of an increasingly isolated, frustrated, and assertive African American community. The riots altered America's perception of race problems and underlined the urgency of confronting race issues.[90]

Unlike the "soft rebellion" of jazz, the Harlem Riots of 1935 and 1943 were rebellions of the hardest sort. Yet, they paralleled jazz in origin, spirit, and consequence. The cultural protest of the Harlem Renaissance, the racial protest of Garveyism, the economic protest of the job boycotts and the popular protest of the riots were related facets of the New Negro. They emerged from the fact that, as Hughes observed, Harlem was "an island within an island" harboring "a dream within a dream." In 1935 and 1943, the dream deferred definitely exploded, but the line between anger and affirmation, despair and hope, remained permeable. Reflecting on the significance of Harlem in 1945, Hughes celebrated its intellectuals and artists, its politicians and preachers, the Savoy Ballroom, and the Schomburg library. He knew that Harlem was a blend of "half-soled shoes. . .dancing shoes. . .a tear. . .a smile. . .the blues." He saw in its people "the strength to make our dreams come true."[91]

Realism, resistance, and resiliency revealed that Harlem was both typical and atypical of the city as a whole. The struggle for survival was always greater in Harlem and it was always about more than survival. Although Harlem underlined the special nature of the struggle for one group, it articulated the ongoing quest for other groups. As Hughes put it, "To save the dream for one/ It must be saved for all." Movement after movement and riot after riot promoted self-determination within the black community and affirmed the need for equity beyond the black community. In this sense, conflict in Harlem mirrored the dynamics of conflict in the city and the nation. Whether uptown or downtown, east side or west side, struggle presumed that the American Dream was attainable for everyone. The issue was whether society was ready to fully implement LaGuardia's vision of "government with a soul."[92]

8

World City
Redefining Gotham, 1945–1969

By selecting Manhattan for its permanent home in 1945, the United Nations (U.N.) officially made New York the world's preeminent city. It was already considered world class but, with all the major European cities devastated by World War II, Gotham stood out as the sole intact Western center of power, wealth, culture, and hope. In 1949, the writer E. B. White pointed out how ironic it was that, although the capitol of neither a state nor a country, New York City was fast "becoming the capitol of the world."[1]

It was Nelson Rockefeller, president of Rockefeller Center, who got his father, John D. Jr., to donate $8.5 million to the U.N. in order to insure that it would settle in New York City rather than Boston, Philadelphia, or San Francisco. Nelson Rockefeller believed that the world organization should be located in the world's center of finance, culture, and communications. In order to solidify that role, the Rockefellers helped develop Lincoln Center, which, when completed in 1969, made New York "the World Center of the Performing Arts." Also during the sixties, Nelson, as governor of New York State, and his brother, David, as president of Chase Manhattan Bank, conceived the World Trade Center. The Rockefellers used their immense wealth and power to translate the idea of a world city into reality.[2]

During the post–World War II era, New York City's economic prominence reached amazing new heights. It had the greatest population (7.5 million), the most factories, the busiest port, and the largest markets—wholesale, retail, and financial. Moreover, it became "headquarters city" because it was home to 136 of the nation's top 500 industrial companies. Their huge, linear, glass, and steel skyscrapers with their soaring shapes and gleaming facades created what the architect Le Corbusier called a "vertical city." This "international school" of architecture was paralleled by abstract expressionism in painting. Called "the New York School," it was really a universal school that rejected both place and representation. In all of these ways, Gotham was greater than itself. As Le Corbusier observed, "Today it belongs to the world. Without anyone expecting it, it has become the jewel in the crown of universal cities. . .New York is a great diamond, hard and dry, sparkling, triumphant."[3]

Ironically, while New York City was excelling externally, it was fragmenting internally and developing an almost schizophrenic urban personality. Le Corbusier sensed the problem when he decried "the violence of the city," its "diminution of life," its "hard, implacably soulless streets." In the forties, Gotham was caught up in Cold War conflicts. Tensions mounted and protests multiplied during the fifties as New Yorkers argued over urban planning. In the sixties, conflict peaked over race, education, and gay rights. Old pains were intensified, hidden fears exposed, new wounds inflicted, and daring patterns established. As Gotham's liberal heritage was weakened in some ways but strengthened in others, its identity seemed increasingly bifurcated.[4]

Local priorities were complicated by national and international struggles. It was fitting that a World City, which was both a cradle of liberalism and a center of capitalism, should become embroiled in the Cold War controversy over communism. The conflict involved four New York City friends who became influential local, national, and international dissenters. Defying the nation's second postwar Red Scare, Benjamin J. Davis Jr., Paul Robeson, Vito Marcantonio, and W. E. B. Du Bois criticized the limitations of democracy, condemned the callousness of capitalism, and praised the egalitarian ideals of Communism. They were strikingly radical in one of America's most reactionary eras.

Harlem elected African American Benjamin J. Davis Jr. to the City Council in 1943 to represent Harlem when Adam Clayton Powell Jr. became a congressman. A Georgia-born graduate of Amherst College and Harvard Law School, Davis sponsored the 1944 City Council bill prohibiting future restrictive housing like Stuyvesant Town. He consistently opposed police brutality, racial discrimination, and anti-Semitism. Davis was a Communist party leader at a time when the mere suggestion of being pro-Communist doomed many careers. Yet the city's tradition of dissent was so strong that New Yorkers constituted one-third of the party's national membership and Gotham was the sole American city that elected Communists to office. In 1945, Davis was reelected by an interracial coalition that even included Tammany Hall. Victory convinced him that New York was fast becoming "the most liberal city in America."[5]

By 1948, however, Davis found himself one of twelve Communists tried for conspiracy against the government at the federal courthouse on Foley Square.

The historian Martin Duberman considers it the most important "symbolic judicial battle of the Cold War." At issue was the threat to free speech embodied in the 1940 Smith Act, which prohibited criticism of the government and was later ruled unconstitutional. After nine months in court, Davis was sentenced to five years in a federal penetentiary. He lost his 1949 reelection bid in a campaign run by Du Bois with aid from Robeson and Marcantonio. Moreover, before his term ran out, Davis was expelled from the City Council for his controversial opinions. Like *The Masses* trials, the case was a critical test of democracy, said Langston Hughes, because it persecuted "all who question the status quo."[6]

When Paul Robeson tried to testify for Davis, he was muzzled by a judge who had taught him at Columbia Law School, which Robeson attended after excelling at Rutgers. The internationally renowned actor, singer, and political activist was already under scrutiny by the Federal Bureau of Investigation's (FBI) director, J. Edgar Hoover, who insisted that Robeson was a Communist even though he never joined the party. To be sure, Robeson traveled across the country and the world giving concerts while condemning lynching, poverty, prejudice, war, and colonialism. In the spirit of the Harlem Renaissance, Robeson saw art as a vehicle for social change. He dedicated his life to the proposition that "the song of freedom must prevail" over "the choirs of hate."[7]

Robeson's worldwide fame, compounded by his criticisms of the United States, his support for Communist ideals, plus his son's marriage to a Jew, made him a national scapegoat. He was blacklisted by the entertainment industry, branded disloyal by the government, impugned by the House Un-American Activities Committee, and had his passport revoked for seven years. Through it all, he insisted, "I am a radical. I am going to stay one until my people are free to walk the earth."[8]

Hostility to Communists, Jews, African Americans, and New York combined in two 1949 riots against Robeson in Peekskill, New York. Armed with clubs and brass knuckles, white mobs shouting racist and anti-Semitic epithets attacked the concertgoers, threw rocks, and burned crosses. The police stood by or abetted the violence. Robeson's supporters, including Davis, were told to "go back to Jew town," and Robeson was hung in effigy. He barely escaped with his life. The Peekskill riots were reported all over the nation and the world. Moreover, they became an issue in the U.S. House of Representatives where New York City was condemned as a "Communist enclave" and Robeson was excoriated as a "N_____ Communist."[9]

Congressman Vito Marcantonio objected to the use of the denigrating "N" word in the House but was overruled by the Speaker, Sam Rayburn. Marcantonio, an Italian American former protégé of Fiorello LaGuardia, entered politics by organizing an East Harlem rent strike in 1920 when he was only seventeen years old. Although he traveled downtown to attend New

York University Law School, he lived his entire life between 112th and 116th Streets near First Avenue. Until he died in 1954, Marcantonio was an ardent defender of immigrants, the poor, and minorities. As stated on his tombstone (near LaGuardia's grave in Woodlawn Cemetery), he was truly "The People's Congressman."[10]

From the moment he entered the House of Representatives in 1934, Marcantonio was the only congressman in "sympathy" with (although never officially affiliated with) American communism. His persistent war against discrimination in employment, voting, housing, and education was the twentieth century's first concerted campaign for civil rights legislation. Forcing debate on controversial issues, he repeatedly appended "Harlem riders" to other bills, a strategy that was later translated into "Powell Amendments."[11]

Even when his riders failed, Marcantonio upset the status quo. In response, the New York State legislature tried to get him out of Congress by redrawing his district in 1944 to include conservative Italian and Irish voters who would oppose him. In 1947, a state law aimed at Marcantonio required candidates to be nominated only by the party in which they were enrolled. This move limited Marcantonio to running on the line of the small, left-wing American Labor Party (ALP), which he led. Although such a restriction should have spelled defeat, Marcantonio was reelected in 1948 because his followers went to the polls in unprecedented numbers. However, his enemies finally combined to defeat him in 1950.[12]

Marcantonio's success was partly a reflection of his charisma but mostly a result of his indefatigable pursuit of working-class causes. He was dedicated not only to his Italian American constituents, but also to the African Americans and Puerto Ricans in his district, which encompassed El Barrio. Considered the dearest friend of the poor, he gave them a national platform in Washington while often personally paying their rent in New York. In 1951, Marcantonio and Robeson (supported by Davis and Du Bois) went to the U.N. with a petition that accused the U.S. of committing genocide against African Americans. Nothing short of violence could have been more offensive to mainstream America.[13]

Also in 1951, Marcantonio served as chief defense lawyer for W. E. B. Du Bois who, at age eighty-two, was indicted (and handcuffed at his arraignment) as an "unregistered foreign agent" for briefly leading an international peace organization that the FBI considered pro-Communist. Admirers from Latin America, Europe, Russia, Africa, and the Far East joined an international defense committee. It was fortunate that the trial ended in acquittal, noted Hughes, because "if W. E. B. Du Bois goes to jail, a wave of wonder will sweep around the world."[14]

Du Bois had become more radical after 1948 when he was fired as research director from the National Association for the Advancement of Colored

People (NAACP) for criticizing the conservatism of its executive secretary, Walter White. Actually, Du Bois had resigned from the NAACP in 1934 over a similar conflict with White but returned in 1944 to work on issues of international peace. Active in the formation of the U.N., Du Bois argued with White over an NAACP document on racism that Du Bois wanted to submit to the U.N. in 1947.[15]

In 1950, Du Bois ran on Marcantonio's ALP ticket as New York's first African American to seek a U.S. Senate seat. After the 1951 trial, he, like Robeson, was deemed threatening enough for the U.S. government to revoke his passport for six years, but Du Bois would not be silenced. He wrote, spoke out, and worked to get Davis freed from prison. He even criticized his protégé, Hughes, for excluding Robeson from a book about Negro musicians. As they had since the Harlem Renaissance, Robeson and Du Bois persistently promoted the arts in order to validate the black experience, demonstrate black equality, and promote black liberation.[16]

Du Bois criticized America for pursuing profit at the expense of democracy and, like Robeson, he increasingly thought in global terms. As the Father of Pan-Africanism, Du Bois pursued mutual understanding among various peoples of African descent. However, he still rejected Garvey's racial separatism in favor of a broad humanitarianism. So, too, Du Bois' support of Communism emphasized the promise of equality across the color line, not loyalty to any national or political system. Despondent about America's racial future, the ninety-three-year-old scholar joined the Communist Party in 1961 and moved to Ghana, where he was revered until he died on the night before the 1963 March on Washington.[17]

Many Americans saw these four men as the worst manifestations of urban liberalism and the evils of Gotham. Their opinions were so disturbing and their impact so substantial that, as with Emma Goldman, every effort was made to punish them. Trials, riots, legislative maneuverings, passport revocations, FBI harassment, and relentless press attacks attested to the power of their protests. Despite it all, they remained defiant coconspirators in a crusade for human rights that encompassed the city, the nation, and the world.

Strangely enough, the arch-capitalist Rockefeller family had provided the perfect platform for the critics of capitalism. The presence of the U.N. in New York was useful, observed Robeson, because it focused "the eyes of the world" on America and exposed its inconsistencies. As a result, said Du Bois, "an internal and national question becomes inevitably an international question." Although from a distinctly different perspective, the dissenters shared the Rockefellers' vision of New York as a world city.[18]

ROBERT MOSES: POWER, PLANNING, AND PROTEST

The U.N. would never have been built in New York City without Robert Moses. For all their money, the Rockefellers needed someone to navigate the practical obstacles including legal contracts, legislative approval, architectural plans, construction costs, tax exemptions, traffic problems, and housing proposals. Only one man had the knowledge, contacts, and power to seal the deal; only one man could do so in four days.

The brilliant son of wealthy German Jews, Moses was a Yale graduate with a doctorate from Oxford. He never held elective office, but dominated city planning through appointive office under five different mayors from 1934 to 1968. At one point, he held twelve state and city positions simultaneously. His imprint is everywhere—on 16 expressways that dissect the city and 16 parkways leading into the city, on 7 bridges, 660 playgrounds, and over 1,000 public housing buildings. In addition, there are scores of beaches, parks, public swimming pools, libraries, bridges, and the Hudson tubes, not to mention Lincoln Center, LaGuardia Airport, and the U.N. According to his biographer Robert Caro, Moses combined "imagination,. . .iron will. . .and. . .arrogance" to redefine New York.[19]

Many more projects stretched out to Long Island and up to Niagara Falls. Moses ruled his empire from deceptively modest offices on Randall's Island located under the Triborough Bridge near Hell Gate. Boss Tweed without the personal greed, Moses was the imperious monarch of municipal growth until undone by his own ambitions. For a long time, however, Moses was invulnerable because he was solidly supported by large segments of the community as well as by politicians and businessmen who, as in Tweed's time, benefited from "honest graft" in the form of contracts, jobs, legal fees, real estate values, and insurance commissions.[20]

Although he lived lavishly, Moses himself was never accused of corruption. His real interest was in power; his real impact was on policy. Moses believed that cars were more important than mass transit, that office buildings should replace factories, and that slum clearance should outweigh community or neighborhood preservation. Traffic congestion would be solved by more highways placed wherever they were needed, regardless of how many people lived or worked in the way. This bulldozer approach to the social contract applied to all other construction too. His philosophy was simple: "When you operate in an overbuilt metropolis, you have to hack your way with a meat ax."[21]

Caro estimates that Moses displaced at least a quarter million people for his highways and at least a half million more for other projects, earning him the nickname, "the Grand Remover." Most of these people ended up in even more crowded housing in even more marginalized neighborhoods. "Urban renewal" often meant "Negro removal," but it also devastated white working-class communities. Moreover, Moses' parks and playgrounds were extravagant when designed for the rich but parsimonious when intended for the poor. The result, says Caro, was to speed "the ghettoization of the city" and to stimulate urban conflict.[22]

In 1953, Moses clashed with the Jewish working-class community of East Tremont over plans for the Cross Bronx Expressway, which promised to displace sixty thousand people. Many of the residents were veterans of the Bronx rent wars as well as of strikes in their previous homes on the Lower East Side. They valued their apartments and good schools in a safe, familial neighborhood abutting Crotona Park. Consequently, when eviction letters arrived, the community resisted. In the spirit of the food riots a half-century earlier, their leader was a Jewish housewife named Lillian Edelstein who quickly formed a tenants' committee and began ringing doorbells.[23]

The East Tremont Neighborhood Association (ETNA) proposed an alternate route for the Expressway that, by swinging two blocks south and skirting along Crotona Park, could have saved 1,530 apartments from demolition. Moses refused to discuss it. Without financial resources to mount a court fight, Edelstein employed grassroots tactics. She organized rallies, wrote press releases, and chartered buses to City Hall. ETNA managed to get municipal hearings on the proposals and seemed to be making progress with local leaders until the final vote. Then all the politicians suddenly supported Moses. To this day, it is unclear what happened, but the lesson was plain. Lillian Edelstein learned that "Mr. Moses runs the city" and that little people did not matter.[24]

However, Central Park did matter. In the spring of 1956, Moses deployed bulldozers to pull down trees for a new parking lot adjacent to the Tavern On The Green restaurant. Word spread rapidly, bringing out forty women with children and strollers to stop the bulldozers. The human stakes were much higher in the Bronx, but the Upper West Side protesters had better contacts. Soon the press was depicting "The Battle of Central Park" as a war of "Moms vs. Moses," dramatized by photographs of cherubic little children dwarfed by menacing big machines. Even Moses' loyal supporters at the *New York Times* objected to disfiguring the city's "sacred land."[25]

With typical "public be damned" arrogance, Moses razed the trees early one April morning. Immediately, over four thousand letters of protest swamped City Hall and Moses was excoriated for using public land to benefit a private company. Then information surfaced that he had allowed the restaurant's manager, who was an old friend, to pay token fees to the city for operating the facility. Now that his integrity was questioned, Moses' aura of invincibility began to fade and, in 1959, Mayor Robert F. Wagner Jr. began restructuring the city agencies that Moses controlled in order to reduce his power.[26]

Moses met his unlikely match in 1961 when the city announced plans to build a housing project on a sixteen-block West Village site branded "blighted." Some people welcomed the prospect of new housing, but Jane Jacobs vehemently opposed it. A longtime Greenwich Village homeowner, Jacobs had already participated in successful campaigns to keep traffic out of Washington Square Park and to save her cherished Hudson Street from "a mindless, routinized city program of vehicular road widening." In 1961 she was also writing her path-breaking study, *The Death and Life of Great American Cities,* which hallowed the role of neighborhoods in urban life. Accordingly, Jacobs vowed that her community would not be destroyed and she became the most formidable foe of the Moses mentality.[27]

Through a Committee to Save the West Village (CSWV), Jacobs battled Moses for seven months. Although initially dominated by white middle-class professionals, CSWV's membership was expanded to include local Puerto Rican, Irish, and Italian residents of Greenwich Village. Jacobs also won support from the Village Independent Democrats, a reform group intent on replacing the last Tammany boss, Carmine De Sapio, as Greenwich Village district leader. The CSWV was so effective that even De Sapio supported its cause. Nonetheless, he was overthrown by a young politician named Edward I. Koch, thus ending De Sapio's 22-year career and Tammany's 150 years of power in city politics.[28]

The CSWV campaign was waged in petitions, the courts, community rallies, private meetings, public hearings, and the press, especially the *Village Voice.* Money was raised through art shows and book sales. When denied the right to testify at one City Hall session, CSWV members created such a commotion that the police were called in to remove them, dragging out one protester by his feet. Within a week, however, the city abandoned the West Village project. Two years later, Jacobs led a similar coalition that successfully blocked the Lower Manhattan Expressway that would have cut through Greenwich Village, the Lower East Side, and what is today's Soho. Once again, people demanded the right to define the future of their city. They demonstrated that the neighborhood really could be, in Jacobs' words, a "means for civilized self-government."[29]

Moses missed the message and hastened his own demise with the 1964 World's Fair. Scheduled to mark the three hundred years since the British took over the colony in 1664, the Fair was held on the same Flushing Meadows site as in 1939, where Moses hoped to create a vast new park to be named after himself. (Initially, he wanted the U.N. to locate there, but it preferred Manhattan.) Although the event was supposed to be a world's fair, it was not endorsed by the fair's coordinating committee after Moses criticized it. Consequently, most of Europe boycotted the festivities.[30]

The 1964 World's Fair was also marred by protests. A plan by the radical Brooklyn branch of the Congress of Racial Equality (CORE) to have cars stall on all roads leading to the Fair sparked furious charges and countercharges between whites and blacks as well as among blacks. Fears that city traffic would be paralyzed, fair revenues would suffer, violence would erupt, and that the ensuing chaos would erode support for civil rights fueled the debate. Moses, Mayor Robert F. Wagner Jr., Attorney General Robert Kennedy, President Lyndon B. Johnson, the NAACP's Roy Wilkins, the Urban League's Whitney Young Jr., the Student Non-Violent Coordinating Committee's John Lewis and national CORE director James Farmer opposed the tactic. Local activists and Brooklyn's Reverend Milton Galamison, who was arrested twice in pre-Fair protests, supported the stall-in. They advocated aggressive strategies to address pervasive problems as expressed by the slogan, "We Don't Need a World's Fair; We Need a Fair World."[31]

The uproar over the proposed stall-in kept so many people away from the Fair that traffic was too light to block and the tactic flopped. The national CORE actually suspended the Brooklyn CORE over the issue, but on the Fair's opening day Farmer led a demonstration of 750 people, many of them white. They disrupted Johnson's dedication speech and picketed pavilions of companies (such as Ford Motor and Schaefer beer) that were accused of job discrimination. A particular focus was Moses and the New York City pavilion where both Farmer and the civil rights activist Bayard Rustin were arrested. Their objective, said Farmer, was to call attention to "the melancholy contrast between the idealized, fantasy world of the fair and the real world of brutality, prejudice and violence in which the American Negro is forced to live."[32]

All in all, the Fair failed to inspire. Even with attendance low and revenues short, Moses refused to reduce the high admissions and exhibit space rental fees. He denied the mounting deficits and denigrated reporters seeking accurate information about the Fair's finances. Calling them "vultures," he declared, "Those who can, build. Those who can't, criticize." It was the sentiment of an increasingly bitter and marginalized man. In 1968, Moses was maneuvered out of his last governmental positions through the coordinated efforts of Nelson and David Rockefeller, who now considered their former ally an obstacle to their own visions of the future.[33]

After thirty-four years in power, Moses left a large legacy. No other man in history had ever been responsible for so much urban development. However, development was also choking Gotham with traffic, destroying viable neighborhoods, and, writes Caro, further "dividing up the city by color and income." The result was resistance. In the end, one of Moses' greatest contributions was the conflict he caused because it made people realize that a city must be more than the sum of its roads.[34]

BLACK PROTEST
The Crisis

While Moses was pretending that all was well at the World's Fair, a historic urban conflict of national importance proved quite the opposite. The 1964 Harlem Riot precipitated what was to the historian Paul A. Gilje "a contagion of disorder" similar to the Revolutionary era and the 1830s. Although the rioting started in Harlem, it quickly inflamed Bedford Stuyvesant, Brooklyn. Within a week, riots erupted in Rochester, where four people died, and two weeks later riots engulfed three New Jersey cities as well as Chicago and Philadelphia. Ghetto riots continued into 1965, bringing havoc to cities in Florida, Ohio, and Illinois. Violence in the Watts section of Los Angeles was so extensive that it caused thirty-four deaths, making it the worst riot since Detroit in 1943. In the opinion of the Charleston, West Virginia *Gazette,* "a dreadful restlessness... among Negroes" was shaking the very foundations of American society.[35]

In 1966, the nation witnessed forty-three riots, the largest in Chicago and Cleveland. 1967 brought riots to Atlanta, Cincinnati, Grand Rapids, Tampa, Toledo, Plainfield, and New Brunswick. Twenty-three people died in Newark and forty-three in Detroit, topping Watts. In addition, there were seventy-five serious riots costing eighty-three lives in 1967 alone. Martin Luther King Jr.'s assassination in 1968 triggered riots in a hundred cities across the country, causing forty-six more deaths. Because the 1964 Harlem riot sparked this extended nationwide black protest, it marked a turning point in American history. New York's Senator Robert F. Kennedy considered it "the gravest domestic crisis since the Civil War."[36]

The 1964 riot resounded across the country precisely because it took place in Harlem—the most famous, most infamous Negro ghetto. From Des Moines to Detroit, Long Island to Little Rock, people feared similar explosions of what Whitney Young called "smoldering powder kegs of resentment and denial." Already horrified by carnage in Vietnam and the murder of three civil rights workers in Mississippi, the nation was haunted by the specter of violence in the Freedom Summer of 1964. Although the sense of crisis confirmed the need for change among some people, it made others resist change and react against the civil rights movement. Events heightened emotions in all camps.[37] (See Figure 17 following page 150)

The riot also astonished international observers of the World City, who sent extensive press reports back to London, Madrid, Paris, Stockholm, Bombay, and Moscow. As an English journalist commented, his previously "pretty picture of Harlem" had given way to images of "heat and dirt, anger and fury." From Peking, the Chinese Communist Party urged African Americans to join their revolution. Africans working at the World's Fair expressed "surprise, shock, and sometimes fear over the racial violence." Everyone appreciated the traumatic significance of the Harlem riots.[38]

The Chaos

On July 16, 1964, a fifteen-year-old African American youth was shot and killed by a white off-duty policeman. There was confusion over the circumstances of the shooting and over whether or not the boy carried a knife. However, there was no confusion in the minds of many African Americans who saw a direct connection between one child's tragedy and their collective tragedy or, as Langston Hughes put it, between that bullet, "the slave chain," and "the lynch rope."[39]

On July 17, a demonstration against police brutality caused sporadic violence. On July 18, a CORE-sponsored rally led to more violence that quickly engulfed Central Harlem. Rocks, garbage cans, bricks, and bottles sailed through the air and rained down from rooftops. Fires were set, Molotov cocktails thrown, and windows broken. Radicals railed on street corners. Gangs and looters took advantage of the situation to ravage the length of 125th Street, after which they moved along Lenox and Eighth Avenues all the way up to 135th Street.

The police dispatched four hundred men and the Tactical Police Force. They repeatedly charged the crowd, beating people with fists and nightsticks. Police fired their guns through tenement windows or at the rooftops, causing yet more panic and one death. The community activist Jesse Gray told blacks to arm and defend themselves. The heightened police brutality infuriated a community where, said Langston Hughes, police beat people's heads so regularly ("bop, bop") that it made them "MAD crazy, SAD crazy, FRANTIC WILD CRAZY." That anger could be channeled into "Be Bop" music or it could erupt into riot.[40]

The mayhem in Harlem continued for three days and nights. Then it spread to the Bedford-Stuyvesant section of Brooklyn, which, like Harlem, was a previously white community now predominantly African American and Caribbean, a previously middle-class community now predominantly a slum. Once more, a CORE rally intended to calm tempers only aroused them, and fighting broke out between police and demonstrators. Again windows were broken, stores looted, fires set, and rocks hurled. Cops used their clubs freely and shot bullets into the air; mounted police charged the crowds. The chaos lasted two more days, during which police shot five people, none fatally.[41]

A third CORE-sponsored march against police brutality at the Mulberry Street police headquarters on July 22 was met by local Italian Americans throwing eggs, bottles, and firecrackers while the police stood by passively. White protestors were called "degenerates" and Communists; blacks were told to go back to Harlem or Africa. Several spectators expressed anger that blacks were getting "more freedom than we have." After the two-hour confrontation, police provided an escort to the subway, but still the protesters were assailed by bricks, garbage can lids, and bottles. Altogether, reported one observer, "This is worse than anything I ever saw in Mississippi."[42]

Throughout the conflict, moderate black leaders walked the streets appealing for calm. Whitney M. Young Jr., executive director of the National Urban League, asked whites to support integration and Negroes to pursue education, but the people's patience had worn thin. When told to go home, they responded, "We *are* home, baby." Veteran civil rights activists Bayard Rustin and James Farmer were jeered as "Uncle Toms." Rustin was humbled by the experience. "It educates me," he admitted. "Neither of us deals daily with their problems…. The people now say, 'We want Farmer and Rustin to get off their behinds and produce results.'"[43]

That was easier said than done. Kenneth B. Clark, the City College psychologist, who was CUNY's first tenured African American professor, was skeptical about the future. "What disgusts me," he said, "is the pretense of shock, surprise, horror" when everyone knew about and ignored reality for years. "But do you know what I think we're going to get?" he asked. "Quiet the natives; then go on with business as usual." Clark was largely correct and later expressed his concern that riot after riot, report after report offered "the same analysis, the same recommendations, the same inaction."[44]

The Causes

The 1964 riots emerged from old conditions but also reflected new developments. On the national level, the Civil Rights movement energized African Americans and legitimized protest, albeit in the nonviolent form advocated by King. Although sidelined by illness, Paul Robeson was gratified that "the concept of mass militancy, or mass action, is no longer deemed 'too radical' in Negro life." By the same token most of the civil rights activism focused on the South with little change in the North. The result was disappointment and frustration. In this sense, wrote Clark, the riots were "an SOS from the ghetto."[45]

On the local level, the economic situation of Harlem had worsened. In the very years when there was a major new migration of African Americans from the South and of Puerto Ricans from the island, manufacturers left the city in search of lower rents and cheaper labor. So, too, federal housing policies, highway construction, and the car culture drew the middle classes to the suburbs along with the tax base needed to address urban problems. For Harlem, it all meant more poverty, disease, crowding, crime, infant mortality, dilapidated housing, inferior schools, and rats. Considering such realities, commented Clark, "the wonder is there have been so few riots."[46]

Enter Malcolm X. After a dramatic metamorphosis from star student to criminal to Muslim minister, he came to New York in 1954 to lead the Nation of Islam's Temple #7 on Lenox Avenue and 116th Street. Starting from virtually nothing, he systematically built a black Muslim movement in Gotham, expanding from Harlem into Brooklyn and Queens. His eloquence and charisma immediately attracted followers and media attention. So did his ability to create and disperse a crowd. In 1957, when a black Muslim was badly beaten by cops, Malcolm amassed protestors at the precinct demanding that the man be sent to a hospital. Facing thousands of angry blacks at their door, the police finally relented, and, with a wave, Malcolm sent his followers home. The police were thoroughly dismayed by Malcolm's power.[47]

Articulate, witty, and hard-hitting, this grassroots leader upset whites by calling them devils and daring them to face racism. As his biographer Peter Goldman points out, Malcolm "saw his life as combat, and words as his weapon. . . . Malcolm didn't teach hate, or need to; he exploited a vein of hate that was there already. . . ." A 1959 television documentary on the Nation of Islam entitled *The Hate That Hate Produced* exacerbated the anxiety that Malcolm's message aroused in whites and created an uproar throughout New York City. It also made Malcolm the nation's most controversial African American and catapulted him to prominence in newspapers, on television and at college campuses.[48]

The son of a Garveyite, Malcolm emphasized racial pride and criticized the integrationist, nonviolent strategies espoused by Martin Luther King Jr. Instead, Malcolm advocated black nationalism, meaning black self-determination, and black liberation "by whatever means necessary." The time for patience was long over, he said. "In 1964, it's the ballot or the bullet." Well aware not only of his influence but also of what Malcolm called the "black social dynamite" of the city, whites considered him "the only Negro who could stop a race riot—or start one." No wonder they were upset when the 1964 Harlem rioters called out "Malcolm! We want Malcolm. Wait 'till Malcolm comes."[49]

At the time, however, Malcolm was on a pilgrimage to Mecca and a tour of Africa, after which he decided that the African American struggle was part of a global struggle against oppression. Like Du Bois and Robeson, he urged blacks to shift their attention to the larger issue of human rights and take their case to the U.N. In 1964, he left the Nation of Islam in order to become more active politically while fostering cooperation between blacks in America and Africa. Until his 1965 assassination at Harlem's Audubon Ballroom, Malcolm mesmerized the nation because, says Goldman, he was "a revolutionary of the spirit, which is the most subversive of all."[50]

Other forms of pre-1964 protests heightened the volatility of Harlem. Demonstrations against police brutality in Harlem and East Harlem were increasingly frequent. Jesse Gray revived the rent strike, which spread to so many communities that Mayor Wagner unofficially condoned the practice and sought renter relief in Albany. Brooklyn's CORE picketed several major companies that began hiring blacks. Less successful was the 1963 protest against the Downstate Medical Center, which was being built in the black community of Bedford Stuyvesant using white labor from other neighborhoods. Brooklyn's black churches held rallies and sit-ins at City Hall. Twelve hundred people demonstrated at the construction site where over two hundred were arrested, the most for a single event since the riot of 1943. However, the struggle petered out over time and no gains were made.[51]

In February 1964, the campaign to desegregate New York City's schools resulted in a one-day boycott, organized by Bayard Rustin and Milton Galamison, president of Brooklyn's NAACP. More than 460,000 students (44 percent of the student body) participated, including many white students. Galamison proclaimed it "the greatest civil rights demonstration on record." Protesters picketed at the Board of Education headquarters and at three hundred city schools, but the movement did not endure and the city made promises without making changes. The combination of deteriorating conditions and accelerating protests, powerful local leadership, and compelling national movements created a combustible mix.[52]

The Consequences

As the first major ghetto uprising of the sixties, the 1964 Harlem Riot took New York and America by surprise. City officials tried to blame the riot on outside agitators, Communists, criminals, wild teenagers, and new migrants from the South. However, the people arrested during the riot turned out to be Northern-born young adults who had lived in Harlem for some time and who held jobs. As in 1935 and 1943, their violence focused on symbols of white oppression—the police and white-owned stores. This "deliberateness within the hysteria," wrote Clark, reflected "a desperate assertion of [the rioter's] desire to be treated as a man."[53]

The city did not meet that need. As Clark had predicted, there was a flurry of studies on conditions in Harlem, but little action beyond the appointment of the first black commander at the Harlem police precinct and the provision of summer jobs for black youth. Mayor Wagner emphasized restoring order and bolstering security, especially as he and Moses worried that the riots would hurt tourism and World's Fair revenues. Most important, Wagner refused to establish a civilian review board to check police brutality, a step that all African American leaders considered crucial for assuaging Harlem's anger. President Johnson was more responsive and pledged federal aid "in correcting the evil social conditions that breed despair and disorder." In January,

Johnson had declared a War on Poverty; in July he signed the Civil Rights Act; in August, he signed the Economic Opportunity Act.[54]

The national importance of the riots brought Martin Luther King Jr. up from the South for a summit of African American leaders. He emphasized the fact that the riot was in New York City, which he called "the center of the Negro struggle for equality, the capital of Negro life, and the most liberal city in the country." Urging New York and America to take Harlem's grievances seriously, King called for reducing police brutality and establishing a civilian review board while also improving housing, jobs, and schools. "What happens here," he said, "affects the whole country."[55]

After meeting with Wagner, King urged Harlemites not just to adopt nonviolent tactics but also to stop demonstrating altogether so that the new Civil Rights Act could be given a chance to work. However, some local African American leaders saw King as an interloper and were offended that he failed to confer with them either before or after seeing the mayor. To Powell, King was just being "used by the white power structure." To Farmer, it was essential that CORE continue protesting loudly in order to keep key issues in the public consciousness.[56]

The prospects for change increased in 1966 when a glamorous, idealistic, Yale-educated liberal Republican congressman named John V. Lindsay became mayor. Committed to Johnson's Great Society, he renewed the city's optimism but failed to quell its antagonisms. In fact, Lindsay's two administrations were profoundly polarizing. That summer brought five days of fighting in East New York, Brooklyn, not only between African Americans and Puerto Ricans, but also between African Americans and Italian Americans who belonged to a Society for the Prevention of Negroes Getting Everything (SPONGE). Lindsay avoided a full-blown riot by visiting the scene to calm the crowds. Like LaGuardia in 1935 and 1943, the mayor wanted to show "that the city government cared."[57]

After the 1966 riot, Lindsay brought blacks and whites together for peace talks in City Hall, set up outreach offices in the neighborhood, and established a Summer Action Task Force to alleviate tension. He changed the police department's leadership and shifted its antiriot policy from confrontation and riot control to containment and self-control. Summer jobs for youth, bus trips to the beach, more frequent sanitation pickups, and the repair of playground equipment all contributed to a sense of official responsiveness. Powell helped by insisting that "instead of 'Burn, baby, burn,' we should be shouting 'Learn, baby, learn' and 'Earn, baby, earn.'"[58]

Nonetheless, riots erupted again in 1967, this time in East Harlem, when a policeman shot and killed a Puerto Rican man involved in a fight. Three days of violence resulted in arson, looting, and one fatality. The riot spread to Brownsville, Brooklyn for four nights and then engulfed the South Bronx where a second person died. A cartoon in the *Amsterdam News* depicted the Statue of Liberty entangled in a snake labeled Riots and Race Hate. Meeting again in New York City, four key African American leaders (King, Wilkins, Young, and Randolph) appealed for calm. Some community activists responded by picketing City Hall for better educational and employment opportunities.[59] (See Figure 18 following page 150)

As the 1967 riots spread across the nation, they motivated President Johnson to create a special federal commission under Illinois's Governor Otto Kerner to investigate the causes of and solutions to civil disorder. Serving as vice chair, Lindsay dominated the Commission's final report, which concluded that "Our nation is moving toward two societies, one black, one white—separate and unequal." Moreover, it jolted mainstream America by claiming that "white racism is essentially responsible for the explosive mixture which has been accumulating in our cities since the end of World War II." The statement was typical not only of Lindsay's sincere idealism but also, contends the historian Vincent J. Cannato, of the "heated and moralistic rhetoric" that made him so controversial.[60]

Although critical of the nation, Lindsay protected the image of his city as being under control. Its many riots notwithstanding, Gotham was not among the places investigated by the Kerner Commission. Similarly, Lindsay minimized accounts of the New York City riots that lasted for four days after King's assassination in 1968. There was, however, no denying that the riots of the sixties definitively dramatized the depth of discrimination and despair that was devastating urban America. New York seemed to have a "Big City Sickness" that could easily infect the whole body politic.[61]

LINDSAY, LIBERALISM, AND THE WHITE BACKLASH

One legacy of 1964 was "the white backlash." It was a reaction against the civil rights movement, the confrontations it involved, and the changes it brought. Rather than accept national responsibility for the plight of minorities (as suggested by the Kerner Commission), many whites increasingly blamed minorities for their own problems and concluded that helping others would only hurt themselves. Moderate blacks and liberal whites feared that the 1964 riots would reinforce the white backlash and reverse the gains of the civil rights movement. After 1964, the term "the white backlash" permanently altered the nation's political vocabulary.[62]

On the local level, the white backlash embroiled Mayor Lindsay in three conflicts and three riots that defined his first term and redefined the character of the city. The struggles over labor unions, the police, and education polarized the city and placed Lindsay right in the middle of the contest over liberalism. His clear preference for change made him anathema to those who were resisting change. Consequently, Lindsay became the focal point for a series of struggles that dismantled the old New Deal coalition of minorities, middle-class liberals, and working-class, union-based whites of Jewish, Italian, and Irish descent.

Lindsay was less central to the riots over Columbia College, the City University of New York (CUNY), and gay rights. Nonetheless, because these events so definitively promoted liberal causes, they crystallized the debate over liberalism and fortified the anti-Lindsay sentiment. Ironically, although the three conflicts undermined Gotham's tradition of liberalism, the three riots promoted it. The result was a city torn between incompatible identities.

Only five hours after being sworn into office, Lindsay faced his first challenge—a walkout of thirty-five thousand bus and subway workers. The 1966 transit strike was engineered by Michael Quill, feisty head of the Transit Workers Union (TWU), a working-class, Irish-born immigrant to whom Lindsay was an elitist Protestant of British stock. Departing from former Mayor Wagner's tradition of friendly negotiations with unions, Lindsay adopted a confrontational approach. Once Quill called the strike, technically an illegal action by public employees, the city obtained an injunction and Quill was sent to jail where he had a heart attack that led to his death shortly after the strike ended.[63]

Thousands of New Yorkers walked to work, but hundreds of thousands more could not get to work at all, including 65 percent of garment district workers. The *Times* deemed it the biggest disruption since the 1863 Draft Riots. After a huge union rally, the burning of Lindsay in effigy, and twelve days of citywide paralysis, the mayor granted Quill his demands. Lindsay's labor disaster avalanched in the form of nurses' and doctors' strikes, a firemen's slowdown, and police pickets at City Hall. Teachers and welfare workers struck in 1967 and sanitation men in 1968. Increasingly, municipal workers defined their own interests in opposition to Lindsay's sympathy for minorities. One sanitation leader explained that "Lindsay is a WASP. He treats labor with contempt. He cares only for the very rich and the very poor. The middle class bores him."[64]

A second major conflict revolved around police brutality. Lindsay endorsed the idea of a Civilian Complaint Review Board (CCRB) so that accusations of police misconduct would go to an independent body not controlled by the police. Pressure for this reform increased after the officer who shot the boy in the 1964 riot was exonerated by the police department. Accordingly, Lindsay hired as police commissioner Timothy Leary, an outsider from Philadephia, which had a civilian review board. Leary then appointed two more outsiders—a Jew and an African American—to run Gotham's traditionally Irish Catholic force. Finally, the new administration added four civilians to the existing three-man police review board, thus tipping the balance of power against the police.[65]

In response, the police mounted one of the most divisive campaigns in New York City history. The Patrolmen's Benevolent Association (PBA) allotted $500,000 of its own union funds and raised a million more from supporters in Gotham and across the country. The campaign intertwined the anxieties created by racial tensions and rising crime rates. The 1964 case of Kitty Genovese, a white woman killed by a black man in Queens while civilians failed to act, provided a perfect rallying cry. In a PBA television ad, a white girl was stalked by dark shadows; in a PBA poster, a cop had his hands tied behind his back over the caption "Don't handcuff the police."[66]

Supporters of the CCRB represented a broad spectrum of civil rights groups that were poorly financed and badly coordinated. By contrast, the PBA was so well organized that it easily secured many more than the forty-five thousand signatures needed to get the CCRB issue on the ballot as a referendum in the fall of 1966. Over 60 percent of New Yorkers rejected the CCRB proposal and, for the first time, the normally liberal Jewish vote split. Majority opposition to the CCRB revealed the strength of the white backlash and the dissolution of New York's old liberal coalition.[67]

The third major policy conflict of 1968 occurred over public education in Ocean Hill-Brownsville, Brooklyn. To Lindsay, it was a tragic collision between "two historic allies in progressive causes—the black and Jewish communities." It derived, says the historian Jerald Podair, from changes in the post–World War II city as its manufacturing sector contracted and its service sector expanded. This shift was accelerated by Moses' elimination of many buildings that housed small factories in poor neighborhoods and by LaGuardia's increase of white-collar government jobs. Those who had access to better schools through which they could acquire white-collar skills benefited. Conversely, those who lived in neighborhoods with inferior schools lost out. The latter were usually minorities whose access to jobs was limited anyway and who were more dependent than whites on the manufacturing sector. Both whites and blacks understood how critical public education was to their futures.[68]

Led by Rhody McCoy, an educational administrator and a follower of Malcolm X, the black community of Ocean Hill-Brownsville believed that white teachers and administrators were not serving the black community well. They thought that community control of the schools would improve education for minority children. Led by Albert Shanker, a mathematics teacher from a liberal Jewish background, The United Federation of Teachers (UFT) was equally convinced that hard-won contracts, jobs, tenure, work rules, and professional integrity would be undermined if educational decision making was vested in parents. Each man was more determined and more vitriolic than the other.[69]

The issue in 1968 was whether to promote community participation in the schools, which, in turn, raised larger issues about the meaning of community itself. On one level, the conflict was a power struggle between the white professional education community and the black neighborhood community. On a deeper level, says Podair, it was a philosophical struggle over the social contract as applied to public education. Shanker's followers upheld the city's long-standing commitment to a diversity of interests orchestrated by central leadership. McCoy's followers considered centralization to be elitist and white-dominated. To them, community control meant less discrimination, more grassroots participation, and, therefore, more democracy. To the UFT, community control meant the replacement of liberalism and pluralism by a divisive emphasis on "racial chauvinism."[70]

The Board of Education, the teachers' union, and the supervisors' union opposed decentralization. Lindsay, black parents' groups, the Public Education Society, civil rights groups, liberal intellectuals, and radicals supported decentralization. When, as head of the local planning board, McCoy demanded total community control of the schools, including the right to hire and fire teachers, the UFT held a brief strike in the fall of 1967. After McCoy dismissed thirteen UFT teachers, Shanker called a second strike in the fall of 1968 to get them reinstated. Harassment of the teachers by protesting parents and a riot at one school resulted in a third strike that fall that lasted thirty-six days. The extended disruption profoundly influenced education and politics in New York City.[71]

Nasty accusations of anti-Semitism were met by equally nasty accusations of racism. Rallies of five thousand supporters of decentralization were outmatched by rallies of forty thousand opponents of decentralization. Police protected the UFT picket lines, often at the expense of community protestors. UFT signs read: "John Lindsay, master of the bungle; he turned New York into a jungle." In tune with the civil rights movement, black parents formed Freedom Schools. Several attempts by the Lindsay administration to reach a settlement failed. Finally, the state intervened and rehired the UFT teachers while suspending McCoy's local board, principals, and teachers.[72]

McCoy, African Americans, and the concept of community control suffered a resounding defeat. Although Shanker and the bureaucracy won, the unions seemed too hostile to reform and too insensitive to minorities. Again Lindsay was portrayed as too pro-minority and too antiunion. Beyond individuals, the 1968 Ocean Hill-Brownsville struggle embittered Gotham's African American communities, contributed to "white flight" from the public schools, and further strained New York City's already fragile liberal coalition. It raised Gotham's volume of contention to an ear-piercing level.[73]

According to scholars Nathan Glazer and Daniel P. Moynihan, Ocean Hill-Brownsville may have been more important than the 1964 riots in creating "the great divide in race relations in New York." Podair agrees, but goes further to suggest that Ocean Hill-Brownsville "symbolized the closing of doors, the end of illusions, for both New York City and America." Compared to the cooperative spirit of the civil rights movement, whites and blacks no longer were speaking the same language and, what was worse, no longer were listening to each other. As a result, long-standing commitments to cosmopolitanism and pluralism seemed doomed to atrophy.[74]

Three riots in 1968 and 1969 complicated the future of liberalism in New York City even more. Two dealt with higher education and the third was about gay rights. All challenged the status quo and brazenly promoted the liberal agenda. The 1968 and 1969 uprisings at Columbia College and the City College of New York (CCNY) were part of a series of protests by students across the nation starting with the Free Speech movement at the University of California at Berkeley in 1964. As an extension of the civil rights movement, students insisted that colleges be more responsive to student concerns and less hostile to their communities. The ensuing conflicts, said the sociologist Nathan Glazer, exposed the hazards colleges faced when confronting "the problems of an enormous world city."[75]

Ivy League traditionalism was under fire at Columbia on several fronts. Since 1965, students had opposed recruiting on campus by the military, the Central Intelligence Agency (CIA), and chemical companies associated with the war in Vietnam. They also objected to Columbia's research affiliation with the Institute for Defense Analysis (IDA), which included on its board of trustees Columbia's president, Grayson Kirk. In 1967 the Students for a Democratic Society (SDS), led by the radical Mark Rudd, obtained fifteen hundred faculty and student signatures on a petition condemning the Columbia-IDA tie, and one hundred students demonstrated in Low Library. When only SDS leaders were disciplined for the action, critics pointed out that Columbia was still using a 1754 regulation vesting punitive power in the University's president. Columbia seemed painfully obsolete.[76]

In 1968, Columbia's few African American students formed a Students Afro-American Society (SAS) to demand more black faculty and students as well as more courses in African American studies. They also joined the Harlem community in opposing Columbia's plans to build a gymnasium on public land in Morningside Heights Park. As originally arranged with Robert Moses, Columbia would clean up the park and allow the Harlem community some access to the facility using a separate community entrance. In April 1968 student and community pickets managed to stop construction amid accusations of "Gym Crow."[77]

After the gym protest, students took over a college building and held three administrators hostage. The standoff between the administration and the students continued for a week and grew more serious as other groups of students took over three additional academic buildings. Although the administrators were released and faculty members tried to negotiate a compromise, neither Rudd nor Kirk would budge. The crisis accelerated as over two thousand students and faculty participated in campus demonstrations. Finally, breaking with the traditional view that a college campus was an oasis from society, Kirk called in the police.[78]

The resulting violence astounded the college community and the nation. The police attacked students with nightsticks and blackjacks, ganged up on individuals, beat injured persons already on stretchers, and dragged people on the ground or down concrete stairs by their hair. They kicked, pushed, and punched both students and faculty. Students in the dormitories retaliated by throwing down bottles and plants. The confrontation was one of the worst on any college campus in U.S. history and "The Battle for Morningside Heights" became symbolic of student protest nationwide.[79]

The behavior of the police was consistent with their behavior in other riots but unexpected on a predominantly white, elite college campus. Indeed, class may have been one undercurrent of the clash with derogatory venom spewing from both sides. Another sore point was liberalism, and several students reported being called "commies" by the police. The Columbia riots revealed the peculiar position of private, elite colleges in cities. Its gates notwithstanding, Columbia was unable to keep social problems out of its quad. As one professor observed, "Columbia is diffused into New York. And in the process something happens that transforms it from the Ivy League school that its alumni and administrators imagine it to be to the urban university that it is in reality."[80]

The student rebellion at Columbia made national news and inspired thousands of student protests at colleges across the nation that spring as well as the formation of 150 new SDS chapters by fall. University administrators started taking student dissent more seriously. Old rules were relaxed and curriculum was revisited. Moreover, the pressure for change, says the historian Irwin Unger, "now widened into a national, and even international, radical sensibility" known as "the Movement" of the New Left. At the same time, liberalism was wounded by affiliation with its aggressive student offspring. A conservative countermovement developed within academia, and more people outside academia equated liberalism with radicalism, lawlessness, and spoiled rich kids.[81]

Merely a mile up Broadway, another conflict was developing over the role of the university in the city and the nation. Here, too, students opposed the war in Vietnam, objected to military recruiting on campus, and criticized the college's insensitivity to its minority neighbors. Nonetheless, the two colleges were really worlds apart. The City College of New York (CCNY) was founded in 1847 as the Free Academy for the express purpose of providing educational opportunity to young men who could not afford to attend private colleges like Columbia. Over time it grew into a multiunit system called the City University of New York (CUNY), which was open to immigrants, women, and minorities. CCNY itself was lauded as the "Harvard for the Proletariat."[82]

The problem was that by the sixties CUNY only admitted 13 percent of all New York City's high school graduates and only 5 percent of New York City's minority high school graduates. Albert H. Bowker, the chancellor appointed in 1963, attempted to alleviate the situation by starting special programs to increase the number of minority students and by planning to offer seats to all high school graduates by 1975. Events accelerated the schedule when, early in 1969, a group of African American and Puerto Rican students demanded that CCNY "utilize whatever means necessary" to increase minorities in the student body and to expand curricular offerings in black and Puerto Rican studies. For emphasis, they briefly took over a college building.[83]

In April, two hundred minority students seized control of CCNY's south campus, proclaiming it the "University of Harlem." (See Figure 19 following page 150) Refusing to call in the police, CCNY's President Buell Gallagher closed the college until the students voluntarily evacuated the buildings two weeks later, despite Adam Clayton Powell Jr.'s advice to hold firm. The violence actually began when the college reopened in early May. However, this time it was not between police and students but among the students—white against minority, conservative against radical, science and engineering majors against social science and humanities majors. When the Board of Higher Education ordered the police on campus, Gallagher resigned. Every day for the next three days, the police arrived in riot gear (but not in riot mode), and the campus was closed only to open again the next morning. The crisis culminated with a fire in the college auditorium, after which CUNY officials decided to "let everybody in."[84]

The resulting policy of open admissions was adopted on July 9, 1969, to be implemented in the coming academic year. Overnight, CUNY became a national and international model for democratic higher education. The CUNY plan was more radical than other open admissions programs because it provided remedial and support services for underprepared students in baccalaureate (not just associate) degree programs. The object was to keep the open door from becoming a revolving door. The key, cautioned Kenneth Clark, was to do so with academic integrity rather than patronizing sentimentality. Lindsay and liberals considered open admissions a victory, but many faculty and alumni saw it as CUNY's death knell. Although white working-class students benefited most from the new policy, open admissions (like affirmative action) became a code word for lowering standards and favoring minorities over whites. The backlash had acquired another rallying cry.[85]

Meanwhile, more changes were brewing at the other end of Manhattan. Greenwich Village gay bars had an arrangement whereby, in exchange for bribes, the police would warn them of impending raids. This system worked well until 1:00 a.m. on June 27, 1969, when the Stonewall Inn, a popular night-spot for gays and transvestites, was raided without prior notice. Planned by federal liquor agents, the raid caught the patrons by surprise, and they responded in a surprising way. For the first time, they fought back.[86]

When the transvestites were herded and prodded like cattle into the police van, one punched a cop. Suddenly wigs came off and fists were flying everywhere. The cops yelled at the crowd and sprayed fire hoses, but neither strategy worked. In fact, the crowd got angrier by the minute, motivated by a long-suppressed rage at police abuse and general societal derision. With the situation out of control, the cops called in the Tactical Patrol Force (TPF). Even then, the gay rioters refused to give up. Every time the police attacked a crowd, another crowd assailed them from the rear. At one point, several queens formed an impromptu chorus line of "Stonewall girls," singing and kicking in what the historian Martin Duberman styled "a deliciously witty, contemptuous counterpoint to the TPF's brute force."[87]

The riot was big news the next day in the mainstream media as well as on the streets. That evening, a large crowd gathered in front of the Stonewall Inn. As the TPF assembled across the street, the crowd grew into the thou-sands. When the TPF moved to break up the crowd, another riot broke out. Bitter about their losses the previous night, the cops attacked with fervor. Exhilarated by their victory, the gays responded in kind. Casualties were seri-ous on both sides by the time the fighting finally stopped at 4:00 a.m. Tension stalked the streets of Greenwich Village for three more nights, with a smaller-scale riot erupting on the fourth night.[88]

The violence finally abated, but the repercussions had just begun. Although many ridiculed the rioters, others suggested that "Stonewall was just the flip side of the Black revolt." Stonewall's spirit of self-assertion spread through the country, giving birth to the gay liberation movement. Within a decade, gay and lesbian activist groups emerged on many college campuses and in all major cities. Homosexuality was declassified as a mental disorder; homosexuals were included in antidiscrimination laws and they became a potent political force. The 1969 riot was such a significant turning point in American attitudes toward homosexuality that, as one Stonewall participant declared, "It's the revolution!"[89]

New York City's turmoil made the mayoral election of 1969 a referen-dum on the white backlash. Resentment had long been building among work-ing- and middle-class whites who felt that their quality of life was declining just as (if not because) the nation was pouring resources into helping blacks. Crime, riots, and endless protests added instability to insecurity and turned anxiety into anger. Lindsay's sympathy for blacks seemed to parallel a lack of sympathy for whites. "What the hell does Lindsay care about me?" asked an ironworker. "None of them politicians gives a goddam. All they worry about is the niggers."[90]

The welfare rights movement exacerbated that anxiety, especially since New York City had the strongest, most aggressive welfare rights organization in the country. 1968 witnessed sit-ins and demonstrations, vandalism of welfare offices, and conflict with the police. In response, the Lindsay administration relaxed restrictive welfare procedures and grants. The result was a huge increase in the number of welfare recipients at a massive cost to the city. Then, in January 1969, the *New York Times* revealed extensive embezzlement and theft of welfare-related monies. New Yorkers and the nation, including President Richard Nixon, were incensed. Taxpayers became increasingly hostile to welfare and blamed Lindsay for "the welfare crisis."[91]

The demonization of Lindsay avalanched when fifteen inches of snow blanketed Gotham on February 9, 1969. The city was caught unawares and unprepared. Its trucks were in disrepair, its snow removal administrator was out of town, and its sanitation union was less than eager to help the mayor. For three days, schools, airports, train stations, and subways remained closed. Half of the forty-two people who died as a result of the storm lived in Queens, the last borough to be plowed. Ralph Bunche, under-secretary general of the U.N. and a Queens resident, indignantly called it "a shameful performance by the great City of New York" and criticized Lindsay for treating Queens like a "second-class borough."[92]

That refrain resonated widely during the 1969 mayoral election and solidified anti-Lindsay sentiment. The city seemed to be out of control and Lindsay was heckled wherever he went. Among others, former Mayor Wagner entered the Democratic primary and berated Lindsay for having created "the Cold City, the Heartless City, the Unlivable City." The author Norman Mailer and the journalist Jimmy Breslin campaigned to save New York from "a hideous death" by making it independent of the state, just as Fernando Wood had suggested a century earlier.[93]

In the end, the Democrats chose Mario Procaccino, an unassuming civil court judge who had spent his life working in the city bureaucracy. With Governor Rockefeller pointedly withholding his support for Lindsay, the Republicans chose John Marchi, a state senator from Staten Island who also was nominated by the Conservative Party. Rejected by the Republicans, the mayor created his own party for the election. In addition, he was endorsed by the Liberal Party, which believed that a Lindsay loss would kill liberalism nationwide. In their opinion, "the backlash had to be turned back."[94]

Marchi and Procaccino both appealed to the white backlash by emphasizing Ocean Hill-Brownsville, open admissions, and law and order. Marchi claimed to represent the "forgotten New Yorker," the little guys whom Lindsay had so often offended. Procaccino called Lindsay a "limousine liberal," meaning that he was too rich, too Manhattan-oriented, and too out of touch with the real people who lived in the outer boroughs.[95]

Opinion polls indicated that the public was predominantly concerned with racial issues. Consequently, voters split on racial lines, pitting minorities and Manhattan's white liberals against most ethnic whites, especially from the other four boroughs. As Breslin put it, the whole contest was about "one word—black." Accordingly, Glazer and Moynihan concluded that the 1969 election was "the first time in New York City's history [that] racial conflict... became determinative for the city's politics."[96]

Lindsay responded by combining contrition with assertion. Although apologizing for his mistakes, he affirmed his commitment to liberal principles. He focused on the Jewish vote, campaigned heavily in minority districts, and explained how the Vietnam War was draining federal financial resources from New York. Luckily, the New York Mets won their first World Series in October, providing the campaign with a timely boost. The strategy worked, but barely, with Lindsay winning only 42 percent of the electorate. Marchi and Proccacino split the white backlash vote, while Lindsay cornered 80 percent of the black vote and 60 percent of the Puerto Rican vote. The Jewish vote divided along class lines, with the middle class favoring Lindsay, but with most Jews voting against him. The white backlash had reshaped metropolitan politics.[97]

During his first term, Lindsay learned the hard way that, as he put it, Gotham was "a collection of separate, disparate interest groups" and that the mayor was "something like a circus performer walking a tightrope and juggling at the same time." Lindsay did not always perform skillfully, but he used his star power to make America consider "how greatness will remain with a country that does not act to insure greatness in the centers where its people live and work." He was encouraged by the fact that, awful as it was, the urban crisis emanating from the riots of 1964 had put the cities on America's agenda.[98]

In fact, Lindsay's national and international image was better than his local reputation because he was an advocate not just for Gotham but also for all big cities. He joined Fernando Wood, Abram Hewitt, and Fiorello LaGuardia in viewing New York expansively. He even suggested that America's big cities be totally redefined as national cities, that is, as valued federal resources rather than mere appendages of the states. Despite all the setbacks he experienced, Lindsay remained determined "to make our great city civil again, the Empire City of the world."[99]

9

Big Apple Redux
Leadership under Fire, 1970–1993

> Being Mayor of New York is an exacting if not a killing job. Any mayor of any great American city—and our mayor in particular—never has leisure and time for reflection, is always in the limelight, and is subject to the pressure of events, the impact of the unexpected and unguessable, the demand for quick decisions, the dangers of misrepresentation and error.... It is as hard for a mayor to get into the Hall of Fame as it is for a camel to pass through the eye of a needle.
>
> **—Robert Moses, 1957**[1]

Shortly after being elected to his first term as mayor in 1966, John V. Lindsay called New York "fun city," a remark for which he was resoundingly ridiculed. In his second term, people were more likely to damn New York as "fear city," decry its "mean streets," or predict its death. The rise of prostitution in Times Square further earned Gotham the label "sin city." A startling conglomeration of ills confirmed New York's image as the worst of all possible worlds. Rampant arson, ravaging disease, surging welfare roles, high unemployment, untrammeled drug use, brazen crime, filthy streets, sprawling graffiti, crumbling schools, huge rats, extensive homelessness, fiscal bankruptcy, police corruption, and political scandals horrified the nation. Gotham epitomized the problems everyone else hoped to avoid. It symbolized the urban crisis.[2]

The situation presented daunting challenges for the mayoralty, making it, as Moses pointed out, "a killing job." Yet, four men eagerly sought the limelight and the heat of urban turmoil. John V. Lindsay, Abraham D. Beame, Edward I. Koch, and David N. Dinkins had contrasting approaches to conflict. Alternately, they let the embers burn, fanned the flames, built fire-walls, or attacked the blaze so vigorously that sparks ignited new conflagrations. They risked "misrepresentation and error" rather, said Koch, than "let this city dwindle or diminish." The moment was critical, the challenge immense. For all their differences, they agreed with Koch that "We must not, we cannot, fail."[3]

In the midst of this general sense of anxiety, the president of the New York Convention and Visitors Bureau decided to offset the city's negative image by reviving the old Big Apple symbol. Considerable polishing brought about a magical rehabilitation, one that paralleled the city's economic revival after 1977. In 1975, the year of the fiscal crisis, the graphic artist Milton Glaser designed his famous "I Love New York" poster, which became an instant success. To be sure, it was a public relations ploy that glossed over social problems, but it met a dire psychic need. Ultimately, the Big Apple was redeemed—in image as well as in reality.[4]

The World Trade Center was the physical manifestation of the city's ups and downs during this period. In order to revitalize the downtown business district, David Rockefeller, president of Chase Manhattan Bank, and his brother, Nelson Rockefeller, governor of New York State, used their influence to get the Port Authority of New York and New Jersey to float bonds and condemn land in order to build a massive office plaza downtown. An upscale residential community called Battery Park City would complete the "golden ghetto."[5]

To many less prominent people, such construction meant the destruction of the Hudson River docks along with the small businesses and industries dependent on them. The city lost at least thirty thousand jobs and important elements of the economic diversity that had rendered it resilient over time. Instead, financial and real estate interests (FIRE) now dominated Gotham's economy. As in the 1820s, control over the land bespoke a major shift of economic priorities.[6]

Begun in 1966 and completed in 1973, the World Trade Center's two 110-story skyscrapers (sometimes dubbed Nelson and David) became icons of the city's economic and political power. For years, however, they remained largely vacant because of a recession and a glut of office space in Manhattan. Even with New York State and the Port Authority as tax-free tenants, the buildings were not fully rented until the boom of the nineties. After one bombing attempt in 1993, the Twin Towers collapsed on September 11, 2001, when terrorists intentionally crashed two jumbo jets into them. The subsequent fires caused the structures to implode, killing the greatest number of civilians in the most brazen attack on American soil. Significantly, Milton Glaser revised his poster to reflect the fact that, because of its wounded heart, many people now loved New York "more than ever."[7]

Gotham was always subject to forces beyond its control. A recession lasting from 1969 to 1977, punctuated by the 1975 fiscal crisis, spelled serious economic losses in terms of population, jobs, manufactures, shipping, and corporate headquarters. In time, the city's economy rebounded through growth in the corporate and consumer service sectors. A quarter of the biggest multinational corporations were located in the city, with sixteen others nearby. Although the stock market crash of 1987 led to a three-year recession, it was followed by recovery in the 1990s. Again Gotham became a magnet for the ambitious and a haven for the rich, but the boom and bust cycles exacted a price.[8]

During this same period, New York City experienced regeneration by immigration. In 1965, the federal government reversed forty years of immigration restriction to welcome peoples from around the world. The newest immigrants hailed less from Europe than from the Caribbean, Latin America, the Middle East, Russia, South Asia, East Asia, and Africa. Like previous groups, they generated their own ethnic economic niches and neighborhood revivals. As they flocked to New York and as older residents moved out, the city's complexion changed. By 1990, people of color comprised the majority of New Yorkers, making it truly "a global city" and changing its politics accordingly.[9]

The political scene was already complicated by diverse constituencies and multiple sources of power. The old days of centralized control under one party boss boosted by patronage were over. Instead, there was a vast bureaucracy staffed by a civil service system that had a life of its own divorced from elected leaders. The mayor also was constrained by power struggles between ethnic interests, neighborhood interests, and borough interests, each with its own political machine. In addition, the state remained an important (and often hostile) policy maker. It would take a leader of consummate skill to negotiate this political minefield. When Dinkins was inaugurated in 1990, Lindsay, Beame, and Koch warned that he faced "overwhelming" odds. In truth, said the *New York Times,* they had all been thrown "into the fire" on becoming mayor. The job was inherently hot.[10]

After the divisive sixties, the demands on the mayor were immense. One wonders with Moses whether any human being could have fulfilled all the expectations, met all the needs, withstood all the pressures, and performed all the roles of being the most visible representative of the nation's most visible city. From 1970 to 1996, conflict in New York tested the nature of leadership as Gotham reeled from protest to protest over local, national, and international issues. They ranged from prison conditions, education, housing, and homelessness to racism, police brutality, women's rights, AIDS, and the Vietnam War. As the city weathered some of the most difficult storms of its history, it served as a barometer of America's anxieties.

New York's fiscal crisis became a code word for urban irresponsibility. The South Bronx was the symbol of urban despair. Place names like Forest Hills,

Bensonhurst, Howard Beach, and Crown Heights were emblems of urban strife. Blacks, Jews, Italians, Koreans, Haitians, and Dominicans intensified the conflicts. It was all overwhelming. At his 1978 inauguration, Koch acknowledged that "These have been hard times. We have been tested by fire." Nevertheless, he insisted that Gotham would prevail because, even "in adversity," New York "towers above any other city in the world."[11]

LINDSAY AND LEADERSHIP

Controversy is part of New York's vitality and none of us would have it any different. But we can at least recognize another loyalty beyond politics, and that is loyalty to this city and to its future—our future.

—John V. Lindsay, January 1, 1970[12]

Lindsay's 1969 campaign slogan acknowledged that being mayor of New York City was "the second toughest job in America" and his 1970 inaugural address reflected that challenge. He recognized (even if he did not resolve) the dilemmas of mayoral leadership in a conflict-ridden city. After what had been a strenuous first term, Lindsay knew all too well that "it is not easy to live with difficulty and turmoil. At times it is barely endurable." His encounters with reality had taught him "not to plan on promises and dreams." Nevertheless, he was still motivated to work for "the kind of city that speaks to the best within us." Lindsay's idealism had dimmed, but it had not died. In fact, his enduring liberal commitments were his undoing.[13]

The events of Lindsay's second term challenged his resolve and exposed his shortcomings. For example, in 1970 inmates mounted protests against horrific prison conditions in five jails in three boroughs involving thirty-two hostages. The first riot occurred in August at the Tombs in lower Manhattan, where inmates held three guards hostage for seven hours and controlled the facility for nine days. The riots were organized by two radical groups—the Black Panther Party and the Puerto Rican Young Lords. As they ignited mattresses, clothing, and furniture, the prisoners declared their intention "to burn ourselves out of here."[14]

In October, more riots erupted at the Tombs as well as at the Queens House of Detention in Long Island City, the Kew Gardens, Queens prison, and the Brooklyn House of Detention. Lindsay considered it "the most difficult moment" of his mayoralty because of the potential for bloodshed. The administration managed to secure surrender without having to storm the jails, but the guards later took revenge on their own. Although Lindsay won praise for talking with the prisoners for three hours, he also was criticized for legitimizing minority radicals and for allowing prison conditions to deteriorate in the first place. He seemed long on liberal sympathies and crisis management, but short on serious problem solving.[15]

Lindsay dismayed many people by supporting the women's liberation movement. Formed in 1966, the National Organization of Women (NOW) conducted some of its most effective protests in Gotham, such as a demonstration against gender-based job advertisements in the *New York Times* and a sit-in against gender stereotyping at the *Ladies Home Journal*. In 1970, NOW sponsored a nationwide Women's Strike for Equality. Between ten thousand and fifty thousand marchers took over Fifth Avenue despite police efforts to block them. That summer, following a suit involving McSorley's, an all-male bar on East 7th Street near Cooper Union, Lindsay signed legislation making it illegal to discriminate against women in public facilities.[16]

Lindsay's liberalism made him vulnerable to attack, especially as the nation became polarized by the Vietnam War, which Lindsay often criticized for diverting funds away from the cities. The shooting death of four antiwar protesters by National Guardsmen at Ohio's Kent State University inspired a Wall Street antiwar rally by a thousand college and high school students on May 8, 1970. In a counterdemonstration, two hundred construction workers attacked the students with fists, pipes, tools, and hard hats. On what became known as "Bloody Friday," ten thousand spectators witnessed construction workers taking over the steps of Federal Hall while waving U.S. flags and singing "God Bless America."[17]

Descending on City Hall, the men demanded that officials raise the flag, which was flying at half-mast in memory of the students killed at Kent State. Then they crossed the street to Pace College, where they beat up students and vandalized the building. Lindsay defended the students' right to protest, criticized the cops for failing to protect them, and called the violence "appalling." His position inflamed the hard hats, who continued to demonstrate during lunch hour for two more weeks. On May 20, they led a march of between 60,000 and 150,000 people through downtown Manhattan. Lindsay was burned in effigy and vilified as the "Red Mayor."[18]

The historian Joshua Freeman explains that the demonstrations converted construction workers into social symbols. They became icons of traditional masculinity during an era when conventional gender roles were being challenged. In addition, they represented the white working classes, that is, loyal laborers who were the backbone of the country but who felt ignored by "bleeding-heart" liberals like Lindsay. President Richard Nixon capitalized on the event to seek support from labor union leaders who gladly gave him a ceremonial hard hat. Nixon relished championing the "forgotten American" and embarrassing his elegant critic, the liberal Republican mayor of New York.[19]

Lindsay antagonized the middle classes, too. In 1971, the mayor announced plans to build "scatter-site housing" in Forest Hills, Queens for the purpose of promoting integration and providing affordable shelter for 840 poor families. If he assumed that the middle-class Jewish community would be too liberal to oppose the new public housing project, events soon proved otherwise. Marches were orchestrated and rallies were held; racial rhetoric escalated, and physical fights erupted. Surprising his liberal friends, Manhattan Congressman Edward Koch went to Queens to lend support.[20]

Activists called the mayor "Adolf Lindsay" and carried torches in front of the home of the African American chairman of the city's Housing Authority, reminding him of the Ku Klux Klan. There were dire predictions that criminals, drug addicts, and teenage gangs (often code words for minorities) would overrun the neighborhood. The struggle to "Save Forest Hills" became a struggle to "Save Middle Class America." Still, Lindsay held firm, believing that his policy was morally right.[21]

The endless rancor forced Lindsay to seek help from Mario Cuomo, the lawyer (and future governor) who had resolved a similar situation in Corona, Queens in 1966. After several more months of negotiations with the community, local politicians, city administrators, commissions, and boards, Cuomo proposed smaller buildings, primarily for the elderly, which were successfully absorbed into the neighborhood. Nonetheless, the debacle had been destructive and the mayor admitted that it caused more acrimony than it was worth. For his critics, it was just another example of how "John Lindsay gave good intentions a bad name."[22]

In 1972, the Lindsay administration tangled with residents in Canarsie, Brooklyn over a plan to bus thirty-two minority children from a local housing project to a neighborhood junior high school. Because the school was already 30 percent minority, the issue was not integration, per se, but the prospect of gradually "tipping" the student body to the point where the school became predominantly black. The Jewish and Italian residents of Canarsie were determined to protect their neighborhood from the fate of Brownsville, from which they had recently fled. Accordingly, parents occupied the school for three days and kept 90 percent of the children home for two weeks. Racial fevers rose. Bands of black and white youths roamed the streets armed with pipes and chains. "Both in Canarsie and the nation," concludes the historian Jonathan Reider, "the system choked on its conflicts."

From 1970 to 1972, the image of the mayor and his city was further damaged by the Knapp Commission's hearings on police corruption. After trying to get the administration to address the issue for years, two policemen, David Durk and Frank Serpico, took their evidence to the *New York Times*, which, as in the Tweed case a century earlier, emblazoned its account of official graft on the front page. Four days of damning articles forced Lindsay to stop defending his police commissioner and condone an inquiry. Lindsay's reluctance in this instance contrasted with his frequent moralisms and undercut his credibility.[23]

The Commission discovered that corruption was systemic in the New York City police department. It encompassed minor offenses like taking free meals and major transgressions like selling heroin, cooperating with the Mafia, or accepting monthly payoffs to protect illegal businesses. Cops covered up the corruption with a "blue code of silence" and anyone who broke the code faced isolation as "a rotten apple." Retribution also could be more serious, possibly accounting for the bullet lodged in Serpico's head during a drug raid. The Knapp Commission blamed the Lindsay administration for neglecting the whole situation.[24]

The police commissioner left, three hundred cops were indicted, and sixty more resigned. Antagonism toward the police intensified and they were commonly called "pigs," particularly in minority communities. The police responded by hardening their code of silence, staging slowdowns, and avoiding dangerous assignments. As a result, crime rates surged and, ironically, cops themselves were ambushed and assassinated, one at Malcolm X's old Mosque #7. In 1970 and 1971, eighteen cops were targeted and killed on the streets. Conflict in Gotham had acquired calamitous new proportions.[25]

Suspicion that New York was out of control seemed confirmed when the Brooklyn slum of Brownsville went up in flames in 1970 and again in 1971. Fires of garbage piled high in the streets and fires set in local stores reflected desperation turned to rage. The riot of May 7, 1971, which emerged from a protest against state retrenchment of social services, logged one hundred fires, fifty burned-out buildings, and scores of injuries, including over thirty police and firemen. Lindsay criticized the rioting, but not the rioters, and blamed events on the state. Brownsville became the latest evidence of his inability to defuse the tinderbox that passed for a city.[26]

Frustrated by local realities and convinced that New York City's problems were part of a larger dynamic, Lindsay turned to national politics. In August 1971, he joined the Democratic Party in order to seek its presidential nomination. Lindsay ran as a liberal, antiwar, pro-city candidate pledged to a vigorous federal attack on urban problems. However, his causes had limited appeal and his Forest Hills enemies shadowed him on the campaign trail, embarrassing him before Miami's retired New York Jews. By April 1972, Lindsay was out of the race, having garnered a mere 7 percent of the vote in both the Florida and Wisconsin primaries. Chastened, he returned to Gotham.[27]

Nationally, Lindsay faced indifference to his urban crusade; locally, he faced disagreement over his urban priorities. The more he stood by his principles, the less successful he was. In March 1973, he decided not to run for mayor again. Lindsay could take credit for being the one who, as he put it, "woke up the nation to the urban crisis." Nonetheless, his sense of purpose often backfired and his charisma did not compensate for his contentiousness. In 1965, Robert Moses had predicted that "if you elect a matinee idol mayor, you're going to get a musical-comedy administration." By 1973, Lindsay had become a tragic figure.[28]

BEAME AND LEADERSHIP

Subjecting America's largest city to humiliation and impoverishment does not enhance either the economy or the moral fiber of our nation. It is unimaginable to me that any other head of state in this world would abandon the premier city of his nation or punish its people as an object lesson.

—**Abraham D. Beame, 1975**[29]

The 1975 fiscal crisis was a devastating phenomenon for this city, other cities, and the nation. Because of its role as a world financial center, New York City's financial plight also affected cities around the globe. A debacle long in coming, but previously unimaginable, the prospect of New York's insolvency underscored national hostility to cities in general and Gotham in particular. It doomed the liberalism that had dominated the city's politics since the LaGuardia era and had distinguished its social contract since colonial times. For labor, the poor, and public services the fiscal crisis was a true disaster. New York would never be the same again.[30]

Abraham D. Beame was an unlikely leader for such a critical moment. He was a well-meaning but uninspiring and unimposing product of working-class Brooklyn and the Democratic machine. Trained in accounting at the City College of New York (CCNY), Beame was a career civil servant who was appointed deputy budget director in 1948 and budget director in 1952. He was elected comptroller in 1961 and 1969, lost a mayoralty bid to Lindsay in 1965, but won in 1973. New York's first Jewish mayor, Beame was deeply indebted to the city that had given him such a successful career, the Everyman's American Dream. As he commented in 1973, "All I ever wanted in life was to be mayor of the greatest city in the world."[31]

When Beame took office, he faced a crisis that was partly of his own making. He had campaigned as the man who "knows the buck" and, having been the city's chief financial officer, he was well aware of its desperate straits. For years he allowed the city to spend more than it earned and to borrow more than it could ever hope to repay. Most objectionably, he used bookkeeping tricks to hide the shortfall between revenues and expenditures. Anticipated income was optimistically inflated and one year's deficit was rolled over into the next year's budget.[32]

At the same time, Beame was far from being the only culprit. The exodus of middle-class taxpayers to the suburbs hardly helped and a national recession lasting from 1969 to 1977 compounded the problem. Moreover, benefits granted to the large municipal workforce were expensive. Special favors, leases, and contracts reminiscent of the Tweed era were costly. So, too, were efforts to alleviate poverty, provide services, and stimulate social mobility. Among urban institutions considered especially extravagant were the municipal hospital system and the City University of New York (CUNY).[33]

Even when programs like welfare and Medicaid were cosponsored by state and federal governments, the city's costs were astronomical because of its size. Not only did the federal government impose expensive financial obligations on the city for every federal grant, but it also started defunding the Great Society programs in the 1970s while shifting national resources from the Northeast to the Sunbelt states. The city paid far more into the federal treasury than it got back. To make matters worse, New York State absorbed less of the bill for social services than other states. Gotham was stuck between a policy rock and a financial hard place.[34]

By the time Beame became mayor, the city's debt was so huge that bankers lost confidence in New York's ability to pay its bills and redeem its loans. When the financial community finally refused to support any more municipal bonds in April 1975, the city faced bankruptcy. Appeals to President Gerald R. Ford were of no avail. He chastized the city for its liberal policies and declared that the federal government should not be expected to cure an "insidious disease" it had not caused. The president's words were so harsh that they inspired the infamous *Daily News* headline, "FORD TO CITY: DROP DEAD."[35]

Nelson Rockefeller, now vice president, tried to influence the president, but, in the Capitol, contempt for Gotham's "fiscal obscenities" was strong. Incredibly, said Beame, the federal government seemed to believe "that sacrificing our city will somehow exorcise the demons plaguing all of Urban America." Ultimately, pressure from fifteen other American cities and several abroad (all afraid that New York's fall would harm their own financial stability) forced the federal government to provide high-interest loans that the city is still paying off. Ironically, it was the municipal workers who really rescued the city by agreeing to use their pension funds to buy city bonds.[36]

In what would have been Fernando Wood's worst nightmare, New York State acquired almost total power over city finances. It created two independent monitoring agencies—the Municipal Assistance Corporation (MAC) and the Emergency Financial Control Board (EFCB)—both of which were dominated by bankers and businessmen with token input from elected officials. Mayor Beame became irrelevant. Now Gotham's future was in the hands of an investment banker, Felix G. Rohatyn, who, as chairman of the MAC and key member of the EFCB, seemed heir to J. P. Morgan. As in the 1930s, the banks once again ran New York City and Rohatyn set about making cuts that, in his own words, would have a "shock impact."[37]

A strike by sanitation men made New York "stink city," but demonstrations by teachers and hospital workers failed to stop the cutbacks. Nor did a police union pamphlet warning tourists to avoid "Fear City." Sixty thousand municipal employees were fired, many of them minorities. The Board of Education lost fully a quarter of its teachers. Class sizes were increased while counseling, athletics, the arts, adult education, and summer school were drastically decreased. At CUNY, two thousand full-time faculty members were fired and 130 years of free tuition came to a close. Welfare grants were reduced. A transit fare hike imposed a regressive tax on the working and middle classes.[38]

The fiscal crisis formalized a major shift in public policy, whereby the city's private interests prevailed over its public interests. In New York, as in the nation, disinvestment in social services became a panacea. The new ethos was best captured by Roger Starr, head of the city's Housing Development Administration, who wanted to "reverse the role of the city" by reducing services for the poor so that they would move elsewhere. Breaking with centuries of history, Starr's concept of "planned shrinkage" was based on the premise that New York "can no longer be the place of opportunity." The firestorm that resulted from this statement cost Starr his job, but the man and his ideas remained influential.[39]

The poor, the working classes, and the middle classes suffered the most from the fiscal crisis. The beneficiaries were the FIRE power holders—the bankers, realtors, and businessmen—who translated their control over public policy into lower taxes on stock transfers, real estate, and personal income. Taxes on everyone else were increased. To the writer Ken Auletta, the fiscal crisis was "liberalism's Vietnam," a traumatic event that inaugurated and legitimized the conservative revolution of the 1980s. The long-term impact of New York City's fiscal crisis was even greater than the short-term pain it induced.[40]

In 1977, a major electrical blackout precipitated riots and demonstrated that the fiscal crisis had only intensified the ghetto crisis. Everyone seemed to agree that bad conditions had gotten worse. Unlike the upheavals of the sixties, these riots were not part of a larger social movement or racial protest. Rather, they were perpetrated by people who, with a 30 percent unemployment rate (60 percent among young minority men), had "nothing to lose." An earlier riot-free blackout had occurred during the winter of 1965 at 5:30 p.m. when proprietors were still in their stores. By contrast, the 1977 blackout occurred during a July heat wave at 9:30 p.m. Almost immediately, riots erupted, and, for the first time in Gotham's history, poor neighborhoods in all five boroughs were engulfed by violence simultaneously.[41]

Thirty neighborhoods suffered substantial damage and over sixteen hundred businesses, white owned as well as black owned, reported property losses. People brazenly stole clothing, food, appliances, furniture, and even cars. The scene combined carnival, criminality, and chaos. Under orders not to shoot, the police made over thirty-seven hundred arrests, forcing the city to reopen the Tombs, which had been shut down as "too decrepit." Prisoners took over the Bronx House of Detention and the South Bronx went up in flames. Facing thirty-nine hundred alarms citywide, firemen focused on the thousand worst fires and neglected the rest. The most devastated area was Bushwick, Brooklyn, which became one "mass conflagration." For Beame, it was "a night of terror."[42]

Fire and looting were lethal partners. Stores were looted and then set ablaze, but arson predated the riots. By the 1970s, arson accounted for the majority of structural fires in the city's most depressed areas. As Dennis Smith explained in his *Report from Engine Co. 82* (1972), arson made fire-fighting particularly treacherous. Many of these fires were not mere vandalism because property owners seeking fire insurance were paying teenagers to torch abandoned buildings. It was more profitable to burn than to build after banks stopped granting loans in poor neighborhoods, a practice called "redlining" for the red marks drawn around those areas on real estate maps. Fire fed and was fed by the urban crisis. Soon it was being memorialized in popular movies such as *The Warriors*.[43]

When off-duty policemen were asked to report for work during the riots, over a thousand refused, so the force was undermanned. State troopers were sent in to help restore order. However, because the National Guard was not requested, Beame was accused of coddling the rioters. He gave press briefings, held staff meetings, visited various neighborhoods, blamed Con Edison, and asked New Yorkers to help rebuild. For starters, he contributed one hundred dollars. The press coverage was welcome in an election year, but Beame's dull, bureaucratic style never inspired the kind of confidence that Lindsay's charisma had evoked during the riots of the 1960s. Instead, the seventy-one-year-old mayor seemed "tired and withered."[44]

Reaction to the riot was mixed. Dismayed by all the fires and theft, urban leaders in the United States and Europe reassessed their own electrical systems. New Yorkers were particularly distressed. When a CUNY historian, Herbert Gutman, suggested some similarity between the blackout riots of 1977 and the food riots of 1902, *New York Times* readers protested that the earlier riot was justified by hunger while the current one was an unjustifiable rampage by "animals." The *Times* editors were less disparaging and called on the nation to face the persistent problems of race and poverty. The warnings of the sixties had not been heeded, and the nation had been "put on notice again." It ignored reality at its own risk.[45]

Mayor Beame and Governor Hugh Carey asked that New York City be declared a disaster area, but President Jimmy Carter denied their request. Many thought the city had "been told to drop dead again" and the *Times* chastised Carter for focusing on foreign affairs while its greatest city proved so "flammable." Vernon E. Jordan, executive director of the National Urban League, urged his friend Carter not to dismiss the riots as merely a "New York tragedy." The challenge, he suggested, was to see beyond the "technical" problem of electrical failure in order to appreciate the "human" problem of failing to create a fairer society.[46]

President Carter was stung by all the criticism and, while speaking at the United Nations that fall, decided to visit a riot-torn site. The famous photograph of the president amidst the ruins of Charlotte Street in the South Bronx brought the Blackout Riots and the urban crisis into focus. Instantly, the South Bronx became a metaphor for disaster in the nation's cities, a modern Five Points. Literally and figuratively, it seemed to be *The Fire Next Time*, about which writer James Baldwin had warned America in 1963. At the very least, it was *The Fire Next Door*, which investigative television reporter Bill Moyers had recently depicted in a devastating critique of the burning Bronx. To Carter and the nation, the whole situation was truly "sobering."[47]

Although he had not been able to control events, Beame understood their significance. Like Lindsay, he called for a redefinition of the role of cities in the country and an appreciation of their vital national functions as markets, cultural centers, and the gateway for immigrants. Sadly, he asked, "If we allow our cities to decay and die, who will, when that day of reckoning comes, bail out America?" Beame was a lackluster leader, but he loved New York.[48]

KOCH AND LEADERSHIP

Without question, this city has made mistakes. But our mistakes have been those of the heart. In my administration, I intend to bring the heart and the head together.

—**Edward I. Koch, January 2, 1978**[49]

The Blackout Riots had an immediate impact on the 1977 Democratic mayoral primary. Liberal and minority candidates were thrown on the defensive, including Manhattan African American Borough President Percy Sutton, Bronx Puerto Rican Borough President Herman Badillo, and feminist former Congresswoman Bella Abzug. New York's secretary of state, Mario M. Cuomo, hoped to ride out the crisis as a compromiser. However, one candidate took full advantage of the moment by attacking Mayor Beame for not suppressing the riots more aggressively. For him, the situation justified using more head than heart.[50]

Edward I. Koch, graduate of the City College and New York University Law School, had been getting tougher for a while. A Jew who was associated with liberal causes, reform politics, and the civil rights movement, Koch served as a one-term councilman and a five-term congressman representing Greenwich Village and Lindsay's old Upper East Side "silk stocking" district. By backing conservatives during the 1972 Forest Hills controversy, Koch consciously crossed "my Rubicon" in order to broaden his base of support. In the 1977 campaign, he cleverly conflated talk of the death penalty with the Blackout Riots and the "Son of Sam" serial murders in Queens. Koch cultivated a new persona as "a liberal with sanity."[51]

At the same time, in meetings with key African American politicians, Koch promised to keep Harlem's Sydenham Hospital open, to appoint minorities to administrative positions, and to stop calling welfare program administrators "poverty pimps." Meanwhile, he deftly forged alliances with county Democratic bosses—the very men he so often derided as clubhouse hacks. In order to quell rumors that he was homosexual, he campaigned with former Miss America, Bess Myerson. This unique liberal-conservative, reformer-establishment coalition enabled Koch to win the Democratic nomination and the general election. Serving three terms from 1978 to 1989, he revitalized the mayoralty and dominated the city as no one had since LaGuardia.[52]

Once in office, Koch not only solidified his coalition but expanded it by pursuing taxation and real estate policies that benefited Manhattan's FIRE sector. With the economy rebounding after 1977, he was able to balance the budget again. The most draconian cuts had already been made under Beame, but Koch continued to pare down public services in his first term while increasing spending in his second and third terms. Thus, earning a reputation as a fiscal conservative early on enabled him to protect his political base later on. Koch was so skillful politically that, in 1981, he received the endorsement of both the Democratic and the Republican parties and won three-quarters of the vote. However, he was too identified with Gotham to defeat Cuomo for the governor's seat in 1982.[53]

Koch was one of New York's most contentious, albeit charming, cheerful, and witty, mayors. He bounded through the city asking anyone and everyone, "How'm I doin'?" Like LaGuardia, Koch was a master of drama and symbolism. For example, his war on subway graffiti broadcast his resolve to restore order and public confidence in the city. Unlike LaGuardia, whose desk he proudly used, Koch promoted conservative social priorities. In fact, Koch felt so secure about his power base that he openly defied his liberal white and black allies by eliminating the Commission on the Status of Women, cutting funds for CUNY's community colleges, opposing affirmative-action hiring and retrenching poverty programs.[54]

In the summer of 1979, Koch violated his preelection pledge and announced plans to close Harlem's Sydenham Hospital, which was New York's first full-service hospital to hire African American doctors. Although old and small, the hospital at 123rd Street and Manhattan Avenue was considered essential for a neighborhood with a high mortality rate and few medical facilities. Harlem's Congressman Charles Rangel, who replaced Adam Clayton Powell Jr. in 1971, accused Koch of "planned genocide." The community created a Coalition to Save Sydenham Hospital. Opposition mounted as the NAACP, the New York Urban League, labor leaders, and local politicians pressured the mayor to keep Sydenham open. Koch was pelted by tomatoes and eggs whenever he appeared in public.[55]

On September 15, 1980, sixty people occupied the hospital, renamed it Fort Sydenham, and hung the mayor in effigy. Crowds gathered and there was a brief riot. One thousand demonstrators turned out the next day and hundreds returned every day. After ten days, Rangel, who had supported the protests, helped defuse the situation and the remaining nine protesters, including Brooklyn's activist Reverend Herbert Daughtry, were removed from the hospital peacefully. Although replacing the hospital with a clinic was a real defeat, the protesters saw their struggle as part of a new spirit of resistance that would eventually forge "a new day for Blacks and Puerto Ricans here in the Big Apple."[56]

By closing Sydenham, Koch opened an unbridgeable gulf between himself and New York City's minorities. That gap had grown since his 1977 "poverty pimps" remark and a 1978 article citing his comment that "the black community is very anti-Semitic." To African Americans and Puerto Ricans, Koch was not only "anti-poor," but also "anti-black." Consequently, saving Sydenham developed into a major cause for African American churches, politicians, labor, and civic groups in and beyond the city. Nationally it was seen as part of the continuing struggle of African Americans for "self-determination, self-respect and the fight for dignity."[57]

Koch also alienated labor unions. From the start, he had campaigned as a fiscal belt-tightener who would control municipal workers and change the climate of labor negotiations in Gotham. Decrying the fact that "under Beame and Lindsay, the labor unions owned the city," he resolved that they would do so "No more!" Consequently, when the Transit Workers Union (TWU) called a strike on April 1, 1980, Koch was defiant. Instead of sitting at the bargaining table, he rushed to the Brooklyn Bridge, where he applauded New Yorkers walking to work and dismissed his critics as "Wackos."[58]

The strike was complicated by division within the union between the old-line white leadership and a membership increasingly comprised of minorities who were skeptical of backroom deals made by union leaders with administration officials. In a post-fiscal crisis world, the workers understood that the financial community had vast influence over public policy and that anti-union sentiment was strong. Determined to counter these trends, the dissident TWU locals opposed the initial agreement made by their parent union with the city and walked out. For eleven days, the city's mass transit system was paralyzed.[59]

Disregarding widespread support for Koch, the state-run Metropolitan Transportation Authority (MTA) granted the TWU a surprisingly generous settlement. The mayor proclaimed it a sellout. However, in a larger sense, Koch had prevailed by galvanizing the public opposition to municipal labor unions that had been germinating since the sixties. In fact, says Joshua Freeman, the 1980 transit strike was the last gasp of workers' resistance to the austerity fostered by the fiscal crisis. Antilabor, pro-business economic policies reigned supreme.[60] (See Figure 20 following page 150)

Although he had defended gay rights in Congress, Koch reacted slowly to the Acquired Immune Deficiency Syndrome (AIDS) epidemic. With one-fifth of America's AIDS patients, New York City was "the world capitol of AIDS." Mainstream society, politicians, the medical profession, and many gays themselves ignored the problem until spurred to action by Larry Kramer, a New York novelist and playwright. In 1983, he helped form the Gay Men's Health Crisis (GMHC) and, in 1987, organized a more "impolite, abrasive, rude" organization. Aggressive to the core, ACT UP (an acronym for AIDS Coalition to Unleash Power) adopted the slogan: Silence=Death.[61]

In December of 1989, ACT UP staged a spectacular protest at St. Patrick's Cathedral targeting John Cardinal O'Connor's role in preventing politicians from addressing the AIDS crisis. While five thousand people marched outside the church with a huge mock condom labeled Cardinal O'Condom, some went inside and orchestrated a "die-in" during which they threw condoms in the air and chained themselves to the pews. One man crushed a communion wafer, threw it down, and proclaimed that "opposing safe sex is murder." He was immediately arrested along with over a hundred others.[62]

Not to be outdone, O'Connor ceremoniously purified the church and solemnly condemned the protest as sacrilege. ACT UP was left defending itself to a largely unsympathetic public because, said the Times, they had "turned honorable dissent into dishonorable disruption." In other words, they had been too offensive. Over time, however, it was precisely these bold tactics that pushed the AIDS crisis onto the public agenda. By the end of his mayoralty, Koch was allotting substantial funds for AIDS clinics, housing, and counseling, although not for preventive programs.[63]

Koch's inaction on AIDS may have been partly a result of his preoccupation with scandals that were tearing apart his administration. As the exposures and arrests expanded during 1986 and 1987, it appeared that the city government Koch claimed to have reformed was actually rife with corruption. Ultimately, six of his highest officials and almost 250 lower officials faced jail sentences. Although Koch himself was never implicated in the malfeasance, the scandals devastated him personally and professionally. The 1987 stock market crash made matters worse. Perhaps it was no accident that *The Bonfire of the Vanities*, Tom Wolfe's New York novel about the limits of arrogance, wealth, and power, was published in 1987.[64]

Koch also was battered politically by several conflicts that occurred from 1986 to 1989, dominating his third term and further polarizing the city. The first incident was in Howard Beach, Queens, in December 1986 when three African American men were stranded after their car broke down in a predominantly Italian American neighborhood. As they left a pizza parlor on Cross Bay Boulevard where they had tried to use a telephone, the blacks were attacked by a dozen whites with baseball bats, bricks, and tire irons shouting "Niggers, you don't belong here." Trying to get away, one of the black men ran onto a highway, where he was struck by a car and killed.[65]

Koch condemned "racial bigotry" and compared the attack to a Southern lynching. Furor emanated from the black community and a new grassroots protest movement emerged. It was led by the brash civil rights activist, Reverend Al Sharpton, a Brooklyn College dropout who had been preaching since the age of ten. Asserting the right of blacks to enter any neighborhood in the city, Sharpton conducted a hundred-car motorcade through Howard Beach and treated all the protesters to pizza. He was intentionally confrontational. Boldly, the marchers proclaimed, "Howard Beach, have you heard? This is not Johannesburg!" In retaliation, the protesters were cursed at, called Mau Maus, and told to go home.[66]

Anger grew as the arrests were delayed. On a freezing January 21, 1987 (Martin Luther King Jr.'s birthday), Sharpton and five thousand people marched down Fifth Avenue for a "Day of Outrage." Blacks across the country held sympathetic marches, but Koch termed the protests "ridiculous" and "racist." Rangel led a delegation of African American politicians to City Hall to express concern. Sharpton led march after march and tied up the subways when he and others jumped onto the tracks at Brooklyn's Borough Hall station in December 1987. Sharpton wanted to "expose New York before the nation," but he was often dismissed as a publicity-seeking clown and rabble-rouser.[67]

Public pressure forced Governor Cuomo to appoint a special prosecutor for the case. The trial brought three convictions for manslaughter (instead of murder) followed by a two-year delay before the sentences actually began. Blacks were bitter. Howard Beach seemed to show how alienated from each other the black and white communities had grown since the sixties, and many blamed Koch for the divide. According to Rangel, the problem was that Koch was "not just insensitive. He knows exactly what he's doing. He has consciously cultivated the backlash."[68]

A second conflict occurred in the sweltering heat of August 7, 1988, when Tompkins Square once again became the center of struggle. As in 1874, the East Village park was a gathering place for the homeless, but it had also become a haven for loud music and hard drugs. Concerns over noise were paralleled by concerns over real estate values as the neighborhood was slowly gentrifying. To some park-goers, this subtext made the conflict a "class war." Pressured by realtors and residents, the Koch administration started enforcing a previously neglected 1:00 a.m. curfew. Hundreds of people staged a protest that led to a full-scale, five-hour riot approximating those of the sixties.[69]

When it became clear, however, that it was the 450 policemen, not the protesters, who were to blame for the riot, the city was stunned. Reports emerged of cops shouting racial epithets, clubbing protesters, attacking bystanders, and assaulting photographers. Admitting that his force was at fault, African American Police Commissioner Benjamin Ward quickly reorganized the department and led an investigation. Videotapes of the police brutality were aired on television for all to see. The Koch administration seemed increasingly beholden to its real estate allies and entrapped by the tough image it cultivated. Uncharacteristically, Koch refused to give an opinion about the matter.[70]

In 1989, two unrelated violent acts became related aspects of a city under stress. In April, a young white female investment banker was brutally beaten and raped in Central Park. A group of black and Puerto Rican youths were blamed for the incident, which was labeled a "wilding." The city was horrified and the African American Manhattan borough president, David Dinkins, called the men "urban terrorists." Sharpton feared that they were scapegoats, an unpopular position that was vindicated when a career criminal confessed to the crime in 2002. Nonetheless, at the time, the crime and its surrounding connotations appalled Gotham.[71]

Four months later, in August, Yusef Hawkins, a sixteen-year-old African American male, was shot dead when attacked by a gang of ten to thirty youths in the predominantly Italian American community of Bensonhurst, Brooklyn. Accompanying friends to view a secondhand car, Hawkins was mistaken for another black male who was purportedly dating a local white female.

Learning from Howard Beach, the police moved quickly to make arrests and Mayor Koch declared the crime "chilling to all New Yorkers." However, when Sharpton led marchers into Bensonhurst, Koch said it was unfair to blame the whole neighborhood and irresponsible to aggravate the situation. In turn, Koch was condemned as the "number one racist in the city." Together Koch and Sharpton raised "the temperature of the city," which, noted the *Times,* "was already overheated." Occurring right in the middle of a mayoral campaign, the incident was explosive and may have cost Koch his job.[72]

Bensonhurst residents greeted marchers with cries of "Niggers go home," pointed obscenities, mocking renditions of calypso songs, and watermelons held up as symbols of contempt. Taunts of "Central Park" were met with counter-taunts of "Howard Beach." Conflict continued for weeks as Sharpton organized more "Days of Outrage." An attempt by seventy-five hundred protesters to cross the Brooklyn Bridge ended in a major confrontation with the police. Sharpton warned that the city would "burn" if the defendants were set free, and, during one march, he was stabbed in the chest. "New York is a powder keg," declared Daughtry. "African Americans have had enough. . . . Something has got to give. A change must come."[73]

While Koch criticized the protesters, they received support from national figures such as Martin Luther King Jr.'s wife, Coretta, civil rights leader, the Reverend Jesse Jackson, and NAACP executive director, Benjamin Hooks. Bensonhurst became a national issue because, said the *Times*, it was increasingly difficult to dismiss the death of Yusef Hawkins as an "isolated incident." Rather, it was linked to a recent race riot in Virginia Beach, an attack on Hispanics in Chicago, and the murder of a Chinese-American autoworker in Raleigh, North Carolina. According to the *Times* columnist Anthony Lewis, anyone who considered America's race problem solved should have been profoundly disturbed by Bensonhurst.[74]

Koch originally sought the mayoralty in order "to rescue the city from itself." On the surface, he seemed successful as New York moved from fiscal crisis to financial boom. Confidence was restored, the mayoralty was revived, and Koch became the city's chief booster. He loved the limelight and gloated over the fact that, once again, the "Big Apple shines in the world's markets." However, Koch was also a lightning rod whose punitive policies and inflammatory rhetoric scorched the city's sensibilities. He himself admitted that at times he was "too strident."[75]

After twelve years of the head ruling the heart, Rangel concluded that the city needed "someone with the heart. . .[to] lower the angry voices and cut through the strife. . . ." He called for "a new kind of leadership," one that would reject divisiveness in favor of "toughness tempered by compassion." Above all, said Rangel, it was imperative to "reclaim" the liberal heritage that had always distinguished Gotham from other places because "that's what makes New York great." No one could accuse Koch of weak leadership but, in the end, his aggressive persona backfired.[76]

DINKINS AND LEADERSHIP

I see New York as a gorgeous mosaic of race and religious faith, of national origin and sexual orientation. . . . I intend to be the mayor of all of the people of New York. This administration will never lead by dividing, by setting some of us against the rest of us, or by favoring one group over others.

—David N. Dinkins, January 2, 1990[77]

Manhattan Borough President David N. Dinkins was the dapper, mild-mannered, moderate product of the Marines, Howard University, Brooklyn Law School, Harlem's Democratic Party organization, and various government jobs. After successfully challenging Koch for the Democratic mayoralty nomination in 1989, Dinkins narrowly defeated Republican U.S. Attorney Rudolph Giuliani in the general election to become Gotham's first African American mayor. He did so by appealing to Blacks, Latinos, and liberal whites, including a significant number of Jews. The result was a coalition that cut across race, class, and ethnicity to momentarily revive New York's liberal traditions. In contrast to Koch, Dinkins pledged to "renew the quest for social justice" and to "never be mean spirited." His "gorgeous mosaic" metaphor offered New Yorkers the hope that harmony could outweigh hatred.[78]

Unfortunately, the qualities that got Dinkins elected did not serve him well in office. Where Koch had been too emotional, inflammatory, and quick to respond, Dinkins proved too passive, formal, and slow to act. Where Koch had seemed too close to real estate and business interests, Dinkins seemed too close to labor unions. Failing to respond forcefully to a sudden increase in drive-by shootings made him look weak on crime. Expensive labor settlements accompanied by tax increases, service cutbacks, and threats of another fiscal crisis made him seem incompetent. Rather than explaining his perspective, Dinkins promoted tennis, presided at social events, and traveled abroad. He appeared to be fiddling while Rome burned.[79]

Under Dinkins's watch, New York City experienced a three-year recession, a year-long boycott, a major strike, and three riots. Conflicts involving blacks, Koreans, Dominicans, and Jews proved too hot to handle. Controversy over the police fanned political flames that Dinkins could not extinguish. Like Lindsay in 1966, Dinkins had no political honeymoon. On January 18, just seventeen days after his inauguration, a Korean grocer was accused of assaulting a Haitian woman whom he suspected of shoplifting in the Family Red Apple store in Flatbush, Brooklyn. Three weeks later, the federal government forbade Haitians from donating blood on the presumption that they were AIDS carriers. The result was a massive protest march by Haitians across the Brooklyn Bridge and the intensification of communal anger.[80]

Black Power advocates, who had staged a similar boycott against Korean grocers in 1988, bridged cultural differences with Haitians and other Caribbeans by emphasizing a common racial identity. They painted Koreans as outsiders exploiting blacks just as whites had for centuries. Key to this effort

was Brooklyn's radical activist Sonny Carson, a controversial black national-
ist who was active in Ocean Hill-Brownsville, Howard Beach, and the 1988
Korean store boycotts. For the entire year of 1990, he mobilized thousands
of people to boycott the Red Apple store. Some saw it as a revival of Powell's
1930s boycott movement, but former Mayor Koch dismissed it as "an organized hustle and extortion operation by Sonny Carson."[81]

Departing from their previously passive political stance, Korean businessmen mobilized against the boycott. They turned the tables on the protesters by claiming to be the victims of racial persecution themselves. Not only
were Koreans being unjustly demonized, they said, but the Korean American
Dream was being destroyed. Appealing to mainstream notions of hard work,
equality, and opportunity, they called for a truly colorblind society. A successful Peace Rally for Racial Harmony held on September 8 marked the emergence of Korean Americans as an organized political force in New York City.
The dynamics of Gotham's ethnic politics had been permanently altered.[82]

Dinkins was caught in the middle of a conflict so complicated that even
Sharpton and Daughtry sympathized with his dilemma. Militant blacks considered him "a traitor to his people" for not supporting the boycott. Koreans
accused him of pandering to his race for not stopping the boycott. Mainstream
politicians and the press sympathized with the Koreans, whom they viewed as
a "model minority," a group that worked hard and made no trouble. Moderate
African Americans, who did not want Sonny Carson defining "how to be
black," ran a counter-boycott of "6:30 Shoppers," making purchases at the Red
Apple on their way home from work. With CORE, they joined the Koreans'
call for enforcement of a rule to keep protesters fifty feet from the store.[83]

The longer the boycott lasted, the more divisive it became. Dinkins
tried to remain neutral, called for an investigation, and began negotiations.
However, as the boycott dragged on and criticism multiplied, Dinkins had to
take a public stand. In May, he spoke out against "any boycott based on race."
When he finally crossed the picket line to shop in the Red Apple store on
September 21, he tacitly admitted his failure to bring harmony to Gotham. It
was too little too late. Thus, the man who wanted to be a "healer" started his
administration by antagonizing blacks, whites, and Koreans. The "gorgeous
mosaic" had already been stained.[84]

In October, a boycott he backed further dimmed Dinkins' future. The
1990 *Daily News* strike lasted 147 days, pitting a powerful big business against
a faltering labor movement. Led by the journalist Juan Gonzalez, a veteran
of the 1968 Columbia protests and the 1970s Young Lords movement, labor
orchestrated a consumer boycott of the paper and, with some violence,
kept replacement workers at bay. Massive rallies clogged 42nd Street at the
News headquarters near Lexington Avenue. Jesse Jackson, Mayor Dinkins,
Governor Cuomo, Cardinal O'Connor, prominent entertainers, and other

unions offered support. Finally, a new owner settled the strike but, over the next few years, labor made concession after concession just to survive. The heyday of New York's labor movement was over and a key segment of the Dinkins coalition had been weakened.[85]

In August 1991, Crown Heights, Brooklyn exploded. Neighborhood relations had long been strained between African Americans, Afro-Caribbeans, Hispanics, and Hasidic Jews. They argued over crime, housing, the observance of Jewish religious rituals in public space, and the control of community boards. Special Jewish street patrols and ambulance services heightened resentment. Then, when a car driven by a Hasidic Jew jumped the curb and killed a seven-year-old Guyanese boy, tension turned to turmoil.[86]

A rumor quickly spread that a Jewish ambulance crew had refused to treat the mortally wounded black child in favor of whisking away the uninjured Jewish driver. Television, radio, and word-of mouth accounts brought crowds of people onto the streets. They fought with one another and with the police. Later that evening, Yankel Rosenbaum, a rabbinical student from Australia, was surrounded by a group of youths and stabbed four times. Because the hospital staff failed to properly treat his wounds, he died, but not before identifying Limerick Nelson, a sixteen-year-old African American, as his assailant. The mayor and police commissioner rushed to the scene and stayed until the early morning trying to calm residents. They failed.[87]

The rioting continued for two more days and nights. Rocks and bottles flew, fires were set, cars were overturned, and stores were looted. Several reporters were attacked by both the protesters and the police. Young Hasidic men threw bricks and threatened blacks; young black men threw bottles and threatened Hasidim. However, only blacks were arrested. Fifty members of the Jewish Defense League patrolled the area as self-appointed vigilantes; policemen were the perpetrators and the victims of violence.[88]

Although his aides were in Crown Heights speaking to residents, the mayor stayed away and missed the Rosenbaum funeral. When Dinkins resurfaced on the third day of the riots, he was booed by everyone. Whites accused him of allowing the riots to continue because the rioters were black. Meanwhile, his role as a leader of blacks had been usurped by Sharpton and Daughtry, who led protest marches, spoke for the bereaved family, and negotiated for the release of the black youth. Seizing the drama of the moment, Sharpton flew to Israel to serve a subpoena against the Jewish driver who fled abroad after being exonerated by a grand jury. Sharpton's slogan, "No Justice, No Peace," echoed loudly in Crown Heights.[89]

The volatile combination of race and ethnicity, reinforced by stereotypes, lack of communication, and a strong sense of historic oppression felt by both groups, made Crown Heights an emblem of the urban nightmare. The tension lasted for weeks, fueled when a black professor at CCNY made anti-Semitic statements and when three white St. John's University athletes were cleared of raping a black coed. Finally, the police brought order to Crown Heights, but Dinkins suffered a severe political blow and was branded as a weak leader. Instead of being a "melting pot," said the *Times,* the city had become a "cauldron of hate."[90]

Similar issues surfaced in Washington Heights during July 1992 when a twenty-four-year-old Dominican immigrant was killed by a policeman in the lobby of a building where he had sought refuge from pursuit. The cop claimed that he shot in self-defense and produced a gun that he said he found on the dead man, a purported drug dealer. Witnesses claimed that the cop beat the man and shot him while he was down on the floor with his hands in the air. They also suggested that this particular cop had a reputation for violence and corruption. In both New York and the Dominican Republic, a cry was raised for "Justicia."[91]

Unemployment, overcrowding, and poor schools aggravated by frequent confrontations with the police created the preconditions of riot. For six days, young men set fire to cars and looted stores. They were met by police in riot gear who made many arrests and foiled an attempt to stop traffic on the George Washington Bridge. On the third day, just when emotions seemed to be subsiding, the death of a rioter reignited the anger and a police officer was burned in effigy. Two days later, at a rally attended by two thousand, Sharpton got a rousing reception when he asked "Why are people of color always the victims of police brutality?" Again, he was assailed for exploiting the "politics of victimization."[92]

Afraid of replicating recent riots in Los Angeles and anxious to restore peace before the Democratic National Convention came to New York, Mayor Dinkins made several visits to Washington Heights with John Cardinal O'Connor, local leaders, the police commissioner, and the Puerto Rican singer Willie Colon. Policemen blanketed the area, but they deeply resented the mayor's expressions of sympathy for the bereaved family and his reaffirmation of support for a Civilian Review Board. While the local residents complained of harassment by white policemen, the cops complained of being unappreciated for risking their lives trying to contain urban crime. The Washington Heights riot deepened the divide between liberals and conservatives, minorities and whites.[93]

The Crown Heights and Washington Heights riots set the stage for the 1993 mayoral campaign and illuminated the differences between the two major candidates. While Dinkins was suggesting that "sometimes a quiet meeting, a kind word says, and does, more than a line of officers in riot gear," former U.S. prosecutor Rudolph Giuliani was leading police officers in an anti-Dinkins demonstration that turned ugly. On September 16, 1992, ten thousand off-duty police officers rallied at City Hall and stopped traffic on the Brooklyn Bridge for an hour. They stomped on cars, jumped barricades, and used offensive language regarding Dinkins, including "nigger," other epithets, and profanity.

Besides Giuliani, the crowd was addressed by the head of the police union and the officer involved in the Washington Heights riot. Mocking Sharpton's slogan, the cops chanted "No Justice! No Police!" For them, the riot was "a symbolic burst of fury," a justifiable response to a mayor who restrained them and a populace that demeaned them. The *Times* worried that "fearsome flames have been ignited." It urged that "instead of fanning them, or arguing about who lit the match," the mayoral candidates should try to "put out the fire."[94]

The police riot heated up the already intense debate over Dinkins's support for an all-civilian police review board (CRB). On the one hand, the riot convinced many New Yorkers that the police were racist and unable to patrol themselves. On the other hand, the riot brought to the surface extensive support for the police and strong resentment against minority protests. Echoing the debate over Lindsay's CRB proposal, attitudes toward the police became a core campaign issue with race relations as the subtext. After a jury acquitted the black man accused of having stabbed the Jewish man in Crown Heights, over forty-five hundred people protested in Brooklyn and, once again, Dinkins was caught in the crossfire.[95]

In order to prove that he was tough on crime, Dinkins pointed to his "Safe Streets, Safe City" campaign, which added over six thousand police to the force. However, he never offset Giuliani's close affinity to the police nor countered the negative legacy of both Crown Heights and Washington Heights. Dinkins' antipolice image was underscored by his administration's refusal to let the police use semi-automatic guns and by new police corruption hearings. Then, Governor Cuomo issued a report criticizing Dinkins' handling of Crown Heights. From every angle, Dinkins' liberalism seemed to be more defect than asset and, wrote the journalist Andrew Kirtzman, gave "compassion a bad name."[96]

The Korean store boycott, Crown Heights, Washington Heights, and the police riot dominated the 1993 campaign. As the *Times* saw it, the candidates were diametrically opposite personalities—one "too mild" and the other "too mean." Giuliani softened his image by rolling up his sleeves and including his wife in campaign ads. Simultaneously, he toughened his image by pledging to eliminate affirmative action programs for city contracts and to decrease services for the homeless. Giuliani benefited from the angry Italian American response to a black preacher who called him a fascist. He basked in the endorsement of key Democrats such as Ed Koch. When, three weeks before the election, a cop was killed in Washington Heights, Giuliani accused the mayor of surrendering the city to "urban terrorists," the very phrase Dinkins had used after the Central Park "wilding" incident.[97]

The election was close, with Dinkins losing to Giuliani by only forty-four thousand votes. On Staten Island the turnout was large, not only because of the issues at stake but also because of a referendum on whether that borough should secede from the larger city. Catholics voted in record numbers, accounting for almost 60 percent of Giuliani's total. In addition, enough white Protestants, Jews, and Latinos supported Giuliani to tip the scales. African Americans overwhelmingly backed Dinkins, but fewer of them actually voted in 1993 than in 1989. Any doubts about the racial context of the election were erased by the fact that the Giuliani vote was 87 percent white and the Dinkins vote was 83 percent black. The colors of the "gorgeous mosaic" had been reduced to two clashing hues.[98]

A Democratic loss in such a heavily Democratic city was notable, but this loss was particularly painful because Dinkins' 1989 victory had been hailed as proof that Gotham's liberalism could survive. By 1993, frustration had outweighed faith in reform; strife had smothered the spirit of cooperation. New York faced a crisis of confidence. Lindsay's moralisms, Beame's bookkeeping, Koch's rancor, Dinkins' ineffectiveness, the fiscal crisis, and endless incendiary incidents had all fostered what *Time* magazine called "The Rotting of the Big Apple."[99]

Giuliani won the mayoralty by capitalizing on a quarter century of public anxiety, but, at his inauguration, he declared the end of "the era of fear. . . doubt [and] cynicism." Insisting that New York's problems could be solved by strong leadership, he promised that "the indomitable spirit of LaGuardia will infuse our city. The common sense approach of Ed Koch will echo again." Like his predecessors, Giuliani was confident of his own ability to affect history. He was determined to be the one mayor to get into the Hall of Fame, the one man to transform raging fires into sparkling fireworks. Bursting with enthusiasm, Giuliani boldly declared that "New York City is poised for dramatic change." He meant it.[100]

10

The Supercity and the Supermayor, 1994–2001

Rudolph Giuliani was audacious. His mayoralty challenged the conventions of urban life and revised urban priorities. In both public policies and personal style, he consistently defied expectation by insisting on doing what was considered undoable. Even though his actions were often at odds with core elements of the New York spirit, his brashness and brazenness were quintessentially New York. Moreover, the contradictions of his character captured the complexity of his city. As Giuliani became a national and international figure, he underlined New York's role as a mirror of national dilemmas and a harbinger of national change.

There was never a dull moment when Giuliani was mayor. He tried to sell off the city's water, declared that dead people have no rights to privacy, dressed in drag for media affairs, insisted that the education system be blown up, attacked the Brooklyn Museum, publicly announced that he was divorcing his wife before telling her, and pranced around town with his mistress. Then, just as the city was tiring of his bombast and his marital troubles, Giuliani became a superhero. The events of September 11, 2001 evoked his least contentious leadership qualities and forever enshrined him as a symbol of compassionate strength. In crisis, Giuliani became "America's mayor."[1]

Giuliani's advocacy of what he himself called "the politics of provocation" made him Gotham's most contentious leader. During his two terms (1994–2001), he initiated more civil law suits than any previous mayor and instigated some of the city's most strident controversies over race, the police, welfare, education, the arts, and civil liberties. He antagonized minorities and labor unions, barricaded city streets and City Hall, tangled with taxi drivers and food vendors, gutted neighborhood gardens, tried to privatize public hospitals, killed open admissions at CUNY, fought with three public school chancellors, ran a popular police commissioner out of town, and twice tried to revise the city charter to punish his critics. Despite supporting many of his policies and being quite combative himself, even former mayor Ed Koch criticized Giuliani as a *Nasty Man* (1999).[2]

At the same time, Giuliani has been judged the city's savior, a nononsense, effective leader whose sheer willpower tamed New York. Prime evidence was reducing crime and salvaging Times Square. "He restored the notion that the city was governable," declared the historian Thomas Kessner. The proud product of New York's working-class immigrant tradition, Giuliani possessed a sense of special destiny since childhood. His success at a Catholic high school and a Catholic college, New York University Law School, and the U.S. Department of Justice strengthened his self-confidence and his ambition. After beating David Dinkins in 1993, Giuliani's joy was palpable. Here was his chance to save Gotham from itself and make it once "again the capital of the world." In the process, he shook the city to its foundations.[3]

In April 1999, the journalist Craig Horowitz published an article for *New York Magazine* entitled "The Fall of Supermayor." It included a graphic by Mark Zingarelli depicting Giuliani as Superman. Red cape and "I Love New York" belt notwithstanding, the mayor was being pummeled by angry citizens throwing food. In testimony to his prosecutorial style, one fist was clenched and the building in the background was a courthouse, not City Hall or the skyline. The analogy is enticing. Giuliani's first-term success as a crime fighter made him seem invulnerable. Like Superman, he was the national champion of "Truth, Justice and the American Way;" his potential for good seemed limitless.[4]

Yet, by Giuliani's second term many people considered him a supervillain. Hubris was his kryptonite. Only the tragedy of September 11, 2001, which occurred right at the end of his tenure, restored his superhero status. Giuliani's rise, fall, and resurrection comprised a stunning political drama. It transformed New York City, which was, after all, Superman's Metropolis (as it was Spiderman's base and Batman's Gotham). In the comics as in life, New York was the prototypical modern city where the line between the good and the bad, the possible and the impossible, the real and the unreal was always thin. Negotiating that line defined the lure of the city and shaped the history of urban conflict since colonial days. It comprised the mythology of the city as symbolized by Superman and tested by the Supermayor.[5]

LAW AND ORDER

Like Superman, Giuliani's first objective was to promote law and order. He, too, would fearlessly and single-handedly fight the forces of evil. A case in point was his success in routing the Mafia from the private garbage collection business and from the Fulton Fish Market, which it had controlled for half a century. However, while Superman was a reluctant crime fighter, Giuliani was a zealous one. Thus, he made New York confront the most difficult challenge of democracy—that of balancing freedom and control by using, without abusing, power. This challenge, says the political scientist Patrick L. Eagan, was central to the symbolism of Superman and the way in which he embodied both the noble ideals and the "disturbing contradictions that mark the national soul."[6]

The same could be said for Giuliani, who understood the need for order in a complex, volatile city, but often did not understand how much Gothamites cherished their liberties, their right to protest, and their heritage of practical toleration. Giuliani contended that "Freedom is about authority. Freedom is about the willingness of every single human being to cede to lawful authority a great deal of discretion about what you do and how you do it." According to Norman Siegel, director of the New York Civil Liberties Union, this philosophy represented "a new New York." Siegal feared that it was an "authoritarian" New York, one that was "antithetical to tradition and our rich history of freedom." The stage was set for conflict.[7]

Concerned with all forms of lawlessness, not just violent crime, Giuliani resolved "to restore a civilized city." Following the "broken windows" theory advanced by the political scientist James Q. Wilson, Giuliani believed that small crimes begat larger ones by creating general disrespect for the law. Consequently, he announced a "zero tolerance" campaign to address "quality of life" offenses such as drinking alcohol, sleeping, or urinating in public. The program was applauded for cleaning up Times Square, closing down strip joints, making the homeless less visible, reducing the number of panhandlers, loiterers, and car window washers (called squeegee men). Nonetheless, questions were raised about harassing the homeless and other members of the city's poor, powerless, or marginalized communities.[8]

The "quality of life" initiative became more controversial when the police started arresting people for littering, jaywalking, lacking a dog leash or a bicycle bell, riding a bicycle on the sidewalk, having a broken bicycle light, or having an unpaid parking ticket. The courts were swamped with cases for minor infractions. Thousands of ordinary citizens were incarcerated for violations once resolved with desk appearance tickets. Some were strip-searched (including an elderly woman). Many had their charges dropped before seeing a judge but after having spent twenty-four hours in jail. Indignation spread. When taxi drivers, food cart vendors, and street artists were targeted, their protests received considerable popular support. Giuliani's policy of "zero tolerance" smacked of an intolerance that offended New York's live-and-let-live spirit.[9]

Giuliani's signature accomplishment was a major reduction in crime that resulted in a general sense that the city was a better place to live and to visit. He proudly pointed out that under his tutelage crime rates fell precipitously, out-pacing similar decreases in other cities. For example, from 1994 through 2001, murders declined by 66 percent and overall crime by 57 percent. He attributed this change partly to his insistence that the public housing police and the transit police merge with the regular police, thus creating a new, better-coordinated force. After years blocking such a move, the transit police finally capitulated when the mayor threatened to defund their salaries. The merger, plus additional hiring (begun by Dinkins), resulted in a total force forty thousand strong. Oddly enough, Giuliani's support for the police stopped at the contract-negotiating table.[10]

Giuliani was particularly proud of the much-lauded Compstat (short for computer comparison statistics) program to track and quantify arrests. It was instituted by Police Commissioner William Bratton, who was so popular that Giuliani forced him to resign in 1996. While the system increased the accountability of the precincts, it also increased pressure on the police to make arrests. According to one cop, the force became consumed by a "go-get-em mentality." According to the mayor, Compstat professionalized the police department and made it more effective. Both inside and outside of the department, Compstat provided, in his words, "true culture shock."[11]

The backbone of Giuliani's anticrime crusade was the Street Crime Unit (SCU), a highly trained corps of undercover cops charged with getting guns off the streets. After Giuliani appointed Fire Commissioner Howard Safir to replace Bratton, Safir increased the unit threefold without providing proper training and supervision. The existing commander resigned in protest. Then the unit accelerated its stop-and-frisk activities, which were widely viewed as racial profiling of young minority men. Indeed, minorities accounted for over 80 percent of the SCU's stop-and-frisk statistics. As the SCU became the police department's "commandos," their slogan, "We own the night," acquired loaded implications for communities of color.[12]

In response to Compstat pressures, stop-and-frisks grew totally out of proportion to actual arrests—not just by the SCU but across the department. Giuliani dismissed public protests as unjustified police bashing and resolved to further disable the already weak Civilian Complaint Review Board. He missed the message when his only black deputy mayor, Rudy Washington, and his only prominent black ally, a former congressman, the Reverend Floyd Flake, related their own confrontations with hostile policemen. By insisting that there was only one standard of justice in the city, Giuliani denied the reality of a double standard. Harlem's Congressman Charles Rangel wondered whether the mayor had "a problem" relating to people of color.[13]

The most disturbing episodes of Giuliani's two terms intertwined race with law and order. Ominously, he had proclaimed in his first inaugural speech that "guns, the handguns, will be a particular source of our efforts" to reduce crime. That promise proved lethal for a black thirteen-year-old killed by cops while playing outside his building in 1994, two Puerto Rican men shot dead in 1995 even though they were already face down on the floor, an Asian honors high school student shot in the head by a cop in 1995, and an unarmed young black veteran shot in the back on a subway platform in 1996. In addition, Anthony Baez, an asthmatic, died in 1994 when a cop, who had fourteen prior brutality complaints against him, held Baez in an illegal choke-hold after Baez's football hit his police car. The problem was so systemic that in 1996 Amnesty International published a study entitled *Police Brutality and Excessive Force in the New York City Police Department*.[14]

Opposition to police brutality crystallized when Haitian immigrant, Abner Louima, was brutally sodomized with a toilet plunger handle by a cop in a Brooklyn police station on August 9, 1997. His internal injuries were so severe that they required two months of hospitalization. Giuliani declared the case "shocking to any decent human being," visited Louima in the hospital, called for a full investigation, and fired the entire precinct command. It was a swift, constructive response and a significant departure from the mayor's pattern of defending cops in all cases whatsoever. It also was an election year.[15]

Giuliani and Safir claimed that the Louima incident was "aberrant... abnormal" behavior, not evidence of any larger pattern of police brutality. When the civil rights leader Al Sharpton pointed out that the furor over the case reflected precisely such a pattern, Giuliani declared it "shameful" to politicize the matter. Many people disagreed, especially Haitians who already disliked Giuliani because of his harsh policies toward Haitian refugees when he worked for the Justice Department in the 1980s. Anger accumulated as the four officers charged with participating in the incident were not questioned until thirty-six hours after the event. Skepticism solidified when few policemen dared testify and risk breaching the "blue wall of silence," behind which cops protected each other.[16]

August witnessed several protests against police brutality, culminating on August 29, when over seven thousand people replicated the Haitian-sponsored AIDS protest of 1990 by marching across the Brooklyn Bridge. Sharpton accompanied the Louima family and addressed the crowd in

Brooklyn. Hearkening back to Howard Beach and Bensonhurst, the Haitian community called it a "Day of Outrage." Norman Siegel and former Mayor Dinkins spoke to the group at City Hall. Signs depicted Giuliani as "Ghouliani," "Crueliani," and "Brutaliani." Toilet plungers were brandished as "a symbol of oppression." Despite the mayor's charge that it was just a "police-bashing rally," Haitians hoped that their collective voice would be heard.[17]

In a sense it was. Although ultimately losing the Democratic mayoral nomination to Manhattan Borough President Ruth Messinger, Sharpton did so well in the primary that he almost forced her into a runoff. Everyone agreed that the police brutality issue was central to Sharpton's support, especially in Brooklyn. Facing such popular uproar, Giuliani appointed a task force, including critics like Norman Siegel, to look into police practices. However, when the Louima report was delivered after Giuliani won reelection, he derided it as "unrealistic," if not absurd. The trial of the four Louima cops was delayed until March 1999, thereby keeping the issue alive and the city on edge for one and a half years.[18]

The Louima case converged with another spectacular case to create what the *Times* deemed "a civic trauma." On February 4, 1999, an unarmed West African immigrant named Amadou Diallo was killed in the entrance of his Bronx apartment house. Mistaking him for a rapist and his wallet for a gun, four SCU cops fired forty-one bullets at Diallo, nineteen of which met their mark. While Giuliani and his police commissioner were defending the police and proposing that they use yet more lethal bullets, Sharpton was organizing a protest movement that communal anger sustained for months. Diallo's death was a galvanizing episode with broad implications for and beyond Gotham. It was, wrote the *New York Times* columnist Maureen Dowd, "one of those moments when you see the ugly worms crawling under the gleaming rock."[19]

The public outcry began at Diallo's home on Wheeler Avenue, where over a thousand people responded to Sharpton's first call for a rally shortly after the shooting. Sharpton took charge of Diallo's parents when they arrived in New York City, providing them with lawyers and living expenses while advising them not to talk to Giuliani. Tensions grew as the Diallo cops refused to make statements, were shielded by the police department, and were backed by the mayor. Still awaiting indictments a month after the killing, Sharpton orchestrated street theater akin to the revolutionary era, the 1830s, and the suffrage movement. With words as his only weapon, Sharpton unnerved and undermined the mayor.[20]

Surprising Sharpton himself, hundreds of New Yorkers turned out for daily protests at police headquarters. As in the sixties, people willingly engaged in civil disobedience and chose to be arrested in the interests of social justice. Sharpton was arrested as were his close friends, the Brooklyn activists Reverend Herbert Daughtry and Charles Barron, a former Black Panther and future city councilman. However, it was the arrest of Rangel and Dinkins, distinguished civic leaders not known for rabble-rousing, that provided high drama and started the avalanche of voluntary arrests. The Diallo demonstrations quickly became the centerpiece of a general anti-Giuliani movement. The mayor called it "a great publicity stunt," but the city and the nation perceived signs of "a serious civic lament."[21]

Almost twelve hundred people were arrested as the protests consumed Gotham and astonished the nation from March 9 to 29, 1999. The participants were an interracial, multigenerational cross section of local citizens, clerics, educators, businessmen, labor leaders, activists, and politicians. In addition, there were national figures such as the civil rights leader Jesse Jackson, NAACP president Kweisi Mfume, the comedian Dick Gregory, and the actors Susan Sarandon, Ossie Davis, and Ruby Dee. Guiliani's former allies Floyd Flake and Ed Koch both supported the cause. Finally overcoming his controversial past, Sharpton energized New York's dormant liberal coalition and, said Flake, may have saved Gotham from riot. Just as his boyhood idol Adam Clayton Powell Jr. was to LaGuardia, so Sharpton became "Giuliani's worst nightmare."[22]

Fighting back, the mayor dismissed the protests as "silly" and the protesters as the "worst elements of society." Few people shared his scorn. In fact, an impressive coalition of prominent religious, business, labor, and civic leaders issued a ten-point program for "a safer and more just New York." As evidence of the struggle's national importance, several thousand people from across the country demonstrated at the Justice Department in Washington D.C. on April 3, 1999. On April 15, ten thousand marched from the federal courts in downtown Brooklyn across the Brooklyn Bridge to the federal courts on Foley Square in downtown Manhattan. The entertainer and civil rights activist Harry Belafonte added luster to the event. Meanwhile, the federal government began investigating the city's police practices.[23]

With his approval ratings plummeting, Giuliani scrambled to recoup. Reluctantly, he met with African American elected officials for the first time since taking office and resuscitated the Louima report that he had previously ridiculed. The SCU was toned down, infused with minority cops, and dispersed throughout the precincts. However, the mayor's efforts were set back when the police shot and killed a deranged orthodox Jewish man in front of his Brooklyn home in August 1999. Fears that the cops were out of control deepened; the sense of pervasive injustice widened.[24]

The Diallo trial was so controversial that it was moved to Albany, where the jury and the judge were expected to be less hostile to the police. Although the shift dampened the protests, they continued in the city while Sharpton and others bore witness in Albany. When the cops were acquitted of murder on February 25, 2000, Giuliani announced that justice had been served. By contrast, polls revealed that 60 percent of city residents thought the verdict unjust. Public reaction was immediate and intensified days later when another unarmed black man, a parolee, was killed by undercover cops just blocks from Diallo's home. With the Louima case still in the courts and in the press, the police brutality issue seemed strikingly unresolved.[25]

The result was more demonstrations at Diallo's home, the Bronx police station, the police academy, and police headquarters. Hundreds of high school students marched across the Brooklyn Bridge and more than three thousand people swept down Fifth Avenue from 59th Street to 42nd Street shouting "No Justice, No Peace" and "It's a wallet, not a gun." The police were excoriated in song by four rap artists and Bruce Springsteen. Civic leaders of every color and creed demanded a review of police practices and a recognition of racial prejudice. As Dinkins put it, "We did not leave the back of the bus only to place our children in the back of an ambulance." The whole situation, said one minister, was "a wake-up call for the city."[26]

The Diallo case was a local crisis, a national issue, and an international embarrassment. The killing was covered around the globe as a symbol of the immigrant dream destroyed and a world-class city in chaos. Diallo's parents, especially his mother, kept the international dynamic of the case in full view. One Diallo demonstrator from Switzerland carried a telling sign saying, "The whole world is watching." Warning that any person of color, native or foreign, could be the next victim, Sharpton led over two thousand people in a prayer vigil at the United Nations two days after the verdict.[27]

During the next week, Sharpton, Diallo's parents, Rangel, Dinkins, and Mfume, plus hundreds of supporters from several states, went to Washington, D.C. to ask the Justice Department to investigate the violation of Diallo's civil rights. President Bill Clinton criticized the Diallo verdict, as did his wife, Hillary, who was campaigning for the Senate against Giuliani. Concern was registered by the NAACP, the National Urban League, the Civil Liberties Union, the Green Party, various labor unions, plus an array of black, Latino, and white leaders. They all shared Jesse Jackson's opinion that exonerating the Diallo cops marked "a sad day for New York City. . .a sad day for our nation."[28]

A third case cemented the cataclysm. On March 15, 2000, shortly after the four Diallo cops were acquitted, Patrick Dorismond was killed in a fight with plainclothes officers when he took exception to being asked if he sold drugs. Rushing to support the police, Giuliani discredited the victim, another unarmed Haitian, as a violence-prone criminal. Then he released Dorismond's sealed records for charges that had been dropped when he was a juvenile. The mayor justified his action by claiming that once a man is dead, he loses his right to privacy. Even Giuliani's closest friends were appalled by his callousness.[29]

Disregarding calmer voices, Giuliani continued to assail Dorismond. On March 25, there was a riot at Dorismond's funeral, which was attended by ten thousand people met by police in riot gear. Rocks and bottles were counteracted with tear gas. The mob demolished two cop cars and a phone booth; twenty-three cops and an unknown number of civilians suffered injuries, several serious. The crowd carried posters depicting Giuliani as Hitler while chanting "Giuliani Must Go" and "Impeach Giuliani." The situation was so bad that the *New York Daily News,* a pro-Giuliani paper, pleaded with the mayor to alleviate the city's "crisis of confidence."[30] (See Figure 21 following page 150)

The "quality of life" campaign compounded by the Louima, Diallo, and Dorismond cases, forced New York and the nation to reconsider the role of the police in a democracy and its connection to America's racial problems. Reminiscent of reactions to previous violent conflicts from 1849 on, many people felt that the human price society paid for order seemed too great. In 2000, the U.S. Commission on Civil Rights issued a report criticizing New York City's police practices and making racial profiling a national issue. Data emerged showing that other cities reduced crime without police brutality or a massive police presence. One such strategy was community policing, where cops worked with local residents to fight crime, a program promoted by Dinkins but abandoned by Giuliani.[31]

Throughout its history, New York had been ambivalent about a strong police presence and often left its force undermanned, underpaid, and undertrained. Giuliani was the first mayor to champion policing as the primary solution to urban problems. It was a bold departure embodying what both his admirers and critics saw as a determined toughness that was consciously calculated to change attitudes within and toward the city. By emphasizing safety and security, Giuliani restored New York's image as manageable, which was an astounding accomplishment. However, his successes were offset by his excesses. When law and order became an end in itself, his source of strength became a weakness that transformed him from supermayor into supervillain.[32]

THE SOCIAL CONTRACT

A city is an experiment in the social contract. It is a place where people choose to live and work together, a place where the individual interest and the general interest are intertwined in delicate, ever-changing relationships that become public policy. LaGuardia, Lindsay, and Dinkins promoted an expansive public service role for government, especially to help the poor. By contrast, Giuliani focused on the middle classes. He emphasized individual initiative and private enterprise over public activism. Convinced that the profit motive induced efficiency, Giuliani advocated the privatization of public services such as the city's water supply, hospitals, schools, and garbage collection. Although those plans were foiled, others succeeded and his overall objective prevailed. In the end, Giuliani altered the city's basic assumptions and operating principles by reducing the public service role of government and by convincing New Yorkers that what was good for business was good for Gotham. He redefined New York's social contract.[33]

Welfare

Giuliani openly disparaged Lindsay's liberalism, particularly his support for the welfare system, which he thought Lindsay had made too "user-friendly." In line with the 1980s Reagan Revolution, Giuliani believed that social programs, which he called the "compassion industry," promoted the dependency of the lazy at the expense of the hard working. He implied that the city might be better off if the poor moved elsewhere and was the first mayor to request that New York State reduce funding for the city's welfare and Medicaid programs. Whereas Roger Starr had been vilified for suggesting that the city scale down its social programs in the 1970s, Giuliani was praised for doing so in the 1990s.[34]

Stringent new qualifying standards instituted in 1995 enabled the Giuliani administration to reject vast numbers of welfare applicants and to discourage countless more from applying at all. Eliminating over six hundred thousand people from the welfare rolls made him a national star. Proclaiming it "by far the best thing we are doing for the city," he called his plan "compassionate." The record was debatable. Despite Giuliani's claims that the system was full of cheats, 90 percent of those who appealed their rejections were deemed eligible for aid. State and federal reviews concluded that the city was improperly preventing deserving recipients, including thousands of children, from getting food stamps, Medicaid, and AIDS/HIV services. A sudden increase in the homeless and those appearing at food kitchens suggested that leaving welfare did not mean rising out of poverty.[35]

After he reduced the welfare rolls, the mayor turned welfare centers into job centers, "not because we love people less," he explained, "but because we have progressed to loving them more deeply, more maturely." The new workfare program required all able-bodied adult welfare recipients to work for their stipends. A private company received a city contract to find them regular jobs. Those who did not get such jobs had to work in the public sector for twenty hours a week under the Work Experience Program (WEP). Giuliani wanted to replace the city's old social contract that, to him, was based on a "perverted social philosophy" of dependence with a new social contract that was "reciprocal." As he put it, "For every right, there's an obligation, for every privilege, there's a duty." Many people thought that this approach was long overdue.[36]

Others considered the new policy heartless, especially advocates for the homeless who sued successfully to prevent Giuliani from making work a prerequisite for shelter. The courts also ruled against forcing WEP workers to handle filth without being protected by gloves or masks, depriving them of adequate water to drink or sanitary facilities to use while on the job, and requiring sick people (two of whom died) to do manual labor. Moreover, because the work requirement included welfare recipients attending college, it forced over sixteen thousand CUNY students to drop out, thus forfeiting their best chance to escape welfare. As City Council President Peter F. Vallone remarked, welfare reform might have been a "good master plan," but the city needed a better "human plan."[37]

Giuliani's many tax cuts designed to help business, large budget allocations for wealthy private institutions (like Lincoln Center and the Museum of Modern Art), plus tax breaks for big corporations contrasted sharply with policies that hurt minorities and the poor. His budgets protected the overwhelmingly white fire and police departments but savaged the Human Resources Administration and the Health and Hospitals Corporation where both workers and clients were mainly minorities. To the journalist and biographer Wayne Barrett, Giuliani's budgets were a "color-coded stacked deck." Perhaps, Barrett suggested, they also were designed to promote a tough image that would offset Giuliani's support of liberal causes (such as gay rights, immigrant rights, and abortion rights) and broaden his national political appeal.[38]

New York had always been America's symbol of economic opportunity and, therefore, was central to its struggle against poverty. The dog, hog, and land riots, the flour, bread, and food riots, the labor strikes, job boycotts, and rent strikes all attested to the ongoing quest for economic opportunity in the nation's wealthiest city. Over the centuries, New York endeavored to balance its commitment to capitalism with its social conscience, but the 1975 fiscal crisis dealt a body blow to benevolence. By the 1990s, New York's poverty rate was double the national average. Moreover, the gap between rich and poor was wider in Manhattan than almost anywhere else in the nation. Poverty seemed destined to remain what the British historian Asa Briggs considered the major unresolved "problem of problems" for the modern city.[39]

Giuliani's solution was to define urban poverty in personal, not social, terms. While reversing the lessons of the discovery of poverty during the Gilded Age, he asserted the need for new thinking in the modern age. According to the journalist Andrew Kirtzman, the mayor was so effective that, in the end, he "looked like the reformer, while the Democrats seemed the enemies of change." By the time he had successfully rewritten New York's concept of the social contract, says the journalist James Traub, Giuliani had been "internalized."[40]

Education

Embedded in the American Dream, the myth of Superman, and the image of the supercity was the possibility of transformation. Aside from work, the key vehicle for personal advancement in America has always been education through which, as in *Ragged Dick,* anyone from anywhere can become anything. Public schools were central to New York's social contract and its sense of civic responsibility for the general welfare. The key to success in an ambitious city, education was always contested. People as different as William Livingston, Bishop Hughes, Fanny Wright, and Rhody McCoy fought to make education more democratic and more reflective of the city's population. To these people, the school wars were largely about opportunity; to Rudy Giuliani, they were really about power.

The mayor's primary goal was to acquire full control of the school system. On the one hand, he secured some change. After extensive wrangling, he shifted supervision of school security to the police department. In addition, he reduced the educational bureaucracy while obtaining more flexibility regarding the appointment of school superintendents and principals. Although he lost a bitter, protracted fight with the New York State legislature, he laid the groundwork for disbanding the Board of Education. He was particularly proud of instituting citywide testing to raise standards, end "social promotion," and bring uniformity to an unwieldy system.[41]

On the other hand, he was often at war with the educational system. In his first term, he courted union support, but, in his second term, he publicly attacked teachers. Claiming that they were more interested in job benefits than in education, he refused to negotiate their contract. Accusing them of incompetence, he advocated hiring private firms to run schools and allowing public funds to be applied to private school tuition through student vouchers. He also tried to end free public transportation for students.[42]

Although he allotted more money for books and computers, Giuliani made more cuts to the schools' operating and construction budgets than any mayor since the 1975 fiscal crisis. He was the first mayor to support reduced school aid from Albany. Moreover, he got school construction funds shifted from areas in Brooklyn and the Bronx that opposed him to areas in Queens and Staten Island that supported him. Most famously, he declared that the entire system should be "blown up" to which Rangel retorted, "When you have schools that aren't working, you don't blow them up, you build them up."[43]

Giuliani's stormy relationships with the teachers' union and three schools chancellors kept the system in constant turmoil. The public was taken aback when he lambasted one highly respected chancellor as "too sensitive" and too "precious," chastening him to "grow up" and "stop whining" about change. Acknowledging that he was being labeled "a bully," Giuliani defiantly declared, "I won't quit." Similarly, he attacked a second highly respected chancellor (supposedly his friend) and violated their agreement not to promote school vouchers. Giuliani simply refused to talk to the third chancellor who was appointed over his opposition and whom he considered pro-union.[44]

In defiance of the educational establishment, the mayor appointed Herman Badillo, former Bronx borough president and congressman, as special education monitor. Following the agenda of the conservative Manhattan Institute for Policy Research, Giuliani and Badillo advocated uniforms, vouchers, merit pay for teachers, and hiring private companies to run schools. Their panacea was back-to-basics testing designed to end "social promotion." These objectives were part of a "standards movement" that swept the nation in the 1990s, much to the dismay of educators who regretted the routinization of teaching.[45]

A graduate of the City College of New York, Badillo now became chairperson of CUNY's Board of Trustees, where he engineered the demise of open admissions in 1999, a policy he had opposed since it began in 1970. Assuming that access was anathema to excellence, Giuliani and Badillo insisted that democratizing CUNY had destroyed it. This position was widely supported in the press and confirmed by a report that condemned CUNY as "an institution adrift." (Its author was Benno Schmidt, former president of Yale, advocate of school privatization, and vice-chairperson of CUNY's Board of Trustees.) No amount of protests, personal testimony, or statistical evidence to the contrary made a difference.[46]

In the public schools as well as in CUNY, proponents of "standards" claimed to be strengthening the social contract by maximizing accountability. Opponents believed that "standards" were a euphemism for abandoning the social contract by restricting opportunity, especially for minorities and the poor. New York's door to social mobility swung precariously on the hinges of controversy.

The First Amendment

A third component of Gotham's social contract was its historic support for the First Amendment rights of free expression and assembly, which, within limits, tolerated difference, controversy, and protest. Over time, this unconventional urban spirit embraced nonconformists such as Fanny Wright, Henry George, Emma Goldman, and Marcus Garvey. The city's identity drew on Greenwich Village, the Savoy Ballroom, and Times Square as much as on the Empire State Building, Rockefeller Center, and the World Trade Center. These two sides of the municipal character coexisted in dynamic interplay until Giuliani embarked on a crusade to squash dissent, stifle protest, and censor art.

In 1999, the Brooklyn Museum mounted an exhibit called "Sensation." It included a portrait of the Virgin Mary by a British artist of Nigerian descent who used dried elephant dung and pornographic cutouts to decorate the canvas. Calling the show "sick" and "disgusting," Giuliani declared that the museum would lose public funds and its lease because, he said, government should not support "offensive art." For the mayor, who never saw the exhibit, the picture was anti-Catholic. For City Council President Peter Vallone, who was a devout Catholic, the real subject was democracy. He accused Giuliani of abusing power and recommended resistance. "Otherwise there's no reason for the existence of government," he said. "You might as well just turn it over to one person and go back to the days of ol' King George."[47]

The debate caused an uproar. "The personal aesthetic or religious views of public officials," wrote a group of prominent interfaith protesters, should not be allowed to limit the "creative. . .independence of. . .cultural institutions," particularly not in the "world capital for the arts, literature and culture." Accordingly, the Brooklyn Museum hired the nation's best First Amendment lawyer to sue the city in federal court and won. On posters and pins, it ridiculed the mayor by revising the "Danger: Men Working" signs to read "Danger: Art." Giuliani had incited a genuine culture war akin to (but opposite in spirit from) the 1913 Armory Show.[48]

Even the museum's director was impressed when over three hundred protesters and nine thousand viewers arrived on opening day. "Now I know I am in New York," he said, "People are coming to make up their own minds." A *Daily News* poll revealed that 30 percent of New Yorkers agreed with the mayor, 10 percent were unsure, and 60 percent sided with the museum. Ultimately, Giuliani's handpicked Cultural Affairs Advisory Commission, also known as the Decency Panel, avoided endorsing artistic censorship. Furthermore, the courts overruled the mayor on other First Amendment issues such as the right to sell art or play music on the streets, the right of Latino cops to speak out on police issues while off duty, and the right of businesses to joke about the mayor in advertisements.[49]

In the Brooklyn Museum case, the arts community did not rally as one to the cause. Some institutions joined the legal suit, but others were more cautious. The problem was the mayor's penchant for retribution. During the preceding years, Giuliani had used the powers of his office against opposition in unprecedented ways. He threatened to cancel the medallions of taxi drivers protesting higher fines, to defund a social service group that criticized city policies, and to cut off CUNY funds unless a new entrance exam was imposed. Giuliani's strong-arm tactics often worked, but Koch considered them counterproductive, because "leadership based on fear" bred more resentment than respect.[50]

Then there was the issue of access to City Hall. Just as Giuliani put up barriers to control how people crossed the streets, so too he barricaded himself against the media and the masses. Carefully monitoring what information was given to the press, he forbade his staff from granting interviews. Not only journalists and watchdog groups but also state and city public officials had to sue to obtain information about city agencies. As Kirtzman put it, a "bunker mentality" was consuming the government.[51]

Citing security concerns, Giuliani closed City Hall Park for ten months and $13.8 million worth of renovations. New Yorkers appreciated the elegant fountain, but resented the park's formidable fences, metal detectors, and traffic obstacles. With the gates closed most of the time, the park was to be seen, not used. Limits were set on which groups and how many people could demonstrate in City Hall plaza or hold press conferences on City Hall steps, both of which had historically been considered public space. When Giuliani welcomed large celebrations for his beloved New York Yankees but banned small demonstrations by AIDS activists, the City Council objected and the Federal District Court ruled his policies unconstitutional.[52]

Giuliani's impact on the city was immense. For all the conflict he caused and the resistance he met, he revolutionized the city's social contract. To be sure, his most outrageous First Amendment initiatives were reversed by the courts. However, in terms of education and welfare, he managed to change policies that had prevailed for decades and that reflected centuries of commitment to urban liberalism. Many people feared that the Gateway City was becoming a gated city. The process began with the fiscal crisis and accelerated under Koch, but was completed by Giuliani who prided himself on seizing a "historic opportunity. . .to do what was politically unthinkable just a few years ago." He called it "reality therapy;" others considered it shock therapy.[53]

THE RESTLESS CITY

Giuliani was widely criticized for spending another $13 million constructing a state-of-the-art crisis command center on the 23rd floor of 7 World Trade Center, a few blocks from City Hall. Although he later cited the September 11, 2001 attacks as justification for such a facility, the center was totally destroyed when the Twin Towers fell. In his book *Leadership* (2002), Giuliani described the harrowing events of that day as his government ran from place to place searching for a base of operations and a source of solace for a shaken city. With people jumping from the burning buildings, debris raining from the sky, crowds rushing through the streets, and ash engulfing everything, the situation was, as he put it, "primitive, shocking, surreal."[54]

Into the breach stepped the superhero. While President George W. Bush was sequestered by his staff, Giuliani became the face of America at home and abroad, the voice of sanity in an insane world. He urged calm, toured Ground Zero, expressed sympathy, attended funerals, and supported rescuers. His approval ratings soared to 85 percent, even though support for extending his mayoralty never materialized and only 40 percent of New Yorkers said they would reelect him if given the chance. Be that as it may, the man who had so recently been the city's stern schoolmarm now emerged as a benevolent father figure exuding strength as well as sensitivity. In the midst of catastrophe, he was larger than life.[55]

Giuliani's legacy has been measured against LaGuardia's, a comparison Giuliani covets because LaGuardia has long been ranked Gotham's best mayor. In some ways, they were similar. Both men had humble origins, bellicose personalities, domineering leadership styles, a moralistic sense of mission, short fuses, and aggressive reform agendas. They were political mavericks and crime fighters who were intolerant of critics and often hostile to the press. Giuliani's description of LaGuardia as "omnipresent and. . .exceedingly controversial" applied equally well to himself. The historian Fred Siegel regards them both as exceptional because they "fundamentally transformed the city." Furthermore, they both loved New York.[56]

In other ways, LaGuardia and Giuliani were opposites. The former built on his immigrant background to reach out to different ethnic groups and used his legal training to advocate for the poor and the powerless. He restrained the police during riots and sought (but never achieved) real reform of the police force. LaGuardia employed his political power to build housing, expand education, promote the arts, and increase social services. He tried to be responsive to racial issues, albeit with limitations.

By contrast, Giuliani used his ethnic identity to polarize the city while directing his legal training against the poor and the powerless. He was a diehard champion of the police. He employed his political power to attack the education system, censor artists, limit personal freedom, and curtail social services. Moreover, contends the historian Chris McNickle, his unresponsiveness to racial issues was "behavior at odds with greatness."[57]

Nevertheless, Giuliani may ultimately outrank LaGuardia because of September 11, which instantly rendered him, like Superman, the nation's superpatriot. He became the first mayor to address the United Nations and was nominated for a Nobel Peace Prize. *Time* magazine named him person of the year, the Queen of England dubbed him an honorary knight, and Hollywood enshrined him in a movie. At the Manhattan Institute, Fred Seigel proclaimed Giuliani "the greatest mayor that New York has had since Peter Stuyvesant." The characteristics of the supercity, the supermayor, and the superhero merged as never before.[58]

The World Trade Center attacks highlighted New York City's unique role in the nation, the world, and history as the symbol of a way of life. Indeed, to countless people around the globe, "only one city is an emotional location as well as a place."[59] Perhaps that is why its conflicts have resonated so widely over time. New York's expanding economy, fluid social structure, and flexible, tolerant culture have always attracted the ambitious, the creative, and the rebellious. These types were particularly prone to conflict when their status was threatened or their opportunities narrowed. Although the resulting violent and nonviolent struggles strained the social contract, they also reinforced the concept of a unique community based on diversity, freedom, and opportunity. Conflict reflected faith in the future as well as criticism of the present.

Former mayor Philip Hone complained about the city's "annual metamorphosis," but he knew that New York was dynamic and resilient precisely because it was characterized by and dedicated to change.[60] From the Peach Tree War to the Diallo crisis, political, economic, social, and cultural conflicts reflected the challenges created by change. Across the centuries, New York's complexity caused tension while keeping it vibrant and humane. Time and again, the interaction between change and conflict was a source of self-assessment for the city—a refreshing whirlwind as much as a dangerous whirlpool.

Change and conflict clarified the dilemmas of civic life by posing, as Asa Briggs put it, "the most exciting and alarming riddles about present and future."[61] The core questions were how to dovetail the private interest with the public good, how to balance freedom with order, and how to promote both capitalism and democracy. New York never fully answered those questions because it never fully resolved those conflicts, and never will. Indeed, the New York spirit is to forever ask questions. Rather than becoming passive, routine, dull, and content, Gotham will always be aggressive, innovative, exciting, and contentious. New York's restlessness remains its greatest asset.

Suggestions for Further Inquiry

This book covers four hundred years of history through a selective examination of the periods, people, and events that shaped the history of change and conflict in New York City. Instead of a formal bibliography organized alphabetically by author, the endnotes provide a more practical organization of references by period and subject. Every chapter starts with an introduction that cites sources for the broad historical context of each era. The subsequent units identify general and specific sources for each topic that will lead the reader to yet more sources. Because so many people find New York City history so fascinating, there is a wealth of books, documents, articles, and images to investigate.

For basic facts, start with Jeffrey Kroessler, *New York, Year by Year: A Chronology of the Great Metropolis* (New York: New York University Press, 2002); James Trager, *The New York Chronology: The Ultimate Compendium of Events, People and Anecdotes from the Dutch to the Present* (New York: HarperCollins, 2003); and Howard Dodson, Christopher Moore, and Roberta Yancy, *The Black New Yorkers: The Schomburg Illustrated Chronology* (New York: John Wiley and Sons, 2000). For more extensive, but still brief, explanations, consult Kenneth T. Jackson, ed., *The Encyclopedia of New York City* (New Haven: Yale University Press, 1995).

For a skeletal text with interesting graphics, some biographical sketches, a timeline, and a bibliography, see Eric Homburger, *The Historical Atlas of New York City: A Visual Celebration of Nearly 400 Years of New York City's History* (New York: Henry Holt and Company, 1994). For a lively topical text with related visuals and bibliography, see Bernie Bookbinder, *City of the World: New York and Its People* (New York: Harry N. Abrams, 1989).

Short general overviews of New York City history include Selma Berrol, *The Empire City* (New York: Praeger, 1997); Frederick M. Binder and David M. Reimers, *All the Nations Under Heaven* (New York: Columbia University Press, 1995); George Lankevich, *New York City: A Short History* (New York: New York University Press, 2002); and Francois Weil, *A History of New York* (New York: Columbia University Press, 2004). Slightly longer but quite engaging are Oliver Allen, *New York, New York: A History of the World's Most Exhilarating and Challenging City* (New York: Atheneum, 1990); and Edward Robb Ellis, *The Epic of New York City* (New York: Old Town Books, 1966/ Kodansha America Reprint, 1997).

Gotham: A History of New York City to 1898 (New York: Oxford University Press, 1999) by Edwin G. Burrows and Mike Wallace is a hefty but well-written and widely praised book covering every aspect of New York City history from the seventeenth through the nineteenth centuries. Its comprehensive alphabetical bibliography is correlated with a references section for each topical vignette. As a companion to the acclaimed Public Broadcasting System's television series called *New York: A Documentary Film* (available on video, CD, and at http://www.pbs.org/wnet/newyork), Ric Burns and James Sanders with Lisa Ades have published *New York: An Illustrated History* (New York: Alfred A. Knopf, 1999). It provides a rich text, six essays, three interviews, superb visuals, and a selected bibliography.

Key primary source documents can be found in Kenneth T. Jackson and David S. Dunbar, eds., *Empire City: New York Through the Centuries* (New York: Columbia University Press, 2002). Broad cross sections of print and visual primary sources are available in Alexander Klein, ed., *The Empire City: A Treasury of New York* (New York: Rhinehart and Company, 1955); John A. Kouwenhoven, *The Columbia Historical Portrait of New York: An Essay in Graphic History* (New York: Harper and Row, 1953); Philip Lopate, ed., *Writing New York: A Literary Anthology* (New York: Literary Classics of the United States, 1998); Mike Marqusee, ed., *New York, An Illustrated Anthology* (Topsfield, Mass.: Salem House Publishers, 1988); Mike Marqusee and Bill Harris, eds., *New York, An Anthology* (New York: Barnes and Noble, 1985); Howard B. Rock and Deborah Dash Moore, *Cityscapes: A History of New York in Images* (New York: Columbia University Press, 2001); and Bayrd Still, *Mirror for Gotham: New York as Seen by Contemporaries from Dutch Days to the Present* (New York: Fordham University Press, 1994).

On the Web, a good place to start is Virtual New York at http://www. vny.cuny.edu, which contains interesting exhibits and a useful list of New York City history links. Additional resources can be found on the Web sites of the Gotham Center at http://www.gothamcenter.org, the LaGuardia and

Wagner Archives at LaGuardia Community College (CUNY) at http://www. laguardiawagnerarchive.lagcc.cuny.edu, the Municipal Archives at http:// NYC.gov/records, the Museum of the City of New York at http://www.mcny. org, and the New York Historical Society at http://www.nyhistory.org.

These suggestions are just a beginning; the possibilities are endless. Enjoy and, as you investigate, remember the architectural critic Paul Goldberger's observation that

> New York remains what it has always been: a city of ebb and flow, a city of constant shifts of population and economics, a city of virtually no rest. It is harsh, dirty and dangerous, it is whimsical and fanciful, it is beautiful and soaring—it is not one or another of these things but all of them, all at once, and to fail to accept this paradox is to deny the reality of city existence.[1]

Notes

CHAPTER 1

1.   Allan Nevins, ed., *The Diary of Philip Hone, 1828–1851* (New York: Dodd Mead, 1927), 394–395, 730, 785; Edwin G. Burrows and Mike Wallace, *Gotham: A History of New York City to 1898* (New York: Oxford University Press, 1999), xi–xxiv; Ric Burns and James Sanders, *New York, An Illustrated History* (New York: Alfred A. Knopf, 1999), xii–xv, 76–78; Allan Nevins, "The Golden Thread in the History of New York," *The New York Historical Society Quarterly* (January, 1955), 5–22; Bayrd Still, "The Essence of New York City," *The New York Historical Society Quarterly* (October, 1959), 401–423; Jacob Judd, "New York: A City of Constant Change and Accommodation," in *The Knickerbocker Tradition: Washington Irving's New York*, ed. Andrew B. Meyers (Tarrytown: Sleepy Hollow Restorations, 1974), 116–124; George Lankevich, *New York City: A Short History* (New York: New York University Press, 2002), vii–x; Thomas Bender, *The Unfinished City: New York and the Metropolitan Idea* (New York: The New Press, 2002), xii–xvi; Eric Homberger, *New York City. A Cultural and Literary Companion* (New York: Interlink Books, 2003), xxvii; Francois Weil, *A History of New York* (New York: Columbia University Press, 2004), xiii–xv.
2.   Nevins, *The Diary of Philip Hone*, vii–xx, 41, 204–209, 508, 740–742; Louis Auchinloss, *The Hone and Strong Diaries of Old Manhattan* (New York: Abbeville Press, 1989), 11–14, 22–25, 40–59, 111, 115–118.
3.   Lewis Mumford, *The City in History: Its Origins, Its Transformations,and Its Prospects* (New York: Harcourt, Brace, Jovanovich, 1961), 4, 9–10, 17–20, 29, 32.
4.   Ibid., 30–34, 46.
5.   Ibid., 52.

6. Alexis de Tocqueville, *Democracy in America* II (New York: Vintage Books, 1945), 144–147.

7. Richard E. Rubenstein, *Rebels in Eden: Mass Political Violence in the United States* (Boston: Little Brown, 1970), 2–20; Milton M. Klein, "Shaping the American Tradition: The Microcosm of Colonial New York," *New York History* (1978), 174; Warren I. Susman, *Culture as History: The Transformation of American Society in the Twentieth Century* (New York: Pantheon Books, 1973), 237–251.

8. Lewis A. Coser, *Continuities in the Study of Social Conflict* (New York: Free Press, 1967), 78–90; Rubenstein, *Rebels in Eden*, 36–41; Marilynn S. Johnson, *Street Justice: A History of Police Violence in New York City* (Boston: Beacon Press, 2003); Michael Wallace, "The Uses of Violence in American History," *American Scholar* 40 (1970–72), 96–97.

9. Richard Hofstadter and Michael Wallace, eds., *American Violence: A Documentary History* (New York: Alfred A. Knopf, 1970), 3–43; Richard C. Wade, "Violence in the Cities: A Historical Overview," in *Cities Under Siege: An Anatomy of the Ghetto Riots, 1964–1968*, eds. David Boesel and Peter H. Rossi (New York: Basic Books, 1971), 277–296.

10. David Grimsted, *American Mobbing, 1828–1861: Toward Civil War* (New York: Oxford University Press, 1998), vii; Mary P. Ryan, *Civic Wars: Democracy and Public Life in the American City During the Nineteenth Century* (Berkeley: University of California Press, 1997), 313; Edward C. Banfield, "Rioting Mainly for Fun and Profit," in *The Metropolitan Enigma*, ed. James Q. Wilson, (New York: Doubleday, 1970), 312–41; Charles Tilly, "Collective Violence in European Perspective," in *Violence in America: Historical and Comparative Perspectives*, eds. Hugh Davis Graham and Ted Robert Gurr (Washington, D.C.: National Commission on the Causes and Prevention of Violence, 1969), 5–34; Ralph W. Conant, "Rioting, Insurrection and Civil Disobedience," in *Violence: An Element of American Life*, eds. Karl K. Taylor and Fred W. Soady, Jr. (Boston: Holbrook Press, 1972), 262–278.

11. St. Clair Drake, "Urban Violence and American Social Movements," in *Urban Riots: Violence and Social Change*, ed. Robert H. Connery (New York: Vintage, 1969), 15–26.

12. Asa Briggs, *Victorian Cities* (London: Odhams Books, 1963), 94.

13 Ibid., 18, 22–23.

14. Ann Douglas, *Terrible Honesty, Mongrel Manhattan in the 1920s* (New York: The Noonday Press, 1995), 28.

15. Briggs, *Victorian Cities*, 324.

16. Ibid., 56; Burns and Sanders, *New York*, 100.

17. Wallace, "The Uses of Violence," 81–102.

CHAPTER 2

1. Kenneth Jackson, ed., *The Encyclopedia of New York City* (New Haven: Yale University Press, 1995), 718; Henry H. Kessler and Eugene Rachlis, *Peter Stuyvesant and His New York* (New York: Random House, 1959), 41.

2. I. N. Phelps Stokes, *The Iconography of Manhattan Island, 1498–1909* IV (New York: Robert H. Dodd, 1915–1928), 44, 125; Albert Ulmann, *A Landmark History*

of New York (New York: D. Appleton-Century, 1939), 8; Michael Kammen, *Colonial New York, A History* (New York: Oxford University Press, 1975), 6, 25; Edwin G. Burrows and Mike Wallace, *Gotham: A History of New York City to 1898* (New York: Oxford University Press, 1999), 18.

3. Bayard Still, "The Essence of New York City," *New York Historical Society Quarterly* 43 (October, 1959), 401–423; Milton M. Klein, *The Politics of Diversity: Essays in the History of Colonial New York* (Port Washington: Kennikat Press, 1974), 183–211; Russell Shorto, *The Island at the Center of the World: The Epic Story of Dutch Manhattan and the Forgotten Colony that Shaped America* (New York: Doubleday, 2004), 285.

4. George J. Lankevich, *New York City, A Short History* (New York: New York University Press, 1998/2002), 20–30; Thomas Archdeacon, "Anglo-Dutch New York, 1676," in *New York: The Centennial Years,* ed. Milton Klein (Port Washington: Kennikat Press, 1976), 11–39; Milton M. Klein, "Shaping the American Tradition: The Microcosm of Colonial New York," *New York History* 59 (1978), 173–197.

5. Kammen, *Colonial New York,* 23–36

6. Bayard Still, *Mirror for Gotham: New York as Seen by Contemporaries from Dutch Days to the Present* (New York: New York University Press, 1956), 3–14; Kessler and Rachlis, *Stuyvesant,* 3–7; Alexander Hamilton, James Madison and John Jay, *The Federalist Papers* (New York: Mentor, 1961), 324.

7. Burrows and Wallace, *Gotham,* 24, 33–39; Kessler and Rachlis, *Stuyvesant,* 53–61; Allen W. Trelease, *Indian Affairs in Colonial New York: The Seventeenth Century* (Ithaca, N.Y.: Cornell University Press, 1960), 26–29, 93; Edward Robb Ellis, *The Epic of New York City* (New York: Old Town Books, 1966), 23–40; Shorto, *Island,* 118–128.

8. Burrows and Wallace, *Gotham,* 68; Ellis, *Epic,* 65–67; Kessler and Rachlis, *Stuyvesant,* 159–68; Trelease, *Indian Affairs,* 12, 72; Archdeacon, "Anglo-Dutch NY," 17–18; Oliver E. Allen, *New York, New York: A History of the World's Most Exhilarating and Challenging City* (New York: Atheneum, 1990), 28–29; Rink, *Holland on the Hudson,* 214–222, 259; Henri Van Der Zee and Barbara Van Der Zee, *A Sweet and Alien Land: The Story of Dutch New York* (New York: Viking, 1978), 271–279.

9. Thomas Bender, "New York as a Center of Difference: How America's Metropolis Counters American Myth," *Dissent* (Fall, 1987), 429–435.

10. Burrows and Wallace, *Gotham,* 41–50; Shorto, *Island,* 146–170; Ellis *Epic,* 41–46; Rink, *Holland,* 223–237; Kessler and Rachlis, *Stuyvesant,* 45–50; Albert Ulmann, *New Yorkers from Stuyvesant to Roosevelt* (Port Washington: Ira J. Friedman, 1928/1969), 7–30.

11. Burrows and Wallace, *Gotham,* 58–59; Kammen, *Colonial New York,* 64.

12. Kessler and Rachlis, *Stuyvesant,* 66–77; Burrows and Wallace, *Gotham,* 43–47.

13. Burrows and Wallace, *Gotham,* 47; Kammen, *Colonial New York,* 55–57.

14. Burrows and Wallace, *Gotham,* 59–60; Kessler and Rachlis, *Stuyvesant,* 169–186; Rink, *Holland,* 223–233.

15. Burrows and Wallace, *Gotham,* 60, 133–135; Kessler and Rachlis, *Stuyvesant,* 171, 176–186; Rink, *Holland,* 233–235; Ellis, *Epic,* 60–61; Frederick M. Binder and David M. Reimers, *All the Nations Under Heaven: An Ethnic and Racial History*

of New York City (New York: Columbia University Press, 1995), 6–11; Kammen, *Colonial New York*, 86–87.

16. Burrows and Wallace, *Gotham*, 61; Kessler and Rachlis, *Stuyvesant*, 186–193; Rink, *Holland*, 235–237; Ellis, *Epic*, 62–64; Shorto, *Island*, 275–276.

17. Binder and Reimers, *All the Nations*, 7–8; Kessler and Rachlis, *Stuyvesant*, 192–193; Klein, "Shaping American Tradition," 188–197; Eric Homberger, *The Historical Atlas of New York City* (New York: Henry Holt, 1994), 168.

18. Kammen, *Colonial New York*, 54–55; Kessler and Rachlis, *Stuyvesant*, 95–109; Shorto, *Island*, 142–144, 204–207, 216–221, 227–230, 240–243, 280–281.

19. Burrows and Wallace, *Gotham*, 139–140; Archdeacon, "Anglo-Dutch NY," 32–33.

20. Still, *Mirror*, 23; Patricia U. Bonomi, *A Factious People: Politics and Society in Colonial New York* (New York: Columbia University Press, 1971), 22–28.

21. Burrows and Wallace, *Gotham*, 91–103; Bonomi, *Factious People*, 10–16; Kammen, *Colonial NY*, 121–127, Charles Howard McCormick, *Leisler's Rebellion* (New York: Garland, 1971/1989), 382–387.

22. Bonomi, *Factious People*, 75–78; Thomas J. Archdeacon, "The Age of Leisler— New York City, 1689–1710: A Social and Demographic Interpretation," in *Aspects of Early New York Society and Politics*, eds. Jacob Judd and Irwin Polishook (Tarrytown: Sleepy Hollow Restorations, 1974), 63–82; McCormick, *Leisler's Rebellion*, 5, 274–275; Jerome R. Reich, *Leisler's Rebellion: A Story of Democracy in New York, 1664–1720* (Chicago: University of Chicago Press, 1953), 91–92, 172– 173; Gary B. Nash, *The Urban Crucible: The Northern Seaports and the Origins of the American Revolution* (Cambridge, Mass.: Harvard University Press, 1986), 24–28; John M. Murrin, "English Rights as Ethnic Aggression: The English Conquest, the Charter of Liberties of 1683 and Leisler's Rebellion in New York," in *Authority and Resistance in Early New York*, eds. William Pencak and Conrad Edick Wright (New York: New York Historical Society, 1988, 56–94; Mary Lou Lustig, *The Imperial Executive in America: Sir Edmund Andros, 1637–1714* (Madison: Fairleigh Dickinson University Press, 2002), 199–200.

23. Archdeacon, "Age of Leisler," 63–82; Reich, *Leisler's Rebellion*, 122.

24. Burrows and Wallace, *Gotham*, 153–155; Bonomi, *Factious People*, 117–120; Kammen, *Colonial NY*, 206–207; Ulmann, *New Yorkers*, 38–56; Carl Bridenbaugh, *Cities in Revolt* (New York: Knopf, 1955), 388–393, 423.

25. Thomas Bender, *New York Intellect: A History of Intellectual Life in New York City from 1750 to Our Own Time* (New York: Alfred A. Knopf, 1987), 17–25.

26. Bonomi, *Factious People*, 56–75.

27. Klein, *Politics of Diversity*, 74–83.

28. Burrows and Wallace, *Gotham*, 180–181; Kammen, *Colonial NY*, 250–251; Bender, *NY Intellect*, 22–23; Richard Hofstadter and Walter Metzger, *The Development of Academic Freedom in the United States* (New York: Columbia University Press, 1955), 186–191; Richard Hofstadter and Wilson Smith, eds., *American Higher Education: A Documentary History* I (Chicago: University of Chicago Press, 1961), 99–103.

29. Klein, *Politics of Diversity*, 83, 97–107.

30. Bender, *NY Intellect*, 23–25; Klein, *Politics of Diversity*, 183–200; Shorto, *Island*, 310.

31. Edgar J. McManus, *A History of Negro Slavery in New York* (Syracuse: Syracuse University Press, 1966), 1; Eric Foner, *The Story of American Freedom* (New York: W.W. Norton, 1998), 15; Klein, *Politics of Diversity*, 194–195.

32. Burrows and Wallace, *Gotham*, 31–33; McManus, *Negro Slavery*, 2–12; Joyce D. Goodfriend, " Burghers and Blacks: The Evolution of a Slave Society in New Amsterdam," *New York History* 59 (1978), 125–144; Graham Russell Hodges, *Root and Branch: African Americans in New York and East Jersey, 1613–1863* (Chapel Hill: University of North Carolina Press, 1999), 6–9.

33. McManus, *Negro Slavery*, 13–15; Goodfriend, "Burghers and Blacks," 128–131; Binder and Reimers, *All the Nations*, 14–15; Hodges, *Root and Branch*, 12–15, 26; Burrows and Wallace, *Gotham*, 55–56.

34. Kammen, *Colonial NY*, 56–60; Hodges, *Root and Branch*, 9–33; McManus, *Negro Slavery*, 11–22; David Kobrin, *The Black Minority in Early New York* (Albany: State University of New York Press, 1971), 9–13; Herman D. Bloch, *The Circle of Discrimination: An Economic and Social Study of the Black Man in New York* (New York: New York University Press, 1969), 1–8.

35. Burrows and Wallace, *Gotham*, 120–129; Kobrin, *Black Minority*, 13–17; Hodges, *Root and Branch*, 34–63; McManus, *Negro Slavery*, 23–39, 59–99; Shane White, *Somewhat More Independent: The End of Slavery in New York City, 1770–1810* (Athens: University of Georgia Press, 1991), 4–9; Donald R. Wright, *African Americans in the Colonial Era: From African Origins through the American Revolution* (Arlington Heights, Ill.: Harlan Davidson, 1990), 72–75; Kenneth M. Stampp, *The Peculiar Institution: Slavery in the Ante-Bellum South* (New York: Vintage Books, 1956), 86–140 .

36. Burrows and Wallace, *Gotham*, 147–149; Hodges, *Root and Branch*, 63–64; McManus, *Negro Slavery*, 95; Herbert Aptheker, *American Negro Slave Revolts* (New York: Columbia University Press, 1943), 72; Bayard Tuckerman, ed., *The Diary of Philip Hone, 1828–1851* (New York: Dodd Mead, 1889), 116.

37. Joyce D. Goodfriend, *Before the Melting Pot: Society and Culture in Colonial New York City, 1664–1730* (Princeton: Princeton University Press, 1992), 111–124; Thomas F. Archdeacon, *New York City, 1664–1710: Conquest and Change* (Ithaca, N.Y.: Cornell University Press, 1976), 145–146; Kobrin, *Black Minority*, 3–17; Hodges, *Root and Branch*, 65; McManus, *Negro Slavery*, 121–125; Kenneth Scott, "The Slave Insurrection in New York in 1712," *New York Historical Society Quarterly* 45 (January, 1961), 43–62.

38. McManus, *Negro Slavery*, 125; Burrows and Wallace, *Gotham*, 148–149; Aptheker, *Slave Revolts*, 172–173; Kobrin, *Black Minority*, 3–17; Scott, "Slave Insurrection," 47–62, 73; Richard Hofstadter and Michael Wallace, eds., *American Violence: A Documentary History* (New York: Vintage, 1971), 21; Thelma Wills Foote, "Black Life in Colonial Manhattan, 1664–1786" (Ph.D. dissertation, Harvard University, 1991), 197–224; Joel Tyler Headly, *The Great Riots of New York, 1712–1873* (New York: Dover, 1873/1971), 26–28.

39. McManus, *Negro Slavery*, 125; Scott, "Slave Insurrection," 69–73; Ferenc M. Szasz, "The New York Slave Revolt of 1741: A Re-examination," *New York History* 48 (1967), 217–218.

40. Burrows and Wallace, *Gotham*, 159; Hodges, *Root and Branch*, 88–89; Goodfriend, *Melting Pot*, 61–80, 111–132; Kammen, *Colonial NY*, 278–304; Raymond A. Mohl,

"Poverty in Early America, A Reappraisal: The Case of Eighteenth Century New York City," *New York History* 50 (January, 1969), 5–27; Archdeacon, *NYC, 1664–1710,* 148.

41. Nash, *Urban Crucible,* 6–11; Aptheker, *Slave Revolts,* 193–197; Szasz, "Slave Revolt 1741," 218–219; Thomas J. Davis, *A Rumor of Revolt: The "Great Negro Plot" in Colonial New York* (New York: The Free Press, 1985), ix–xii, 261–263.

42. Thomas J. Davis, ed., *The New York Conspiracy by Daniel Horsmanden, 1744* (Boston: Beacon Press, 1971), vii–xx, 13–35; Headley, *Great Riots,* 28–33; Szasz, "Slave Revolt 1741," 220–221; McManus, *Negro Slavery,* 126–128.

43. Aptheker, *Slave Revolts,* 193–195; Davis, *Rumor of Revolt,* 59–127; Szasz, "Slave Revolt 1741," 220–221; McManus, *Negro Slavery,* 128–131; Burrows and Wallace, *Gotham,* 159–161; Hodges, *Root and Branch,* 93–96; *New York Weekly Journal,* May 11, 1741–June 8, 1741.

44. Davis, *Rumor of Revolt,* 129–159, 252, 298 footnote 1; McManus, *Negro Slavery,* 131–133; Szasz, "Slave Revolt 1741," 215; Hodges, *Root and Branch,* 94; *New York Weekly Journal,* June 8, 1741–August 17, 1741.

45. Davis, *Rumor of Revolt,* 160–249; McManus, *Negro Slavery,* 133–138; Szasz, "Slave Revolt 1741," 223–225; Hodges, *Root and Branch,* 94–95; *New York Weekly Journal,* June 15, 1741–August 31, 1741.

46. Headley, *Great Riots,* 28–45; Davis, *Rumor of Revolt,* 250–263; Szasz, "Slave Revolt 1741," 222–227; Hodges, *Root and Branch,* 93–99; T. Wood Clarke, "The Negro Plot of 1741," *New York History* 25 (1944), 167–181; Leopold S. Launitz-Schurer Jr., "Slave Resistance in Colonial New York: An Interpretation of Daniel Horsemanden's New York Conspiracy," *Phylon* 41 (June, 1980), 137–152; Richard Maxwell Brown, *Strain of Violence: Historical Studies of American Violence and Vigilantism* (New York: Oxford University Press, 1975), 190–191.

47. Kammen, *Colonial NY,* 337–338.

48. Burrows and Wallace, *Gotham,* 167–170, 181–184, 190–194; Kammen, *Colonial NY,* 305–332; Patricia U. Bonomi, "New York, The Royal Colony," *New York History* 82 (Winter, 2001), 5–24.

49. Burrows and Wallace, *Gotham,* 196–198; Kammen, *Colonial NY,* 338–356.

50. Burrows and Wallace, *Gotham,* 198–200; Edmund S. Morgan and Helen M. Morgan, *The Stamp Act Crisis: Prologue to Revolution* (New York: Collier, 1953/1962), 75–98; Foner, *Freedom,* 9; Joseph S. Tiedemann, *Reluctant Revolutionaries: New York City and the Road to Independence, 1763–1776* (Ithaca, N.Y.: Cornell University Press, 1997), 67–68; Paul A. Gilje, *The Road to Mobocracy: Popular Disorder in New York City, 1763–1834* (Chapel Hill: University of North Carolina Press, 1987), 44–52.

51. Morgan, *Stamp Act Crisis,* 139–152; Tiedemann, *Reluctant Revolutionaries,* 94–97; Pauline Maier, *From Resistance to Revolution: Colonial Radicals and the Development of American Opposition to Britain, 1765–1776* (New York: Alfred A. Knopf, 1972), 78–79.

52. Tiedemann, *Reluctant Revolutionaries,* 70–73, 171; Ellis, *Epic,* 143–148; Headley, *Great Riots,* 46–49.

53. Ellis, *Epic,* 144–148; Kammen, *Colonial NY,* 350–353; Headley, *Great Riots,* 50–53; Nash, *Urban Crucible,* 189–193; Gilje, *Mobocracy,* 45–51; Edward Countryman, *A People in Revolution: The American Revolution and Political Society in New York,*

1760-1790 (Baltimore: Johns Hopkins University Press, 1981), 55-62; Burrows and Wallace, *Gotham*, 198-200; Jesse Lemish, *Jack Tar vs John Bull: The Role of New York's Seamen in Precipitating the Revolution* (New York: Garland, 1997), 73-87.

54. Burrows and Wallace, *Gotham*, 201-203; Carl Becker, *The History of Political Parties in the Province of New York, 1760-1776* (Madison: University of Wisconsin Press, 1960), 23-52; Tiedemann, *Reluctant Revolutionaries*, 78-32; Bruce M. Wilkenfeld, "Revolutionary NY," 64.

55. Lemish, *Jack Tar*, 16, 51-64; Burrows and Wallace, *Gotham*, 198-201; Gilje, *Mobocracy*, 5-8, 44-52; Paul A. Gilje, *Rioting in America* (Bloomington: Indiana University Press, 1996), 38-40; Morgan, *Stamp Act Riots*, 236-237; Philip S. Foner, *Labor and the American Revolution* (Westport, Conn.: Greenwood Press, 1976), 52-60.

56. Gilje, *Mobocracy*, 52-55; Phelps Stokes, *Iconography* IV, 765, 802-803; Lee R. Boyer, "Lobster Backs, Liberty Boys, and Laborers in the Streets: New York's Golden Hill and Nassau Street Riots," *New York Historical Society Quarterly* 57 (October, 1973), 289-308; Richard M. Ketchum, *Divided Loyalties: How the American Revolution Came to New York* (New York: Henry Holt, 2002), 134-159.

57. Burrows and Wallace, *Gotham*, 200-202; Nash, *Urban Crucible*, 189-199; Gilje, *Mobocracy*, 51; Lemish, *Jack Tar*, 92-104; Tiedemann, *Reluctant Revolutionaries*, 39-41; Maier, *Resistance to Revolution*, 71-112; Philip S. Foner, *Labor and the American Revolution* (Westport, Conn.: Greenwood Press, 1976), 52-60; Staughton Lynd, "The Mechanics in New York City Politics, 1774-1788," *Labor History* 5 (1964), 225-246.

58. Boyer, "Lobster Backs," 292-305; Gilje, *Mobocracy*, 51-58; Bonomi, *Factious People*, 234-236, 267-274; Lemish, *Jack Tar*, 121-142; Countryman, *People in Revolution*, 63-67; Tiedemann, *Reluctant Revolutionaries*, 147-149; Ketchum, *Divided Loyalties*, 176-184, 224-229.

59. Burrows and Wallace, *Gotham*, 210-212; Bonomi, *Factious People*, 267-275; Ketchum, *Divided Loyalties*, 213-219; Roger J. Champagne, *Alexander McDougall and the American Revolution in New York* (Schenectady, N.Y.: Union College Press, 1975), 19-28; Tiedemann, *Reluctant Revolutionaries*, 143-145; Launitz-Schurer Jr., *Loyal Whigs and Revolutionaries: The Making of the Revolution in New York, 1765-1776* (New York: New York University Press, 1980), 200-204.

60. Broadus Mitchell, *Alexander Hamilton, Youth to Maturity, 1755-1788* (New York: Macmillan, 1957), 1-56; Ron Chernow, *Alexander Hamilton* (New York: Penguin, 2004), 7-56.

61. Champagne, *McDougall*, 19-28.

62. Ketchum, *Divided Loyalties*, 213-219; Champagne, *McDougall*, 27-40; Launitz-Schurer, *Loyal Whigs*, 82-86, 194-195.

63. Burrows and Wallace, *Gotham*, 213-217; Champagne, *McDougall*, 35-56; Countryman, *People in Revolution*, 55-63, 66-67, 292-296; Tiedemann, *Reluctant Revolutionaries*, 175-197; Becker, *History of Political Parties*, 5-22, 95-141; Lynd, "Mechanics," 225-246; Howard D. Rock, *Artisans of the New Republic: The Tradesmen of New York City in the Age of Jefferson* (New York: New York University Press, 1984), 19-23.

64. Gilje, *Mobocracy*, 43, 58–61; Maier, *Resistance to Revolution*, 271–296; Kammen, *Colonial NY*, 342–348; Countryman, *People in Revolution*, 66–67, 292–296; Burrows and Wallace, *Gotham*, 224.

65. Willard Sterne Randall, *Alexander Hamilton, A Life* (New York: Harper Collins, 2003), 89–95, 135–137, 295–296; Mitchell, *Hamilton, 1755–1788*, 74–77; Chernow, *Hamilton*, 54–70.

66. Mitchell, *Hamilton, 1755–1788*, 77–84; Randall, *Hamilton*, 95–103; Chernow, *Hamilton*, 70–78; Burrows and Wallace, *Gotham*, 223–225, 230–232; Kammen, *Colonial NY*, 337–375.

67. Burrows and Wallace, *Gotham*, 232–44; Wilbur C. Abbott, *New York in the American Revolution* (New York: Charles Scribner's Sons, 1929), 170; Barnet Schecter, *The Battle for New York: The City at the Heart of the American Revolution* (New York: Penguin, 2003), 141–167, 179–218.

68. Burrows and Wallace, *Gotham*, 244–56; Ellis, *Epic*, 157–175; Allen, *NY, NY*, 55–80.

69. Burrows and Wallace, *Gotham*, 176, 259–261; Allen, *NY, NY*, 81–89.

70. Kammen, *Colonial NY*, 369.

71. Allen, *NY, NY*, 81–82.

72. Burrows and Wallace, *Gotham*, 298–304, 309–312, 321–323; Chernow, *Hamilton*, 488–500; Donald L. Smith, *John Jay, Founder of a State and a Nation* (New York: Columbia University Press, 1968), 1–6; George Pellew, *John Jay* (Boston: Chelsea House, 1898/ 1997), 1–52, 282–283; Richard B. Morris, "The American Revolution Comes to John Jay," in Judd and Polishook, *Aspects of Early NY*, 96–117; Broadus Mitchell, *Alexander Hamilton, The National Adventure, 1788–1804* (New York: Macmillan, 1962), 168–180, 331–350.

73. Randall, *Hamilton*, 349–353; Mitchell, *Hamilton, 1755–1788*, 356–425; Smith, *John Jay*, 128–132.

74. Burrows and Wallace, *Gotham*, 288–96; Mitchell, *Hamilton, 1755–1788*, 426–465; Chernow, *Hamilton*, 219–269.

75. Mitchell, *Hamilton, 1755–1788*, 346–355; Mitchell, *Hamilton, 1788–1804*, 86–108; Randall, *Hamilton*, 369–405; Chernow, *Hamilton*, 199–202, 344–355, 649–650.

76. Chernow, *Hamilton*, 128–153, 379–383, 641–650.

77. Burrows and Wallace, *Gotham*, 386–387; Headley, *Great Riots*, 56–65; Gilje, *Mobocracy*, 62, 79–83; Gilje, *Rioting*, 51–52; Paul A. Gilje, "The Common People and the Constitution: Popular Culture in New York City in the Late-Eighteenth Century," in *New York in the Age of the Constitution, 1775–1800*, eds. Paul A. Gilje and William Pencak (Madison, N.J.: Fairleigh Dickinson University Press, 1992), 48–70.

78. Burrows and Wallace, *Gotham*, 323–324; Gilje, *Mobocracy*, 105–107; Sean Wilentz, *Chants Democratic: New York City and the Rise of the American Working Class, 1788–1850* (New York: Oxford University Press, 1984), 66–67; Rock, *Artisans*, 24–26; Graham Russell Hodges, *New York City Cartmen, 1667–1850* (New York: New York University Press, 1986), 96–100.

79. Randall, *Hamilton*, 328; Elaine F. Crane, "Dependence in the Era of Independence: The Role of Women in a Republican Society," in *The American Revolution: Its Character and Limits*, ed. Jack P. Greene (New York: New York University Press, 1987), 253–275; Jean P. Jordan, "Women Merchants in Colonial New York," *New*

York History (October, 1977), 412–439; Barbara Berg, *The Remembered Gate: Origins of American Feminism, the Woman and the City, 1800–1860* (New York: Oxford University Press, 1978), 11–28.

80. Burrows and Wallace, *Gotham*, 407–408; Gilje, *Rioting*, 67–69; Christine Stansell, *City of Women: Sex and Class in New York, 1789–1860* (New York: Alfred A. Knopf, 1986), 18–26; Timothy J. Gilfoyle, *City of Eros: New York City, Prostitution and the Commercialization of Sex, 1790–1920* (New York: W.W. Norton, 1992), 23–26.

81. Burrows and Wallace, *Gotham*, 248–249; Kobrin, *Black Minority*, 40–41; McManus, *History of Negro Slavery*, 141–59, 174; Morris, *Hamilton*, 454–456; Milton Cantor, ed., *Hamilton* (Englewood Cliffs, N.J.: Prentice Hall, 1971), 15–19.

82. Hodges, *Root and Branch*, 147–161; Chernow, *Hamilton*, 121–123; William Loren Katz, *Black Legacy: A History of New York's African Americans* (New York: Atheneum, 1997), 29–40; Graham Russell Hodges, "Black Revolt in New York City and the Neutral Zone, 1775–83," in *New York in the Age of the Constitution, 1755–1800*, eds. Paul A. Gilje and William Pencak (Madison, N.J.: Fairleigh Dickinson University Press, 1992) 20–40; Gary B. Nash, "Forging Freedom: The Emancipation Experience in the Northern Seaport Cities, 1775–1820," in *Slavery and Freedom in the Age of the American Revolution*, eds. Ira Berlin and Ronald Hoffman (Charlottesville: University Press of Virginia, 1983), 3–48.

83. Burrows and Wallace, *Gotham*, 283–287; Chernow, *Hamilton*, 210–216; Randall, *Hamilton*, 291–294; McManus, *History of Negro Slavery*, 166–174; Hodges, *Root and Branch*, 163–167, 217; Rob N. Weston, "Alexander Hamilton and the Abolition of Slavery in New York," *Afro-Americans in New York Life and History* 18 (January, 1994), 31–45; Daniel C. Littlefield, "John Jay, the Revolutionary Generation and Slavery," *New York History* 81 (January 2000), 91–132.

84. Burrows and Wallace, *Gotham*, 347–349; Chernow, *Hamilton*, 580–581; Hodges, *Root and Branch*, 168–171; Kobrin, *Black Minority*, 41–43; Morris, *Hamilton*, 96–117; Pellew, *John Jay*, 245–256.

85. Burrows and Wallace, *Gotham*, 45, 142; James F. Richardson, *The New York Police, Colonial Times to 1901* (New York: Oxford University Press, 1970), 3–22; Sidney Pomerantz, *New York: An American City, 1783–1803, A Study of Urban Life* (Port Washington, N.Y.: Ira J. Friedman, 1938/1965), 296–305.

86. Binder and Reimers, *All the Nations*, 31; Wilkenfeld, "Revolutionary NY," 64.

87. Launitz-Schurer Jr., *Loyal Whigs*, 200–204; Maier, *Resistance to Revolution*, 271–276.

88. Saul K. Padover, ed., *The Mind of Alexander Hamilton* (New York: Harper, 1958), 1–27; Chernow, *Hamilton*, 4, 30–36.

89. Wilkenfeld, "Revolutionary NY," 68; Carl Bridenbaugh, *Cities in the Wilderness: The First Century of Urban Life in America, 1625–1742* (New York: The Ronald Press, 1938), 69.

CHAPTER 3

1. William Irving, James Kirke Paulding, and Washington Irving, *Salmagundi or the Whimwhams and Opinions of Launcelet Langstaff, Esq., and Others* (Philadelphia:

J.P. Lippincott, 1871), 392–400; William R. Taylor, *In Pursuit of Gotham: Culture and Commerce in New York* (New York: Oxford University Press, 1992), xv–xvi; Edwin G. Burrows and Mike Wallace, *Gotham: A History of New York to 1898* (New York: Oxford University Press, 1999), xii–xiv.

2. Pierre M. Irving, ed., *Biographies and Miscellanies by Washington Irving* (New York: G.P. Putnam's Sons, 1866), 522–530; Burrows and Wallace, *Gotham*, 415–419; Washington Irving, *Diedrich Knickerbocker's A History of New York* (Tarrytown: Sleepy Hollow Press, 1981), 117–119, 124.

3. Robert A. Ferguson, "'Hunting Down a Nation': Irving's A History of New York," in *Washington Irving: The Critical Reaction*, ed. James W. Tuttleton (New York: AMS Press, 1993), 25–41; Donna Hagensick, "Irving: A Litterateur in Politics," in *Essays on Washington Irving*, ed. Ralph M. Aderman (Boston: G. K. Hall, 1990), 178–190; William L. Hedges, "The Theme of Americanism in Irving's Writings," in *Washington Irving, A Tribute*, ed. Andrew B. Meyers (Tarrytown: Sleepy Hollow Restorations, 1972), 29–35; Lorman A. Ratner, "American Nationalism Fifty Years After the Revolution," in Meyers, *Irving, A Tribute*, 43–46.

4. Irving, *History of NY*, 127–128, 158; Burrows and Wallace, *Gotham*, 419–422, 368–370; Oliver E. Allen, *New York, New York, A History of the World's Most Exhilarating and Challenging City* (New York: Atheneum, 1990), 95–99; Bayrd Still, *Mirror for Gotham: New York as Seen by Contemporaries from Dutch Days to the Present* (New York: New York University Press, 1956), 98.

5. Arthur M. Schlesinger Jr., *The Age of Jackson* (Boston: Little, Brown, 1945), 522–523.

6. John D. Stevens, *Sensationalism and the New York Press* (New York: Columbia University Press, 1991), 12–32; Paul O. Weinbaum, *Mobs and Demagogues: The New York Response to Collective Violence in the Early Nineteenth Century* (Ann Arbor: University of Michigan Press, 1979), 56–58; Burrows and Wallace, *Gotham*, 522–527; Gunther Barth, *City People: The Rise of Modern City Culture in Nineteenth Century America* (New York: Oxford University Press, 1980), 58–77.

7. Carl E. Prince, "The Great Riot Year: Jacksonian Democracy and Patterns of Violence in 1834," *Journal of the Early Republic* 5 (Spring, 1985), 1–20; Michael Feldberg, *The Turbulent Era: Riot and Disorder in Jacksonian America* (New York: Oxford University Press, 1980), 3–7; David Grimsted, "Rioting in its Jacksonian Setting," *American Historical Review* 77 (April, 1972), 361–397; Paul A. Gilje, *Rioting in America* (Bloomington: Indiana University Press, 1996), 60–75; Tyler Anbinder, *Five Points: The Nineteenth Century New York City Neighborhood that Invented Tap Dance, Stole Elections, and became the World's Most Notorious Slum* (New York: Free Press, 2001).

8. Irving, *History of NY*, xi–xiv; Andrew B. Meyers, "Introduction," in *The Knickerbocker Tradition: Washington Irving's New York*, ed. Andrew B. Meyers (Tarrytown: Sleepy Hollow Restorations, 1974), 1–11; Andrew B. Meyers, "Introduction," in Meyers, *Irving, A Tribute*, 1–19.

9. Burrows and Wallace, *Gotham*, 455, 469; Irving, *History of NY*, 387.

10. Robert G. Albion, *The Rise of New York Port, 1815–1860* (New York: Charles Scribner's Sons, 1939), 8–37, 235–259; Richard B. Stott, *Workers in the Metropolis: Class, Ethnicity and Youth in Antebellum New York City* (Ithaca, N.Y.: Cornell University Press, 1990), 7–10; Robert Ernst, *Immigrant Life in New York City*,

1825-1863 (New York: King's Crown Press, 1949), 12–16; Edward K. Spann, *The New Metropolis: New York City, 1840-1857* (New York: Columbia University Press, 1981), 1–22.

11. Stott, *Workers in Metropolis*, 10–13, 34–67; Burrows and Wallace, *Gotham*, 427–446.

12. Elizabeth Blackmar, *Manhattan for Rent, 1785-1850* (Ithaca, N.Y.: Cornell University Press, 1989), 72–108; Burrows and Wallace, *Gotham*, 446–449; Edward Robb Ellis, *The Epic of New York City* (New York: Old Town Books, 1966), 244; Hagensink, "Irving: A Litterateur in Politics," 180, 186; Stanley T. Williams, *The Life of Washington Irving* (New York: Oxford University Press, 1935), 74–88, 210.

13. Paul A. Gilje, *The Road to Mobocracy: Popular Disorder in New York City, 1763-1834* (Chapel Hill: University of North Carolina Press, 1987), 220–222; Irving, *History of NY*, 134.

14. Burrows and Wallace, *Gotham*, 353–356; Gilje, *Mobocracy*, 225, 228.

15. Gilje, *Mobocracy*, 224–227.

16. Ibid., 227–232; *New York Evening Post*, Sept. 7, 1826; Howard B. Rock, "A Delicate Balance: The Mechanics and the City in the Age of Jefferson," *New York Historical Society Quarterly* 63 (April 1979), 93–114.

17. Blackmar, *Manhattan for Rent*, 149–169; James F. Richardson, "New York Society, High and Low," in Meyers, *Knickerbocker Tradition*, 36–50; Edward Pessen, "Who Has Power in the Democratic Capitalist Community? Reflections on Antebellum New York City," *New York History* 58 (April, 1977), 131–155.

18. Frederick M. Binder and David M. Reimers, *All the Nations Under Heaven: An Ethnic and Racial History of New York City* (New York: Columbia University Press, 1995), 33–47; Ernst, *Immigrant Life*, 20–24; Anbinder, *Five Points*, 14–27, 42–66; Burrows and Wallace, *Gotham*, 391–392; Gilje, *Mobocracy*, 240.

19. Jerome Mushkat, *Tammany: The Evolution of a Political Machine* (Syracuse: Syracuse University Press, 1971), 367–369; Oliver E. Allen, *The Tiger: The Rise and Fall of Tammany Hall* (New York: Addison-Wesley, 1993), 1–26; Ernst, *Immigrant Life*, 162; Burrows and Wallace, *Gotham*, 822–824.

20. Gilje, *Mobocracy*, 125–142; Mushkat, *Tammany*, 162; Burrows and Wallace, *Gotham*, 544–546; Sean Wilentz, *Chants Democratic: New York City and the Rise of the American Working Class, 1788-1850* (New York: Oxford University Press, 1984), 266–268; Leo Hershkowitz, *New York City, 1834 to 1840, A Study in Local Politics* (Ph.D. dissertation, New York University, 1960), 111–116.

21. Anbinder, *Five Points*, 91–92, 193–195; Burrows and Wallace, *Gotham*, 496–498, 529–537; Gilje, *Mobocracy*, 206–209.

22. Gilje, *Mobocracy*, 125–138, 253–260.

23. Michael Kaplan, "The World of the B'Hoys: Urban Violence and the Political Culture of Antebellum New York City, 1825–1860" (Ph.D. dissertation, New York University, 1996), 74–90; Hershkowitz, *NYC, 1834-1840*, 117–185; Carol Groneman Pernicone, "The Bloody Ould Sixth: A Social Analysis of a New York City Working Class Community in the Mid-Nineteenth Century" (Ph.D. dissertation, University of Rochester, 1973); Anbinder, *Five Points*, 29–31; Burrows and Wallace, *Gotham*, 545.

24. Gilje, *Mobocracy*, 253–257; James F. Richardson, "To Control the City: The New York Police in Historical Perspective," in *Cities in American History*, eds. Kenneth T. Jackson and Stanley K. Schultz (New York: Alfred A, Knopf, 1972), 273; James F. Richardson, *The New York Police, Colonial Times to 1901* (New York: Oxford University Press, 1970), 3–13, 13–22; Irving, *History of NY*, 146–149.

25. Allan Nevins, ed., *The Diary of Philip Hone, 1828–1851* (New York: Dodd Mead, 1927), 9–11.

26. Alice S. Rossi, ed., *The Feminist Papers from Adams to Beauvoir* (New York: Bantam, 1974), 86–91; Celia Morris Eckhart, *Fanny Wright: Rebel in America* (Cambridge, Mass.: Harvard University Press, 1984), 1–48, 49–85, 184; A. J. G. Perkins and Theresa Wolfson, *Frances Wright, Free Enquirer: The Study of a Temperament* (New York: Harper and Brothers, 1939), 3–25, 26–53, 54–84; Lori D. Ginzberg, "Fanny Wright," in *The American Radical*, ed. Mary Jo Buhle, Paul Buhle and Harvey S. Kaye (New York: Routledge, 1994), 17–19; Burrows and Wallace, *Gotham*, 509–512.

27. Irving, *History of NY*, 164–166; Wilentz, *Chants Democratic*, 177; Schlesinger Jr., *Age of Jackson*, 181; Eckhardt, *Fanny Wright*, 189.

28. Rossi, *Feminist Papers*, 91–93; Wilentz, *Chants Democratic*, 178–180; Eckhardt, *Fanny Wright*, 87–93, 99–167; Perkins and Wolfson, *Frances Wright*, 271–294; Ginzberg, "Fanny Wright," 19–20; Edward Pessen, *Most Uncommon Jacksonians: The Radical Leaders of the Early Labor Movement* (Albany: State University of New York Press, 1967), 66–68.

29. Ginzberg, "Fanny Wright," 21; Eckhardt, *Fanny Wright*, 171–175; Schlesinger, Jr., *Age of Jackson*, 183; Burrows and Wallace, *Gotham*, 522.

30. Wilentz, *Chants Democratic*, 183–197; Perkins and Wolfson, *Frances Wright*, 260–261; Walter Hugins, *Jacksonian Democracy and the Working Class: A Study of the New York Workingmen's Movement, 1829–1837* (Stanford: Stanford University Press, 1960), 11–15; Howard B. Rock, *Artisans of the New Republic: The Tradesmen of New York City in the Age of Jefferson* (New York: New York University Press, 1984), 49–63, 101–143.

31. Rock, *Artisans*, 259–262; Eckhardt, *Fanny Wright*, 216–219; Wilentz, *Chants Democratic*, 197–200; Hugins, *Jacksonian Democracy*, 203–219; Edward Pessen, *Uncommon Jacksonians*, 9–33.

32. Pessen, *Uncommon Jacksonians*, 11–15; Schlesinger Jr., *Age of Jackson*, 190–209; Eckhardt, *Fanny Wright*, 266; Wilentz, *Chants Democratic*, 212; Rossi, *Feminist Papers*, 99.

33. Rossi, *Feminist Papers*, 108–117; Wilentz, *Chants Democratic*, 178–179; Perkins and Wolfson, *Frances Wright*, 289–291; Hugins, *Jacksonian Democracy*, 132–134.

34. Wilentz, *Chants Democratic*, 181–182; Perkins and Wolfson, *Frances Wright*, 235–238, 295; Eckhardt, *Fanny Wright*, 191–194.

35. Eckhardt, *Fanny Wright*, 186–194; Wilentz, *Chants Democratic*, 176, 182; Eckhardt, *Fanny Wright*, 175–187.

36. Rossi, *Feminist Papers*, 93, 100–117; Ginzberg, "Fanny Wright," 22–23; Schlesinger Jr., *Age of Jackson*, 182; Eckhardt, *Fanny Wright*, 186, 194; Perkins and Wolfson, *Frances Wright*, 296–298.

37. Christine Stansell, *City of Women: Sex and Class in New York, 1789-1860* (New York: Alfred A. Knopf, 1986), 133; Rossi, *Feminist Papers*, 103; Mary P. Ryan, *Womanhood in America from Colonial Times to the Present* (New York: Franklin Watts, 1979), 54–80.

38. Stansell, *City of Women*, 11–15.

39. Ibid., 171–192; Timothy J. Gilfoyle, "Strumpets and Misogynists: Brothel Riots and the Transformation of Prostitution in Antebellum New York City," *New York History* 68 (January, 1987), 45–65; Timothy J. Gilfoyle, *City of Eros: New York City, Prostitution and the Commercialization of Sex, 1790-1920* (New York: W.W. Norton, 1992), 42-44, 76–91; Rossi, *Feminist Papers*, 115.

40. Stansell, *City of Women*, 105–113, 132–135.

41. Ibid., 130–135; Wilentz, *Chants Democratic*, 168.

42. Eckhardt, *Fanny Wright*, 266–272.

43. Rossi, *Feminist Papers*, 99–107; Burrows and Wallace, *Gotham*, 522, 541, 621.

44. Perkins and Wolfson, *Frances Wright*, 262–268; Eckhardt, *Fanny Wright*, 252.

45. Prince, "Great Riot Year," 1–19; Weinbaum, *Mobs and Demagogues*, 1; John M. Werner, *Reaping the Bloody Harvest: Race Riots in the United States During the Age of Jackson, 1824-1849* (New York: Garland, 1986), 22, 241–242.

46. Robert V. Remini, *The Legacy of Andrew Jackson: Essays on Democracy, Indian Removal, and Slavery* (Baton Rouge: Louisiana State University Press, 1988), 7–44; Alexis de Tocqueville, *Democracy in America* I (New York: Vintage Books, 1945), 264–280.

47. Irving, *History of NY*, 153.

48. Feldberg, *Turbulent Era*, 56–57; Mary P. Ryan, *Civic Wars: Democracy and Public Life in the American City During the Nineteenth Century* (Berkeley: University of California Press, 1997), 109, 129–131.

49. Burrows and Wallace, *Gotham*, 571–575; Hugins, *Jacksonian Democracy*, 28–32; Hershkowitz, *NYC, 1834 to 1840*, 24–30; Bray Hammond, *Banks and Politics in America from the Revolution to the Civil War* (Princeton: Princeton University Press, 1957), 351–359; Glyndon G. Van Deusen, *The Jacksonian Era, 1828-1848* (New York: Harper and Brothers, 1959), 62–67, 82–90; Schlesinger Jr., *Age of Jackson*, 88–102; Weinbaum, *Mobs and Demagogues*, 1–14; Werner, *Reaping the Bloody Harvest*, 17; David Grimsted, *American Mobbing, 1828-1861: Toward Civil War* (New York: Oxford University Press, 1998), 200–205.

50. Grimsted, *American Mobbing, 200-205*; Hershkowitz, *NYC, 1834 to 1840*, 32–43; Schlesinger Jr., *Age of Jackson*, 185; Philip S. Foner, *History of the Labor Movement in the United States* I (New York: International Publishers, 1947), 143–150; Hugins, *Jacksonian Democracy*, 172–202.

51. Marco A. Pamplona, *Riots, Republicanism and Citizenship: New York City and Rio de Janeiro City during the Consolidation of the Republican Order* (New York: Garland, 1996), 139–141; Hugins, *Jacksonian Democracy*, 203–221; Weinbaum, *Mobs and Demagogues*, 5–7; Headley, *Great Riots*, 69–71.

52. Headley, *Great Riots*, 73; Gilje, *Mobocracy*, 139; Kaplan, "World of the B'Hoys," 62–70; *New York Evening Post*, April 11–12, 1834; Grimsted, *American Mobbing*, 200; Nevins, *Hone*, 122–123.

53. Weinbaum, *Mobs and Demagogues*, 7–14; Gilje, *Mobocracy*, 138–141; Leonard L. Richards, *"Gentlemen of Property and Standing": Anti-Abolition Mobs in*

Jacksonian America (New York: Oxford University Press, 1970), 167–170; Headley, *Great Riots,* 74–77; Kaplan, "World of the B'Hoys," 54–72; Grimsted, "Rioting," 361–367; Anbinder, *Five Points,* 27–29; Grimsted, *American Mobbing,* 202.

54. Irving et al., *Salmagundi Papers,* 232–235; *New York Evening Post,* April 12, 1834.

55. *New York Evening Post,* April 12, 1834.

56. Gilje, *Mobocracy,* 165–170; Headly, *Great Riots,* 79–95; Burrows and Wallace, *Gotham,* 556–559.

57. Weinbaum, *Mobs and Demagogues,* 25–30; Werner, *Reaping the Bloody Harvest,* 148; Pamplona, *Riots, Republicanism and Citizenship,* 97–99, 143; *New York Evening Post,* July 12, 1834; Richards, *Gentlemen of Property and Standing,* 150; Linda Kerber, "Abolitionists and Amalgamators: The New York City Race Riots of 1834," *New York History* 48 (1967), 52–58.

58. Anbinder, *Five Points,* 7–10; Werner, *Reaping the Bloody Harvest,* 124–126.

59. Pamplona, *Riots, Republicanism and Citizenship,* 92–94; Headly, *Great Riots,* 83–85; Werner, *Reaping the Bloody Harvest,* 128–130.

60. Pamplona, *Riots, Republicanism and Citizenship,* 94–97; Anbinder, *Five Points,* 10–13; Richards, *Gentlemen of Property and Standing,* 115–118; Kerber, "Abolitionists and Amalgamators," 30–33; Werner, *Reaping the Bloody Harvest,* 130–137; Lewis Tappan, *Life of Arthur Tappan* (Westport, Conn.: Negro Universities Press, 1871/1970), 203–224; Richard Hofstadter and Michael Wallace, eds., *American Violence, A Documentary History* (New York: Vintage, 1970), 341–344; Letters to Mayor Cornelius W. Lawrence in Manuscript Folder on Miscellaneous Riots, 1834, New York Historical Society.

61. Irving et al., *Salmagundi Papers,* 232–235.

62. Burrows and Wallace, *Gotham,* 551–552; Bertram Wyatt-Brown, *Lewis Tappan and the Evangelical War Against Slavery* (Cleveland: Case Western Reserve University Press, 1969), 79–115; John B. Jentz, "The Anti-Slavery Constituency in Jacksonian New York City," *Civil War History* 27 (1981), 101–122; Tappan, *Arthur Tappan,* 207; Gerald Sorin, *The New York Abolitionists: A Case Study of Political Radicalism* (Westport, Conn.: Greenwood, 1971), 71–75.

63. Burrows and Wallace, *Gotham,* 551–552; Ellis, *Epic,* 236; Werner, *Reaping the Bloody Harvest,* 119–124, 265–266; Philip S. Foner, *Business and Slavery: New York Merchants and the Irrepressible Conflict* (Chapel Hill: University of North Carolina Press, 1941), 1–14; Richards, *Gentlemen of Property and Standing,* 61–62, 166–170.

64. Tappan, *Arthur Tappan,* 208–211, 222–224; Wyatt-Brown, *Lewis Tappan,* 117–118; Richards, *Gentlemen of Property and Standing,* 150; Weinbaum, *Mobs and Demagogues,* 21–30; Ellis, *Epic,* 238.

65. Burrows and Wallace, *Gotham,* 547–552; Katz, *Black Legacy,* 57–61; Gilje, *Mobocracy,* 145–170; Kaplan, "World of the B'Hoys," 28–30; Benjamin Quarles, *Black Abolitionists* (New York: Oxford University Press, 1969), 23–41, 149–153, 170; Leonard P. Curry, *The Free Black in Urban America, 1800–1850: The Shadow of a Dream* (Chicago: University of Chicago Press, 1981), 101, 217–218; Richards, *Gentlemen of Property and Standing,* 120, 150–155; Werner, *Reaping the Bloody Harvest,* 265–288.

66. Werner, *Reaping the Bloody Harvest*, 117, 120; Tappan, *Arthur Tappan*, 206–207; Graham Hodges, "'Desirable Companions and Lovers': Irish and African Americans in the Sixth Ward, 1830–1870" in *The New York Irish*, eds. Ronald H. Bayor and Timothy J. Meagher (Baltimore: Johns Hopkins University Press, 1996), 107–124.

67. Werner, *Reaping the Bloody Harvest*, 126, 143, 147, 281–283; Kerber, "Abolitionists and Amalgamators," 30; Richards, *Gentlemen of Property and Standing*, 114–115, 165–166; Gilje, *Mobocracy*, 162–163.

68. Werner, *Reaping the Bloody Harvest*, 132–136; Richards, *Gentlemen of Property and Standing*, 120–121; Weinbaum, *Mobs and Demagogues*, 22.

69. Werner, *Reaping the Bloody Harvest*, 127.

70. Kerber, "Abolitionists and Amalgamators," 35–36.

71. Ibid., 37–38; Werner, *Reaping the Bloody Harvest*, 280–288; Anbinder, *Five Points*, 12; Alexis de Tocqueville, *Democracy in America*, I (New York: Vintage, 1945), 373.

72. Kerber, "Abolitionists and Amalgamators," 34, 37; Werner, *Reaping the Bloody Harvest*, 144–146; *New York Evening Post*, July 12, 1834.

73. Kerber, "Abolitionists and Amalgamators," 34; Werner, *Reaping the Bloody Harvest*, 143; Prince, "The Great Riot Year," 6; Hofstadter and Wallace, *American Violence*, 475–478; Anbinder, *Five Points*, 12–13.

74. Wilentz, *Chants Democratic*, 23–60, 61–103, 107–142; Burrows and Wallace, *Gotham*, 515–518; Irving, *History of NY*, 153.

75. Rock, "A Delicate Balance," 93–114; Rock, *Artisans*, 63–71; Daniel J. Walkowitz, "The Artisans and Builders of Nineteenth Century New York: The Case of the 1834 Stonecutters' Riot" in *Greenwich Village, Culture and Counter Culture*, eds. Rick Beard and Leslie Cohen Berlowitz (New Brunswick, N.J.: Rutgers University Press, 1993), 199–211.

76. Walkowitz, "The Artisans and Builders," 199–201; Burrows and Wallace, *Gotham*, 604–605; Wilentz, *Chants Democratic*, 233; Gilje, *Mobocracy*, 198–199; Hugins, *Jacksonian Democracy*, 156–161; Headly, *Great Riots*, 95–96.

77. Wilentz, *Chants Democratic*, 168–170; Gilje, *Mobocracy*, 175–195.

78. Burrows and Wallace, *Gotham*, 518–521; Pessen, *Uncommon Jacksonians*, 9–33; Wilentz, *Chants Democratic*, 190–216.

79. Wilentz, *Chants Democratic*, 219–230, 286, 411; Gilje, *Mobocracy*, 193–199; Hugins, *Jacksonian Democracy*, 28–43; Burrows and Wallace, *Gotham*, 603–609.

80. Wilentz, *Chants Democratic*, 287–188.

81. Ibid., 289–290.

82. Ibid., 290–294.

83. Ibid., 294–295; Burrows and Wallace, *Gotham*, 611–614; Ellis, *Epic*, 244; Hershkowitz, *NYC, 1834 to 1840*, 226–232, 261–266.

84. Wilentz, *Chants Democratic*, 294–295; Burrows and Wallace, *Gotham*, 610.

85. Burrows and Wallace, *Gotham*, 610–611; Headly, *Great Riots*, 103–110; Hofstadter and Wallace, *American Violence*, 126–129.

86. Hershkowitz, *NYC, 1834 to 1840*, 232–235; Burrows and Wallace, *Gotham*, 619–625.

87. Nevins, *Hone*, 241–242, 245, 252, 259.

88. Weinbaum, *Mobs and Demagogues*, 13–14; Feldberg, *Turbulent Era*, 91.

89. Irving, *History of NY*, 169; P. Irving, *Biographies*, 538; Prince, "The Great Riot Year," 6.

CHAPTER 4

1. Scully Bradley, ed., *Walt Whitman: Leaves of Grass and Selected Prose* (New York: Holt, Rinehart and Winston, 1965), 246, 388–389; Edwin G. Burrows and Mike Wallace, *Gotham: A History of New York City to 1898* (New York: Oxford University Press, 1999), 705–711; Justin Kaplan, *Walt Whitman, A Life* (New York: Simon and Schuster, 1980), 105–113.

2. Kaplan, *Walt Whitman*, 388–389, 413; Ric Burns and James Sanders, *New York, An Illustrated History* (New York: Alfred A. Knopf, 1999), 82–83; George J. Lankevich, *American Metropolis, A History of New York City* (New York: New York University Press, 1998), 70–71; Bayrd Still, *Mirror for Gotham, New York as Seen by Contemporaries from Dutch Days to the Present* (New York: New York University Press, 1956), 125–143; Richard B. Stott, *Workers in the Metropolis: Class, Ethnicity and Youth in Antebellum New York City* (Ithaca, N.Y.: Cornell University Press, 1990), 7–11, 68–86; Tyler Anbinder, *Five Points: The Nineteenth Century New York City Neighborhood that Invented Tap Dance, Stole Elections, and Became the World's Most Notorious Slum* (New York: The Free Press, 2001), 42–66.

3. Burrows and Wallace, *Gotham*, 704–711; Mark Van Doren, ed., *The Portable Walt Whitman* (New York: Penguin, 1973), ix–xxvii; Kaplan, *Walt Whitman*, 95–113.

4. Burrows and Wallace, *Gotham*, 699–670, 790–795; Roy Rosenzweig and Elizabeth Blackmar, *The Park and the People: A History of Central Park* (Ithaca, N.Y.: Cornell University Press, 1992); Edward K. Spann, *The New Metropolis, New York City, 1840–1857* (New York: Columbia University Press, 1981), 163–173; Eric Homberger, *Scenes from the Life of a City: Corruption and Conscience in Old New York* (New Haven: Yale University Press), 1994, 212–293.

5. Burrows and Wallace, *Gotham*, 712–726; Spann, *New Metropolis*, 94–116.

6. Edward Pessen, *Riches, Class and Power: America Before the Civil War* (New Brunswick, N.J.: Transaction Publishers, 1973/1990), 31–35; Anbinder, *Five Points*, 32; Burrows and Wallace, *Gotham*, 474–76.

7. Anbinder, *Five Points*, 32–37, 67–71, 66–110, 207–234; Burrows and Wallace, *Gotham*, 697–700; Bradley, *Whitman*, 246; Still, *Mirror for Gotham*, 123, 136; Herbert Asbury, *The Gangs of New York* (New York: Capricorn Books, 1927/1970), 21–62.

8. *Account of the Terrific and Fatal Riot at the Astor Place Opera House* (New York: H.M. Ranney, 1849), 5–6; Richard Moody, *The Astor Place Riot* (Bloomington: Indiana University Press, 1958), 8–13, 120–121; Joel Tyler Headley, *The Great Riots of New York, 1712–1873* (New York: Dover, 1873/1971), 111–128; Burrows and Wallace, *Gotham*, 761–766; Michael Kaplan, "The World of the B'Hoys: Urban Violence and the Political Culture of Antebellum New York City, 1825–1860" (Ph. D. dissertation, New York University, 1996), 150–151; Richard Hofstadter and Michael Wallace, eds., *American Violence: A Documentary History* (New York: Vintage, 1970), 453–457.

9. *Account of the Riot,* 7–14; Burrows and Wallace, *Gotham,* 761–762; Spann, *The New Metropolis,* 235–236; Moody, *Astor Place Riot,* 27–100; Kaplan, "The World of the B'Hoys," 153; David Grimsted, *Melodrama Unveiled: American Theater and Culture, 1800–1850* (Chicago: University of Chicago Press, 1968), 64–70; Paul A. Gilje, *The Road to Mobocracy: Popular Disorder in New York City, 1763–1834* (Chapel Hill: University of North Carolina Press, 1987), 246–247; Alan Nevins, ed., *The Diary of Philip Hone, 1828–1851* II (New York: Dodd Mead, 1927), 866; Sean Wilentz, *Chants Democratic: New York City and the Rise of the American Working Class, 1780–1850* (New York: Oxford University Press, 1984), 257–259.

10. Burrows and Wallace, *Gotham,* 762; Spann, *The New Metropolis,* 236; Headley, *Great Riots,* 112; Richard Moody, *Edwin Forrest: First Star of the American Stage* (New York: Alfred A. Knopf, 1960), 241; Peter G. Buckley, "Culture, Class and Place in Antebellum New York" in *Power, Culture and Place: Essays on New York City,* ed. John Hull Mollenkopf (New York: Russell Sage, 1988), 34–35.

11. *Account of the Riot,* 15–16; Kaplan, "The World of the B'Hoys," 154–155; Headley, *Great Riots,* 114–119; Herbert Asbury, *The Gangs of New York* (New York: Capricorn Books, 1927/1970), 44.

12. *Account of the Riot,* 17–20; Kaplan, "The World of the B'Hoys," 158–160; Headley, *Great Riots,* 120; Burrows and Wallace, *Gotham,* 762–763; Spann, *The New Metropolis,* 237–238; Grimsted, *Melodrama Unveiled,* 71–72; Louis Auchinloss, *The Hone and Strong Diaries of Old Manhattan* (New York: Abbeville Press, 1989), 115–118.

13. *Account of the Riot,* 20–26; Kaplan, "The World of the B'Hoys," 163–167; Headley, *Great Riots,* 121–128; Burrows and Wallace, *Gotham,* 763–764; Spann, *The New Metropolis,* 238; Nevins, *Hone,* 867–869; Moody, *Forrest,* 136–175.

14. Moody, *Forrest,* 176–199; *Account of the Riot,* 26–27; Kaplan, "The World of the B'Hoys," 170–180; Grimsted, *Melodrama Unveiled,* 72–73; Robert Ernst, "The One and Only Mike Walsh," *New York Historical Society Quarterly* 36 (1952), 43–65; George W. Walling, *Recollections of a New York Chief of Police* (New York: Caxton Book Concern, 1887), 46–47.

15. *Account of the Riot,* 30–32; Iver Bernstein, *The New York City Draft Riots: Their Significance for American Society and Politics in the Age of the Civil War* (New York: Oxford University Press, 1990), 148–150; Ralph W. Conant, "Rioting, Insurrection and Civil Disobedience," in *Violence: An Element of American Life,* eds. Karl Taylor and Fred W. Soady Jr. (Boston: Holbrook Press, 1972), 262–279.

16. Kaplan, "The World of the B'Hoys," 188–199; Burrows and Wallace, *Gotham,* 764–765; Spann, *The New Metropolis,* 239–240; Moody, *Forrest,* 182–185, 225–229; Nevins, *Hone,* 869.

17. *Account of the Riot,* 18–19; Moody, *Forrest,* 226–227; Kaplan, "The World of the B'Hoys," 180–184.

18. Kaplan, "The World of the B'Hoys," 180–184; James F. Richardson, *The New York Police, Colonial Times to 1901* (New York: Oxford University Press, 1970), 28–68; Gilje, *Mobocracy,* 267–282.

19. Kaplan, "The World of the B'Hoys," 192–193; Burrows and Wallace, *Gotham,* 765; Moody, *Forrest,* 228–229; Spann, *The New Metropolis,* 239–240; Anthony Gronowicz, *Race, Class and Politics in New York City Before the Civil War* (Boston: Northeastern University Press, 1998), 123–124.

20. *New York Tribune*, May 15, 1849.

21. Burrows and Wallace, *Gotham*, 770; Wilentz, *Chants Democratic*, 350–356.

22. Wilentz, *Chants Democratic*, 366, 372–374.

23. Ibid., 375–380; Burrows and Wallace, *Gotham*, 771; Carl N. Degler, "Labor in the Economy and Politics of New York City, 1850–1860" (Ph.D. dissertation, Columbia University, 1952), 51–61, 80–81.

24. Wilentz, *Chants Democratic*, 381–389; Kaplan, *Whitman*, 174–175.

25. Bradley, *Whitman*, 246; Frederick M. Binder and David M. Reimers, *All the Nations Under Heaven: An Ethnic and Racial History of New York City* (New York: Columbia University Press, 1995), 59–74; Hasia Diner, "The Most Irish City in the Union: The Era of the Great Migration, 1844–1877," in *The New York Irish*, eds. Ronald H. Bayor and Timothy J. Meagher (Baltimore: Johns Hopkins University Press, 1996), 87–106.

26. Douglas T. Miller, "Immigration and Social Stratification in Pre-Civil War New York," *New York History* 49 (1968), 157–168; Robert Ernst, "Economic Nativism in New York City During the 1840's," *New York History* 29 (1948), 170–184; Burrows and Wallace, *Gotham*, 620–621, 782–784; Charles Loring Brace, *The Dangerous Classes of New York and Twenty Years Working Among Them* (New York: Wynkoop and Hallenbeck, 1872); Robert H. Bremner, *From the Depths: The Discovery of Poverty in the United States* (New York: New York University Press, 1956/1972), 31–45.

27. Kaplan, "The World of the B'Hoys," 2–19; Burrows and Wallace, *Gotham*, 633–635; Spann, *The New Metropolis*, 34–39; Asbury, *Gangs of NY*, 21–45; Wilentz, *Chants Democratic*, 300–301, 315–335; Ira M. Leonard, "The Rise and Fall of the American Republican Party in New York City, 1843–1845," *New York Historical Society Quarterly* 50 (1966), 151–192.

28. Diane Ravitch, *The Great School Wars, New York City, 1805–1973: A History of the Public Schools as Battlefields of Change* (New York: Basic Books, 1974), 8–10, 20–22, 27–35.

29. Ravitch, *Great School Wars*, 44–66; Burrows and Wallace, *Gotham*, 629–31; Spann, *The New Metropolis*, 29–34; George Potter, *To The Golden Door: The Story of the Irish in Ireland and America* (Boston: Little, Brown, 1960), 410–419.

30. Anbinder, *Five Points*, 154–155; Ravitch, *Great School Wars*, 67–70; Marie Fitzgerald, "The St. Patrick's Day Parade: The Conflict of Irish American Identity in New York City, 1840–1900" (Ph.D. dissertation, State University of New York at Stony Brook, 1993), 80–82.

31. Ravitch, *Great School Wars*, 67–76; Burrows and Wallace, *Gotham*, 629–31; Joann P. Krieg, *Whitman and the Irish* (Iowa City: University of Iowa Press, 2000) 16; Potter, *Golden Door*, 414–416; Anbinder, *Five Points*, 154–158; Binder and Reimers, *All the Nations*, 66–70; Vincent P. Lannie, *Public Money and Parochial Education: Bishop Hughes, Governor Seward, and the New York School Controversy* (Cleveland: Case Western Reserve University Press, 1968), 247–251; Jerome Mushkat, *Tammany: The Evolution of a Political Machine* (Syracuse: Syracuse University Press, 1971), 192–207.

32. Leonard, "American Republican Party," 151–192; Burrows and Wallace, *Gotham*, 633–638; Fitzgerald, "The St. Patrick's Day Parade," 82–85; City University of New

York, *Master Plan of the Board of Higher Education* (New York: City University of New York, 1972), 11.

33. Carroll S. Rosenberg, "Protestants and Five Pointers: The Five Points House of Industry, 1850–1870," *New York Historical Society Quarterly* 48 (1964), 327–347; Anbinder, *Five Points*, 245–252; Burrows and Wallace, *Gotham*, 750–751; Kaplan, "The World of the B'Hoys," 205–206, 220.

34. Kaplan, "The World of the B'Hoys," 221–238, 249–250; Anbinder, *Five Points*, 253.

35. Kaplan, "The World of the B'Hoys," 250–263.

36. Ernst, "Economic Nativism," 170–184; Elliott J. Gorn, "'Good-Bye Boys, I Die a True American': Homicide, Nativism, and Working-Class Culture in Antebellum New York City," *Journal of American History* 74 (September, 1987), 388–410.

37. Amy Bridges, *A City in the Republic: Antebellum New York and the Origins of Machine Politics* (Ithaca, N.Y.: Cornell University Press, 1987), 83–98; Fitzgerald, "The St. Patrick's Day Parade," 57–58, 65–79; Michael Lind, *The Next American Nation: The New Nationalism and the Fourth American Revolution* (New York: The Free Press, 1995), 84; Mary P. Ryan, *Civic Wars: Democracy and Public Life in the American City During the Nineteenth Century* (Berkeley: University of California Press, 1997), 84–85.

38. Jerome Mushkat, *Fernando Wood, A Political Biography* (Kent, Ohio; Kent State University Press, 1990), 8–10; Jerome Mushkat, "Fernando Wood and the Commercial Growth of New York City," in *New York and the Rise of American Capitalism: Economic Development and the Social and Political History of an American State, 1770–1870*, eds. William Pencak and Conrad Edick Wright (New York: New York Historical Society, 1989), 202–206; Spann, *The New Metropolis*, 358–385; Oliver Allen, *The Tiger: The Rise and Fall of Tammany Hall* (Reading, Mass: Addison-Wesley, 1993), 51–63.

39. Mushkat, "Wood and Commercial Growth," 207–212; Burrows and Wallace, *Gotham*, 831–832; Spann, *The New Metropolis*, 364–377; Allen, *The Tiger*, 64–66.

40. Mushkat, "Wood and Commercial Growth," 204; Mushkat, *Fernando Wood*, 8–10, 95, 243–247; Burrows and Wallace, *Gotham*, 832; Allen, *The Tiger*, 67–71.

41. Burrows and Wallace, *Gotham*, 835–838; Tyler Anbinder, "Fernando Wood and New York City's Secession from the Union: A Political Reappraisal," *New York History* 68 (January, 1987), 67–92; Leonard Chalmers, "Tammany Hall, Fernando Wood, and the Struggle to Control New York City, 1857–1859," *New York Historical Society Quarterly* 53 (January, 1969), 7–33.

42. Burrows and Wallace, *Gotham*, 836–838; Spann, *The New Metropolis*, 384–390.

43. Spann, *The New Metropolis*, 372–375; Tyler Anbinder, *Nativism and Slavery: The Northern Know Nothings and the Politics of the 1850's* (New York: Oxford University Press, 1992), 67–79; W. J. Rorabaugh, "Rising Democratic Spirits: Immigrants, Temperance and Tammany Hall, 1854–1860," *Civil War History* 22 (1976), 138–157; Alice Felt Tyler, *Freedom's Ferment: Phases of American Social History from the Colonial Period to the Outbreak of the Civil War* (New York: Harper and Row, 1944/1962), 308–350; Paul O. Weinbaum, "Temperance, Politics and the New York City Riots of 1857," *New York Historical Society Quarterly* 59 (1975), 246–270.

44. Anbinder, "Wood and Secession," 71–75; Rorabaugh, "Rising Democratic Spirits," 141–157; Spann, *The New Metropolis,* 372–375; Kaplan, "The World of the B'Hoys," 2–19; Joshua Brown, "The Dead Rabbit-Bowery Boy Riot: An Analysis of the Antebellum Gang" (M.A. dissertation, Columbia University, 1976), 7–10.

45. Anbinder, "Wood and Secession," 75–76; Burrows and Wallace, *Gotham,* 782, 830–831; James F. Richardson, "Mayor Fernando Wood and the New York Police Force, 1855–1857," *New York Historical Society Quarterly* 50 (January, 1966), 5–33; Richardson, *The New York Police,* 82–102; Bernstein, *NYC Draft Riots,* 92–93.

46. Anbinder, "Wood and Secession," 70–77; Anbinder, *Five Points,* 278–289; Richardson, "Wood and the Police," 33–34; Richardson, *The New York Police,* 102–104; Brown, "Dead Rabbit Riot," 10–16; Burrows and Wallace, *Gotham,* 638–641; Weinbaum, "Temperance, Politics and Riots," 246–248.

47. Walling, *Recollections,* 54–60; Anbinder, "Wood and Secession," 70–71; Mushkat, *Fernando Wood,* 72–75; Burrows and Wallace, *Gotham,* 838–839; Richardson, "Wood and the Police," 34–40; Richardson, *The New York Police,* 104–108; Brown, "Dead Rabbit Riot," 17–19; Allen, *The Tiger,* 71–73; Headley, *Great Riots,* 128–131; Spann, *The New Metropolis,* 391–394. Weinbaum, "Temperance, Politics and Riots," 250–253, 269.

48. Weinbaum, "Temperance, Politics and Riots," 251–257; Brown, "Dead Rabbit Riot," 24–32; Anbinder, *Five Points,* 282–292; Burrows and Wallace, *Gotham,* 839; Headley, *Great Riots,* 131–134; Asbury, *Gangs of NY,* 112–116; Denis Tilden Lynch, *Boss Tweed: The Story of a Grim Generation* (New York: Boni and Liverright, 1927), 184–199.

49. Weinbaum, "Temperance, Politics and Riots," 258–262; Brown, "Dead Rabbit Riot," 34–37; Burrows and Wallace, *Gotham,* 840; Still, *Mirror for Gotham,* 163.

50. Carol Groneman Pernicone, "The Bloody Ould Sixth: A Social Analysis of a New York City Working Class Community in the Mid-Nineteenth Century" (Ph.D. dissertation, University of Rochester, 1973), iv–vii, 53–84; Weinbaum, "Temperance, Politics and Riots," 263–270; Brown, "Dead Rabbit Riot," 100–106, 114–117, 144–155; Anbinder, *Five Points,* 290–292; Mushkat, *Tammany,* 300–306.

51. Mushkat, *Fernando Wood,* 75; Allen, *The Tiger,* 73; Spann, *The New Metropolis,* 393; Louis Auchinloss, ed., *The Hone and Strong Diaries of Old Manhattan* (New York: Abbeville Press, 1989), 170–171; Kenneth M. Stampp, *America in 1857: A Nation on the Brink* (New York: Oxford University Press, 1990), 208–210.

52. Mushkat, *Fernando Wood,* 77; Burrows and Wallace, *Gotham,* 842–846.

53. Burrows and Wallace, *Gotham,* 848; Bernstein, *NYC Draft Riots,* 138–139; Spann, *The New Metropolis,* 394–395; Chalmers, "Tammany Hall, Fernando Wood," 13–14; Mushkat, *Fernando Wood,* 77–78.

54. Bernstein, *NYC Draft Riots,* 139; Mushkat, "Wood and Commercial Growth," 209, 214–215; Lynch, *Boss Tweed,* 122–127, 151.

55. Burrows and Wallace, *Gotham,* 849–851; Headley, *Great Riots,* 134–135; Bernstein, *NYC Draft Riots,* 140–142; Stampp, *America in 1857,* 213–238; Mushkat, "Wood and Commercial Growth," 211–212; Rosenzweig and Blackmar, *The Park and the People,* 65–71, 152–153; Bridges, *A City in the Republic,* 116–119; James L. Huston, *The Panic of 1857 and the Coming of the Civil War* (Baton Rouge: Louisiana State

University Press, 1987), 15–27; Philip S. Foner, *History of the Labor Movement in the United States from Colonial Times to the Founding of the American Federation of Labor* I (New York: International Publishers, 1947), 238–239.

56. Mushkat, *Tammany* 308–319; Mushkat, *Fernando Wood*, 82–97; Chalmers, "Tammany Hall, Fernando Wood," 15–33.

57. Chalmers, "Tammany Hall, Fernando Wood," 94–115; Philip S. Foner, *Business and Slavery: New York Merchants and the Irrepressible Conflict* (Chapel Hill: University of North Carolina Press, 1941), 1–14, 144–168, 302; Basil L. Lee, *Discontent in New York City, 1861–1865* (Washington, D.C., The Catholic University of America Press, 1943), 125–164.

58. Foner, *Business and Slavery*, 162–168.

59. Ibid., 285–305; Mushkat, *Fernando Wood*, 94–97, 126–129; Lee, *Discontent in NY*, 16–19; Anbinder, "Wood and Secession," 83–92; Lynch, *Boss Tweed*, 222–226; Allen, *The Tiger*, 77.

60. Foner, *Business and Slavery*, 285–322; Anbinder, "Wood and Secession," 87–92; Mushkat, "Wood and Commercial Growth," 221; Lee, *Discontent in NY*, 264–295.

61. Mushkat, "Wood and Commercial Growth," 223–225; Mushkat, *Fernando Wood*, 243–247; Allen, *The Tiger*, 51–79.

62. Paul A. Gilje, *Rioting in America* (Bloomington: Indiana University Press, 1996) 91–94; Adrian Cook, *The Armies of the Streets: The New York City Draft Riots of 1863* (Lexington: University of Kentucky Press, 1974), 193–195; Headley, *Great Riots*, 271–276; Lawrence Lader, "New York's Bloodiest Week," *American Heritage* 10 (June, 1959), 98; James McCague, *The Second Rebellion: The Story of the New York City Draft Riots of 1863* (New York: The Dial Press, 1968); Ernest A. McKay, *The Civil War and New York City* (Syracuse: Syracuse University Press, 1990), 195–215; Burrows and Wallace, *Gotham*, 887–899; Irving Werstein, *July, 1863* (New York: Julian Messner, 1957); Hofstadter and Wallace, *American Violence*, 211–217; Burns and Sanders, *New York*, 119–127.

63. Mary P. Ryan, *Civic Wars: Democracy and Public Life in the American City During the Nineteenth Century* (Berkeley: University of California Press, 1997), 139; Albon Man, "Labor Competition and the New York Draft Riots of 1863," *Journal of Negro History* 36 (1951), 400–401.

64. Bernstein, *NYC Draft Riots*, 18–19, 22; Edward K. Spann, *Gotham at War: New York City, 1860–1865* (Wilmington, Del.: Scholarly Resources, 2002), 93–97; Mushkat, *Fernando Wood*, 136–139; Burrows and Wallace, *Gotham*, 887–888.

65. *New York Times*, July 15 and 24, 1863; Lader, "New York's Bloodiest Week," 44; Foner, *History of Labor* I, 322; Headley, *Great Riots*, 152–159.

66. Headley, *Great Riots*, 169, 215–218; Bernstein, *NYC Draft Riots*, 21, 32–33.

67. Bernstein, *NYC Draft Riots*, 25–38; Headley, *Great Riots*, 166–168; Burrows and Wallace, *Gotham*, 889–890.

68. Burrows and Wallace, *Gotham* 889–893; Bernstein, *NYC Draft Riots*, 21, 35–37; Headley, *Great Riots*, 160–164; Elmer Davis, *History of the New York Times, 1851–1921* (New York: New York Times, 1921), 58–60; Francis Brown, *Raymond of the Times* (New York: W. W. Norton, 1951), 229–230.

69. Headley, *Great Riots*, 168–170; Bernstein, *NYC Draft Riots*, 20–21, 27–30; Asbury, *Gangs of NY*, 136; Cook, *Armies of the Streets*, 136; Walling, *Recollections*, 79;

Anbinder, *Five Points*, 315–316; Spann, *Gotham at War*, 98–99; Graham Russell Hodges, *Root and Branch: African Americans in New York and East Jersey, 1613–1863* (Chapel Hill: University of North Carolina Press, 1999), 263–270.

70. Bernstein, *NYC Draft Riots*, 28–35; Cook, *Armies of the Streets*, 97–100; Williston H. Lofton, "Northern Labor and the Negro During the Civil War, " *Journal of Negro History* 34 (July, 1949), 266.

71. Bernstein, *NYC Draft Riots*, 21, 27–29; Cook, *Armies of the Streets*, 141–142; Lofton, "Northern Labor," 267; Craig Steven Wilder, *A Covenant with Color: Race and Social Power in Brooklyn* (New York: Columbia University Press, 2000), 99–101; John Tebbel, *From Rags to Riches: Horatio Alger, Jr. and the American Dream (New York: Macmillan, 1963)*, 60–63.

72. Tebbel, *From Rags to Riches*, 60–63; Bernstein, *NYC Draft Riots*, 30–34.

73. Bernstein, *NYC Draft Riots*, 8–10; Man, "Labor Competition," 375–405; Lofton, "Northern Labor," 251–273; Lee, *Discontent in NY*, 125–142; Spann, *Gotham at War*, 121–133; Burrows and Wallace, *Gotham*, 884–887.

74. Burrows and Wallace, *Gotham*, 884–887; Man, "Labor Competition," 394–400; Lee, *Discontent in NY*, 139–154; Richardson, *NY Police*, 129–132; Bernstein, *NYC Draft Riots*, 27, 119–120; McKay, *Civil War and NYC*, 196–197; Gronowicz, *Race and Class Politics*, 135; Edward K. Spann, "Union Green: The Irish Community and the Civil War," in Ronald H. Bayor and Timothy J. Meagher, *The New York Irish* (Baltimore: Johns Hopkins University Press, 1996), 203–205.

75. Burrows and Wallace, *Gotham*, 854–57, 884–885; William Loren Katz, *Black Legacy: A History of New York's African Americans* (New York: Atheneum, 1997), 75–86; John H. Hewitt, "The Search for Elizabeth Jennings, Heroine of a Sunday Afternoon in New York City," *New York History* 71 (October, 1990), 387–415.

76. Burrows and Wallace, *Gotham*, 856–859; Katz, *Black Legacy*, 61–86; Hodges, *Root and Branch*, 245–262.

77. Headley, *Great Riots*, 253–257; Bernstein, *NYC Draft Riots*, 23–24, 36, 40–48; Lee, *Discontent in NY*, 142; Lofton, "Northern Labor," 269; Foner, *History of the Labor Movement* I, 323; Burrows and Wallace, *Gotham*, 882.

78. Richardson, *NY Police*, 134–138; Walling, *Recollections*, 78–86.

79. Walling, *Recollections*, 78–86.

80. Ibid.; Burrows and Wallace, *Gotham*, 894–895; Headley, *Great Riots*, 244–252; Richardson, *NY Police*, 139–142; Edward Robb Ellis, *The Epic of New York City* (New York: Old Town Books, 1966), 316.

81. *New York Times*, July 17, 1863; Richardson, *NY Police*, 133–134; Lader, "NY's Bloodiest Week," 44; Bernstein, *NYC Draft Riots*, 48–51.

82. Bernstein, *NYC Draft Riots*, 64–66; Cook, *Armies of the Streets*, 174–175.

83. Bernstein, *NYC Draft Riots*, 56–57, 130; Burrows and Wallace, *Gotham*, 887, 895–899; Brown, *Raymond*, 229–230; *New York Times*, July 21, 1863; Lofton, "Northern Labor," 267–268; Spann, *Gotham at War*, 128–133.

84. *New York Times*, July 17–18, 1863; *New York Commercial Advertiser*, July 20, 1863; *New York Herald*, July 16 and 18, 1863; Lofton, "Northern Labor," 272; Man, "Labor Competition," 375.

85. *New York Commercial Advertiser*, July 18, 20, 1863; *New York Herald*, July 16, 1863; *New York Times*, July 16, 18, 24, 1863; McCague, *Second Rebellion*, 182–183.

86. *New York Commercial Advertiser*, July 21, 1863.

87. *New York Times,* July 15, 16, 18, 21, 22, 24, 1863.
88. Bradley, *Whitman,* 246, 509–510; Burns and Sanders, *New York,* 126.

CHAPTER 5

1. Horatio Alger Jr., *Ragged Dick and Mark, the Match Boy* (New York: Crowell-Collier, 1962), 108–109; Gary Scharnhorst with Jack Bales, *The Lost Life of Horatio Alger, Jr.* (Bloomington: Indiana University Press, 1985), 81–87; Samuel P. Hays, *The Response to Industrialism, 1885–1914* (Chicago: University of Chicago Press, 1957), 24–47.

2. Gunther Barth, *City People: The Rise of Modern City Culture in Nineteenth-Century America* (New York: Oxford University Press, 1980), 58–109; Richard R. Wohl, "The Rags to Riches Story: An Episode of Secular Idealism" in *Class, Status and Power: A Reader in Social Stratification,* eds. Richard Bendik and Seymour Martin Lipset (New York: Crowell-Collier, 1953/1961), 388–393; John Tebbel, *From Rags to Riches: Horatio Alger, Jr. and the American Dream* (New York: Macmillan, 1963); Ralph D. Gardner, *Horatio Alger, or the American Hero Era* (Mattituck, N.Y.: Amereon, 1964/1990), 323–330; Carol Nackenoff, *The Fictional Republic: Horatio Alger and American Political Discourse* (New York: Oxford University Press, 1994), 261–271; Scharnhorst, *The Lost Life of Horatio Alger,* 77–83; Louis Hartz, *The Liberal Tradition in America* (New York: Harcourt, Brace and World, 1955), 203–237; Richard Hofstadter, *Social Darwinism in American Thought* (Boston: Beacon, 1944/1955).

3. Stephen Crane, *Maggie: A Girl of the Streets and George's Mother* (Greenwich, Conn.: Fawcett, 1960), 15, 29, 45, 53; Thomas A. Gullason "Tragedy and Melodrama in Stephen Crane's *Maggie,"* in *Stephen Crane, Maggie: A Girl of the Streets (A Story of New York, 1893),* ed. Thomas A. Gullason (New York: W. W. Norton, 1979), 245–253.

4. David Scobey, *Empire City: The Making and Meaning of the New York City Landscape* (Philadelphia: Temple University Press, 2002), 23–33, 43–52; *New York Commercial Advertiser,* August 26, 1871; Bayrd Still, *Mirror for Gotham* (New York: New York University Press, 1956), 184, 209, 218, 231; Alan Trachtenberg, *The Incorporation of America: Culture and Society in the Gilded Age* (New York: Hill and Wang, 1982), 3–10.

5. Robert H. Wiebe, *The Search for Order, 1877–1920* (New York: Hill and Wang, 1967), 11–43; David C. Hammack, *Power and Society: Greater New York at the Turn of the Century* (New York: Columbia University Press, 1987), 193.

6. Henry George, *Progress and Poverty: An Inquiry into the Causes of Industrial Depressions and of Increase of Want with Increase of Wealth* (New York: Robert Schalkenbach Foundation, 1879/1937), 3–13.

7. Mark Twain and Charles Dudley Warner, *The Gilded Age* (Seattle: University of Washington Press, 1873/1968); Hofstadter, *Social Darwinism,* 38–66; Robert Green McCloskey, *American Conservatism in the Age of Enterprise, 1865–1910* (New York: Harper and Row, 1951), 42–71; Ric Burns and James Sanders, *New York, An Illustrated History* (New York: Alfred A. Knopf, 1999), 146–153.

8. Mark Twain, "Life As I Find It," in *Life As I Find It: A Treasury of Mark Twain Rarities,* ed. Charles Neider (New York: Cooper Square Press, 2000), 3–4.

9. Edwin G. Burrows and Mike Wallace, *Gotham: A History of New York City to 1898* (New York: Oxford University Press, 1999), 1041–1049; Thomas Kessner, *Capital City: New York City and the Men Behind America's Rise to Economic Dominance, 1860–1900* (New York: Simon and Schuster, 2003), xi–xix, 1–43, 45–91, 128, 329–331.

10. Kessner, *Capital City*, 227; Matthew Josephson, *The Robber Barons: The Great American Capitalists, 1861–1901* (New York: Harcourt, Brace and World, 1934/1962), 275–277; John D. Rockefeller, *Random Reminiscences of Men and Events* (Tarrytown, N.Y.: Sleepy Hollow Press, 1909/1984), 40–55; Edward C. Kirkland, *Industry Comes of Age: Business, Labor and Public Policy, 1860–1897* (Chicago: Quadrangle, 1961), 195–215; Glenn Porter, "Industrialization and the Rise of Big Business," in *The Gilded Age: Essays on the Origins of Modern America*, ed. Charles W. Calhoun (Wilmington, Del.: Scholarly Resources, 1996), 1–18; Ron Chernow, *Titan: The Life of John D. Rockefeller, Sr.* (New York: Vintage, 1998), ix, 3–72, 227–228.

11. Kessner, *Capital City*, 230; Josephson, *Robber Barons*, 264–280; Rockefeller, *Random Reminiscences*, 6–11, 56–77; Chernow, *Titan*, 197–230; Ida M. Tarbell, *The History of the Standard Oil Company* I and II (New York: Peter Smith, 1904/1950).

12. Chernow, *Titan*, 148; Porter, "Industrialization," 16; Rockefeller, *Random Reminiscences*, 65.

13. Henry Demarest Lloyd, *Wealth against Commonwealth* (New York: Harper and Brothers, 1894); John A. Garraty, *The New Commonwealth, 1877–1890* (New York: Harper and Row, 1968), 78–127.

14. Burrows and Wallace, *Gotham*, 1044–1046; Kessner, 150, 207–237, 260, 330–331; Oliver E. Allen, *New York, New York: A History of the World's Most Exhilarating and Challenging City* (New York: Atheneum, 1990), 199–200; Rockefeller, *Random Reminiscences*, 12–13; Kirkland, *Industry Comes of Age*, 195–215; Chernow, *Titan*, 227–228.

15. Scobey, *Empire City*, 1–13, 161–165; Burrows and Wallace, *Gotham*, 935–937; Alan Trachtenberg, *Brooklyn Bridge: Fact and Symbol* (Chicago: University of Chicago Press, 1970), 115–127; David McCullough, *The Great Bridge: The Epic Story of the Building of the Brooklyn Bridge* (New York: Simon and Schuster, 1972), 533–536.

16. Thomas Kessner, *The Golden Door: Italian and Jewish Immigrant Mobility in New York City, 1880–1915* (New York: Oxford University Press, 1977), 3–23, 24–43; Burrows and Wallace, *Gotham*, 1111–1125; Moses Rischin, *The Promised City: New York Jews, 1970–1914* (New York: Corinth Books, 1964), 76–94; Selma Berrol, *The Empire City: New York and its People, 1624–1996* (Westport, Conn.: Praeger, 1997), 75–102; Frederick M. Binder and David M. Reimers, *All the Nations Under Heaven: An Ethnic and Racial History of New York City* (New York: Columbia University Press, 1995), 114–148.

17. *New York Times*, Oct. 5, 1971.

18. Hammack, *Power and Society*, 189–193, 209–229; Burrows and Wallace, *Gotham*, 1219–1226; *New York Times*, Jan. 1, 1898; *Public Opinion* (London), Jan. 7, 1898; *The Newtown Register*, Jan. 6, 1898; *New York Tribune*, Jan. 1, 1898.

19. William Irvine, *Apes, Angels and Victorians: Darwin, Huxley and Evolution* (Cleveland: Meridian Books, 1955), 296.

20. Alger, *Ragged Dick*, 122–123; Lincoln Steffens, *The Shame of the Cities* (New York: Hill and Wang, 1904/1957); James W. Mooney, "The Problem of the Cities Revisited," in *Honest Graft, The World of George Washington Plunkitt, Plunkitt of Tammany Hall, 1905*, ed. William L. Riordan, (St. James, N.Y.: Brandywine Press, 1993), 25–41.

21. Oliver E. Allen, *The Tiger: The Rise and Fall of Tammany Hall* (Reading, Mass.: Addison-Wesley, 1993), 80; Alexander B. Callow Jr., *The Tweed Ring* (New York: Oxford University Press, 1965), 299; Thomas Nast St. Hill, *Thomas Nast: Cartoons and Illustrations* (New York: Dover, 1974), 19; Seymour J. Mandlebaum, *Boss Tweed's New York* (New York: John Wiley and Sons, 1965), 66–75.

22. Callow, *The Tweed Ring*, 12–32; Allen, *The Tiger*, 80–100; Kenneth D. Ackerman, *Boss Tweed: The Rise and Fall of the Corrupt Pol Who Conceived the Soul of Modern New York* (New York: Carroll and Graf, 2005), 18–29.

23. Callow, *The Tweed Ring*, 110–114, 174–181, 208–213; Allen, *The Tiger*, 100–105.

24. Callow, *The Tweed Ring*, 91–114, 152–160, 207–208, 221; Allen, *The Tiger*, 110–112; Ackerman, *Boss Tweed*, 71–82.

25. Callow, *The Tweed Ring*, 163–197, 218–219; Riordon, *Honest Graft*, 51–55; Allen, *The Tiger*, 109; Iver Bernstein, *The New York City Draft Riots: Their Significance for American Society and Politics in the Age of the Civil War* (New York: Oxford University Press, 1990), 202–209.

26. Callow, *The Tweed Ring*, 115–131, 247–252; Allen, *The Tiger*, 114–117; Riordon, *Honest Graft*, 55.

27. Callow, *The Tweed Ring*, 253–259; Eric Homberger, *Scenes from the Life of a City: Corruption and Conscience in Old New York* (New Haven: Yale University Press, 1994), 175–188; Albert Bigelow Paine, *Th. Nast, His Period and His Pictures* (Princeton: The Pyne Press, 1904), 137–139.

28. Callow, *The Tweed Ring*, 222–235, 262–263; Bernstein, *Draft Riots*, 228–233.

29. Headley, *Great Riots*, 289–293; Michael A. Gordon, *The Orange Riots: Irish Political Violence in New York City, 1870 and 1871* (Ithaca, N.Y.: Cornell University Press, 1993), 27–51.

30. Gordon, *The Orange Riots*, 52–92, 93–113; Headley, *Great Riots*, 293–302; Burrows and Wallace, *Gotham*, 1003–1005.

31. Burrows and Wallace, *Gotham*, 1005–1008; Headley, *Great Riots*, 302–306; Gordon, *The Orange Riots*, 113–148; Mary P. Ryan, *Civic Wars: Democracy and Public Life in the American City During the Nineteenth Century* (Berkeley: University of California Press, 1997), 229–234.

32. Gordon, *The Orange Riots*, 154, 165, 172; Richard Hofstadter and Michael Wallace, eds., *American Violence: A Documentary History* (New York: Vintage, 1970), 321–324; *New York Times*, July 13, 1871; Ackerman, *Boss Tweed*, 153–160.

33. *New York Tribune*, July 13, 1871; St. Hill, *Thomas Nast*, 17–29; Paine, *Th. Nast*, 137–165; Gordon, *The Orange Riots*, 149–187; Callow, *The Tweed Ring*, 254.

34. Callow, *The Tweed Ring*, 198–206, 253–60; Allen, *The Tiger*, 118–124.

35. James Bryce, *The American Commonwealth* II (New York: Macmillan, 1895), 377–403; Callow, *The Tweed Ring*, 198–206.

36. Allen, *The Tiger*, 122–126; *New York Times*, Sept. 2, 1871; Elmer Davis, *History of the New York Times, 1851–1921* (New York: New York Times, 1921), 81–116; St. Hill, *Thomas Nast*, 21.

37. Callow, *The Tweed Ring*, 261–278; *New York Times*, Sept. 9 and 11, 1871; Allen, *The Tiger*, 126–128; Homberger, *Scenes from the Life of a City*, 198–202; Ackerman, *Boss Tweed*, 100–104, 191–201; Sven Beckert, "The Making of New York City's Bourgeoisie, 1850–1886" (Ph.D. dissertation, Columbia University, 1995), 272–88.

38. Callow, *The Tweed Ring*, 279–300; Burrows and Wallace, *Gotham*, 1108–1010; Allen, *The Tiger*, 128–133.

39. Mandlebaum, *Boss Tweed's NY*, 76–86; Callow, *The Tweed Ring*, 279–300; Allen, *The Tiger*, 134–43; Homberger, *Scenes from the Life of a City*, 202–211.

40. Homberger, *Scenes from the Life of a City*, 144–169; Callow, *The Tweed Ring*, 2–12, 91–114, 211, 298–300; Bryce, *The American Commonwealth* II, 377–403; Amy Bridges, *A City in the Republic: Antebellum New York and the Origins of Machine Politics* (Ithaca, N.Y.: Cornell University Press, 1987), 150–154; *New York Times*, April 13, 1878; Daniel Czitrom, "Underworlds and Underdogs: Big Tim Sullivan and Metropolitan Politics in New York, 1889–1913," *Journal of American History* (September, 1991), 536–558.

41. *New York Times*, Sept. 11, 1871, Oct. 2, 9, 11, 16, 22, 1871, May 5, 1871; *New York Evening Post*, Sept. 7, 1871; Callow, *The Tweed Ring*, 265; Bryce, *The American Commonwealth* II, 377; Steffens, *The Shame of the Cities*, 195; Burns and Sanders, *New York*, 156–162.

42. Robert H. Bremner, *From the Depths, The Discovery of Poverty in the United States* (New York: New York University Press, 1956/1972), 3–15; Beckert, *NYC's Bourgeoisie*, 377–80; Wiebe, *The Search for Order*, 62.

43. Bremner, *From the Depths*, 16–45; Kessner, *Capital City*, 244.

44. Jacob A. Riis, *A Ten Year's War: An Account of the Battle With the Slum in New York* (Freeport, N.Y.: Books for Libraries Press, 1900/1969), 28; Alexander Alland, Sr., *Jacob A. Riis: Photographer and Citizen* (Millerton, N.Y.: Aperture, Inc., 1974), 5–7, 11, 36–39.

45. Alland, *Jacob A. Riis* 17–25; David Leviatin, ed., *How the Other Half Lives: Studies Among the Tenements of New York by Jacob A. Riis* (Boston: Bedford, 1996), 3–16; Jacob A. Riis, *The Making of an American* (New York: Macmillan, 1901/1970), 170–176; Louise Ware, *Jacob A. Riis: Police Reporter, Reformer, Useful Citizen* (New York: D. Appleton Century, 1939), 16–48.

46. Alland, *Jacob A. Riis*, 26–31; Beaumont Newhall, *The History of Photography* (New York: The Museum of Modern Art, 1982), 132–133; Tyler Anbinder, *Five Points: The 19th Century New York Neighborhood That Invented Tap Dance, Stole Elections, and Became the World's Most Notorious Slum* (New York: The Free Press, 2001), 424–428.

47. Ware, *Jacob A. Riis*, 73–78, 234, 254; Burrows and Wallace, *Gotham*, 1180–1183; Leviatin, *How the Other Half Lives*, 36–37; Bremner, *From the Depths*, 67–85; Thomas A. Gullason, "A Minister, a Social Reformer, and Maggie" in Gullason, *Maggie*, 103–108; Riis, *The Making of an American*, 212–219; Anbinder, *Five Points*, 429–431; Burns and Sanders, *New York*, 163–164, 191–195, 213–214.

48. Leviatin, *How the Other Half Lives*, 23, 150.

49. Ibid., 61, 177–187.

50. Burrows and Wallace, *Gotham*, 1167–1169, 1192–1193; James F. Richardson, *The New York Police, Colonial Times to 1901* (New York: Oxford University Press,

1970), 165–213, 214–245; Warren Sloat, *A Battle for the Soul of New York* (New York: Cooper Square, 2002).

51. Alland, *Jacob A. Riis*, 32–35; Burrows and Wallace, *Gotham*, 1194–1203; Ware, *Jacob A. Riis*, 49–59, 128–139, 152–168; Richardson, *The New York Police*, 246–267, 269–283; Riis, *The Making of an American*, 166–167, 179–182; Anbinder, *Five Points*, 428.

52. Diane Ravitch, *The Great School Wars, New York City, 1805–1973: A History of the Public Schools as Battlefields of Change* (New York: Basic Books, 1974), 107–143, 161–180; David Nasaw, *Schooled to Order: A Social History of Public Schooling in the United States* (New York: Oxford University Press, 1979), 105–113; Israel Zangwill, *The Melting-Pot, Drama in Four Acts* (New York: The Macmillan Company, 1909/1928).

53. Ravitch, *The Great School Wars*, 144–158, 161; Deborah Dash Moore, *At Home in America: Second Generation New York Jews* (New York: Columbia University Press, 1981), 89–104; Burns and Sanders, *New York*, 250–252.

54. Carleton Mabee, "Long Island's Black School War and the Decline of Segregation in New York State," *New York History* 58 (October, 1977), 385–411; Leviatin, *How the Other Half Lives*, 155–162; Mary White Ovington, *The Walls Came Tumbling Down* (New York: Harcourt, Brace, 1947), 13–19; Ena L. Farley, *The Underside of Reconstruction in New York: The Struggle over the Issue of Black Equality* (New York: Garland, 1993), 122–133.

55. Leviatin, *How the Other Half Lives*, 233; Burrows and Wallace, *Gotham*, 1031–1032, 1158—1161; Josephine Shaw Lowell, *Public Relief and Private Charity* (New York: Arno Press, 1884/1971), 58–69, 94–96; Joan Waugh, *Unsentimental Reformer: The Life of Josephine Shaw Lowell* (Cambridge, Mass: Harvard University Press, 1997), 1–40, 163–176; Lloyd C. Taylor, "Josephine Shaw Lowell and American Philanthropy," *New York History* 44 (October, 1963), 336–350; Bremner, *From the Depths*, 46–57.

56. Burrows and Wallace, *Gotham*, 1176–1177; Waugh, *Unsentimental Reformer*, 179–196, 202.

57. Waugh, *Unsentimental Reformer*, 11, 165, 196–231; Burrows and Wallace, *Gotham*, 1187–1188; Samuel Gompers, *Seventy Years of Life and Labor* I (New York: E. P. Dutton, 1925), 481–482; Charles A. Barker, *Henry George* (New York: Robert Schalkenbach Foundation, 1955/1991), 478; Taylor, "Josephine Shaw Lowell," 351–64.

58. Burrows and Wallace, *Gotham*, 1178; Waugh, *Unsentimental Reformer*, 197–202; Helen Campbell, *Prisoners of Poverty: Women Wage Workers, Their Trades and their Lives* (Westport, Conn.: Greenwood, 1887/1970), 173–185; Maud Nathan, *The Story of an Epoch-Making Movement* (Garden City: Doubleday, 1926), 17–25; Barth, *City People*, 110–147; Blanche Wiesen Cook, *Eleanor Roosevelt* I (New York: Penguin Books, 1992), 135–136.

59. Nathan, *Epoch-Making Movement*, 26–59; Allis Rosenberg Wolfe, "Women, Consumerism, and the National Consumers' League in the Progressive Era, 1900–1923," *Labor History* 16 (Summer, 1975), 378–384; Jacob A. Riis, *The Battle With the Slum* (New York: Macmillan, 1902), 196–201.

60. Wolfe, "Women, Consumerism, and the National Consumers' League," 384–392; Nathan, *Epoch-Making Movement*, 60–103, 141; Bremner, *From the Depths*, 79.

61. Bremner, *From the Depths*, 46–66; Burrows and Wallace, *Gotham*, 1174–1176; Rischin, *The Promised City*, 95–111, 194–207; Elizabeth Ewen, *Immigrant Women in the Land of Dollars: Life and Culture on the Lower East Side, 1890–1925* (New York: Monthly Review Press, 1985), 76–91.

62. Leviatin, *How the Other Half Lives*, 182–197, 214–219; Rischin, *The Promised City*, 95–111; Bremner, *From the Depths*, 41–42; Jacob A, Riis, *The Children of the Poor* (New York: Arno Press, 1892/1971), 291–300; Selma Berrol, "In Their Image: German Jews and the Americanization of the OstJuden in New York City," *New York History* 63 (October, 1982), 417–433; Priscilla Murolo, *The Common Ground of Womanhood: Class, Gender and Working Girls Clubs, 1884–1928* (Urbana: University of Illinois Press, 1997); Joanne Reitano, "Working Girls Unite!" *American Quarterly* 36 (Spring, 1984), 112–134; Allan Nevins, "The Golden Thread in the History of New York," *The New York Historical Society Quarterly* 39 (January, 1955), 16.

63. Leviatin, *How the Other Half Lives*, 59–62, 185, 233–235, 244.

64. Ibid., 69; Anbinder, *Five Points*, 428.

65. Wiebe, *The Search for Order*, 133–163; Hays, *Response to Industrialism*, 48–70; Gompers, *Seventy Years* I, 61–62; Melvin Dubovsky, *When Workers Organize: New York City in the Progressive Era* (Amherst: University of Massachusetts Press, 1968), 1–4.

66. Waugh, *Unsentimental Reformer*, 190–196; Sven Beckert, *The Monied Metropolis: New York City and the Consolidation of the American Bourgeoisie, 1850–1896* (Cambridge, UK: Cambridge University Press, 2001), 190–195; Hays, *The Response to Industrialism*, 37.

67. Herbert G. Gutman, "The Tompkins Square 'Riot' in New York City on January 13, 1874: A Re-examination of its Causes and Aftermath," *Labor History* 6 (Winter, 1965), 47; Burrows and Wallace, *Gotham*, 1022–1025.

68. Gutman, "The Tompkins Square Riot," 44–55; Richard Hofstadter and Michael Wallace, eds., *American Violence: A Documentary History* (New York: Vintage, 1970), 345–347.

69. Richardson, *The New York Police*, 197, 287–288; Gutman, "The Tompkins Square Riot," 56–64; Burrows and Wallace, *Gotham*, 1022–1027; *Harper's Weekly*, July 11, 1874 in William Loren Katz, *Black Legacy: A History of New York's African Americans* (New York: Atheneum, 1997), 102; David Quigley, *Second Founding: New York City, Reconstruction and the Making of American Democracy* (New York: Hill and Wang, 2004), 104–108.

70. Richardson, *The New York Police*, 198–199; James Lardner and Thomas Repetto, *NYPD: A City and its Police* (New York: Henry Holt, 2000), 55–59: Marilynn S. Johnson, *Street Justice: A History of Police Violence in New York City* (Boston: Beacon, 2003), 30–34.

71. Burrows and Wallace, *Gotham*, 1035–1038; Henry F. May, *Protestant Churches and Industrial America* (New York: Harper and Row, 1949/1967), 93–94; Beckert, *The Monied Metropolis*, 232–236, 293–297.

72. Gompers, *Seventy Years* I, 28–30, 97; Will Chasan, *Samuel Gompers, Leader of American Labor* (New York: Praeger, 1971), 11–33.

73. Gompers, *Seventy Years* I, 264–287; Joseph Rayback, *A History of American Labor* (New York: The Free Press, 1966), 142–159; Thomas R. Brooks, *Toil and Trouble: A History of American Labor* (New York: Dell, 1971), 56–76.

74. Dorothee Schneider, "The New York Cigarmakers Strike of 1877," *Labor History* 26 (Summer, 1985), 325–338, 345–347.

75. Ibid., 333, 343–352; Gompers, *Seventy Years* I, 148–155; Leon Litwack, ed., *The American Labor Movement* (Englewood Cliffs: Prentice Hall, 1962), 35; John R. Commons, "Karl Marx and Samuel Gompers," in *Gompers*, ed. Gerald Emanuel Stearn (Englewood Cliffs: Prentice Hall, 1971), 137–142.

76. Burrows and Wallace, *Gotham*, 1089–1091; Philip S. Foner, *History of the Labor Movement*, II (New York: International Publishers, 1955), 33–34; David Scobey, "Boycotting the Politics Factory: Labor Radicalism and the New York City Mayoral Election of 1884" [*sic*] *Radical History Review* 28–30 (1984), 287–295.

77. Lardner and Repetto, *NYPD*, 64–71; Richardson, *The New York Police*, 199; Johnson, *Street Justice*, 12–43; Beckert, *The Monied Metropolis*, 279–288; Richard K. Lieberman, *Steinway & Sons* (New Haven: Yale University Press, 1995), 95.

78. Scobey, "Boycotting the Politics Factory," 287–294; Burrows and Wallace, *Gotham*, 1095–1096, 1179–1180; William Dean Howells, *A Hazard of New Fortunes* (New York: Signet, 1965), 352–369.

79. Scobey, "Boycotting the Politics Factory," 295–303; Foner, *History of the Labor Movement* II, 117–119; Michael A. Gordon, "The Labor Boycott in New York City," *Labor History* 16 (Spring 1975), 184–229.

80. Gordon, "The Labor Boycott in New York City," 184–229; Burrows and Wallace, *Gotham*, 1098; Gompers, *Seventy Years* I, 311.

81. Barker, *Henry George*, 458–467; Scobey, "Boycotting the Politics Factory," 281–287; Foner, *History of the Labor Movement* II, 122–125.

82. Burrows and Wallace, *Gotham*, 1100–1103; Barker, *Henry George*, 463–468; Alan Nevins, *Abram S. Hewitt with Some Account of Peter Cooper* (New York: Harper, 1935), 461–462; Agnes George De Mille, *Henry George, Citizen of the World* (Chapel Hill: University of North Carolina Press, 1950), 142–147; Louis F. Post, *The Prophet of San Francisco: Personal Memories and Interpretations of Henry George* (New York: The Vanguard Press, 1930), 67–73.

83. Nevins, *Hewitt*, 410–419, 460–463; Barker, *Henry George*, 328–329; Burrows and Wallace, *Gotham*, 1103–1105; De Mille, *Henry George*, 89–90.

84. Nevins, *Hewitt*, 467; Barker, *Henry George*, 462, 472–475; Gompers, *Seventy Years*, 311–318; Scobey, "Boycotting the Politics Factory," 284–285; Hammack, *Power and Society*, 174–175; Phillip S. Foner, "Class Collaborator" in Stearn, *Gompers*, 143–151.

85. Barker, *Henry George*, 472–475; Richardson, *New York Police*, 199; Burrows and Wallace, *Gotham*, 1098–1100; De Mille, *Henry George*, 146–147; Henry George Jr., *Henry George* (New York: Chelsea House, 1981), 467–470; Post, *The Prophet of San Francisco*, 71–72.

86. Hammack, *Power and Society*, 114–115; Nevins, *Hewitt*, 463–466; Burrows and Wallace, *Gotham*, 1105; Beckert, *The Monied Metropolis*, 273–279, 320; Foner, *History of the Labor Movement*, II, 125–126; Richard Samuel West, *Satire on Stone: The Political Cartoons of Joseph Keppler* (Urbana: University of Illinois Press,

1988), 232–233; *New York Daily Tribune,* October 14 and 29, 1886, November 4, 1886; *New York Times,* November 1, 1886.

87. Burrows and Wallace, *Gotham,* 1105; Scobey, "Boycotting the Politics Factory," 280–281; Nevins, *Hewitt,* 465–467; Gompers, *Seventy Years* I, 318; Barker, *Henry George,* 477; Foner, *History of the Labor Movement,* II, 121–125; De Mille, *Henry George,* 146–151; Post, *The Prophet of San Francisco,* 74–78.

88. Burrows and Wallace, *Gotham,* 1105–1108; Barker, *Henry George,* 464–467, 476–481; Hammack, *Power and Society,* 175–176; Nevins, *Hewitt,* 468–469; De Mille, *Henry George,* 152; Foner, *History of the Labor Movement,* II, 126–127; Post, *The Prophet of San Francisco,* 78–80.

89. *New York Daily Tribune,* Nov. 4, 1886; *New York Evening Post,* November 3 and 6, 1886; *Public Opinion* (London), November 19, 1886; Burrows and Wallace, *Gotham,* 1101; Nevins, *Hewitt,* 469; Barker, *Henry George,* 464; De Mille, *Henry George,* 152–154.

90. Hammack, *Power and Society,* 176; Foner, *History of the Labor Movement* II, 128–129.

91. *New York Daily Tribune,* Nov. 4, 1886; Foner, *History of the Labor Movement* II, 129–130; Scobey, "Boycotting the Politics Factory," 313.

92. Foner, *History of the Labor Movement,* II, 32–46, 132–156; Rayback, *A History of American Labor,* 171–184; Gompers, *Seventy Years* I, 264–287, 321.

93. Gompers, *Seventy Years* I, 381–402; Foner, *History of the Labor Movement,* II, 171–188; Rayback, *A History of American Labor,* 194–207; Burrows and Wallace, *Gotham,* 1095–1098; Leon Litwack, ed., *The American Labor Movement* (Englewood Cliffs: Prentice Hall, 1962), 37–42; Kessner, *Capital City,* 251.

94. Sarah Henry, "The Strikers and their Sympathizers: Brooklyn in the Trolley Strike of 1895," *Labor History* 32 (1991), 329–336, 351; Theodore Dreiser, *An American Tragedy* (New York: Signet, 1981), 386–407.

95. Henry, "The Strikers and their Sympathizers," 336–353; Nancy Groce, *New York: Songs of the City* (New York: Watson-Guptill, 1999), 133.

96. Gunther Barth, *City People: The Rise of Modern City Culture in Nineteenth Century America* (New York: Oxford University Press, 1980), 58–109.

97. David Nasaw, *Children of the City at Work and at Play* (New York: Oxford University Press, 1985), 62–87, 167–177; Barth, *City People,* 90.

98. Nasaw, *Children of the City,* 171–175.

99. Ibid., 172–181.

100. Riis, *The Children of the Poor,* 1–2; Riis, *A Ten Year's War,* 266–267; Leviatin, *How the Other Half Lives,* 187–197, 254.

CHAPTER 6

1. Elizabeth Sussman with John Hanhardt, *City of Ambition: Artists and New York, 1900–1960* (New York: Whitney Museum of American Art, 1996), 10–11.

2. Frederick Lewis Allen, *The Great Pierpont Morgan* (New York: Harper and Row, 1949/1965), 163; Ron Chernow, *The House of Morgan: An American Banking Dynasty and the Rise of Modern Finance* (New York: Grove Press, 1990), 86.

3. Chernow, *The House of Morgan,* 66–69, 88–94, 99, 108–109, 152–3; Allen, *The Great Pierpont Morgan,* 66–79; Thomas Kessner, *Capital City: New York City and*

the Men Behind America's Rise to Economic Dominance, 1860–1900 (New York: Simon and Schuster, 1903), 269–72, 284–289; Harold U. Faulkner, *The Decline of Laissez Faire, 1897–1917* (New York: Harper and Row, 1951), 187–210.

4. Faulkner, *The Decline of Laissez Faire*, 35–45, 153–170; Allen, *The Great Pierpont Morgan*, 123–148; Chernow, *The House of Morgan*, 81–86, 100–102; Kessner, *Capital City*, 298–309.

5. Allen, *The Great Pierpont Morgan*, 80–101, 192–213; Chernow, *The House of Morgan*, 71–77, 93, 121–128; Ric Burns and James Sanders, *New York: An Illustrated History* (New York: Alfred A. Knopf, 1999), 270–271.

6. Burns and Sanders, *New York*, 270; Faulkner, *The Decline of Laissez Faire*, 366–382; Richard Hofstadter, *The Age of Reform* (New York: Vintage Books, 1955), 231–240; Chernow, *The House of Morgan*, 204; Kessner, *Capital City*, 309.

7. Edmund Morris, *Theodore Rex* (New York: Random House, 2001), 3–30; Kathleen Dalton, *Theodore Roosevelt, A Strenuous Life* (New York: Alfred A. Knopf, 2002), 182–184.

8. Richard Hofstadter, *The American Political Tradition* (New York: Vintage, 1948), 206–237; Dalton, *Theodore Roosevelt*, 224–226; Jacob A. Riis, *Theodore Roosevelt, The Citizen* (New York: Grosset and Dunlap, 1907), 302.

9. Morris, *Theodore Rex*, 87–94; Morton Keller, ed., *Theodore Roosevelt. A Profile* (New York: Hill and Wang, 1967); Hofstadter, *The American Political Tradition*, 227–231; Chernow, *The House of Morgan*, 106, 130, 150–161; Allen, *The Great Pierpont Morgan*, 175–178; Kessner, *Capital City*, 313–318.

10. Allen, *The Great Pierpont Morgan*, 114, 150, 205; Chernow, *The House of Morgan*, 119; William R. Taylor, *In Pursuit of Gotham: Culture and Commerce in New York* (New York: Oxford University Press, 1992), xv; William B. Scott and Peter M. Rutkoff, *New York Modern: The Arts and the City* (Baltimore: Johns Hopkins Press, 1999), 1–13; David Garrard Lowe, *Beaux Arts New York* (New York: Whitney Library of Design, 1998); Donald Martin Reynolds, *The Architecture of New York City: Histories and Views of Important Structures, Sites and Symbols* (New York: Collier Books, 1984), 205–227.

11. Burns and Sanders, *New York*, 230–238, 344; Taylor, *In Pursuit of Gotham*, 30–31, 51–67; Scott and Rutkoff, *New York Modern*, 20–22; Reynolds, *The Architecture of New York City*, 147, 169–179.

12. Burns and Sanders, *New York*, 243–250, 272–273; Jacob A. Riis, *The Battle With The Slum* (New York: Macmillan, 1902); Robert H. Bremner, *From the Depths: The Discovery of Poverty in the United States* (New York: New York University Press, 1972), 208–210; Frederick M. Binder and David M. Reimers, *All the Nations Under Heaven: An Ethnic and Racial History of New York City* (New York: Columbia University Press, 1995), 93–148; Hofstadter, *The Age of Reform*, 241–242.

13. David Nasaw, *The Chief: The Life of William Randolph Hearst* (Boston: Houghton Mifflin, 2000), 194–201.

14. William R. Taylor, ed., *Inventing Times Square: Commerce and Culture at the Crossroads of the World* (Baltimore: Johns Hopkins University Press, 1991), xi–xxvi.

15. Burns and Sanders, *New York*, 293–294; Taylor, *In Pursuit of Gotham*, 93–108; Scott and Rutkoff, *New York Modern*, 14–20; David C. Hammack, "Developing

for Commercial Culture" in Taylor, *Inventing Times Square*, 36–50; James Traub, *The Devil's Playground: A Century of Pleasure and Profit in Times Square* (New York: Random House, 2004), 17–52; Lewis Allen, *The City in Slang: New York Life and Popular Speech* (New York: Oxford University Press, 1993), 57–61.

16. Christine Stansell, *American Moderns: Bohemian New York and the Creation of a New Century* (New York: Henry Holt, 2000), 1–8, 40–69, 73; Ross Wetzsteon, *Republic of Dreams, Greenwich Village: The American Bohemia, 1910–1960* (New York: Simon and Schuster, 2002), ix–xvii, 1–24.

17. Stansell, *American Moderns*, 100–111; Taylor, *In Pursuit of Gotham*, 119–132; Leslie Fischbein, "The Culture of Contradiction: The Greenwich Village Rebellion," in *Greenwich Village: Culture and Counterculture*, eds. Rick Beard and Leslie Cohen Berlowitz (New Brunswick, N.J.: Rutgers University Press, 1993), 212–228; Malcolm Cowley, *Exile's Return, A Literary Odyssey of the 1920s* (New York: Viking, 1934/1968), 52–65.

18. Stansell, *American Moderns*, 28–39, 231; Wetzsteon, *Republic of Dreams*, 162–236; James R. McGovern, "The American Woman's Pre-World War I Freedom in Manners and Morals," in *Our American Sisters: Women in American Life and Thought*, eds. Jean E. Friedman and William G. Shade (Boston: Allyn and Bacon, 1976), 345–365; Blanche Wiesen Cook, "The Radical Women of Greenwich Village from Crystal Eastman to Eleanor Roosevelt" in Beard and Berlowitz, *Greenwich Village*, 243–257.

19. Scott and Rutkoff, *New York Modern*, xvii–xx, 48–52; Beaumont Newhall, *The History of Photography* (New York: The Museum of Modern Art, 1993), 160–168.

20. Rebecca Zurier, "The Making of Six New York Artists," in *Metropolitan Lives: The Ashcan Artists and Their New York*, eds. Rebecca Zurier, Robert W. Snyder, Virginia M. Mecklenburg (New York: W. W. Norton, 1995), 59–68; Elizabeth Milroy, *Painters of a New Century: The Eight and American Art* (Milwaukee: Milwaukee Art Museum, 1991), 15–26; Scott and Rutkoff, *New York Modern*, 22–27; Rebecca Zurier, "Picturing the City: New York in the Press and the Art of the Ashcan School, 1890–1917" (Ph.D. dissertation, Yale University, 1988), 1–18, 53.

21. Zurier, "Picturing the City," 179–181; Elizabeth Milroy, *Painters of a New Century*, 45–51; Scott and Rutkoff, *New York Modern*, 25–27; Zurier, "Picturing the City," 179–181.

22. Milton W. Brown, *The Story of the Armory Show* (Washington, D.C.: Joseph H. Hirschorn Foundation, 1963), 89–93, 205–213; Scott and Rutkoff, *New York Modern*, 58–62; Stansell, *American Moderns*, 102; Wetzsteon, *Republic of Dreams*, 28–29.

23. Rebecca Zurier, *Art for the Masses: A Radical Magazine and Its Graphics* (Philadelphia: Temple University Press, 1988), 29–38; Stansell, *American Moderns*, 166–177; Wetzsteon, *Republic of Dreams*, 48–56; Ann Douglas, *Terrible Honesty: Mongrel Manhattan in the 1920's* (New York: Noonday Press, 1995), 3–8; Cowley, *Exile's Return*, 53.

24. Zurier, *Art for the Masses*, 39–42; Stansell, *American Moderns*, 173–177; Wetzsteon, *Republic of Dreams*, 68; Henry F. May, *The End of American*

Innocence: A Study of the First Years of Our Own Time, 1912-1917 (Chicago: Quadrangle Books, 1959), 314-317.

25. Zurier, *Art for the Masses,* 44-45; Wetzsteon, *Republic of Dreams,* 68-69.

26. Zurier, *Art for the Masses,* 107; Burns and Sanders, *New York,* 336; Scott and Rutkoff, *New York Modern,* 81; Stansell, *American Moderns,* 183-184; May, *The End of American Innocence,* 314-318; Thomas Bender, *New York Intellect: A History of Intellectual Life in New York City from 1750 to the Beginnings of Our Own Time* (New York: Alfred A, Knopf, 1987), 228-231.

27. Zurier, *Art for the Masses,* 46-57, 148-151.

28. Ibid., 25-27, 59-64; Wetzsteon, *Republic of Dreams,* 75-78.

29. Wetzsteon, *Republic of Dreams,* 78-83; Zurier, *Art for the Masses,* 61-65.

30. Zurier, *Art for the Masses,* 148-151; Stansell, *American Moderns,* 336-337; Bender, *New York Intellect,* 231.

31. John Hope Franklin and Alfred A. Moss Jr., *From Slavery to Freedom, A History of African Americans* 7th Edition (New York: McGraw Hill, 1994), 317-322; Nancy J. Weiss, *The National Urban League, 1910-1940* (New York: Oxford University Press, 1974), 47-70; W. E. B. Du Bois, *The Souls of Black Folk* (New York: Signet, 1903/1969), 45-46.

32. Franklin and Moss, *From Slavery to Freedom,* 247-263, 309; Jacqueline Jones Royster, ed., *Southern Horrors and Other Writings: The Anti-Lynching Campaign of Ida B. Wells, 1892-1900* (Boston: Bedford Books, 1997), 65, 206.

33. Emma Lou Thornbrough, "The National Afro-American League, 1887-1908" in *The Black Man in America Since Reconstruction,* ed. David Reimers (New York: Crowell, 1970), 94-109; Emma Lou Thronbrough, *T. Thomas Fortune, Militant Journalist* (Chicago: Chicago University Press, 1972), 117-135; Emma Lou Thornbrough, "T. Thomas Fortune, Militant Editor in the Age of Accommodation," in *Black Leaders of the Twentieth Century,* eds. John Hope Franklin and August Meier (Urbana: University of Chicago Press, 1982), 19-37; Emma Lou Thornbrough, "The National Afro-American League, 1887-1908" in Reimers, *The Black Man in America Since Reconstruction,* 94-109; T. Thomas Fortune, "Constitution and Address to the Nation of The Afro-American League, New York, January 25, 1890" in *The Black American: A Documentary History,* eds. Leslie H. Fishel Jr. and Benjamin Quarles (Glenview, Ill.: Scott, Foresman, 1970), 325-327.

34. Gilbert Osofsky, "Race Riot, 1900: A Study of Ethnic Violence," *Journal of Negro Education* 36 (1963), 16-24; Gilbert Osofsky, *Harlem: The Making of a Ghetto, Negro New York, 1890-1930* (New York: Harper, 1963/1971), 46-49; *New York Evening Post,* August 16 and 17, 1900; [Frank Moss, ed.] Citizens' Protective League of New York, *Story of the Riot* (New York: Arno Press, 1900/1969), 2, 8-22, 76-79.

35. *New York Tribune,* Aug. 19, 1900; *New York Times,* Aug. 19-20, 1900; *New York Evening Post,* Aug. 16-18, 1900.

36. Osofsky, *Harlem,* 49-52; Osofsky, "Race Riot," 22-24; Citizens' Protective League, *Story of the Riot,* 1-8, 15; James Weldon Johnson, *Black Manhattan* (New York: Da Capo Press, 1930/1991), 126-130; *New York Evening Post,* Aug. 16, 1900; *New York Times,* Aug. 17-20, 1900; *New York Tribune,* Aug. 19, 1900.

37. Eric J. Sundquist, ed., *The Oxford W. E. B. Du Bois Reader* (New York: Oxford University Press, 1996), 362; Marilynn S. Johnson, *Street Justice: A History of Police Violence in New York City* (Boston: Beacon Press, 2003), 80–86.

38. Franklin and Moss, *From Slavery to Freedom*, 317–322; Osofsky, *Harlem*, 53–67.

39. Osofsky, *Harlem*, 64–67; Weiss, *The National Urban League*, 3–28.

40. David Levering Lewis, *W. E. B. Du Bois, Biography of a Race, 1868–1919* (New York: Henry Holt, 1993), 386–407; Johnson, *Black Manhattan*, 135–144; Richard Kluger, *Simple Justice: The History of Brown v. Board of Education and Black America's Struggle for Equality* (New York: Alfred A. Knopf, 1987), 91–104; Du Bois, *The Souls of Black Folk*, 88; Franklin and Moss, *From Slavery to Freedom*, 281–289.

41. Zurier, Snyder, Mecklenburg, *Metropolitan Lives*, 47; Geoffrey C. Ward, *Unforgivable Blackness: The Rise and Fall of Jack Johnson* (New York: Alfred A. Knopf, 2004); Jeffrey T. Sammons, *Beyond the Ring: The Role of Boxing in American Society* (Urbana: University of Illinois Press, 1988), 37–40.

42. Sammons, *Beyond the Ring*, 37–40; Ward, *Unforgivable Blackness*, 166–201; Randy Roberts, *Papa Jack: Jack Johnson and the Era of White Hopes* (New York: The Free Press, 1983), 109–110; *New York Times*, July 6, 1910.

43. *New York Times*, July 6, 1910.

44. Arthur Bonner, *Alas, What Brought Thee Thither? The Chinese in New York, 1800–1950* (np: 1997), 135–151; Peter Kwong, *The New Chinatown* (New York: The Noonday Press, 1987), 11–16, 97–99; Ronald Takaki, *Strangers From a Different Shore: A History of Asian Americans* (New York: Penguin, 1989), 230–237; Binder and Reimers, *All the Nations Under Heaven*, 52, 107–108; Selma Berrol, *The Empire City, New York and its People, 1624–1996* (Westport, Conn.: Praeger, 1997), 48–49, 86–87; Du Bois, *The Souls of Black Folk*, 78; Sundquist, *W. E .B. Du Bois Reader*, 53–54; Lewis, *Du Bois Biography*, 42–43, 90–95.

45. Lewis, *Du Bois Biography*, 9–15; Johnson, *Black Manhattan*, 236–239; Ann Douglas, *Terrible Honesty: Mongrel Manhattan in the 1920s* (New York: The Noonday Press, 1995), 325–326; Herbert Aptheker, *A Documentary History of the Negro People in the United States, 1910–1932* (New York: Citadel Press, 1973), 181–183, 196.

46. Aptheker, *A Documentary History, 1910–1932*, 190–222; Johnson, *Black Manhattan*, 131–134, 233–236; Lewis, *Du Bois Biography*, 3–9, 15, 386–434; Jervis Anderson, *This Was Harlem: A Cultural Portrait, 1900–1950* (New York: Farrar Straus Giroux, 1981), 118–119; Nathan Irvin Huggins, *Harlem Renaissance* (New York: Oxford University Press, 1971), 54–56; Burns and Sanders, *New York*, 312–314; Eliot Rudwick, "Du Bois: Protagonist of the Afro-American Protest" in Franklin and Meier, *Black Leaders*, 62–83.

47. Paula Hyman, "Immigrant Women and Consumer Protest: The New York City Kosher Meat Boycott of 1902," *American Jewish History* 70 (September, 1980), 96–103.

48. Ibid., 91–100; Irving Howe, *World of Our Fathers* (New York: Harcourt, Brace, Jovanovich, 1976), 123–124.

49. Hyman, "Kosher Meat Boycott," 92–94.

50. Hyman, "Kosher Meat Boycott," 94–95; Rosalyn Baxandall, Linda Gordon and Susan Reverby, eds., *America's Working Women* (New York: Random House, 1976), 184–185.

51. Baxandall, Gordon, and Reverby, *America's Working Women,* 186; Hyman, "Kosher Meat Boycott," 95, 103.

52. Hyman, "Kosher Meat Boycott," 91–96; Herbert G. Gutman, *Work, Culture and Society in Industrializing America* (New York: Vintage Books, 1966), 62.

53. Johnson, *Street Justice,* 69–72.

54. Marie Ganz, *Rebels Into Anarchy and Out Again* (New York: Dodd, Mead and Company, 1919), 246–248; William Frieberger, "War Prosperity and Hunger: The New York Food Riots of 1917," *Labor History* 25 (Spring, 1984), 217–220; Dana Frank, "Housewives, Socialists, and the Politics of Food: The 1917 New York Cost of Living Protests," *Feminist Studies* 11 (Summer, 1985), 255–258.

55. Frank, "Housewives, Socialists, and the Politics of Food," 259–273; Ganz, *Rebels,* 258–260; Frieberger, "War Prosperity and Hunger," 223–229.

56. Frieberger, "War Prosperity and Hunger," 231–239.

57. Hyman, "Kosher Meat Boycott," 96–103; Howe, *World of Our Fathers,* 124–125.

58. Hyman, "Kosher Meat Boycott," 104–105; Joan M. Jensen, "The Great Uprisings: 1900–1920," in *A Needle, A Bobbin, A Strike: Women Needle Workers in America,* eds. Joan M. Jensen and Sue Davidson (Philadelphia: Temple University Press, 1984), 83–87; Roger Waldinger, "Another Look at the International Ladies' Garment Workers' Union: Women, Industry Structure, and Collective Action," in *Women, Work and Protest: A Century of United States' Women's Labor History,* ed. Ruth Milkman (New York: Routledge, Kegan, Paul, 1985), 89–95; Elizabeth Ewen, *Immigrant Women in the Land of Dollars: Life and Culture on the Lower East Side, 1890–1925* (New York: Monthly Review Press, 1985), 242–255; Leslie W. Tentler, *Wage-Earning Women: Industrial Work and Family Life in the United States, 1900–1935* (New York: Oxford University Press, 1979), 38–45; Alice Kessler-Harris, "Organizing the Unorganizable: Three Jewish Women and their Union," *Labor History* 17 (Winter, 1976), 5–23; Nancy Schrom Dye, *As Equals and As Sisters* (Columbia: University of Missouri Press, 1980), 13–33; Melvin Dubovsky, *When Workers Organize: New York City in the Progressive Era* (Amherst: University of Massachusetts Press, 1968), 40–49; Philip S. Foner, *Women and the American Labor Movement from Colonial Times to the Eve of World War I* (New York: The Free Press, 1979), 344.

59. Foner, *Women and American Labor,* 344.

60. Ibid., 12; Jensen, "The Great Uprisings," 88–92; Sandra Adickes, *To Be Young Was Very Heaven: Women in New York Before the First World War* (New York: St. Martin's Griffin, 1997), 108–114; Alice Henry, *The Trade Union Woman* (New York: D. Appleton, 1915), 90–91; John F. McClymer, *Triangle Strike and Fire* (Orlando, Fla.: Harcourt Brace, 1998), 20–25; David Von Drehle, *Triangle: The Fire that Changed America* (New York: Grove Press, 2003), 35–54.

61. Ann Schofield, "The Uprising of the 20,000: The Making of a Labor Legend," in Jensen and Davidson, *A Needle, A Bobbin, A Strike,* 167–182; Ewen, *Immigrant Women,* 256–257; Foner, *Women and American Labor,* 324–332.

62. McClymer, *Triangle Strike and Fire,* 26–50; Henry, *Trade Union Woman,* 89–95; Dye, *As Equals and As Sisters,* 88–94; Von Drehle, *Triangle,* 55–77.

63. Dye, *As Equals and As Sisters*, 88–94; Von Drehle, *Triangle*, 77–86; Ewen, *Immigrant Women*, 259; Foner, *Women and American Labor*, 333–338.

64. McClymer, *Triangle Strike and Fire*, 35–83; Schofield, "The Uprising of the 20,000," 169–171; Ewen, *Immigrant Women*, 242; Leon Stein, *The Triangle Fire* (New York: J.B. Lippincott, 1962), 158–168; Dubovsky, *When Workers Organize*, 4, 49–58.

65. McClymer, *Triangle Strike and Fire*, 2–6; Von Drehle, *Triangle*, 86.

66. Von Drehle, *Triangle*, 116–170; Stein, *The Triangle Fire*, 11–21; McClymer, *Triangle Strike and Fire*, 84–100; Burns and Sanders, *New York*, 284–287; Adickes, *To Be Young*, 114–115.

67. McClymer, *Triangle Strike and Fire*, 101–110; Von Drehle, *Triangle*, 171–193; Stein, *The Triangle Fire*, 73–157; *New York Sun*, March 29, 1911; *New York Tribune*, March 29, 1911, April 6, 1911; *New York Times*, March 29, 1911.

68. McClymer, *Triangle Strike and Fire*, 99–102; Bonnie Mittleman, "Rose Schneiderman and the Triangle Fire," in Frederick M. Binder and David M. Reimers, *The Way We Lived* II (Lexington, Massachusetts: D.C. Heath, 1992), 91–99; Dye, *As Equals and As Sisters*, 96–97.

69. McClymer, *Triangle Strike and Fire*, 110–127; Burns and Sanders, *New York*, 288; Von Drehle, *Triangle*, 219–258; Stein, *The Triangle Fire*, 157–176.

70. Stein, *The Triangle Fire*, 177–207; McClymer, *Triangle Strike and Fire*, 109–110; Jensen, "The Great Uprisings," 91.

71. *New York Times*, March 27–28, 1911; *New York Tribune*, March 27–29, 1911; *Literary Digest*, April 8, 1911.

72. McClymer, *Triangle Strike and Fire*, 40, 139–163; Oscar Handlin, *Al Smith and His America* (Boston: Northeastern University Press, 1958/1987), 56–60; Burns and Sanders, *New York*, 288–293; Robert A. Slayton, *Empire Statesman, The Rise and Redemption of Al Smith* (New York: The Free Press, 2001), 89–100; Von Drehle, *Triangle*, 194–218; Daniel Czitrom, "Underworlds and Underdogs: Big Tim Sullivan and Metropolitan Politics in New York, 1889–1913," *Journal of American History* (September, 1991), 536–558.

73. John D. Buenker, *Urban Liberalism and Progressive Reform* (New York: Charles Scribner's Sons, 1973), 48–49; Elizabeth Israels Perry, *Belle Moskowitz: Feminine Politics and the Exercise of Power in the Age of Alfred E. Smith* (New York: Oxford University Press, 1987), 82–83; Frances B. Jensen, "The Triangle Fire and the Limits of Progressivism" (Ph.D. dissertation, University of Massachusetts at Amherst, 1996), 236–262; Thomas J. Kerr IV, "The New York Factory Investigating Commission and the Minimum Wage Movement," *Labor History* (Summer, 1971), 373–391; Robert F. Wesser, *A Response to Progressivism: The Democratic Party and New York Politics, 1902–1918* (New York: New York University Press, 1986), 70–74.

74. McClymer, *Triangle Strike and Fire*, 163–170; Von Drehle, *Triangle*, 195–200, 263.

75. Stansell, *American Moderns*, 228–229.

76. Ibid.; Ronald Schaffer, "The New York City Woman Suffrage Party, 1909–1919," *New York History* 43 (July, 1962), 269–270; Rosalyn Terborg-Penn, "Discontented Black Feminists," in *Major Problems in American Women's History*, ed. Mary Beth Norton (Lexington, Massachusetts: D.C. Heath, 1989), 341–342; Frances

Diodato Bzowski, "Spectacular Suffrage; Or, How Women Came Out of the Home and into the Streets and Theaters of New York City to Win the Vote," *New York History* (January, 1995), 57–67; David Levering Lewis, ed., *W. E .B. Du Bois: A Reader* (New York: Henry Holt, 1995), 297–298.

77. Schaffer, "The New York City Woman Suffrage Party," 270–283; Bzowski, "Spectacular Suffrage," 57–94; Adickes, *To Be Young,* 84–88; Eleanor Flexner, *Century of Struggle: The Woman's Rights Movement in the United States* (New York: Atheneum, 1974), 249–253.

78. Flexner, *Century of Struggle,* 290; Schaffer, "The New York City Woman Suffrage Party," 283–285; Bzowski, "Spectacular Suffrage," 68; Adickes, *To Be Young,* 91–102; Aileen Kraditor, *The Ideas of the Woman Suffrage Movement, 1890–1920* (New York: W. W. Norton, 1981), 6, 249–264; Elinor Lerner, "Jewish Involvement in the New York City Woman Suffrage Movement," *American Jewish History* 70 (June 1981), 442–461.

79. Bzowski, "Spectacular Suffrage," 70–79.

80. Schaffer, "The New York City Woman Suffrage Party," 271–272; Kraditor, *The Ideas of the Woman Suffrage Movement,* 14–74; Hyman, "Immigrant Women and Consumer Protest," 99.

81. Emma Goldman, *Anarchism and Other Essays* (New York: Dover, 1910/1969), 195–211; Alix Shulman, ed., *Red Emma Speaks* (New York: Random House, 1972), 386–398; Alice Wexler, "Emma Goldman," in *The American Radical,* eds. Mary Jo Buhle, Paul Buhle, and Harvey J. Kaye (New York: Routledge, 1994), 97.

82. Buhle, Buhle, and Kaye, *The American Radical,* 97–103; Cecyle S. Neidle, *America's Immigrant Women, Their Contribution to the Development of a Nation from 1609 to the Present* (New York: Hippocrene Books, 1975), 169.

83. Stansell, *American Moderns,* 22–24; Wexler, "Emma Goldman," 97–98; Alice Wexler, *Emma Goldman in America* (Boston: Beacon Press, 1984), 3–38; Shulman, *Red Emma Speaks,* 387–388; Richard Drinnon, *Rebel in Paradise, A Biography of Emma Goldman* (New York: Harper and Row, 1976), 3–38.

84. Wexler, *Emma Goldman in America,* 61–66, 74–79; Drinnon, *Rebel in Paradise,* 39–61; Neidle, *America's Immigrant Women,* 170–171.

85. Neidle, *America's Immigrant Women,* 62–94, 112–120; Wexler, *Emma Goldman in America,* 100–112; Goldman, *Anarchism,* 88–93.

86. Stansell, *American Moderns,* 75–88, 122–123; Drinnon, *Rebel in Paradise,* 126–130.

87. Drinnon, *Rebel in Paradise,* 94, 102–105, 160–162; Goldman, *Anarchism,* 47–67; Emma Goldman, *Living My Life* (New York: Alfred A. Knopf, 1931) 231, 528–529.

88. Shulman , *Red Emma Speaks,* 78–85; Goldman, *Living My Life,* 230.

89. Goldman, *Living My Life,* 523–524; Stansell, *American Moderns,* 112–114.

90. Zurier, *Art for the Masses,* 90; Wexler, "Emma Goldman," 100; Goldman, *Living My Life,* 523–524; Dubovsky, *When Workers Organize,* 72–85; Philip S. Foner, *Hisory of the Labor Movement in the United States IV* (New York: International Publishers, 1965), 442–450; Neidle, *America's Immigrant Women,* 172.

91. Drinnon, *Rebel in Paradise,* 167–169.

92. Ibid., 147–152, 164–171; Goldman, *Anarchism*, 213–225; Wexler, *Emma Goldman in America*, 209–215; Alice S. Rossi, ed., *The Feminist Papers from Adams to de Beauvoir* (New York: Bantam, 1974), 506–516.

93. Wexler, *Emma Goldman in America*, 226–244; Drinnon, *Rebel in Paradise*, 155–164.

94. Drinnon, *Rebel in Paradise*, 184–223.

95. Ibid., 224–314; Stansell, *American Moderns*, 323–326.

96. Shulman, *Red Emma Speaks*, 78–85; Goldman, *Living My Life*, 528–529; Goldman, *Anarchism*, 69–78.

97. Shulman, *Red Emma Speaks*, 386–398; Drinnon, *Rebel in Paradise*, 154.

CHAPTER 7

1. Arnold Rampersad, *The Life of Langston Hughes* I (New York: Oxford University Press, 1986), 50.

2. Langston Hughes, *The First Book of Jazz* (Hopewell, N.J.: The Ecco Press, 1955), 3, 40; Irving Lewis Allen, *The City in Slang: New York Life and Popular Speech* (New York: Oxford University Press, 1993), 62–63; Jervis Anderson, *This Was Harlem: A Cultural Portrait, 1900–1950* (New York: Farrar Straus Giroux, 1981), 315; Gerard L. Cohen, *Origin of New York City's Nickname, "The Big Apple"* (Frankfurt am Main: PeterLang, 1991), 1–7; Nancy Groce, *New York: Songs of the City* (New York: Watson-Guptill, 1999), 165; Elizabeth Sussman with John G. Hanhardt, *City of Ambition: Artists and New York, 1900–1960* (New York: Whitney Museum of Art, 1996), 10–11; Arnold Rampersad, ed., *The Collected Poems of Langston Hughes* (New York: Alfred A. Knopf, 1995), 32.

3. Bayrd Still, *Mirror for Gotham* (New York: New York University Press, 1956), 292, 297.

4. David A. Shannon, *Between the Wars: America, 1919–1941* (Boston: Houghton Mifflin, 1965), 65–68; James H. Timberlake, *Prohibition and the Progressive Movement, 1900–1920* (New York: Atheneum, 1970), 57–66.

5. Thomas G. Aylesworth and Virginia L. Aylesworth, *New York, The Glamour Years, 1919–1945* (New York: Gallery Books, 1987), 29–33; Thomas Kessner, *Fiorello H. La Guardia and the Making of Modern New York* (New York: McGraw Hill, 1989), 110–114; Robert A. Slayton, *Empire Statesman, The Rise and Redemption of Al Smith* (New York: The Free Press, 2001), 189–201.

6. Shannon, *Between the Wars*, 68–72; Ric Burns and James Sanders, *New York: An Illustrated History* (New York: Alfred A. Knopf, 1999), 318; Frederick Lewis Allen, *Only Yesterday: An Informal History of the 1920s* (New York: Harper and Row, 1931/1964), 204–224, 260–261; Herbert Asbury, "The Noble Experiment of Izzie and Moe," in *The Aspirin Age, 1919–1941*, ed. Isabel Leighton (New York: Simon and Schuster, 1949), 34–49.

7. William E. Leuchtenberg, *The Perils of Prosperity, 1914–1932* (Chicago: University of Chicago Press, 1958), 204–208, 226.

8. Ibid., 80, 204–224; Ron Chernow, *The House of Morgan: An American Banking Dynasty and the Rise of Modern Finance* (New York: Grove Press, 1990), 212–214.

9. Burns and Sanders, *New York*, 340–353; Aylesworth, *New York*, 36–93.

10. William R. Taylor, *In Pursuit of Gotham: Culture and Commerce in New York* (New York: Oxford University Press, 1992), 23, 30–33, 65.

11. Burns and Sanders, *New York*, 399–400; Clifton Hood, "Subways, Transit Politics, and Metropolitan Spatial Expansion," in *The Landscape of Modernity, New York City, 1900–1940*, eds. David Ward and Oliver Zunz (Baltimore: Johns Hopkins University Press, 1992), 191–212; Deborah Dash Moore, "On the Fringes of the City: Jewish Neighborhoods in Three Boroughs" in Ward and Zunz, *The Landscape of Modernity*, 252–272.

12. Burns and Sanders, *New York*, 450–454; W. Parker Chase, *New York, 1932: The Wonder City* (New York: New York Bound, 1932/1983), 3, 9, 211, 233, 249; Daniel Okrent, *Great Fortune: The Epic of Rockefeller Center* (New York: Viking, 2003); Ron Chernow, *Titan: The Life of John D. Rockefeller, Sr.* (New York: Vintage, 1998), 667–670.

13. David Galernter, *1939: The Lost World of the Fair* (New York: The Free Press, 1995); Burns and Sanders, *New York*, 455–457; Aylesworth, *New York*, 105–108; Frederick Lewis Allen, *Since Yesterday: The 1930's in America* (New York: Harper and Row, 1939/1972), 266; Robert Wojtowicz, ed., *Sidewalk Critic: Lewis Mumford's Writings on New York* (New York: Princeton Architectural Press, 2000), 234–241.

14. Kessner, *La Guardia*, 271, 570, 588–591.

15. Rampersad, *The Life of Langston Hughes* I, 131; Anderson, *This Was Harlem*, 199–200.

16. David Levering Lewis, *When Harlem Was in Vogue* (New York: Oxford University Press, 1989), 24, 115–117.

17. Rampersad, *The Life of Langston Hughes* I, 3–55, 69–73, 145–146, 180, 315; II, 6; Faith Berry, *Langston Hughes, Before and Beyond Harlem* (New York: Wing Books, 1992), 32–34, 86, 314, 320–321.

18. Anderson, *This Was Harlem*, 3–56; Gilbert Osofsky, *Harlem, The Making of a Ghetto: Negro New York, 1890–1930* (New York: Harper, 1963/1971), 9–13, 92–123; Lewis, *When Harlem Was in Vogue*, 34.

19. Lewis, *When Harlem Was in Vogue*, 89–118; Anderson, *This Was Harlem*, 137–144; Burns and Sanders, *New York*, 323–328; Nathan Irvin Huggins, *Harlem Renaissance* (New York: Oxford University Press, 1971), 13–26.

20. Huggins, *Harlem Renaissance*, 26–30; James Weldon Johnson, *Black Manhattan* (New York: Da Capo Press, 1930/1991), 246–248.

21. Johnson, *Black Manhattan*, 246–251; Benjamin Quarles, "A. Philip Randolph: Labor Leader at Large," in *Black Leaders of the Twentieth Century*, ed. John Hope Franklin and August Meier, (Urbana: University of Illinois Press, 1982), 139–165; Thomas R. Brooks, *Toil and Trouble: A History of American Labor* (New York: Dell, 1971), 250–254; Paula Pfeffer, *A. Philip Randolph, Pioneer of the Civil Rights Movement* (Baton Rouge: Louisiana State University Press, 1990); Daniel S. Davis, *Mr. Black Labor: The Story of A. Philip Randolph, Father of the Civil Rights Movement* (New York: E. P. Dutton, 1972).

22. Anderson, *This Was Harlem*, 307–315; Ann Douglas, *Terrible Honesty: Mongrel Manhattan in the 1920s* (New York: Noonday Press, 1995), 14–15, 74; Lewis, *When Harlem Was in Vogue*, 169–173.

23. Lewis, *When Harlem Was in Vogue*, 169–173; Burns and Sanders, *New York*, 329–334; Aylesworth, *New York*, 36–44; Groce, *New York Songs*, 82–89; Geoffrey C. Ward, *Jazz: A History of America's Music* (New York: Alfred A. Knopf, 2000), 166, 174, 217.

24. Osofsky, *Harlem*, 180–187; Anderson, *This Was Harlem*, 59–71, 199–200; Huggins, *Harlem Renaissance*, 3–30; Lewis, *When Harlem Was in Vogue*, xv–xvi; Douglas, *Terrible Honesty*, 5, 345; Johnson, *Black Manhattan*, 260–261.

25. Anderson, *This Was Harlem*, 121; Huggins, *Harlem Renaissance*, 41–47; E. Franklin Frazier, "Garvey, A Mass Leader," in *Marcus Garvey and the Vision of Africa*, ed. John Hendrik Clarke (New York: Vintage, 1974), 236–241; Amy Jacques Garvey, ed., *The Philosophy and Opinions of Marcus Garvey* (Dover, Mass.: The Majority Press, 1923/ 1986), 53; William Loren Katz, *Black Legacy: A History of New York's African Americans* (New York: Atheneum, 1997), 128–138; Lawrence W. Levine, "Marcus Garvey and the Politics of Revitalization," in *Black Leaders of the Twentieth Century* eds. John Hope Franklin and August Meier (Urbana: University of Illinois Press, 1982), 105–138.

26. Levine, "Marcus Garvey," E. David Cronon, *Black Moses: The Story of Marcus Garvey and the Universal Negro Improvement Association* (Madison: University of Wisconsin Press, 1964), 39–49; E. David Cronon, "Marcus Garvey: 'One Aim, One God, One Destiny,'" in *Black History, A Reappraisal*, ed. Melvin Drimmer (New York: Anchor Books, 1969), 386–408; Howard Dodson, Christopher Moore, Roberta Yancy, *The Black New Yorkers, The Schomburg Illustrated Chronology* (New York: John Wiley and Sons, 2000), 159.

27. Lewis, *When Harlem Was in Vogue*, 17–24; Herbert Aptheker, ed., *A Documentary History of the Negro People in the United States, 1910–1932* (Secaucus, N.J.: The Citadel Press, 1973), 190–232; C. Eric Lincoln, "Political Nationalism: The Garvey Movement," in *The Black Man in America Since Reconstruction*, ed. David M. Reimers (New York: Thomas Y. Crowell, 1970), 252.

28. Cronon, *Black Moses*, 31–36; Levine, "Marcus Garvey," 105–120; Huggins, *Harlem Renaissance*, 41–47, 71; Anderson, *This Was Harlem*, 125–126; Lincoln, "Political Nationalism," 257–258.

29. Cronon, *Black Moses*, 60–61, 73–102; Levine, "Marcus Garvey," 120–125; Frazier, "Garvey," 236–241; Johnson, *Black Manhattan*, 251–259; Lewis, *When Harlem Was in Vogue*, 34–39; Anderson, *This Was Harlem*, 125–127; Aptheker, *A Documentary History, 1910–1932*, 366–411.

30. Cronon, *Black Moses*, 63; Katz, *Black Legacy*, 132; Lincoln, "Political Nationalism," 254–259.

31. Lincoln, "Political Nationalism," 254–255; Cronon, *Black Moses*, 65–69; Cary D. Wintz, ed., *African American Political Thought, 1890–1930* (Armonk, NY: M. E. Sharpe, 1996), 208–214.

32. Cronon, *Black Moses*, 103–112; Levine, "Marcus Garvey," 132–134; Johnson, *Black Manhattan*, 259; Lewis, *When Harlem Was in Vogue*, 41–44; Anderson, *This Was Harlem*, 123–125; Lincoln, "Political Nationalism," 254, 260–261; Huggins, *Harlem Renaissance*, 41–47; Katz, *Black Legacy*, 133–135.

33. Katz, *Black Legacy*, 136–138; Emma Lou Thornbrough, "T. Thomas Fortune: Militant Editor in the Age of Accommodation" in Franklin and Meier, *Black Leaders*, 35.

34. Cronon, *Black Moses*, 112–137; Levine, Marcus Garvey, 135–137; Gunnar Myrdal, *An American Dilemma: The Negro Problem and Modern Democracy* (New York: Harper and Brothers, 1944), 746–749.
35. Rampersad, *Poems of Langston Hughes*, 311; Douglas, *Terrible Honesty*, 376.
36. Burns and Sanders, *New York*, 291.
37. Groce, *New York Songs*, 136, 144; Frederick Lewis Allen, *Since Yesterday: The 1930s in America* (New York: Harper and Row, 1939/1972), 266.
38. Caroline F. Ware, *Greenwich Village, 1920–1930* (Berkeley: University of California Press, 1963), 105–126; Ronald H. Bayor, *Neighbors in Conflict: The Irish, Germans, Jews and Italians of New York City, 1929–1941* (Urbana: University of Illinois Press, 1988), 150–167; Craig Steven Wilder, *A Covenant With Color: Race and Social Power in Brooklyn* (New York: Columbia University Press, 2000), 107–133.
39. Virginia E. Sanchez-Korroll, *From Colonia to Community: The History of Puerto Ricans in New York City* (Berkeley: University of California Press, 1983), 11–38.
40. Ibid., 53–62.
41. Ibid., 68–71, 150–151.
42. Ibid., 68–81, 142–152, 235.
43. Burns and Sanders, *New York*, 164, 181–182; Oscar Handlin, *Al Smith and His America* (Boston: Northeastern University Press, 1958/1987), 8–12; Slayton, *Empire Statesman*, 3–49; Ralph D. Gardner, *Horatio Alger, or the American Hero Era* (Mattituck, NY: Amereon, 1964/1990), 346.
44. Burns and Sanders, *New York*, 289–291; Handlin, *Al Smith*, 53–60, 90–111; Christopher M. Finan, *Alfred E. Smith, The Happy Warrior* (New York: Hill and Wang, 2002), 27, 111, 117, 120, 233; Kessner, *La Guardia*, 67–69.
45. Groce, *New York Songs*, 136, 142–144.
46. Burns and Sanders, *New York*, 364–366; Handlin, *Al Smith*, 112–136; Finan, *Alfred E. Smith*, 187–230; Elizabeth Israels Perry, *Belle Moskowitz: Feminine Politics and the Exercise of Power in the Age of Alfred E. Smith* (New York: Oxford University Press, 1987), 184–218; Alfred E. Smith, *Up to Now: An Autobiography* (New York: Viking, 1929), 384–418; Matthew Josephson and Hannah Josephson, *Al Smith: Hero of the Cities* (Boston: Houghton Mifflin, 1969), 350–400.
47. Edward Robb Ellis, *The Epic of New York City* (New York: Old Town Books, 1966), 540–548; Burns and Sanders, *New York*, 418–419; Kessner, *La Guardia*, 157–159, 222–237.
48. Burns and Sanders, *New York*, 416; Kessner, *La Guardia*, 165–171; Ellis, *Epic*, 552; Leuchtenberg, *The Perils of Prosperity*, 246–256; Irving Bernstein, *The Lean Years: A History of the American Worker, 1920–1933* (Boston: Houghton Mifflin, 1960), 292–296.
49. Burns and Sanders, *New York*, 413–416; Kessner, *La Guardia*, 216; Bernstein, *The Lean Years*, 292–296.
50. Kessner, *La Guardia*, 73–74; Burns and Sanders, *New York*, 438; Bernstein, *The Lean Years*, 292–296; David A. Shannon, *The Decline of American Communism: A History of the Communist Party of the United States Since 1945* (New York: Harcourt Brace, 1959), 204–206.
51. Michael Gold, *Jews Without Money* (New York: Carroll and Graff, 1930/1985); Ronald Lawson with Mark Naison, eds., *The Tenant Movement in New York*

City, 1904–1984 (New Brunswick: Rutgers University Press, 1986), 1–7; Mark Naison, "From Eviction Resistance to Rent Control: Tenant Activism in the Great Depression," in Lawson, *The Tenant Movement*, 102–130.

52. Naison, "From Eviction Resistance to Rent Control," 94–130.

53. Ellis, *Epic*, 536–539; Burns and Sanders, *New York*, 416–417; Bernstein, *The Lean Years*, 427; Kessner, *La Guardia*, 201; Naison, "From Eviction Resistance to Rent Control," 94–130; Mark Naison, *Communists in Harlem During the Depression* (Urbana: University of Illinois Press, 1983), 35–36.

54. Kessner, *La Guardia*, 102; Ronald H. Bayor, *Fiorello La Guardia: Ethnicity and Reform* (Wheeling, Ill.: Harlan Davidson, 1993), 59.

55. Bayor, *La Guardia*, 1–21; Kessner, *La Guardia*, 117–126; H. Paul Jeffers, *The Napoleon of New York: Mayor Fiorello La Guardia* (New York: John Wiley and Sons, 2002), 244; Alyn Brodsky, *The Great Mayor: Fiorello La Guardia and the Making of the City of New York* (New York: St. Martin's, 2003), 487–488; Arthur Mann, *La Guardia, A Fighter Against his Times, 1882–1933* (Chicago: University of Chicago Press, 1959), 19–42; Fiorello H. La Guardia, *An Autobiography, 1882–1919* (New York: Capricorn Books, 1948/1961); Lawrence Elliott, *Little Flower: The Life and Times of Fiorello La Guardia* (New York: William Morrow, 1983), 11–68, 228.

56. Bayor, *La Guardia*, 50–81; Kessner, *La Guardia*, 115–133, 191; Mann, *La Guardia, A Fighter*, 181–230; Elliott, *Little Flower*, 71–145.

57. Kessner, *La Guardia*, 233–261.

58. Ibid., 287–289, 342–368; Charles Garrett, *The La Guardia Years,: Machine and Reform Politics in New York City* (New Brunswick, N.J.: Rutgers University Press, 1961), 152–219; Elliott, *Little Flower*, 205–222; Bayor, *La Guardia*, 104–127; Bayor, *Neighbors in Conflict*, 30–86.

59. Kessner, *La Guardia*, 29–30, 186–190, 353–355, 386; La Guardia, *An Autobiography*, 95–100.

60. Kessner, *La Guardia*, 257–291; Bayor, *La Guardia*, 123–127; Garrett, *The La Guardia Years*, 178–219.

61. *New York Times*, Sept. 8, 1996, 41; Bayor, *La Guardia*, 111.

62. Rampersad, *Poems of Hughes*, 426–428.

63. Paul A. Gilje, *Rioting in America* (Bloomington: Indiana University Press, 1996), 152–158; Richard Hofstadter and Michael Wallace, eds., *American Violence: A Documentary History* (New York: Vintage, 1970), 258–259; Joseph Boskin, ed., *Urban Racial Violence in the Twentieth Century* (Beverley Hills: Glencoe Press, 1969), 51–52.

64. Cheryl Lynn Greenberg, *"Or Does It Explode?" Black Harlem in the Great Depression* (New York: Oxford University Press, 1991), 13–67; Osofsky, *Harlem*, 128–148.

65. Greenberg, *Or Does It Explode*, 59–61, 103–105; Anderson, *This Was Harlem*, 242–253; Osofsky, *Harlem*, 155.

66. Greenberg, *Or Does It Explode*, 103–105; Dominic J. Capeci Jr., *The Harlem Riot of 1943* (Philadelphia: Temple University Press, 1977), 19; Charles V. Hamilton, *Adam Clayton Powell Jr.: The Political Biography of an American Dilemma* (New York: Atheneum, 1991), 87–89; Wil Haygood, *King of the Cats: The Life and Times of Adam Clayton Powell Jr.* (Boston: Houghton Mifflin, 1993), 33–37;

Adam Clayton Powell Jr., *Keep the Faith, Baby!* (New York: Trident Press, 1967), 55–60.

67. Greenberg, *Or Does It Explode*, 94, 214–223; Osofsky, *Harlem Ghetto*, 150–158.

68. William Muraskin, "The Harlem Boycott of 1934: Black Nationalism and the Rise of Labor-Union Consciousness," *Labor History* 13 (1972), 361–373; Greenberg, *Or Does It Explode*, 114–125; Hamilton, *Powell*, 90–94; John Hendrik Clarke, ed., *Marcus Garvey and the Vision of Africa* (New York: Vintage, 1974), 64.

69. Greenberg, *Or Does It Explode*, 3–5; Hofstadter and Wallace, *American Violence*, 258–262; Hamilton Basso, "The Riot of 1935" in Boskin, *Urban Racial Violence*, 52–56.

70. Kessner, *La Guardia*, 368–370; Hamilton, *Powell*, 56–60; Marilynn S. Johnson, *Street Justice: A History of Police Violence in New York City* (Boston: Beacon Press, 2003), 184–187.

71. *New York Post*, March 23, 1935; *New York Times*, March 22, 1935; *New York Amsterdam News*, March 30, 1935; *New York Age*, March 30, 1935, April 6, 1935; Hamilton, *Powell*, 56–60; Naison, *Communists in Harlem*, 140–148.

72. *The Complete Report of Mayor La Guardia's Commission on the Harlem Riot of March 19, 1935* (New York: Arno Press, 1969), 113–121; Kessner, *La Guardia*, 374–375; Naison, *Communists in Harlem*, 144–147; James Lardner and Thomas Repetto, *NYPD: A City and its Police* (New York: Henry Holt, 2000), 243–245; Johnson, *Street Justice*, 188–189.

73. *Commission on the Harlem Riot*, 122–135.

74. Kessner, *La Guardia*, 374–377; Bayor, *La Guardia*, 130–134; Capeci, *The Harlem Riot*, 3–8; Joel Schwartz, *The New York Approach: Robert Moses, Urban Liberals and the Redevelopment of the Inner City* (Columbus: Ohio State University Press, 1993), 184–107; Martha Biondi, *To Stand and Fight: The Struggle for Civil Rights in Postwar New York City* (Cambridge, Mass.: Harvard University Press, 2003), 121–136.

75. Greenberg, *Or Does It Explode*, 132–134; *The WPA Guide to New York City* (New York: Pantheon Books, 1939/1982), 235; Powell, *Keep the Faith, Baby!*, 62–64.

76. Greenberg, *Or Does It Explode*, 133–136; Capeci, *The Harlem Riot*, 25–27; Hamilton, *Powell*, 102–105; Powell, *Keep the Faith, Baby!* 64–69.

77. Capeci, *The Harlem Riot*, 54–55, 70–76; Powell, *Keep the Faith, Baby!* 57; Greenberg, *Or Does It Explode*, 211–223; Quarles, *Randolph*, 154–156.

78. Capeci, *The Harlem Riot*, 10–11, 26–27, 136–139; Hamilton, *Powell*, 122–124.

79. Kessner, *La Guardia*, 528; Bayor, *La Guardia*, 167–170; Dominic J. Capeci Jr., "Fiorello La Guardia and the Stuyvesant Town Controversy," *New York Historical Society Quarterly* 62 (October, 1978), 289–310.

80. Capeci, *The Harlem Riot*, 140–142; Kenneth Clark, "Group Violence: A Preliminary Study of the Attitudinal Pattern of its Acceptance and Rejection: A Study of the 1843 Harlem Riot," *Journal of Social Psychology* 14 (1944), 319–337; Hamilton, *Powell*, 126–135; Arthur Simon, *Stuyvesant Town, USA: Pattern for Two Americas* (New York: New York University Press, 1970).

81. Capeci, *The Harlem Riot*, 68–78; Kessner, *La Guardia*, 530–531; Alex L. Swan, "The Harlem and Detroit Riots of 1943: A Comparative Analysis," in *Black Communities and Urban Development in America, 1720–1990* Volume 6, ed. Kenneth L. Kusmer (New York: Garland, 1991), 139–157.

82. Capeci, *The Harlem Riot*, 81–98.
83. Rampersad, *Poems*, 282–283; Marilynn S. Johnson, "Gender, Race and Rumours: Re-examining the 1943 Race Riots," *Gender and History* 10 (August, 1998), 252–277.
84. Capeci, *The Harlem Riot*, 99–102; Greenberg, *Or Does It Explode*, 211; Kessner, *La Guardia*, 531; Johnson, *Street Justice*, 267–271.
85. Capeci, *The Harlem Riot*, 102–108; Kessner, *La Guardia*, 532; Lardner and Repetto, *NYPD*, 246–248; Walter White, "Behind the Harlem Riot of 1943," in Boskin, *Urban Racial Violence*, 56–61; *New York Times*, August 3, 1943; *New York Amsterdam News*, August 7, 1943.
86. *New York Times*, Aug. 3, 1943; *New York Amsterdam News*, Aug. 7 and 14, 1943; *New York Age*, Aug. 7, 1943.
87. Capeci, *The Harlem Riot*, 148–168.
88. Ibid.; *New York Age*, Aug. 23, 1943.
89. *New York Times*, Aug. 3, 4, 7, 1943; *New York Amsterdam News*, Aug. 7, 14, 21, 1943; Swan, "The Harlem and Detroit Riots," 139–157; Gunnar Myrdal, *An American Dilemma: The Negro Problem and American Democracy* (New York: Harper and Brothers, 1944), liii, 4.
90. Capeci, *The Harlem Riot*, 169–176; Swan, "The Harlem and Detroit Riots," 139–157; Johnson, "Gender, Race and Rumours," 267–271; Joe R. Feagin and Harlan Hahn, *Ghetto Revolts: The Politics of Violence in American Cities* (New York: Macmillan, 1973), 89–90; Robert M. Fogelson, "Violence as Protest," in *Urban Riots: Violence and Social Change*, ed. Robert H. Connery (New York: Random House, 1969), 40–44.
91. Rampersad, *Poems*, 273, 311–312, 429.
92. Ibid., 542.

CHAPTER 8

1. Oliver E. Allen, *New York, New York: A History of the World's Most Exhilarating and Challenging City* (New York: Atheneum, 1990), 283–284; E. B. White, *Here is New York* (New York: Warner Books, 1949/1988), 54; Bayrd Still, *Mirror for Gotham* (New York: New York University Press, 1956), 338–340.
2. Ric Burns and James Sanders, *New York: An Illustrated History* (New York: Alfred A. Knopf, 1999), 481–484, 532; William B. Scott and Peter M. Rutkoff, *New York Modern: The Arts and the City* (Baltimore: Johns Hopkins University Press, 1999), 354–360; Eric Homberger, *The Historical Atlas of New York City: A Visual Celebration of Nearly 400 Years of New York City's History* (New York: Henry Holt, 1994), 158–159; Robert Moses, "Remarks on Groundbreaking at Lincoln Square," in *Empire City: New York Through the Centuries*, eds. Kenneth Jackson and David Dunbar (New York: Columbia University Press, 2002), 736–738.
3. Burns and Sanders, *New York*, 484–488; Homberger, *Historical Atlas*, 152; Scott and Rutkoff, *New York Modern*, 289–320; Still, *Mirror for Gotham*, 333–336.
4. Still, *Mirror for Gotham*, 333–336.
5. Benjamin J. Davis, *Communist Councilman from Harlem: Autobiographical Notes Written in a Federal Penitentiary* (New York: International Publishers, 1969), 1–52, 101–144; David Shannon, *The Decline of American Communism: A History of*

the Communist Party of the United States Since 1945 (New York: Harcourt Brace, 1959), 92–100; Martha Biondi, *To Stand and Fight: The Struggle for Civil Rights in Postwar New York City* (Cambridge, Mass.: Harvard University Press, 2003), 43–45.

6. Davis, *Communist Councilman*, 161–186; Gerald Horne, *Black Liberation/Red Scare: Ben Davis and the Communist Party* (Newark: University of Delaware Press, 1994), 210–243, 254–304; Shannon, *The Decline of American Communism*, 196–200; Biondi, *To Stand and Fight*, 153–155; Philip S. Foner, ed., *Paul Robeson Speaks: Writings, Speeches, Interviews, 1918–1974* (New York: Citadel Press, 1978), 230–231; Martin B. Duberman, *Paul Robeson* (New York: Knopf, 1988), 338; Arnold Rampersad, *The Life of Langston Hughes* II (New York: Oxford University Press, 1988), 171.

7. Duberman, *Robeson*, 1–30, 68–86, 280–311; Foner, *Robeson Speaks*, 230–233.

8. Duberman, *Robeson*, 336–362.

9. Ibid., 363–380; Biondi, *To Stand and Fight*, 155–159; Foner, *Robeson Speaks*, 230–233; Lamont H. Leakey, "Paul Robeson," in *The American Radical*, eds. Mari Jo Buhle, Paul Buhle, and Harvey J. Kaye (New York: Routledge, 1994), 279–286.

10. Gerald Meyer, *Vito Marcantonio: Radical Politician, 1902–1954* (Albany: SUNY Press, 1989), 5, 39, 183–184; Alan Schaffer, *Vito Marcantonio, Radical in Congress* (Syracuse: Syracuse University Press, 1966), 10–12; Biondi, *To Stand and Fight*, 209.

11. Meyer, *Marcantonio*, 53–86; Charles V. Hamilton, *Adam Clayton Powell, Jr.: The Political Biography of an American Dilemma* (New York: Atheneum, 1991), 226–235.

12. Meyer, *Marcantonio*, 25–38; Schaffer, *Marcantonio*, 58–60, 185–190; Biondi, *To Stand and Fight*, 55, 209; Duberman, *Robeson*, 373.

13. Meyer, *Marcantonio*, 1–6, 35–44, 173–184; Joshua B. Freeman, *Working-Class New York: Life and Labor Since World War II* (New York: The New Press, 2000), 58–59, 74–90; Mark Naison, *Communists in Harlem During the Depression* (Urbana: University of Illinois Press, 1983), 217–218; David Levering Lewis, *W. E. B. Du Bois, The Fight for Equality and the American Century, 1919–1963* II (New York: Henry Holt, 2000), 555; Gerald Meyer, "Vito Marcantonio," in Buhle, Buhle, and Kaye, *American Radical*, 269–277.

14. Meyer, *Marcantonio*, 84; Manning Marable, *W. E. B. Du Bois: Black Radical Democrat* (Boston: Thayne, 1986), 178–189; Gerald Horne, *Black and Red: W. E. B. Du Bois and the Afro-American Response to the Cold War, 1944–1963* (Albany: SUNY Press, 1986), 151–182; Biondi, *To Stand and Fight*, 160–161.

15. Marable, *Du Bois*, 162–189; Horne, *Black and Red*, 75–111; Lewis, *Du Bois*, 498–553.

16. Marable, *Du Bois*, 175–181; Horne, *Black and Red*, 137–146, 201–221; Duberman, *Robeson*, 392; Keith E. Byerman, *Seizing the Word: History, Art and Self in the Work of W. E. B. Du Bois* (Athens: University of Georgia Press, 1994), 100–106.

17. Marable, *Du Bois*, 194–212; Horne, *Black and Red*, 188–198, 289–311; Lewis, *Du Bois*, 567–571; Thomas C. Holt, "W. E. B. Du Bois," in Buhle, Buhle, and Kaye, *American Radical*, 113–120; Adolph L. Reed Jr., *W. E. B. Du Bois and American Political Thought: Fabianism and the Color Line* (New York: Oxford University Press, 1997), 79–89; W. E. B. Du Bois, *The Education of Black People: Ten*

Critiques, 1906–1960 (New York: Monthly Review Press, 1973), 149–158; Elliott Rudwick, "W. E. B. Du Bois: Protagonist of African American Protest," in *Black Leaders of the Twentieth Century,* eds. John Hope Franklin and August Meier (Urbana: University of Illinois Press, 1982), 68–83.

18. Biondi, *To Stand and Fight,* 160–161, 272–287; Duberman, *Robeson,* 334, 343, 392; Paul Robeson, *Here I Stand* (Boston: Beacon Press, 1958/1988), 83–84.

19. Robert A. Caro, *The Power Broker: Robert Moses and the Fall of New York* (New York: Vintage Books, 1975), 1–21, 771–775.

20. Ibid., 1–15; Freeman, *Working-Class New York,* 114–124.

21. Caro, *The Power Broker,* 15–19, 849.

22. Ibid., 19–21, 689–698; Burns and Sanders, *New York,* 494–497; Joel Schwartz, *The New York Approach: Robert Moses, Urban Liberals and the Redevelopment of the Inner City* (Columbus: Ohio State University Press, 1993), 107–112, 295–305; Jack Newfield and Paul Du Brul, *The Permanent Government: Who Really Runs New York?* (New York: The Pilgrim Press, 1981), 131.

23. Caro, *The Power Broker,* 641–688, 844–849, 851–863, 886.

24. Ibid., 864–879.

25. Ibid., 399, 614, 984–993; *New York Post,* April 24–27, 1956; *New York Daily News,* April 24–25, 1956; *New York Times,* April 18–24, 1956.

26. Caro, *The Power Broker,* 993–1004.

27. J. Clarence Davies, III, *Neighborhood Groups and Urban Renewal* (New York: Columbia University Press, 1966), 79–82; Jane Jacobs, *The Death and Life of Great American Cities* (New York: Vintage, 1971), 112–140.

28. Davies, *Neighborhood Groups,* 75, 82–92, 102; Oliver E. Allen, *The Tiger: The Rise and Fall of Tammany Hall* (Reading, Mass.: Addison-Wesley, 1993), 260–283; Edward I. Koch, *Mayor: An Autobiography* (New York: Warner Books, 1984), 4–7.

29. Davies, *Neighborhood Groups,* 93–109; Burns and Sanders, *New York,* 514–517, 530–531.

30. Caro, *The Power Broker,* 1082–1094.

31. Fred Halstead, *Harlem Stirs* (New York: Marzani and Munsell, 1966), 110–113.

32. Craig Steven Wilder, *A Covenant With Color: Race and Social Power in Brooklyn* (New York: Columbia University Press, 2000), 235–239; *New York Times,* April 17 and 23, 1964, August 3, 1964; Bruce L. R. Smith, "The Politics of Protest: How Effective Is Violence?" in *Urban Riots: Violence and Social Change,* ed. Robert H. Connery (New York: Vintage, 1968), 115–121.

33. Caro, *The Power Broker,* 1094–1114, 1132–1156; Burns and Sanders, *New York,* 518–519; Newfield and Du Brul, *The Permanent Government,* 133–135.

34. Caro, *The Power Broker,* 1–21; Burns and Sanders, *New York,* 532–534.

35. U.S. Government, *Report of the National Advisory Commission on Civil Disorders* (New York: New York Times, 1968), 35–38; *New York Times,* July 22, 1964; Paul A. Gilje, *Rioting in America* (Bloomington: Indiana University Press, 1996), 157–160.

36. *Commission on Civil Disorders,* 38–113; *Amsterdam News,* July 29, 1967; *New York Times,* Sept. 11, 1964.

37. *New York Times,* Sept. 11, 1964.

38. Ibid., July 21–27, 1964, Aug. 12, 1964, Sept. 11, 1964; Charles R. Morris, *The Cost of Good Intentions: New York City and the Liberal Experiment, 1960–1975* (New York: McGraw Hill, 1981), 72–74; Hugh Davis Graham, "The Paradox of American Violence: A Historical Appraisal," in *Collective Violence*, eds. James F. Short and Marvin E. Wolfgang (Chicago: Aldine-Atherton, 1972), 202–209.

39. Rampersad, *Life of Langston Hughes*, II, 554–555; Langston Hughes, "The Harlem Riot," in *Harlem, A Community in Transition*, ed. John Henrik Clarke (New York: The Citadel Press, 1964), 214–220; Fred Shapiro and James W. Sullivan, *Race Riots, New York 1964* (New York: Thomas Y. Crowell, 1964), 16–42.

40. Shapiro and Sullivan, *Race Riots 1964*, 1–14, 43–103; *New York Times*, July 20–23, 1964; Scott De Veaux, *The Birth of Bebop: A Social and Musical History* (Berkeley: University of California Press, 1997), 20–21; Halstead, *Harlem Stirs*, 119–123.

41. *New York Herald Tribune*, July 19–20, 1964; *New York Times*, July 19–24, 1964; Craig Steven Wilder, *A Covenant With Color*, 175–217; Harold X. Connolly, *A Ghetto Grows in Brooklyn* (New York: New York University Press, 1977), 129–141, 151–153.

42. *New York Times*, July 24, 1964.

43. *Newsweek*, July 27, 1964, 101, 104–106; *Amsterdam News*, Aug. 1, 1964.

44. *Newsweek*, July 27, 1964, 108; *Commission on Civil Disorders*, 29; Marilynn S. Johnson, *Street Justice: A History of Police Violence in New York City* (Boston: Beacon Press, 2003), 234–238.

45. Foner, *Robeson Speaks*, 473; Kenneth B. Clark, "The Wonder Is There Have Been So Few Riots," in *Black Protest in the Sixties*, eds. August Meier and Elliott Rudwick (Chicago: Quadrangle Books, 1970), 107–115; Maurice Isserman and Michael Kazin, *America Divided: The Civil War of the 1960s* (New York: Oxford University Press, 2000), 37–42.

46. Clark, "The Wonder Is There Have Been So Few Riots," 107–115; *New York Times*, July 20, 1964, August 2, 1964.

47. *The Autobiography of Malcolm X* (New York: Grove Press, 1966), 217–220, 233–235; Bruce Perry, *Malcolm: The Life of a Man Who Changed Black America* (New York: The Talman Company, 1991), 160–166; Peter Goldman, *The Death and Life of Malcolm X* (New York: Harper and Row, 1965), 60–65.

48. Perry, *Malcolm*, 174–180; *Autobiography*, 236–247, 267–287; Goldman, *Death and Life*, 8–13.

49. *Autobiography*, 1–2, 236–265, 312; Perry, *Malcolm*, 186–194, 308–313; George Breitman, ed., *Malcolm X Speaks* (New York: Grove Weidenfeld, 1965), 23–44.

50. *Autobiography*, 179, 288–363; Perry, *Malcolm*, 202–212; Goldman, *Death and Life*, 171–172, 434–436; Peter Goldman, "Malcolm X: Witness for the Prosecution," in Franklin and Meier, *Black Leaders*, 305–329; Michael Eric Dyson, "Malcolm X," in Buhle, Buhle, and Kaye, *American Radical*, 321–327; Isserman and Kazin, *America Divided*, 43–47; *New York Times*, July 18, 1964.

51. Johnson, *Street Justice*, 229–234; Goldman, "Malcolm X," 311; Freeman, *Working-Class New York*, 186–190; Connolly, *A Ghetto Grows in Brooklyn*, 151–153.

52. Freeman, *Working-Class New York*, 191; Connolly, *A Ghetto Grows in Brooklyn*, 151–153; Wilder, *A Covenant With Color*, 222; Jerald E. Podair, *The Strike that Changed New York: Blacks, Whites, and the Ocean Hill-Brownsville Crisis* (New Haven: Yale University Press, 2002), 24, 30–32; Diane Ravitch, *The Great School*

Wars: New York City, 1805–1973, A History of the Public Schools as Battlefields of Social Change (New York: Basic Books, 1974), 267–279.

53. *New York Times,* July 22, 1964; Barrington Moore, "Thoughts on Violence and Democracy," in *Urban Riots: Violence and Social Change,* ed. Robert H. Connery (New York: Vintage Books, 1969), 3–14; Robert M. Fogelson, "Violence as Protest," in Connery, *Urban Riots,* 27–44; Kenneth B. Clark, *Dark Ghetto: Dilemmas of Social Power* (New York: Harper and Row, 1965), 15–16; Edward C. Banfield, "Rioting Mainly for Fun and Profit," in *The Metropolitan Enigma,* ed. James Q. Wilson (New York: Doubleday Anchor, 1970), 322–329; Joel R. Feagin and Harlan Hahn, *Ghetto Revolts* (New York: Macmillan, 1973), 6–12.

54. *New York Times,* July 20–27, 1964, Aug. 1–3, 1964, Sept. 11, 1964; *New York Amsterdam News,* July 25, 1964, Aug. 1 and 8, 1964; Robert M. Fogelson, *Big City Police* (Cambridge, Mass.: Harvard University Press, 1977), 239–242; Johnson, *Street Justice,* 237–239.

55. *New York Amsterdam News,* Aug. 8, 1964; *New York Times,* July 22 and 26, 1964; Dominic J. Capeci Jr., *The Harlem Riot of 1943* (Philadelphia: Temple University Press, 1977), 179; Graham, "The Paradox of American Violence," 202–209.

56. *New York Herald Tribune,* Aug. 10, 1964; *New York Times,* July 28–31, 1964.

57. *Commission on Civil Disorders,* 113; Morris, *The Cost of Good Intentions,* 74–78; John V. Lindsay, *The City* (New York: W. W. Norton, 1969), 88–100; James Lardner and Thomas Repetto, *NYPD: A City and its Police* (New York: Henry Holt, 2000), 252–255; Barry Gottehrer, *The Mayor's Man* (New York, Doubleday, 1975), 3–30; Vincent J. Cannato, *The Ungovernable City: John Lindsay and His Struggle to Save New York* (New York: Basic Books, 2001), 120–124.

58. Morris, *The Cost of Good Intentions,* 74–78; Gottehrer, *The Mayor's Man,* 33–51; Lindsay, *The City,* 93–108; Cannato, *Ungovernable City,* 120–129; Adam Clayton Powell Jr., *Keep the Faith, Baby!* (New York: Trident Press, 1967), 11.

59. Gottehrer, *The Mayor's Man,* 71–79; Cannato, *Ungovernable City,* 129–141; Lardner and Repetto, *NYPD,* 259–260; Johnson, *Street Justice,* 257; Henry Etzkowitz and Gerald M. Schaflander, *Ghetto Crisis: Riots or Reconciliation* (Boston: Little Brown, 1969), 142–158; *New York Amsterdam News,* July 29, 1967, August 8, 1967.

60. *Commission on Civil Disorders,* 1; Cannato, *Ungovernable City,* 204–207.

61. *New York Times,* August 8, 1967; *Commission on Civil Disorders,* 1, 10; Cannato, *Ungovernable City,* 204–213; Moore, "Thoughts on Violence," 6–7; Johnson, *Street Justice,* 258; Peter H. Rossi, ed., *Ghetto Revolts* (New York: Transaction Books, 1930), 1–12; Kenneth Fox, *Metropolitan America* (New Brunswick, N.J.: Rutgers University Press, 1985), 137–138.

62. Stephen Steinberg, *Turning Back: The Retreat from Racial Justice in American Thought and Policy* (Boston: Beacon Press, 1995), 107–119; *New York Herald Tribune,* Aug. 3, 1964; *New York Amsterdam News,* Aug. 1, 1964; *New York Times,* July 21–22, 27, 1964.

63. Morris, *The Cost of Good Intentions,* 82–85; Freeman, *Working-Class New York,* 209–211; Cannato, *Ungovernable City,* 78–82, 93; Chris McNickle, *To Be Mayor of New York: Ethnic Politics in the City* (New York: Columbia University Press, 1993), 210–213.

64. Morris, *The Cost of Good Intentions*, 83–106; Freeman, *Working-Class New York*, 209–212; Cannato, *Ungovernable City*, 196–204; McNickle, *To Be Mayor of New York*, 210–213; Lindsay, *The City*, 19–23.

65. Cannato, *Ungovernable City*, 155–167; Chris McNickle, *To Be Mayor of New York*, 214–215; Gottehrer, *The Mayor's Man*, 125–130; Lardner and Repetto, *NYPD*, 256–257; Edward T. Rogowsky, Louis H. Gold, and David W. Abbott, "Police: The Civilian Review Board Controversy," in *Race and Politics in New York City*, eds. Jewell Bellush and Stephen David (New York: Praeger, 1971), 59–67.

66. Cannato, *Ungovernable City*, 168–183; Lardner and Repetto, *NYPD*, 256–258; Joseph P. Viteritti, *Police, Politics and Pluralism in New York City: A Comparative Case Study* (Beverly Hills: Sage Publications, 1973), 25–34.

67. Cannato, *Ungovernable City*, 172–186; McNickle, *To Be Mayor of New York*, 214–215; Morris, *The Cost of Good Intentions*, 92–93; Rogowsky, Gold, and Abbott, "Police," 69–95; Johnson, *Street Justice*, 241–254.

68. Lindsay, *The City*, 20–21; Podair, *The Strike that Changed New York*, 9–20.

69. Gottehrer, *The Mayor's Man*, 183–198; Cannato, *Ungovernable City*, 267–281, 305, 338–341, 351; Freeman, *Working-Class New York*, 217–219; Ravitch, *The Great School Wars*, 317, 322; Marilyn Gitell, "Education: The Decentralization-Community Control Controversy," in *Race and Politics in New York City*, eds. Jewell Bellush and Stephen David (New York: Praeger, 1971), 134–137.

70. Podair, *The Strike that Changed New York*, 21–47.

71. Gitell, "Education," 137–152; Ravitch, *The Great School Wars*, 281–300, 338–361; Cannato, *Ungovernable City*, 281–300, 309–315; Morris, *The Cost of Good Intentions*, 108–115; New York Civil Liberties Union, "The Burden of Blame: A Report on the Ocean Hill-Brownsville School Controversy," in *The Politics of Urban Education*, eds. Marilyn Gitell and Alan G. Hevesi (New York: Frederick A. Praeger, 1969), 346.

72. Podair, *The Strike that Changed New York*, 103–142; Gitell, "Education," 152–160; Ravitch, *The Great School Wars*, 362–376; Cannato, *Ungovernable City*, 315–351; Morris, *The Cost of Good Intentions*, 111–114; Freeman, *Working-Class New York*, 220–226.

73. Podair, *The Strike that Changed New York*, 123–182; Gitell, "Education," 160–161; Ravitch, *The Great School Wars*, 381–398; Cannato, *Ungovernable City*, 345–351; Morris, *The Cost of Good Intentions*, 114–116; Freeman, *Working-Class New York*, 227; McNickle, *To Be Mayor of New York*, 216–218; Martin Mayer, "The Full and Sometimes Very Surprising Story of Ocean Hill, the Teacher's Union and the Teachers' Strike of 1968," in *Black Protest in the Sixties*, eds. August Meier and Elliott Rudwick (Chicago: Quadrangle Books, 1970), 169–229.

74. Nathan Glazer and Daniel Patrick Moynihan, *Beyond the Melting Pot: The Negroes, Puerto Ricans, Jews, Italians, and Irish of New York City* (Cambridge: The M.I.T. Press, 1970), xxix; Podair, *The Strike that Changed New York*, 183–214.

75. Nathan Glazer, "Facing Three Ways: City and University in New York Since World War II," in *The University and the City from Medieval Origins to the Present*, ed. Thomas Bender (New York: Oxford University Press, 1988), 267–289; Norman F. Cantor, *The Age of Protest: Dissent and Rebellion in the Twentieth Century* (New York: Hawthorn Books, 1969), 289–307.

76. Robert Freidman, "Introduction," in Jerry L. Avorn et al, *Up Against the Ivy Wall: A History of the Columbia Crisis* (New York, np, 1968), 3–8, 15–18, 21–22; *Crisis at Columbia: Report of the Fact-Finding Commission Appointed to Investigate the Disturbances at Columbia University in April and May 1968* (The Cox Commission Report) (New York: Vintage Books, 1968), 10–12, 89–98; Cannato, *Ungovernable City*, 237–238; Cantor, *The Age of Protest*, 292–294.

77. Cannato, *Ungovernable City*, 229–236; Cantor, *The Age of Protest*, 294; Smith, "The Politics of Protest," 128–131.

78. *Crisis at Columbia*, 12–17, 76–89, 158–186; Cannato, *Ungovernable City*, 236–253; Freidman, "Introduction," 18–21; Cantor, *The Age of Protest*, 292–295.

79. Cannato, *Ungovernable City*, 253–254; Cantor, *The Age of Protest*, 297–301; Gottehrer, *The Mayor's Man*, 157–164; Johnson, *Street Justice*, 265; Michael Baker et al, *Police on Campus: The Mass Police Action at Columbia University, Spring, 1968* (New York: New York Civil Liberties Union, 1969), 102–104, 109–110, 117–122; Irwin Unger, *The Movement: A History of the American New Left, 1959–1972* (New York: Harper and Row, 1974), 101–114; Ellen Kay Trimberger, "Columbia: The Dynamics of a Student Revolution," in *Campus Power Struggle*, ed. Howard S. Becker (New York: Transaction Books, 1970), 34–45.

80. Freidman, "Introduction," 4; Baker et al, *Police on Campus*, 104; Cannato, *Ungovernable City*, 229, 254–260.

81. Cannato, *Ungovernable City*, 260–265; Cantor, *The Age of Protest*, 303–306; Unger, *The Movement*, 115–118; Johnson, *Street Justice*, 260–265.

82. David E. Lavin, Richard D. Alba, Richard A. Silberstein, *Right versus Privilege: The Open Admissions Experiment at the City University of New York* (New York: The Free Press, 1981), 1–3; Sherry Gorelick, "City College: Rise and Fall of the Free Academy," *Radical America* 14 (September-October, 1980), 21–26; Robert E. Marshak, *Problems and Prospects of an Urban Public University* (New York: The City College, 1973), 6–10; James Traub, *City on a Hill: Testing the American Dream at City College* (Reading, Mass.: Addison-Wesley, 1994), 21–42; Conrad M. Dyer, "Protest and the Politics of Open Admissions: The Impact of the Black and Puerto Rican Students' Community of City College," (Ph.D. Dissertation, the City University of New York, 1990), 48–70.

83. Lavin, Alba, Silberstein, *Right versus Privilege*, 4–11; Allen B. Ballard, *The Education of Black Folk: The Afro-American Struggle for Knowledge in White America* (New York: Harper and Row, 1973), 119–124; Gorelick, "City College," 21–35; Dyer, "Protest and the Politics of Open Admissions," 70–88.

84. Freeman, *Working-Class New York*, 229–230; Traub, *City on a Hill*, 43–68; Lavin, Alba, Silberstein, *Right versus Privilege*, 12–13; David Lavin and David Hyllegard, *Changing the Odds: Open Admissions and the Life Chances of the Disadvantaged* (New Haven: Yale University Press, 1996), 1–13; Gorelick, "City College," 21–35; *New York Post*, May 8–12, 1969; Dyer, "Protest and the Politics of Open Admissions," 93–137.

85. Gorelick, "City College," 21–35; Freeman, *Working-Class New York*, 235–237; Traub, *City on a Hill*, 69–80, 191–226, 291–307; Lavin and Hyllegard, *Changing the Odds*, 14–20; Ballard, *The Education of Black Folk*, 124–141; *New York Times*, October 13, 1970.

86. Martin Duberman, *Stonewall* (New York: Dutton, 1993), 193–196; Charles Kaiser, *The Gay Metropolis, 1940–1996* (Boston: Houghton Mifflin, 1997), 197–198; John D'Emilio, *Sexual Politics, Sexual Communities: The Making of a Homosexual Minority in the United States, 1940–1970* (Chicago: University of Chicago Press, 1983), 231–232.

87. Duberman, *Stonewall*, 196–201.

88. Ibid., 202–209; Kaiser, *The Gay Metropolis*, 201.

89. Duberman, *Stonewall*, 198; Kaiser, *The Gay Metropolis*, 200–206; D'Emilio, *Sexual Politics*, 234–239.

90. Cannato, *Ungovernable City*, 389–395.

91. Morris, *The Cost of Good Intentions*, 67–71; Frances Fox Piven and Richard A. Cloward, *Poor People's Movements: Why They Succeed, How They Fail* (New York: Vintage, 1979), 291–296, 324–343, 354–359; Cannato, *Ungovernable City*, 539–545.

92. Cannato, *Ungovernable City*, 396–397.

93. Ibid., 403–408.

94. McNickle, *To Be Mayor of NY*, 218–229; Cannato, *Ungovernable City*, 389–414; Joe Flaherty, *Managing Mailer* (New York: Coward-McCann, 1969), 39–43.

95. Cannato, *Ungovernable City*, 414–417, 426–431.

96. Ibid., 435; Glazer and Moynihan, *Beyond the Melting Pot*, x, xxvii.

97. Cannato, *Ungovernable City*, 431–441; McNickle, *To Be Mayor of NY*, 229–236; Lindsay, *The City*, 19–46.

98. Lindsay, *The City*, 71, 133–134.

99. Ibid., 194–218; John V. Lindsay, "For New National Cities," in *Political Power and the Urban Crisis*, 2nd ed., ed. Alan Shank (Boston: Holbrook Press, 1974), 392–395; McNickle, *To Be Mayor of NY*, 207; Morris, *The Cost of Good Intentions*, 210–214; William F. Buckley Jr., *The Unmaking of a Mayor* (New York: Viking, 1966), 279–304.

CHAPTER 9

1. Robert Moses, *La Guardia: A Salute and a Memoir* (New York: Simon and Schuster, 1957), 18.

2. Gerard L. Cohen, *Origin of New York City's Nickname, "The Big Apple"* (Frankfurt am Main: Peter Lang, 1991), 2, 70–71; Jack Newfield and Paul Du Brul, *The Permanent Government: Who Really Runs New York?* (New York: The Pilgrim Press, 1981), 3–10.

3. *New York Times*, Jan. 2, 1978.

4. Irving Lewis Allen, *The City in Slang: New York Life and Popular Speech* (New York: Oxford University Press, 1993), 62.

5. Newfield and Du Brul, *The Permanent Government*, 76–96; Robert Fitch, *The Assassination of New York* (London: Verso, 1993), 130–141; James Glanz and Eric Lipton, *City in the Sky: The Rise and Fall of the World Trade Center* (New York: Times Books, 2003), 6–61.

6. Newfield and DuBrul, *The Permanent Government*, 76–96; Fitch, *Assassination of New York*, 130–141; Glanz and Lipton, *City in the Sky*, 62–87.

7. Fitch, *Assassination of New York,* 30; Paul Goldberger, "Groundwork," *The New Yorker* May 20, 2002, 86–96; *New York Daily News,* Sept 19, 2001.

8. Matthew Drennan, "The Decline and Rise of the New York Economy," in *Dual City: Restructuring New York,* eds. John H. Mollenkopf and Manuel Castells (New York: Russell Sage Foundation, 1992), 25–40.

9. Frederick M. Binder and David M. Reimers, *All the Nations Under Heaven: An Ethnic and Racial History of New York City* (New York: Columbia University Press, 1995), 225–242; Margaret E. Crahan and Alberto Vourvoulias-Bush, eds., *The City and the World* (New York: Council on Foreign Relations, 1997), 1–21; Joseph J. Salvo and Arun Peter Lobo, "Immigration and the Changing Demographic Profile of New York," in Crahan and Vourvoulias-Bush, eds., *The City and the World,* 88–109; Peter Hall, *The World Cities* (New York: McGraw Hill, 1977), 178–218.

10. *New York Times,* Jan. 2, 1990; John H.Mollenkopf, "The Crisis of the Public Sector in America's Cities," in *The Fiscal Crisis of American Cities,* eds. Roger E. Alcaly and David Mermelstein (New York: Vintage, 1976), 113–131.

11. *New York Times,* Jan. 2, 1978.

12. Ibid., Jan. 1, 1970.

13. Ibid.; John V. Lindsay, *The City* (New York: W.W. Norton, 1969), 20; Vincent J. Cannato, *The Ungovernable City: Lindsay and His Struggle to Save New York* (New York: Basic Books, 2001), 443–444.

14. *New York Times,* Aug. 11–13, 1970; *New York Amsterdam News,* Aug. 15, 1970; Jose Yglesias, "Right On With the Young Lords," *New York Times,* June 7, 1970.

15. *New York Amsterdam News,* Oct. 10, 17, 24, 1970; Cannato, *Ungovernable City,* 461–465; Barry Gottehrer, *The Mayor's Man* (New York: Doubleday, 1975), 261–287.

16. Cannato, *The Ungovernable City,* 461; Flora Davis, *Moving the Mountain: The Women's Movement in America Since 1960* (New York: Simon and Schuster, 1991), 107–116; Barbara Sinclair Deckard, *The Women's Movement: Political, Socioeconomic and Psychological Issues* (New York: Harper and Row, 1983), 324–335.

17. Joshua B. Freeman, *Working-Class New York: Life and Labor Since World War II* (New York: The Free Press, 2000), 237–238; Cannato, *Ungovernable City,* 448–449.

18. Freeman, *Working-Class NY,* 237–238; Cannato, *Ungovernable City,* 449–453; Charles R. Morris, *The Cost of Good Intentions: New York City and the Liberal Experiment, 1960–1975* (New York: McGraw Hill, 1980), 148.

19. Freeman, *Working-Class NY,* 239–246; Cannato, *Ungovernable City,* 452–453; Joshua B. Freeman, "Hardhats: Construction Workers, Manliness, and the 1970 Pro-War Demonstrations," *Journal of Social History* (Summer 1993), 725–737.

20. Cannato, *Ungovernable City,* 504–512; Jack Newfield and Wayne Barrett, *City For Sale: Ed Koch and the Betrayal of New York* (New York: Harper and Row, 1988), 116–123.

21. Cannato, *Ungovernable City,* 508–515; Jewel Bellush, "Housing: The Scatter Site Controversy," in *Race and Politics in New York City,* eds. Jewel Bellush and Stephen M. David (New York: Praeger, 1971), 98–114.

22. Cannato, *Ungovernable City,* 512–515; Newfield and Du Brul, *The Permanent Government,* 135; Newfield and Barrett, *City For Sale,* 122–123; Mario Cuomo, *Forest Hills Diary: The Crisis of Low-Income Housing* (New York: Vintage, 1974).

23. Cannato, *Ungovernable City,* 466–470; Newfield and Du Brul, *The Permanent Government,* 142–143; James Lardner and Thomas Repetto, *NYPD: A City and Its Police* (New York: Henry Holt, 2000), 265–268.

24. Cannato, *Ungovernable City,* 471–478; Newfield and Du Brul, *The Permanent Government,* 144–146.

25. Cannato, *Ungovernable City,* 478–482; Lardner and Repetto, *NYPD,* 269–274; Marilynn S. Johnson, *Street Justice: A History of Police Violence in New York City* (Boston: Beacon Press, 2003), 273–274; Eli B. Silverman, *NYPD Battles Crime: Innovative Strategies in Policing* (Boston: Northeastern University Press, 1999), 29–32.

26. Cannato, *Ungovernable City,* 482–483.

27. Ibid., 500–504, 515–523.

28. Ibid., 525–566; Newfield and Du Brul, *The Permanent Government,* 139; Robert A. Caro, *The Power Broker: Robert Moses and the Fall of New York* (New York: Vintage, 1975), 1118.

29. Fred Ferretti, *The Year the Big Apple Went Bust* (New York: G.P. Putnam's Sons, 1976), 377.

30. Freeman, *Working-Class NY,* 256, 272.

31. Cannato, *Ungovernable City,* 50–52; Chris McNickle, *To Be Mayor of New York: Ethnic Politics in the City* (New York: Columbia University Press, 1993), 252–255.

32. Ferretti, *The Year the Big Apple Went Bust,* 51–83; Morris, *The Cost of Good Intentions,* 127–146, 218–220; McNickle, *To Be Mayor of NY,* 255–256; Newfield and Du Brul, *The Permanent Government,* 147–148.

33. Ferretti, *The Year the Big Apple Went Bust,* 23–50; Morris, *The Cost of Good Intentions,* 155–170; Ken Auletta, *The Streets Were Paved With Gold: The Decline of New York—An American Tragedy* (New York: Random House, 1980), 29–91; Newfield and Du Brul, *The Permanent Government,* 11–42; Roger E. Alcaly and Helen Bodian, "New York's Fiscal Crisis and the Economy," in *The Fiscal Crisis of American Cities: Essays on the Political Economy of Urban America with Special Reference to New York,* eds. Roger E. Alcaly and David Mermelstein (New York: Random House, 1977), 30–58; Martin Shefter, *Political Crisis/Fiscal Crisis: The Collapse and Revival of New York City* (New York: Basic Books, 1985), 105–124.

34. Morris, *The Cost of Good Intentions,* 218–231; Newfield and Du Brul, *The Permanent Government,* 11–62; Seymour Melman, "The Federal Rip-Off of New York's Money," in Alcaly and Mermelstein, *The Fiscal Crisis,* 181–188; Eli B. Silverman, "New York City Revenues: The Federal and State Role," in Alcaly and Mermelstein, *The Fiscal Crisis,* 339–348.

35. Morris, *The Cost of Good Intentions,* 232–234; Freeman, *Working-Class NY,* 256–260; Ferretti, *The Year the Big Apple Went Bust,* 183–190, 349–357.

36. Morris, *The Cost of Good Intentions,* 232–240; Freeman, *Working-Class NY,* 260; Ferretti, *The Year the Big Apple Went Bust,* 333–406; Eric Lichten, "Fiscal Crisis, Power, and Municipal Labor," in *The Apple Sliced: Sociological Studies of New*

York City, eds. Vernon Boggs, Gerald Handel, and Sylvia F. Fava, (South Hadley, Mass.: Bergin and Garvey, 1984), 196–213.

37. Newfield and Du Brul, *The Permanent Government*, 158–174; Freeman, *Working-Class NY*, 260–268; Morris, *The Cost of Good Intentions*, 232–234; John Darnton, "Banks Rescued the City in a Similar Plight in '33," in Alcaly and Mermelstein, *The Fiscal Crisis*, 225–227; Matthew Edel, "The New York Crisis as Economic History," in Alcaly and Mermelstein, *The Fiscal Crisis*, 228–235.

38. Newfield and Du Brul, *The Permanent Government*, 8–9; Freeman, *Working-Class NY*, 260–272; David E. Lavin, Richard D. Alba, Richard A. Silberstein, *Right versus Privilege: The Open Admissions Experiment at the City University of New York* (New York: The Free Press, 1981), 289–308; John H. Mollenkopf, "The Crisis of the Public Sector in America's Cities," in Alcaly and Mermelstein, *The Fiscal Crisis*, 113–131; Frances Fox Piven, "The Urban Crisis: Who Got What and Why," in Alcaly and Mermelstein, *The Fiscal Crisis*, 132–144; William K. Tabb, *The Long Default* (New York: Monthly Review, 1982), 48–53; *New York Daily News*, July 2–5, 1975.

39. Tabb, *The Long Default*, 9–15, 38–39; William K. Tabb, "Blaming the Victim," in Alcaly and Mermelstein, *The Fiscal Crisis*, 315–326; Freeman, *Working-Class NY*, 277.

40. Piven, "The Urban Crisis," 132–144; Robert Zevin, "New York City Fiscal Crisis: First Act in a New Age of Reaction," in Alcaly and Mermelstein, *The Fiscal Crisis*, 11–29; Tabb, *The Long Default*, 9–15; Newfield and Du Brul, *The Permanent Government*, 11–42, 63–99; Freeman, *Working-Class NY*, 272; Auletta, *The Streets Were Paved With Gold*, 253–271; Martin Shefter, *Political Crisis/Fiscal Crisis*, 127–148.

41. Robert Curvin and Bruce Porter, *Blackout Looting: NYC, July 13, 1977* (New York: np, 1979), xiii–xv, 3–7; *New York Times*, July 14–17, 1977; Freeman, *Working-Class NY*, 276; Jill Jonnes, *South Bronx Rising: The Rise, Fall and Resurrection of an American City* (New York: Fordham University Press, 1986), 308–310.

42. Harold X. Connolly, *A Ghetto Grows in Brooklyn* (New York: New York University Press, 1977), 235–238; Curvin and Porter, *Blackout Looting*, 21–27, 34–41, 57–79, 183–185; *New York Times*, July 14–17, 1977.

43. Curvin and Porter, *Blackout Looting*, 24–27, 135–138; *New York Times*, July 14–17, 1977; Newfield and Du Brul, *The Permanent Government*, 6–7, 89–90, 274–275; Auletta, *The Streets Were Paved With Gold*, 69–72; Jonnes, *South Bronx Rising*, 249–267; Dennis Smith, *Report From Engine Co. 82* (New York: Pocket Books, 1972).

44. Curvin and Porter, *Blackout Looting*, 73–75; *New York Times*, July 15–19, 1977.

45. *New York Times*, July 15, 17, 24, 1977; *New York Amsterdam News*, July 30, 1977; Freeman, *Working-Class NY*, 281–282; Irving Howe, "The 'Animals' and the Moralists," *Dissent* (Fall 1977), 345–346.

46. *New York Times*, July 17, 19, 22, 1977; *New York Amsterdam News*, July 23, 30, 1977.

47. Freeman, *Working-Class NY*, 276; James Baldwin, *The Fire Next Time* (New York: Laurel, 1963); Jonnes, *South Bronx Rising*, 306–317; Jonathan Mahler, *Ladies and Gentlemen, The Bronx Is Burning: 1977, Baseball, Politics, and the Battle for the Soul of a City* (New York: Farrar, Straus and Giroux, 2005).

48. Freeman, *Working-Class NY,* 276; *New York Times,* Oct. 6–7, 1977; Ferretti, *The Year the Big Apple Went Bust,* 381.

49. *New York Times,* Jan. 2, 1978.

50. Ibid., July 21, 1977; Arthur Browne, Dan Collins, and Michael Goodwin, *I, Koch: A Decidedly Unauthorized Biography of the Mayor of New York City, Edward I. Koch* (New York: Dodd Mead, 1985), 143–146.

51. Newfield and Barrett, *City For Sale,* 107–135; John H. Mollenkopf, *Phoenix in the Ashes: The Rise and Fall of the Koch Coalition in New York City Politics* (Princeton: Princeton University Press, 1992), 100–104; Browne, Collins, and Goodwin, *I, Koch,* 87–89, 204–205; Edward I. Koch with Daniel Paisner, *Citizen Koch, An Autobiography* (New York: St. Martins, 1992), 116–118, 121–146; Edward I. Koch with Leland T. Jones, *All the Best: Letters from a Feisty Mayor* (New York: Simon and Schuster, 1990), 17–19.

52. Newfield and Barrett, *City For Sale,* 124–141; Mollenkopf, *Phoenix,* 100–110; Edward I. Koch with William Rauch, *Mayor: An Autobiography* (New York: Simon and Schuster, 1984), 21–41.

53. Newfield and Barrett, *City For Sale,* 2–3; Mollenkopf, *Phoenix,* 110–127; McNickle, *To Be Mayor of NY,* 280–281; Browne, Collins, and Goodwin, *I, Koch,* 227–243.

54. Koch, *Mayor,* 71–86, 107–108, 142–144; Mollenkopf, *Phoenix,* 114; McNickle, *To Be Mayor of NY,* 271–275; Browne, Collins, and Goodwin, *I, Koch,* 163–166; Freeman, *Working-Class New York,* 283.

55. Koch, *Mayor,* 136, 144–151, 209–227; Mollenkopf, *Phoenix,* 110–111; Browne, Collins, and Goodwin, *I, Koch,* 194–195; Newfield and Du Brul, *The Permanent Government,* 248–262; *New York Amsterdam News,* Sept. 20, 1980; *New York Times,* Sept. 18, 1980.

56. Koch, *Mayor,* 211–227; *New York Amsterdam News,* Sept. 27, 1980, Oct. 25, 1980; *New York Times,* Sept. 18–26, 1980.

57. Koch, *Mayor,* 153, 209–227; *New York Amsterdam News,* Oct. 25, 1980; *New York Times,* Sept. 21, 1980; Browne, Collins, and Goodwin, *I, Koch,* 194–197; Newfield and Du Brul, *The Permanent Government,* 257–259; McNickle, *To Be Mayor of NY,* 275–277.

58. Koch, *Mayor,* 271–190; Freeman, *Working-Class NY,* 284–286.

59. Steve Burghardt, "The New York Transit Strike of 1980: The Story of a Rank and File Disaster," in *Social Movements of the Sixties and Seventies,* ed. Jo Freeman (New York: Longman, 1983), 348–360.

60. Koch, *Mayor,* 190–208; Freeman, *Working-Class NY,* 284–287; Newfield and Du Brul, *The Permanent Government,* 248–262; McNickle, *To Be Mayor of NY,* 274–275.

61. Koch, *All the Best,* 112–113; Peter S. Arno and Karyn L. Feiden, eds., *Against the Odds: The Story of AIDS Drug Development, Politics and Profits* (New York: Harper and Collins, 1992), 73; Abigail Halchi, "AIDS, Anger and Activism: ACT-UP as a Social Movement Organization," in *Waves of Protest: Social Movements Since the Sixties,* eds. Jo Freeman and Victoria Johnson (New York: Rowman and Littlefield, 1999), 135–140; Mark Blasius and Shane Phelan, eds., *We Are Everywhere: A Historical Sourcebook of Gay and Lesbian Politics* (New York: Routledge, 1997), 600–615; *New York Times,* Sept. 27, 1989.

62. Halchi, "AIDS, Anger and Activism," 145; Arno and Feiden, *Against the Odds,* 77; *New York Times,* Dec. 12, 1989.

63. Halchi, "AIDS, Anger and Activism," 144–149; Blasius and Phelan, *We Are Everywhere,* 622–634; *New York Times,* Dec. 12, 1989.

64. McNickle, *To Be Mayor of NY,* 287–290; Newfield and Barrett, *City For Sale,* 62–104; Tom Wolfe, *The Bonfire of the Vanities* (New York: Bantam Books, 1987).

65. Charles J. Hynes and Bob Drury, *Incident at Howard Beach: The Case for Murder* (New York: G. P. Putnam's Sons, 1990), 11–25; Koch, *All the Best,* 240; *New York Amsterdam News,* Dec. 27, 1986.

66. Hynes and Drury, *Incident at Howard Beach,* 4, 53–64; Koch, *All the Best,* 241–245; *New York Amsterdam News,* Dec. 27, 1986; Al Sharpton and Anthony Walton, *Go and Tell Pharoah: The Autobiography of the Reverend Al Sharpton* (New York: Doubleday, 1996), 97–103; Al Sharpton and Karen Hunter, *Al on America* (New York: Kensington, 2002), 92–95.

67. Sharpton, *Go and Tell Pharoah,* 109; Sharpton, *Al on America,* 92–95.

68. Sharpton, *Go and Tell Pharoah,* 103–119; Hynes and Drury, *Incident at Howard Beach,* 96–99, 201–303; Browne, Collins, and Goodwin, *I, Koch,* 197; McNickle, *To Be Mayor of NY,* 275–277; Nicolaus Mills, "Howard Beach—Anatomy of a Lynching," *Dissent* (Fall 1987), 479–485; *New York Amsterdam News,* Jan. 3, 10, 17, 31, 1987; Feb. 21, 1987; Dec. 31, 1988; Aug. 5, 1889.

69. *New York Times,* Aug. 8–10, 1988.

70. Ibid., Aug. 8–11, 1988; Aug. 25–27, 1988.

71. McNickle, *To Be Mayor of NY,* 304; Sharpton, *Go and Tell Pharoah,* 173; Hynes and Drury, *Incident at Howard Beach,* 304–305; *New York Amsterdam News,* Dec. 16, 1989; *New York Times,* Sept. 28, 2002.

72. *New York Times,* Aug. 27, 1989; Sept. 1–2, 1989; Sharpton, *Go and Tell Pharoah,* 157–165; Koch, *All the Best,* 230–236; Edward I. Koch with Daniel Paisner, *I'm Not Done Yet: Keeping At It, Remaining Relevant, and Having the Time of My Life* (New York: William Morrow, 2000), 140–153.

73. *New York Times,* Aug. 26, 29, 30, 1989; Sept. 1, 1989; Sharpton, *Go and Tell Pharoah,* 173–177; Koch, *All the Best,* 230–236.

74. *New York Amsterdam News,* Sept. 2, 16, 23, 1989, Oct. 14, 1989; *New York Times,* Aug. 27, 28, 29, 31, 1989, Sept. 1, 2, 3, 10, 11, 1989.

75. Koch, *Citizen Koch,* 122; Koch, *All the Best,* 39–43, 166–168, 269.

76. *New York Amsterdam News,* Sept. 9, 1989; *New York Times,* Aug. 21, 1989; Mollenkopf, *Phoenix,* 165–189.

77. *New York Times,* Jan. 2, 1990.

78. Ibid., Aug. 29, 1989, Sept. 10, 13, 1989; *New York Amsterdam News,* Sept. 2, 9, 1989, Nov. 11, 1989; Mollenkopf, *Phoenix,* 165–189; McNickle, *To Be Mayor of NY,* 293–314; Freeman, *Working-Class NY,* 318–319; Asher Arian, Arthur S. Goldberg, John H. Mollenkopf, and Edward T. Rogowsky, *Changing New York City Politics* (New York: Routledge, 1990), ix–19, 197–205.

79. *New York Times,* Oct. 25, 1993; Jim Sleeper, *The Closest of Strangers: Liberalism and the Politics of Race in New York* (New York: W. W. Norton, 1990), 278–302.

80. Jean Claire Kim, *Bitter Fruit: The Politics of Black-Korean Conflict in New York City* (New Haven: Yale University Press, 2000), 109–118, 140.

81. Ibid., 116–145, 199.

82. Ibid., 156–187.
83. Ibid., 19–20, 145–155, 167–173, 204, 217–218.
84. Ibid., 188–223.
85. Freeman, *Working-Class NY*, 318–323.
86. Carol B. Conaway, "Crown Heights: Politics and Press Coverage of the Race War that Wasn't," *Polity* (Fall 1999), 95–102; *New York Times*, Aug. 20–25, 1991, Sept. 1, 1991; *New York Amsterdam News*, Aug. 24, 29, 31, 1991.
87. Conaway, "Crown Heights," 95–97; *New York Times*, Aug. 21, 1991; *New York Amsterdam News*, Aug. 24 and 31, 1991; *New York Daily News*, Jan. 1, 2002; *Newsday*, Jan. 1, 2002; *Village Voice*, Jan. 22, 2002.
88. *New York Times*, Aug. 22 and 25, 1991; *New York Amsterdam News*, Aug. 31, 1991.
89. *New York Times*, Aug. 22 and 27, 1991, Sept. 1, 1991; *New York Amsterdam News*, Aug. 31, 1991; Sharpton, *Go and Tell Pharoah*, 193–203; Sharpton, *Al on America*, 217–220.
90. *New York Times*, Aug. 25 and 29, 1991; *New York Amsterdam News*, Aug. 31, 1991; Sharpton, *Al on America*, 219–220.
91. *New York Times*, July 8, 10, 16, 1992; *New York Amsterdam News*, July 11, 1992.
92. *New York Times*, July 7–10, 1992; *New York Amsterdam News*, July 11, 1992; Sleeper, *The Closest of Strangers*, 195.
93. *New York Times*, July 7–10, 16, 1992; Sept. 16, 1992.
94. Ibid., Sept. 16, 17, 19, 27, 1992.
95. Ibid., Sept. 16, 20–23, 1992, Nov. 2 and 14, 1992.
96. Ibid., Oct. 3, 11, 14, 1993; Wayne Barrett assisted by Adam Fifiel, *RUDY! An Investigative Biography of Rudolph Giuliani* (New York: Basic Books, 2000), 276–277; Andrew Kirtzman, *Rudy Giuliani, Emperor of the City* (New York: William Morrow, 2000), 42–62.
97. Barrett, *RUDY!* 265–286; *New York Times*, Oct. 1–7, 14–17, 25, 1993, Nov. 4, 1993.
98. Barrett, *RUDY!* 284–287; *New York Times*, Oct. 15, 21, 1993, Nov. 4, 1993; Arian, Goldberg, Mollenkopf, and Rogowsky, *Changing New York City Politics*, 88–201.
99. Kirtzman, *Rudy Giuliani*, 32–62.
100. *New York Times*, Jan. 3, 1994.

CHAPTER 10

1. *Newsday*, Dec. 20, 2001; *New York Times*, Dec. 31, 2001; Andrew Kirtzman, *Rudy Giuliani, Emperor of the City* (New York: William Morrow, 2000), xii.
2. *New York Times*, Dec. 31, 2001; Edward I. Koch, *Giuliani, Nasty Man* (New York: Barricade Books, 1999), 5–22, 107–109.
3. Kirtzman, *Rudy Giuliani*, 44; Wayne Barrett assisted by Adam Fifiel, *RUDY! An Investigative Biography of Rudolph Giuliani* (New York: Basic Books, 2000), 2; *New York Times*, Jan. 3, 1994, Dec. 31, 2001; Fred Siegel with Harry Siegel, *The Prince of the City: Giuliani, New York and the Genius of American Life* (San Francisco: Encounter Books, 2005), vii–xv, 192–193.
4. Craig Horowitz, "The Fall of Supermayor," *New York Magazine*, April 19, 1999, 24–31.

5. Patrick L. Eagan, "A Flag With A Human Face," in *Superman at Fifty: The Persistence of a Legend,* eds. Dennis Dooley and Gary Engle (New York: Collier, 1987), 88–95; Gary Engle, "What Makes Superman So Darned American," in Dooley and Engle, *Superman at Fifty,* 79–87.

6. Kirtzman, *Rudy Giuliani,* 164–165; Siegel, *The Prince of the City,* 167–172; Eagan, "A Flag With A Human Face," 89.

7. *Newsday,* April 20, 1998; Siegel, *The Prince of the City,* 142.

8. Kirtzman, *Rudy Giuliani,* 36–40, 55, 88; Barrett, *RUDY!* 315, 341–345, 364–366; *New York Daily News,* May 14, 2000; Siegel, *The Prince of the City,* 62; Rudolph W. Giuliani, *Leadership* (New York: Hyperion, 2002), xiii, 41–43, 271–272; Marilynn S. Johnson, *Street Justice: A History of Police Violence in New York City* (Boston: Beacon Press, 2003), 291–291.

9. Kirtzman, *Rudy Giuliani,* 223–225; Barrett, *RUDY!* 344–345; Siegel, *The Prince of the City,* 75–77, 220–221; Johnson, *Street Justice,* 291; *New York Times,* Jan. 31, 1999, Feb. 2, 1999, Aug. 23, 1999, Feb. 6, 2000; *Village Voice,* March 14, 2000.

10. Kirtzman, *Rudy Giuliani,* 92–94; Barrett, *RUDY!* 342; Giuliani, *Leadership,* 197–200; Jack Newfield, *The Full Rudy: The Man, The Myth, The Mania* (New York: Nation Books, 2002), 93–94.

11. Kirtzman, *Rudy Giuliani,* 91; Barrett, *RUDY!* 343–366; Giuliani, *Leadership,* 72–82; Siegel, *The Prince of the City,* 146–150; *New York Times,* April 4, 1999.

12. Kirtzman, *Rudy Giuliani,* 95–96, 174–177; Barrett, *RUDY!* 331–335; Siegel, *The Prince of the City,* 186–187, 233; Johnson, *Street Justice,* 299–300; Horowitz, "The Fall of the Supermayor," 24–28.

13. Kirtzman, *Rudy Giuliani,* 245–250; Barrett, *RUDY!* 331–335; Newsday, March 28, 1999; Newfield, *The Full Rudy,* 61–88.

14. Kirtzman, *Rudy Giuliani,* 232; Barrett, *RUDY!* 328–333; *Village Voice,* March 12, 2002; Johnson, *Street Justice,* 292–293; *New York Times,* Jan. 3, 1994, Jan. 6, 1995, Oct. 15, 1996, Nov. 11, 1996, Feb. 15, 1999, May 27, 1999.

15. Johnson, *Street Justice,* 294–295; Siegel, *The Prince of the City,* 206–207; *New York Times,* Aug. 15, 1997; Koch, *Giuliani, Nasty Man,* 70.

16. Johnson, *Street Justice,* 296; *New York Times,* Aug. 8, 14, 15, 18, 21, 1997, Sept. 5, 12, 1997.

17. Barrett, *RUDY!* 115–124; *New York Times,* Aug. 30, 1997.

18. Kirtzman, *Rudy Giuliani,* 204–209; Barrett, *RUDY!* 328; Newfield, *The Full Rudy,* 91–96; Siegel, *The Prince of the City,* 207–211; Elizabeth Kolbert, "The People's Preacher," *The New Yorker,* Feb. 18 and 25, 2002, 165–166; *New York Times,* Aug. 28, 30, 1997, Sept. 10, 1997, March 27, 28, 1998; Koch, *Giuliani, Nasty Man,* 93–95.

19. Kirtzman, *Rudy Giuliani,* 227–244; Newfield, *The Full Rudy,* 96–112; Siegel, *The Prince of the City,* 233–239; *New York Daily News,* Feb. 26, 2000; *New York Times,* March 28, 1999.

20. Siegel, *The Prince of the City,* 235–236; *New York Times,* Feb. 13 and 16, 1999.

21. Johnson, *Street Justice,* 297; Siegel, *The Prince of the City,* 236–237; *New York Times,* March 17, 1999; *Newsday,* March 16, 1999, *New York Amsterdam News,* March 11, 17, 1999; *New York Daily News,* March 21, 1999.

22. Johnson, *Street Justice,* 297–298; Barrett, *RUDY!* 341–366; Elizabeth Kolbert, "The People's Preacher," 136–167; Al Sharpton with Karen Hunter, *Al on America*

(New York: Kensington, 2002), 182–188, 244; *New York Times,* March 3, 4, 17, 25, 29, 30, 1999, April 28, 1999.

23. Johnson, *Street Justice,* 298; Siegel, *The Prince of the City,* 237; *New York Times,* Jan. 14, 1998.

24. Kirtzman, *Rudy Giuliani,* 180–196, 244–253; Barrett, *RUDY!* 291–291, 322–327; Koch, *Nasty Man,* 157–159; *New York Times,* March 17 and 28, 1999, April 4, 1999, May 26, 1999, Dec 31, 2001; *Newsday,* March 28, 1999, Feb. 28, 2000; *New York Observer,* April 26, 1999; *New York Daily News,* Feb. 26, 2000; *Village Voice,* Feb. 28, 2000.

25. *New York Times,* Feb. 26–29, 2000; *Newsday,* March 3–4, 2000.

26. *New York Times,* March 28, 1999, Feb. 21, 27–29, 2000, March 3–5, 2000; *Newsday,* Feb. 16 and 28, 2000; *New York Daily News,* March 3–4, 2000; *New York Amsterdam News,* Feb. 11–17, 2000, March 2–8, 2000; *New York Post,* Feb. 28, 2000.

27. *New York Times,* March 2, 9, 15, 17, 21, 2000; *New York Daily News,* March 28, 2000; Kadiatou Diallo and Craig Wolff, *My Heart Will Cross This Ocean: My Story, My Son, Amadou* (New York: Ballantine Books, 2003).

28. *New York Times,* March 3 and 21, 2000; *Newsday,* March 3, 4, 28, 2000; *New York Daily News,* March 3–4, 2000; *New York Amsterdam News,* March 2–8, 2000; Sharpton, *Al on America,* 241–245; Barrett, *RUDY!* 338.

29. *Newsday,* March 21, 2000; Siegel, *The Prince of the City,* 273.

30. Kirtzman, *Rudy Giuliani,* 204–206, 232–233, 246, 272–275; Barrett, *RUDY!* 335–340; Sharpton, *Al on America,* 245–246; Newfield, *The Full Rudy,* 112–119; *New York Times,* March 28, 1999, Feb. 28, 2000, March 22, 2000; Horowitz, "The Fall of Supermayor," 26.

31. Johnson, *Street Justice,* 298–299; Barrett, *RUDY!* 241–266; Siegel, *The Prince of the City,* 144–145; *New York Times,* March 29, 1999, April 4, 1999, Feb. 27, 2000, March 4, 5, 13, 2000, April 1, 2000.

32. Barrett, *RUDY!* 290–291; Kirtzman, *Rudy Giuliani,* ix–xv; Siegel, *The Prince of the City,* 99–110, 141–150, 331; Horowitz, "The Fall of Supermayor," 24–31; Newfield, *The Full Rudy,* 1–14, 159–169; James Traub, "Giuliani Internalized," *The New York Times Magazine,* Feb. 11, 2001, 65.

33. Traub, "Giuliani Internalized," 62–67, 91, 100, 104; Siegel, *The Prince of the City,* xiii–xiv, 1–33, 216–218.

34. Siegel, *The Prince of the City,* 151–163; Barrett, *RUDY!* 310–311; Kirtzman, *Rudy Giuliani,* 170–174; *New York Times,* Jan. 14, 1998, March 31, 1999.

35. Barrett, *RUDY!* 310–318; Kirtzman, *Rudy Giuliani,* 171–174; *New York Times,* Dec. 9, 1999, Dec. 31, 2001; Giuliani, *Leadership,* 160–163.

36. Siegel, *The Prince of the City,* 151–163; Barrett, *RUDY!* 319; Giuliani, *Leadership,* 160–163; *New York Times,* Jan. 14, 1998.

37. Barrett, *RUDY!* 317–320; Kirtzman, *Rudy Giuliani,* 170–173; *New York Times,* Dec. 9, 1999, July 5, 2000, Dec. 31, 2001.

38. Barrett, *RUDY!* 309–320; Kirtzman, *Rudy Giuliani,* 75–78, 114, 172–174; *New York Times,* Dec. 9–10, 1999, July 25, 2000, Dec. 31, 2001; *Newsday,* Dec. 20, 2001.

39. *New York Times,* Dec. 25, 1994, Oct. 10, 1999; Asa Briggs, *Victorian Cities* (London: Odhams Books, 1963), 325.

40. Traub, "Giuliani Internalized," 65–67; Kirtzman, *Rudy Guiliani,* 174.

41. Giuliani, *Leadership*, 175–176, 384.

42. Jack Newfield, "The Full Rudy," *The Nation*, June 17, 2002, 13–14; Newfield, *The Full Rudy*, 37–60.

43. Barrett, *RUDY!* 367–378; Kirtzman, *Rudy Giuliani*, 270–271.

44. Barrett, *RUDY!* 367–394; Kirtzman, *Rudy Giuliani*, 112–126, 270–271; Siegel, *The Prince of the City*, 114–117, 185–186; Koch, *Giuliani, Nasty Man*, 39–46.

45. Siegel, *The Prince of the City*, 60–66; Barrett, *RUDY!* 290, 367–394; Kirtzman, *Rudy Giuliani*, 114–118, 271.

46. Siegel, *The Prince of the City*, 218, 241–247; Barrett, *RUDY!* 310, 318; *New York Times*, Jan. 1, 1998, Oct. 31, 1999; David E. Lavin, Richard D. Alba, Richard A. Silberstein, *Right Versus Privilege: The Open Admissions Experiment at the City University of New York* (New York: The Free Press, 1981); David E. Lavin and David Hyllegard, *Changing the Odds: Open Admissions and the Life Chances of the Disadvantaged* (New Haven: Yale University Press, 1996); James Traub, *City on a Hill: Testing the American Dream at City College* (Reading, Mass.: Addison-Wesley, 1994); Joanne Reitano, "CUNY's Community Colleges: Democratic Education on Trial," *Gateways to Democracy: Six Urban Community College Systems* (San Francisco: Jossey-Bass, 1999), 23–40; Benno C. Schmidt, "The City University of New York: An Institution Adrift," Report of the Mayor's Advisory Task Force on the City University of New York, June 7, 1999; Alisa Solomon with Dierdre Hussey, "Enemies of Public Education: Who is Behind the Attacks on CUNY and SUNY?" *Village Voice*, Education Supplement, April 21, 1998.

47. Giuliani, *Leadership*, 225–226; Siegel, *The Prince of the City*, 249–251; *New York Times*, Sept. 23, 25, 28, 30, 1999, Oct. 1, 3, 5, 1999; *New York Post*, Sept. 30, 1999; *Daily News*, Oct. 1, 1999.

48. *New York Times*, Sept. 30, 1999, Oct. 1, 7, 9, 10, 1999; Newfield, *The Full Rudy*, 26–36.

49. *New York Times*, Jan. 21, 1999, Feb. 25, 1999, April 2, 1999, Sept. 30, 1999, Oct. 3, 7, 1999, Nov. 13, 1999, Aug. 3, 2001, Dec. 28, 2001; *Daily News*, Oct. 8, 1999; *Newsday*, Sept. 3, 1999; Barrett, *RUDY!* 381; Kirtzman, *Rudy Giuliani*, 262–266; Koch, *Giuliani, Nasty Man*, 89–92; Siegel, *The Prince of the City*, 219.

50. *New York Times*, Oct. 3, 7, 10, 11, 1999, Nov. 13, 1999, Dec. 28, 31, 2001; *Newsday*, Oct. 3, 1999; *Daily News*, Oct. 8, 1999; Kirtzman, *Rudy Giuliani*, 103; Newfield, *The Full Rudy*, 20–26; Koch, *Giuliani, Nasty Man*, 35–38, 107–109.

51. *Newsday*, March 2, 2000; Kirtzman, *Rudy Giuliani*, xiii, 103, 170, 183–184.

52. Barrett, *RUDY!* 381; *New York Times*, Jan. 1, 1999, Feb. 25, 1999, April 2, 1999, Oct. 7, 1999, Nov. 13, 1999, April 7, 2000.

53. *New York Times*, March 31, 1999; Siegel, *The Prince of the City*, 216–217; Kirtzman, *Rudy Giuliani*, 170–174; Barrett, *RUDY!* 310–311; Giuliani, *Leadership*, 40–50.

54. Giuliani, *Leadership*, 3–26, 226; *New York Times*, July 17, 1999; *New York Daily News*, June 8, 1999.

55. Siegel, *The Prince of the City*, 301–308; Traub, "Giuliani Internalized," 36–38; Frank Rich, "The Father Figure," *New York Times Magazine*, Sept. 30, 2001, 23.

56. *New York Times*, Dec. 31, 2001; Kirtzman, *Rudy Giuliani*, 153.

57. *New York Times*, Dec. 31, 2001.

58. Ibid., Newfield, "The Full Rudy," 11.

59. Michael Pye, *Maximum City: The Biography of New York* (London: Sinclair Stevenson, 1994), 27.
60. Alan Nevins, ed., *The Diary of Philip Hone, 1828–1851* (New York: Dodd Mead, 1927), 41.
61. Briggs, *Victorian Cities*, 324.

SUGGESTIONS FOR FURTHER INQUIRY

1. Paul Goldberger, *The City Observed: New York, A Guide to the Architecture of Manhattan* (New York: Random House, 1979), xvi.

Index

Van Der Donck, Adriaen, 12
Vaux, Calvert, 56
Vietnam War, 164, 174, 175, 179, 190;
  see also Hardhat Riot
Village Independent Democrats, 162
Village Voice, 162
Virginia, 14, 15

W

Wagner, Robert F., Jr., 163, 168,
  169, 171, 178
Wagner, Robert F., Sr., 124
Walker, James, 131, 142
Walkowitz, Daniel, 50
Wallace, Mike, 5, 101
Walling, George W., 67, 76
Wall Street, 9, 16, 142, 143, 185; see
  also J. P. Morgan
Walsh, Mike, 59
Ward, Benjamin, 197
Washington, Booker T., 114, 116
Washington, D.C., 49, 71, 106, 211–212
Washington, George, 24–26
Washington, Rudy, 209
Washington Heights, 140
Washington Heights Riot, 202–203
Washington Square, 50, 110, 123, 162
Weavers' Strike, 50
Webb, James Watson, 43, 44, 46, 48, 60
Weeksville, Brooklyn, 47, 75
Weinbaum, Paul, 53
Welfare, 178, 189, 190, 214–215
Wells-Barnett, Ida, 114
Westchester, 12, 129, 76–77
West Indies; see Caribbean
Whig Party, 14, 36, 43–44
White Backlash, 170–171, 178–179;
  see also Civilian Review
  Board, Canarsie, CUNY
  riots, Forest Hills, Ocean
  Hill-Brownsville
White, E. B., 155
White, Walter, 151, 152, 159
Whitman, Walt, 37, 55–57, 62, 63, 78
  influence of, 111, 128, 133, 135
Whitney, Stephen, 34, 67, 71
Wiebe, Robert H., 80, 95
Wilentz, Sean, 50, 51

Wilkenfeld, Bruce, 30
Wilkins, Roy, 163, 170
Williams, Peter, 29
Williams, Peter Jr., 48
Wilson, James Q., 207
Wolfe, Tom, 196
Women
  18th Century, 18, 19, 23, 28
  Early-19th century, 35, 61, 75, 77; see
    also Elizabeth Jennings,
    Frances Wright,
  Late-19th century, 97; see also
    Josephine Shaw
    Lowell, Settlements,
    Ida Wells-Barnett
  Early-20th century, 116; see also food
    riots, Emma Goldman,
    New Woman, Triangle
    Shirtwaist Company,
    Margaret Sanger, rent
    strikes, suffrage
  Late-20th century; see Bella Abzug,
    Lillian Edelstein,
    Jane Jacobs, Ruth
    Messinger, National
    Organization of Women
Women's Trade Union League, 122–125
Wood, Benjamin, 75
Wood, Fernando, 56, 65–66, 69–72, 85;
  see also free city, liquor
  riot, Metropolitan police,
  Municipal Assistance
  Corporation, Tammany
Work Experience Program, 214–215
Working Girls Clubs, 94
Working Women's Protective Union, 94
World City, 12, 29
  20th century, 155–156, 174,
    179, 183, 206
World's Fairs, 56
  1939, 133–134, 140, 149
  1964, 162–163, 168
World Trade Center, 182, 205, 206,
    219, 220; see also David
    and Nelson Rockefeller
World War I, 113, 118, 121, 130
World War II, 149, 150

- this book is more descriptive than analytical
- 400+ years in 200+ pages
- really a textbook for an urban hx class on NYC class